I0762237

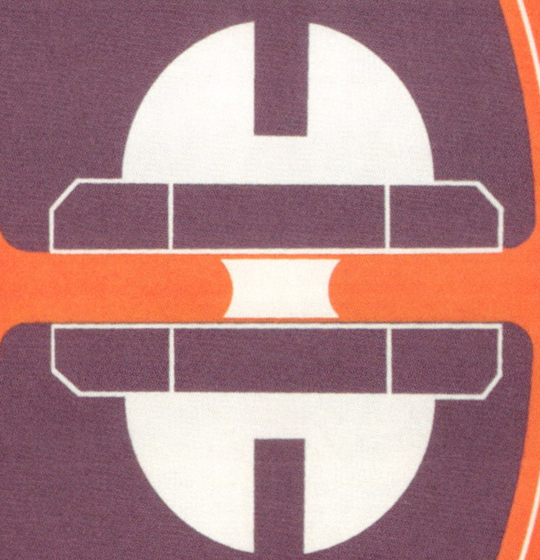

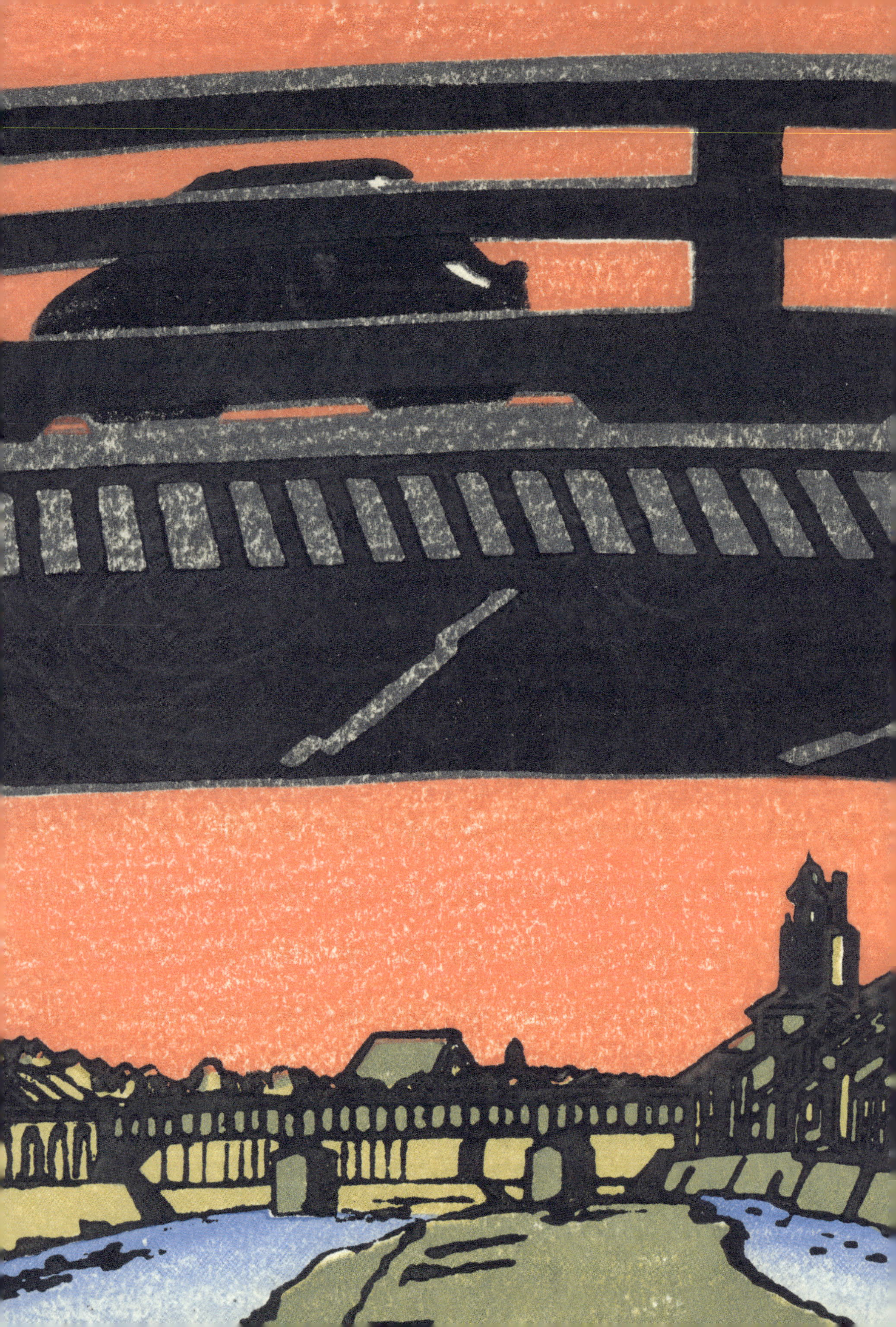

Modern Japanese Printmakers

New Waves *and* Eruptions

Malene Wagner

ASAWA Ruth Aiko
Ay-O
AZECHI Umetarō
FOUJITA Léonard Tsuguharu
FUKITA Fumiaki
FUNASAKA Yoshisuke
HAMAGUCHI Yōzō
HIRATSUKA Un'ichi
INAGAKI Tomoo
KASAMATSU Shirō
KAWANO Kaoru
KINOSHITA Tomio
KUROSAKI Akira
KUSAMA Yayoi
MORI Yoshitoshi
MUNAKATA Shikō
NAGAI Kazumasa
NARA Yoshitomo
NODA Tetsuya
OKUYAMA Gihachirō
ONCHI Kōshirō
ONOSATO Toshinobu
SAITŌ Kiyoshi
SATŌ Ado
SHINODA Tōkō
SHINOHARA Ushio
SHIOMI Nana
SUGAÏ Kumi
TAKEDA Hideo
TAKEI Takeo
TERAOKA Masami
TOKURIKI Tomikichirō
TSURUYA Kōkei
URUSHIBARA Yoshijirō
YAMAMOTO Kanae
YAYANAGI Go
YOKOO Tadanori
YOSHIDA Hiroshi
YOSHIDA Fujio
YOSHIDA Hodaka
YOSHIDA Chizuko
YOSHIDA Ayomi
YOSHIDA Hideshi

PRESTEL
Munich • London • New York

To Ay-O – from the beginning to the end of the rainbow

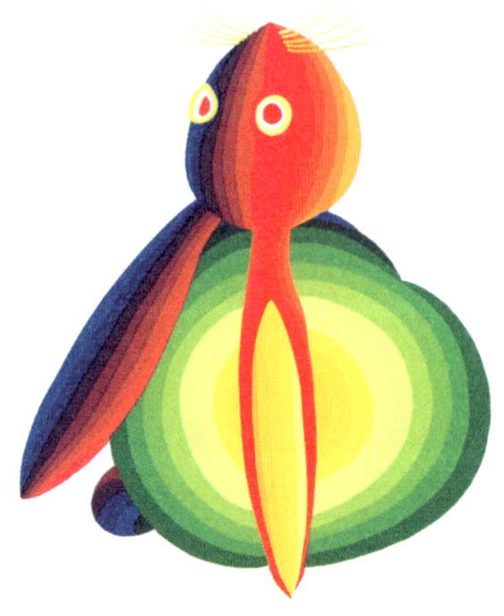

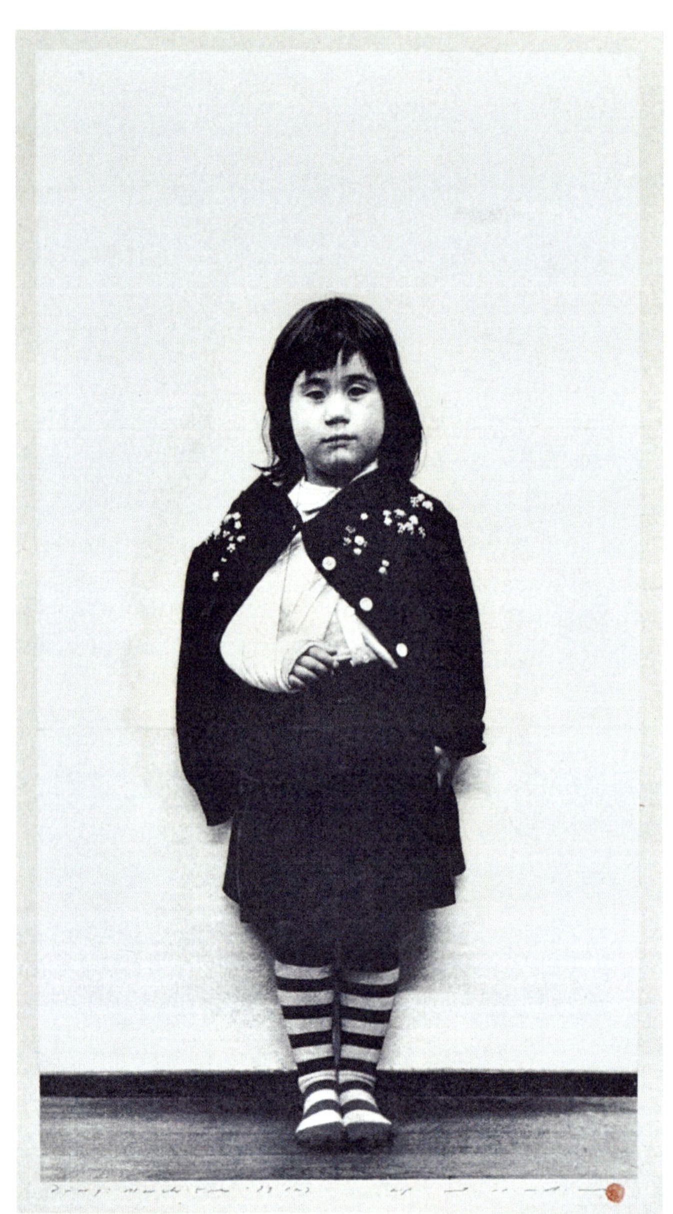

Prints were initially created by hand for making reproductions – multiple copies from one creation. At first, these prints were mainly of religious texts such as Buddhist scriptures, but later on people began printing Buddhist paintings. Gradually, various innovations were made in printing methods and the techniques improved, allowing more beautiful prints to be reproduced. *Ukiyo-e* woodblock prints, perfected in the eighteenth century during Japan's Edo period, are a prime example of the genre. However, as mechanisation progressed, hand-made production gradually declined.

People with an aesthetic sensibility found that with these printmaking techniques, they could achieve expressions and effects that could never be produced by oil or watercolour. There are things that can only be expressed by printmaking. Contemporary printmakers use such techniques to create their own original print works.

Japan has a long tradition of woodblock printmaking. However, many works were created using techniques other than woodblock printing, such as copperplate printing, lithography and silkscreen printing.

I am very pleased and grateful for this book, which expresses the artistic quality of modern and contemporary Japanese printmaking. I sincerely hope that it will help to extend the understanding of Japanese prints to a wider audience all over the world, and especially in Europe.

Noda Tetsuya, 2025

Preface

These are the stories of 43 modern Japanese artists who form a significant part of the long history of Japanese printmaking. A few were active at the beginning of the twentieth century, some worked leading up to the Second World War, while the majority took the print medium into the post-war era. A handful or so are active today, but most of the artists represented have passed away. Many gained recognition during their lifetime but are not known to a wide audience today.

Some of those who are still here have kindly shared insights into their connection with the Japanese print tradition in interviews I have conducted over the past six years. The artists in this book are my personal selection, based on the variety of styles, techniques and motifs they encompass as well as, importantly, their stories. I hope this introduction to their work will inspire further interest in, and investigation of, other print artists of the past, present and future.

The history of the modern Japanese print is not an isolated story, and the aim here is to place modern Japanese printmaking in a wider international art historical context. This book therefore includes artists who do not define themselves as printmakers but who have worked with the medium at some point in their career, many of them outside Japan, as well as a few earlier artists who were pioneers in the field.

The content of this book was inspired by the artists themselves. But the idea and form owe a great deal to the academic work of four particular individuals: from the very first generation of post-war collectors and specialists, Oliver Statler, who wrote the groundbreaking book *Modern Japanese Prints: An Art Reborn* (1956); the art dealer Frances Blakemore and her book *Who's Who in Modern Japanese Prints* (1975); Lawrence Smith, former Keeper of Japanese Antiquities at the British Museum, who organised exhibitions and wrote several publications on modern Japanese print artists during the 1980s and 1990s; and Helen Merritt, whose deep research into modern Japanese printmakers helped form the core of this book.

I am especially indebted to the artists and their families for letting me into their homes and for sharing their stories: Ay-O and his daughter Hanako, as well as Ay-O's printer Mr Sukeda; Funasaka Yoshisuke; Noda Tetsuya and his wife Dorit; the children of Satō Ado, Eko, Ako and Vinci Satō; Shinohara Ushio and his wife Noriko; Shiomi Nana; Takeda Hideo; Yayanagi Go and his son Yayanagi Seiichi; Yoshida Ayomi and her husband Yamaguchi Bidou; and Yoshida Hideshi.

I owe special gratitude to Matsuhashi Eiichi, Director of Karuizawa New Art Museum, who has supported this project from the very beginning and helped contact artists as well as organise interviews, attending several of them with me. I would also like to thank Yagura Naoko and her colleagues at the College Women's Association of Japan: their continuing work in promoting and supporting modern print artists in Japan is significant. I am very grateful to all the copyright holders who have given us permission to use the images in this book, including the Japan Print Association for their help.

Thanks also to Ogawa Remiko, Curator at the Matsudo City Board of Education, and the team at Catharine Clark Gallery, San Francisco; the Daiwa Anglo-Japanese Foundation, for supporting me with a travel grant in the early phase of my interviews; and the friends who have acted as translators and whose help has been invaluable: Ando Tomoro, Morita Miki, Nakane Kokoro, Yoshida Aya and Yuko Jørgensen. Thank you to my editor, Rochelle Roberts at Prestel, who took on the book with stoic calm and led us through to the end; book designers Luke Hall and Jason Wolfe of Wolfe Hall, for bringing the book to life and honouring the aesthetics of the artists; and Aimee Selby for her sharp eye in the proofreading stages.

And not least my four 'mentors', Israel Goldman, Michael Fornitz, Flemming Friborg and Peter Titelbech, for the abundance of encouragement, advice – and refreshments when needed. Lastly, I am grateful to my parents, who took me to Japan for the first time at the age of two, which opened my eyes and heart to the wonders of this special country.

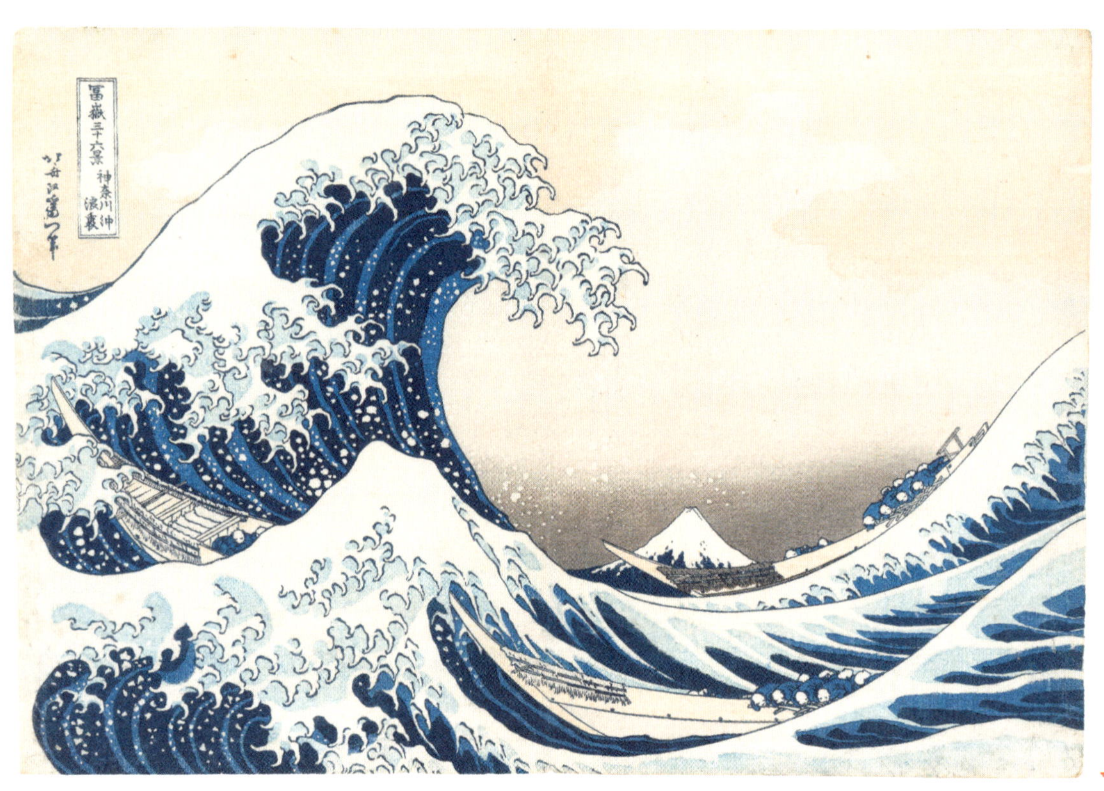

1

1 KATSUSHIKA Hokusai *Under the Wave off Kanagawa*, c. 1830–32. Woodblock print

The Japanese Print: Perception and Appreciation

As is well-known, ukiyo-e *prints have long enjoyed a world-wide fame. But Japanese wood-block prints are not represented solely by* ukiyo-e, *there being also modern prints, produced by a new technique and showing a modern sense of beauty.*[1]

Fujikake Shizuya, 1949

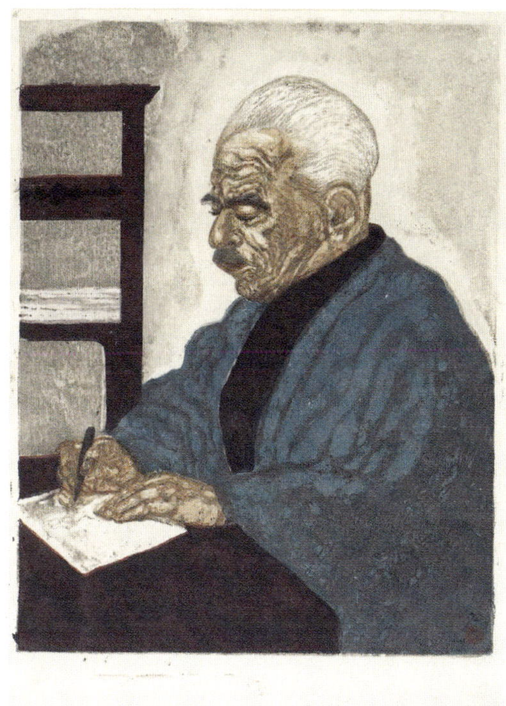

2 ONCHI Kōshirō *Portrait of Dr Shizuya Fujikake*, 1949. Woodblock print

3 KITAGAWA Utamaro *Courtesans after the Bath*, c. 1801. Woodblock print

Despite major developments in the Japanese print in the twentieth and twenty-first centuries, it is still the colourful woodblock prints known as *ukiyo-e* ('pictures of the floating world') from the age of Katsushika Hokusai (1760–1849) and his contemporaries that are the main point of recognition when it comes to the graphic art of Japan, and perhaps even Japanese art in general. The subject matters are familiar: kabuki actors, samurai, beautiful women (*bijin*), cherry blossoms, Mt Fuji – and who doesn't recognise the impressive motif of the towering blue wave, perhaps from a museum exhibition or more likely a T-shirt or a little emoji (fig. 1)?

When Dr Fujikake Shizuya (fig. 2) touched upon the subject of 'modern Japanese prints' in his book *Japanese Wood-Block Prints*, published by the Japan Travel Bureau in 1949,[2] Hokusai had been dead for one hundred years and new generations of artists had moved Japan's age-old print tradition into the twentieth century, largely following two routes. While some artists worked in the genre known as *shin hanga* (new prints), reviving the spirit of the classic prints of the Edo period (c. 1603–1868), others looked to more creative and personal expressions in what became broadly termed *sōsaku hanga* (creative prints). Not generic in style or technique, many *sōsaku hanga* artists continued using the traditional technique of woodblock

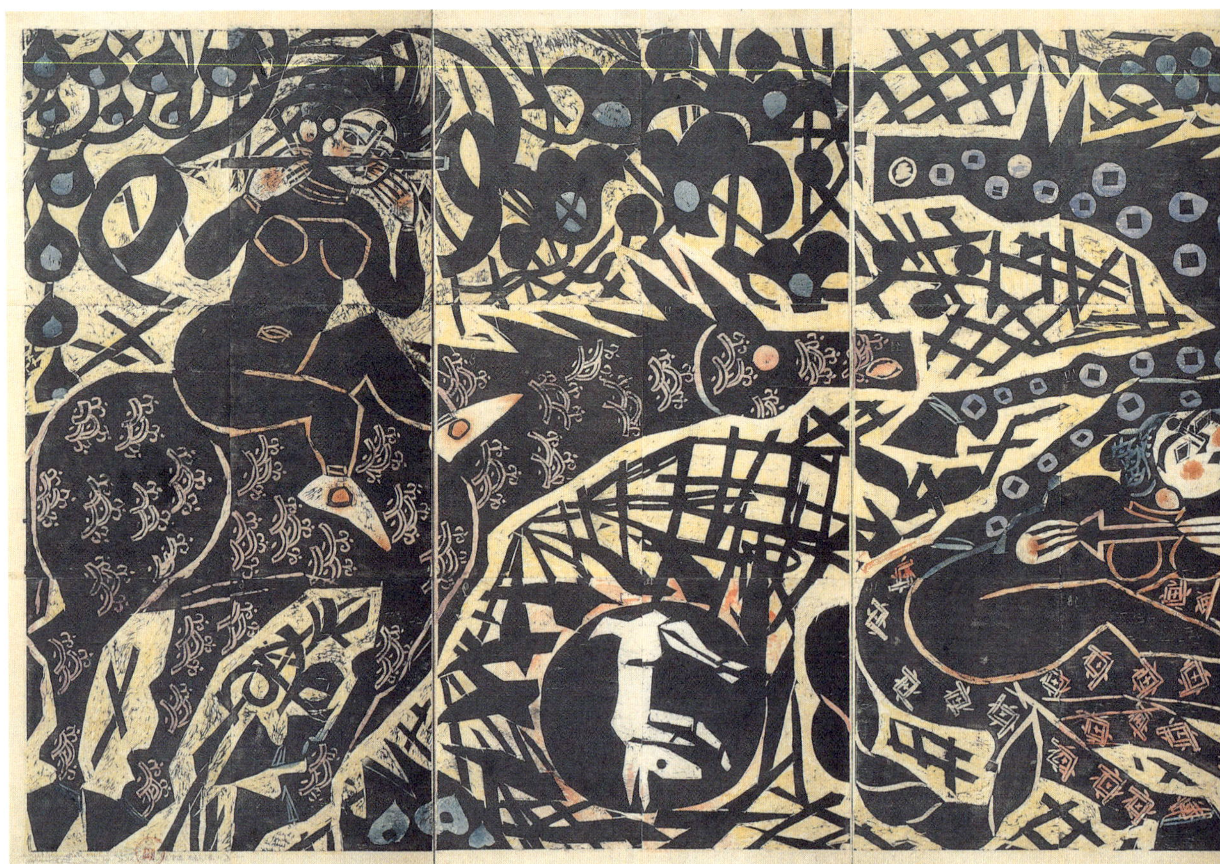

printing (*moku hanga*) but approached it in new ways, some using the traditional blocks of cherry wood, some plywood or other wood types that allowed for larger formats. Others embraced Western techniques such as lithography, silkscreen printing and etching. The majority printed in limited editions, emphasising the authenticity of their work, as opposed to the massive editions of *ukiyo-e*, which could run from several hundred impressions into the thousands. A few artists moved in the realms of both *shin hanga* and *sōsaku hanga*.[3]

In the 1950s, contemporary Japanese printmakers began exhibiting and winning awards at international shows and biennials, owing much to foreign appreciation and putting the Japanese print on the global map yet again, as during its glory days in late nineteenth-century Europe. However, in Japan, printmaking in the mid-twentieth century was yet to be re-established as an academic discipline following its short appearance in 1935–44 at the Tokyo School of Fine Arts (today Tokyo University of the Arts), and the art establishment was still not fully accepting of the print medium as an art form equal to that of painting.[4]

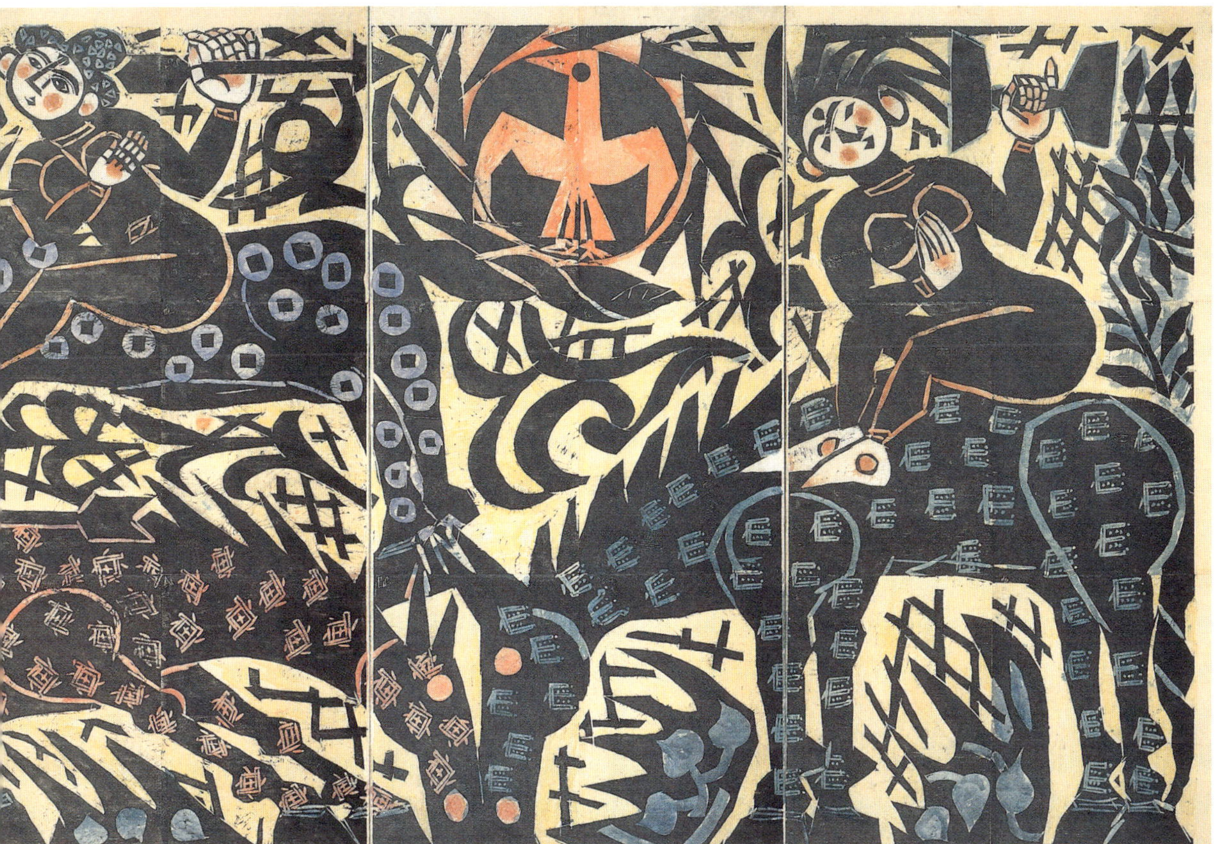

4 MUNAKATA Shikō *Flower Arrow*, 1961. Woodblock print

In fact, with the development of the new genre of *ukiyo-e* in the Edo period, the woodblock print became associated with consumerism and the urban middle class. Indeed it became a fully fledged commercial medium for mass production, used to depict the latest news and events of Edo (present-day Tokyo) and Osaka, particularly the entertainment districts and the 'pop stars' of the day – kabuki actors, courtesans and sumo wrestlers (fig. 3).

Essentially, *ukiyo-e* were the Edo period's answer to today's posters and postcards. Hokusai's *The Great Wave*, in its day, would have cost little more than a bowl of soba noodles.[5] However, while comparable in terms of pricing and subject matter, in quality the traditional woodblock print far exceeds that of today's machine-printed poster, as they were not only meticulously crafted by hand in a collaborative system consisting of an artist, a carver, a printer and a publisher, called *hanmoto*, but also reflected the high creative standards of the artist.

Paris print mania

And the most sharp-sighted had discovered in their searches some images of ravishing effect. They were collected in made-up albums representing fantastic scenes, in a new style of coloring which fascinated.[6]

Siegfried Bing, 1894

While not considered 'fine art' in Japan, ironically, more than any other Japanese art form, the woodblock print has probably been the most celebrated and influential in the West. In fact, *ukiyo-e* became collector's items and played a key role in fuelling the craze for all things Japanese in the second half of the nineteenth century – a phenomenon termed Japonisme – with Paris as its epicentre.[7]

Admiration for the 'exotic' Japanese print was centred around a group of Paris-based art dealers, collectors, critics and artists. Through the publication of books and journals, the establishment of private museums and dedicated exhibitions, they promoted Japanese art, including the very popular *ukiyo-e*. A leading figure was Siegfried Bing (1838–1905), an art dealer and connoisseur who published the journal *Le Japon artistique* (Artistic Japan; 1888–91), a source of inspiration for many artists and designers in Europe with its full-page colour reproductions of Japanese artworks (fig. 7).

In his shop at 19 rue Chauchat, Bing would receive visits from enthusiastic collectors, eager to see his latest stock freshly arrived from Japan (fig. 5).[8] Among his many clients were the actress Sarah Bernhardt (1844–1923), writer and connoisseur Edmond de Goncourt (1822–1896), and artists Claude Monet (1840–1926) – who owned an edition of *The Great Wave* – Paul Gauguin (1848–1903), Vincent van Gogh (1853–1890) and Henri de Toulouse-Lautrec (1964–1901).[9] They not only collected but took inspiration from, and at times even copied, the Japanese woodblock prints in terms of motifs, colours, composition and atmosphere (fig. 6). In 1888 Van Gogh wrote to his brother Theo, an art dealer, concerning the stock of *ukiyo-e* prints at Bing's gallery and conveying his enthusiasm for the genre: 'But take the Hokusais as well then, 300 views of the sacred mountain and scenes of manners and customs. There's an attic at Bing's, and in it there's a heap of 10 thousand Japanese prints, landscapes, figures, old Japanese prints too.'[10]

The inflow of Japanese prints to Europe was directly connected to the political situation in Japan. Following repeated pressure from Western powers,[11] in 1854 Japan's ruling Tokugawa shogunate was forced to abandon the closed-door policy (*sakoku*) that had allowed for financial and cultural progress for nearly 250 years.[12] Besides tea and silk, it was porcelain, lacquerware and bronzes (some authentic antiques, some manufactured specifically for the Western market) as well as cheap commercial art such as *ukiyo-e* prints and books – 'virtually fresh off the block' – that became major export commodities following the opening of Japan.[13]

Foreign pressure combined with existing domestic unrest led to the Tokugawa shogunate being overthrown in 1868. The Edo period, and with it the feudal system, came to an end. The following Meiji period (1868–1912) saw Japan enter a transformative time during which the country was strongly influenced by Western ideas, not least within the cultural sector. Under the slogan *Bunmei kaika* (civilisation and enlightenment), the new imperial government chose to embrace a Westernisation of Japan[14] by hiring foreign advisers (*oyatoi gaikokujin*), including teachers to conduct courses in European art and techniques at the Kōbu Bijutsu Gakkō (Technical Fine Arts School), founded in 1876 as Japan's first academy of Western art.[15]

While Japan became influenced by Western culture, the opposite could be seen in Paris, as the capital of European art. The Exposition Universelle hosted by Paris in 1867, and again in 1878, offered an opportunity to experience a wide variety of Japanese art and artefacts, including *ukiyo-e*. However, it was not until 1890 that the first major exhibition dedicated to Japanese prints, the *Exposition de la gravure japonaise* (fig. 8), took place. Held at the École des Beaux-Arts and organised by Siegfried Bing, it presented Japanese prints from the early *ukiyo-e* artists of the Torii school in the early eighteenth century to one of the last great *ukiyo-e* masters, Kawanabe Kyōsai (1831–1889). Apart from Bing's own impressive collection of woodblock prints, including an early edition of *The Great Wave*,[16] loans came from many of his clients and fellow Japan enthusiasts, including collector Charles Gillot (1853–1903), critic Philippe Burty (1830–1890), jeweller Henri Vever (1854–1942) and, notably, the leading *ukiyo-e* expert Hayashi Tadamasa (1856–1906). Apart from being a significant dealer of *ukiyo-e*, importing more than 16,000 prints from Japan between 1890 and 1901,[17] Hayashi also acquired works by French artists, including Monet, in exchange for prints.[18]

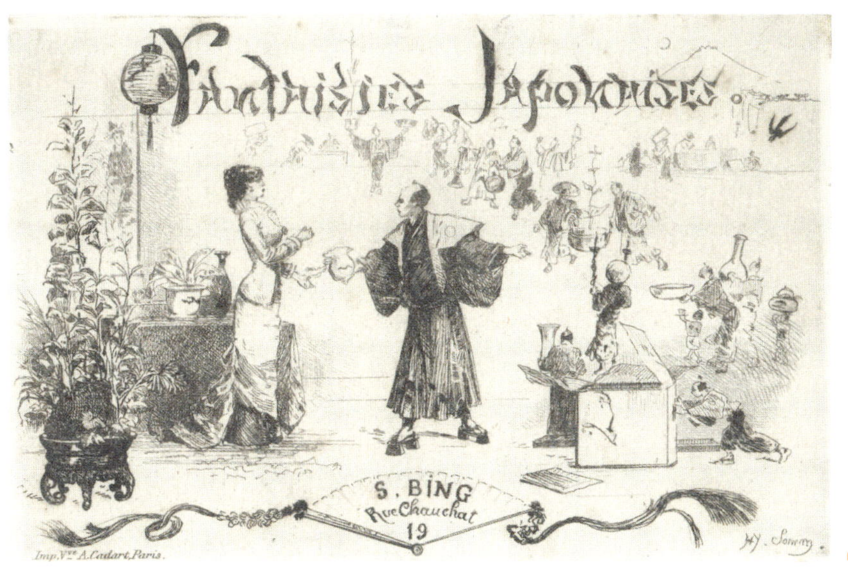

5

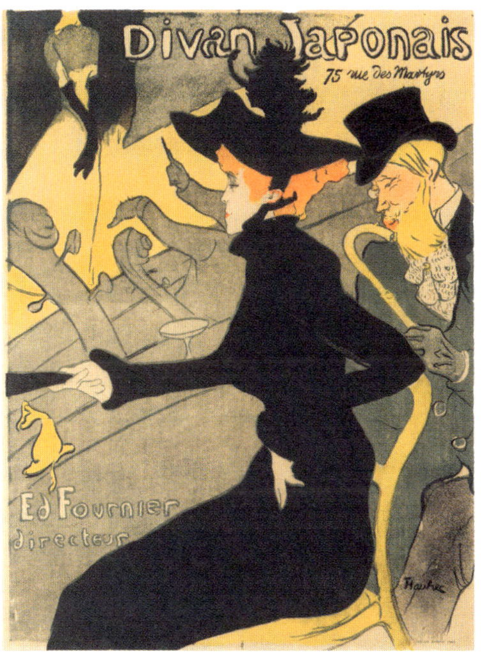

6

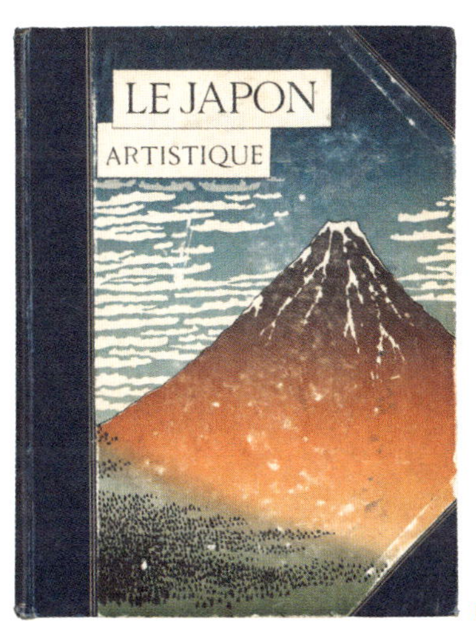

7

5 Henry Somm — *'Fantaisies Japonaises', S. Bing, rue Chauchat 19,* c. 1879. Etching and drypoint

6 Henri de Toulouse-Lautrec — *Divan Japonais*, 1893. Lithograph poster

7 — Cover of *Le Japon artistique*, volume 2, 1888–91, showing KATSUSHIKA Hokusai, *Fine Wind, Clear Morning*, c. 1830–32

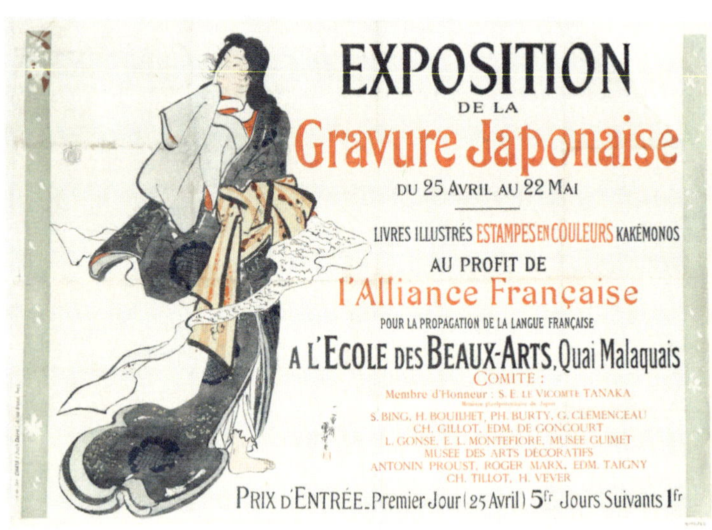

8

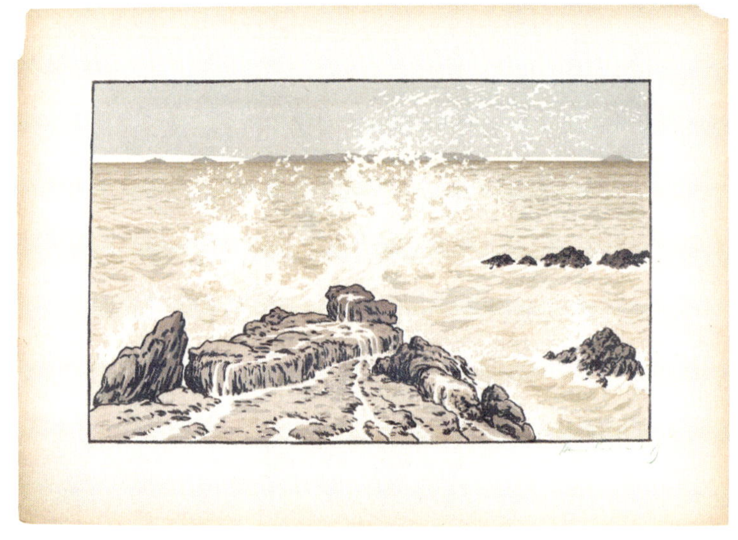

9

The poster for the 1890 exhibition was designed by none other than the 'father of the modern poster', lithographer Jules Chéret (1836–1932). Chéret himself participated the following year in the third exhibition of the Société de Peintres-Graveurs Français, which also included contemporary 'painter-engravers' and Japan admirers Henri Rivière (1864–1951) (fig. 9), Félix Bracquemond (1833–1914) and Auguste Rodin (1840–1917). Among the techniques represented were lithography, wood engraving, woodblock and more.[19] Only European artists participated.

Bing also initiated the establishment of the Société des Amis de l'Art Japonais (Society of Friends of Japanese Art) in 1892, whose members included Vever, Gillot and other figures mentioned above, as well as artists like Félix Régamey (1844–1907) and Prosper-Alphonse Isaac (1858–1924). In 1906, the year after Bing's death, the group started a tradition of making invitations to their monthly dinners, hosted at the Restaurant du Cardinal on boulevard des Italiens. These were small prints with Japanese-inspired motifs, mostly made by woodblock and designed by the members themselves, testifying to the enthusiasm for the print medium in French avant-garde circles at the time. An invitation from 14 December 1912 carries the monogram of a Japanese artist, Urushibara Yoshijirō (pp. 208–11), a London-based artisan turned artist who was invited to Paris by Isaac, who wanted to learn Japanese woodblock printing (fig. 10).

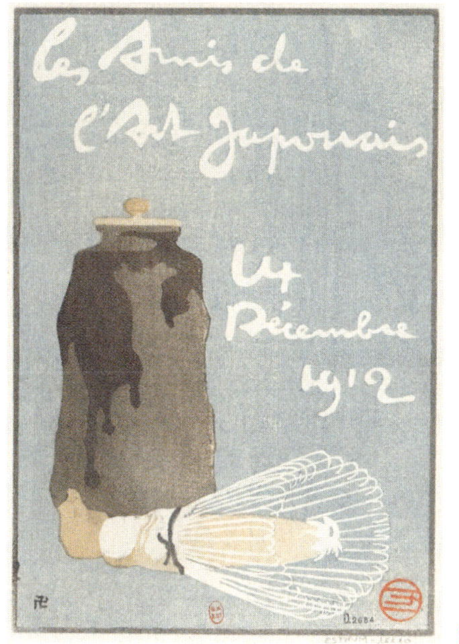

10

'A new vision of an old medium'

The ukiyo-e spirit had died ... By the 20th century there was a new world, a new outlook, and the artforms that that earlier spirit had given rise to were bound to be obsolete.[20]

Jack Hillier, 1960

In 1904, the year Japan participated in the St Louis World's Fair as a full-blown 'modern' nation, cementing its dominant position in Asia,[21] what has become regarded as the first *sōsaku hanga* print was published (fig. 12). The name of the young Japanese artist was Yamamoto Kanae (pp. 212–17), and in the spirit of the *peintre-graveur* he had designed, carved and printed the work himself, emphasising the concept of the artist as sole creator in opposition to the traditional collaborative *hanmoto* system of artists and artisans.[22]

Meanwhile, that same year in Paris, a young artist named Pablo Picasso (1881–1973), coming to the end of his Blue Period, made his second attempt at printmaking. The result was an etching titled *Le repas frugal* (The Frugal Meal) (fig. 13).[23] While Picasso's print was executed using a chemical process, etching, Kanae's *Fisherman* was created via a physical process: carving a woodblock using a chisel. Here were two young artists worlds apart, experimenting with different printing techniques for graphic works that each represented a new phase in their artistic career. However remote in technique and geography – Yamamoto did not move to Paris until 1912 – the two also shared artistic influences in European artists like Edgar Degas (1834–1917), Toulouse-Lautrec and Van Gogh.

The ideas and techniques of this generation of Impressionists and Post-Impressionists, we now know, ironically owed much to *ukiyo-e*,[24] and even Picasso himself later started collecting Japanese prints.[25] While many creative roads led to Paris, one could argue that they arrived there 'via' Japan.

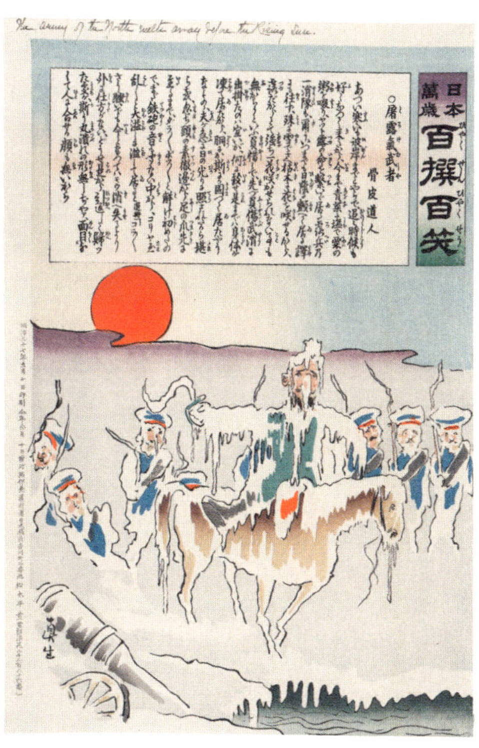

11

8 Jules Chéret — Poster for the *Exposition de la gravure japonaise*, held from 25 April to 22 May 1890. Lithograph
9 Henri Rivière — *The Wave*, 1893. Lithograph
10 URUSHIBARA Yoshijirō — Invitation card for the Société des Amis de l'Art Japonais, 14 December 1912. Woodblock print
11 KOBAYASHI Kiyochika — *The Army of the North Melts Away before the Rising Sun*, 1904. Woodblock print

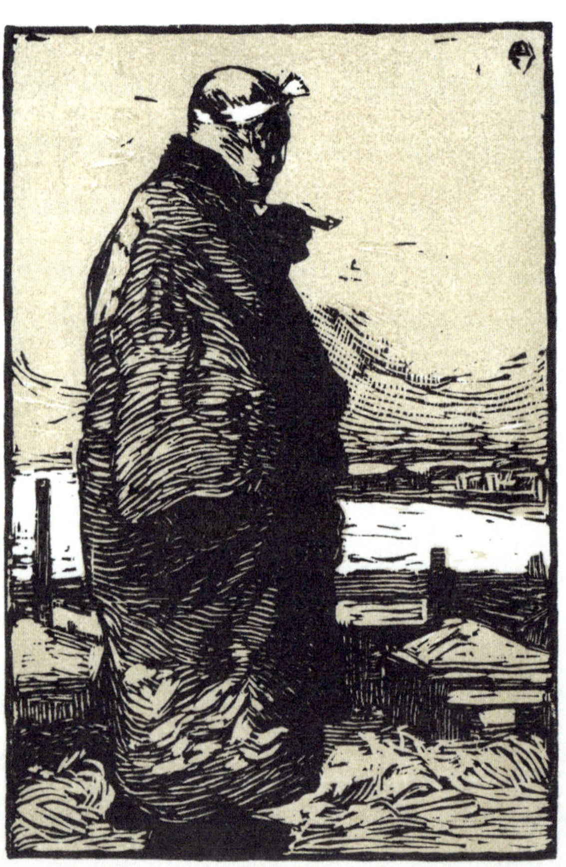

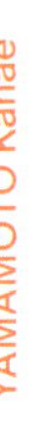

12 YAMAMOTO Kanae

Fisherman, 1904. Woodblock print

East to West to East

The stretches of water make patches of a beautiful emerald and a rich blue in the landscapes, as we see it in the Japanese prints.[26]

Vincent van Gogh, 1888

While to Van Gogh Japan was an idealised place and source of immense inspiration, he in turn was a significant figure for many modern Japanese printmakers, some of whom decided to become artists after seeing his work.[27] A leading Japanese source in the introduction to Japanese audiences of European artists including Van Gogh and Edvard Munch (1863–1944) (fig. 14) – another influential figure for twentieth-century artists in Japan – was the avant-garde literary and art magazine *Shirakaba* (White Birch), published monthly between 1910 and 1923 by a group of young writers and thinkers of the same name. *Shirakaba* continued the Meiji period's craving for Western culture and art,[28] and, among other activities, in 1911 organised an exhibition in Japan of European prints. This was followed in 1915 with *Der Sturm*, the German equivalent to *Shirakaba* (and also founded in 1911), sponsoring an exhibition in Japan centred around woodblock prints by European Expressionists. It was organised by Japanese artists who had just returned from Europe, bringing back with them the prints. These two exhibitions bear witness to the many cross-currents in Japanese and European art and printmaking in the early twentieth century.[29]

The year 1915 also turned out to be an important one in the development of a parallel Japanese print movement, *shin hanga*. The term, referring to what can be regarded as a modern interpretation of the classic *ukiyo-e* of the Edo period, was coined by the man behind the new genre, Watanabe Shōzaburō (1885–1962).[30] At the time a publisher of *ukiyo-e* reproductions made by skilled artisans working under him,[31] Watanabe understood the Western market's demand for original *ukiyo-e*, which had become very expensive and low in supply in Japan following the mass exports of the Meiji period. Watanabe wished to create new original prints, but unlike Yamamoto Kanae's creative prints he sought to keep the atmosphere of the traditional woodblock prints, catering to a Western taste. *Shin hanga* were also produced following the old *hanmoto* system. Producing works that were Japanese in style and spirit, and with similar themes as *ukiyo-e* – beautiful women, actors, landscapes and city scenes – but

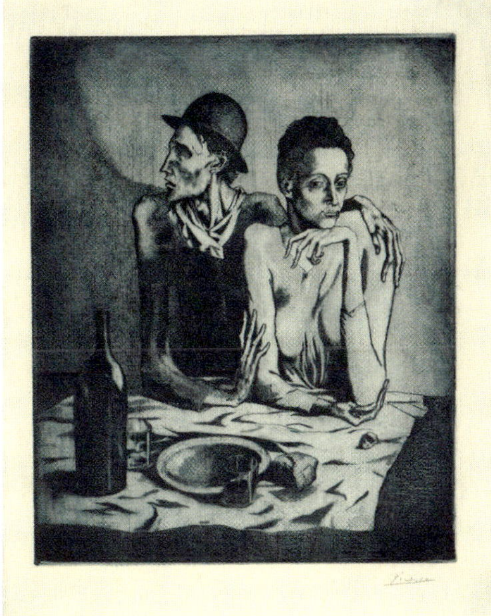

13 Pablo Picasso *The Frugal Meal*, 1904. Etching

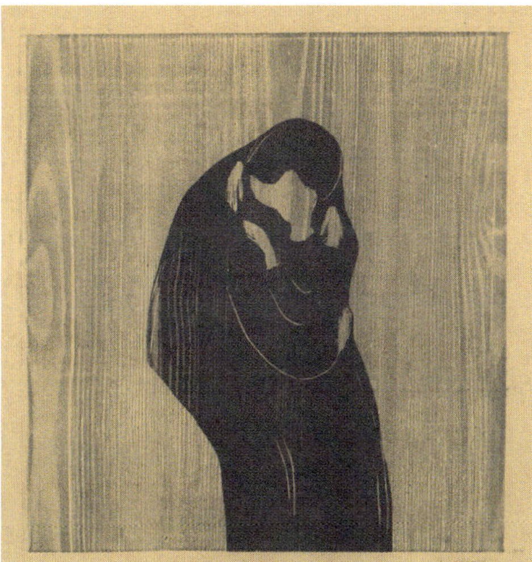

14 Edvard Munch *The Kiss*, 1898. Woodblock print

employing Western artistic effects such as light and shade, Watanabe in collaboration with contemporary artists brought the classic woodblock print into the twentieth century.[32]

The first print, *Woman at the Bath*, was designed in 1915 by Hashiguchi Goyō (1880–1921), a Western-style (*yōga*) painter (fig. 15). Goyō was followed by artists such as Itō Shinsui (1989–1972), Kawase Hasui (1883–1957), Kasamatsu Shirō (pp. 76–81), Yoshida Hiroshi (pp. 232–33) and Ohara Koson (or Shōson; 1877–1945), who all pursued the *shin hanga* route thanks to encouragement and commissions by Watanabe, who promoted and sold the 'new prints' in Japan.

Meanwhile, Yoshida, a Western-style painter turned printmaker who collaborated with Watanabe for a few years (fig. 16), became the prime promoter of *shin hanga* in the United States, where they turned out to be a commercial success.[33] Yoshida helped organise exhibitions of his and fellow artists' prints, including at the Toledo Museum of Art in Ohio in 1930 and 1936. As curator Dorothy Blair wrote on the occasion of the first exhibition:

> *We are now introduced to a new era of Japanese woodblock prints which may be called a period of Renaissance in this particular field. In any event, the last decade has seen a wonderful improvement in Japan in this phase of graphic arts ... It has been possible to acquire 342 titles representing the work of Japanese artists in this field, including Hashiguchi Goyo, Ito Shinsui, Kawase Hasui, Ohara Shoson and Yoshida Hiroshi.*[34]

While *shin hanga* was gaining momentum, the *sōsaku hanga* movement, led by Yamamoto, cemented itself with the establishment of the Japan Creative Print Association (Nihon Sōsaku Hanga Kyōkai) in 1918.[35] The group's objective was to promote *hanga* by arranging shows as part of government-sponsored exhibitions, which had yet to include the print medium, as well as by having a printmaking course included at the Tokyo School of Fine Arts.[36] These ideas, and the fundamental belief that the print was an important and rewarding medium, worthy of as much attention as painting,[37] continued with Onchi Kōshirō (pp. 130–33), who took the reins after Yamamoto.

'Creative prints', Onchi later wrote, 'are pictures made by a printing process, just as oil paintings are made by brush on canvas. The *hanga* method itself is a creative process ... The printing process requires various steps or stages – the engraving of the block, and the printing from the block.'[38] The idea of self-carving and self-printing was a matter of principle to Onchi, although in practice this was not a consistent approach, as many *sōsaku hanga* artists also worked with artisans who helped them carve.

In 1931 the Japan Print Association (Nihon Hanga Kyōkai) was established with members of the then dissolved Japan Creative Print Association, the Yōfū Hangakai (Western-Style Print Society), which consisted of etchers and lithographers, and other independent artists who also joined.[39] The office for the new society was Onchi's house in Tokyo.

A few years later, in 1934, the Japan Print Association organised the first major exhibition of contemporary Japanese prints abroad. *L'estampe japonaise moderne et ses origines* (Modern Japanese Prints and their Origins) was held in Paris at the Musée des Arts Décoratifs from February to March and showcased about 250 modern prints alongside 350 *ukiyo-e* works. In Japan, Yamamoto and Onchi were part of the organising committee, while Hasegawa Kiyoshi (1891–1980), a renowned artist and engraver based in Paris since 1919, who also compiled the catalogue (fig. 17; published in French),[40] was the main organiser and representative of the Japan Print Association. The focus of the exhibition was clearly to promote *sōsaku hanga* abroad, presenting artists of the first generation like Yamamoto as

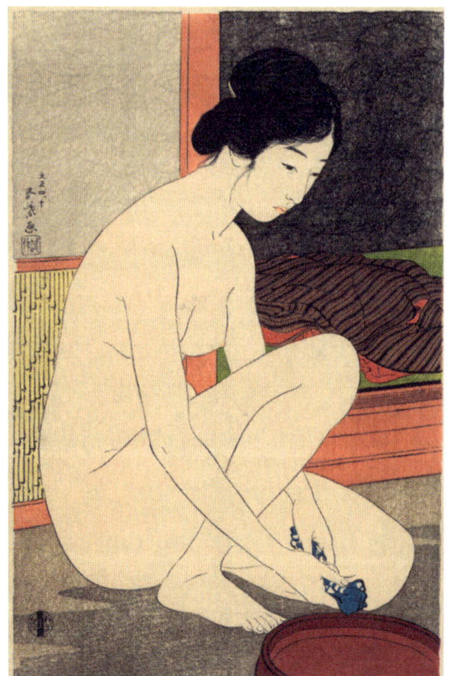

15 HASHIGUCHI Goyō *Woman at the Bath*, 1915. Woodblock print

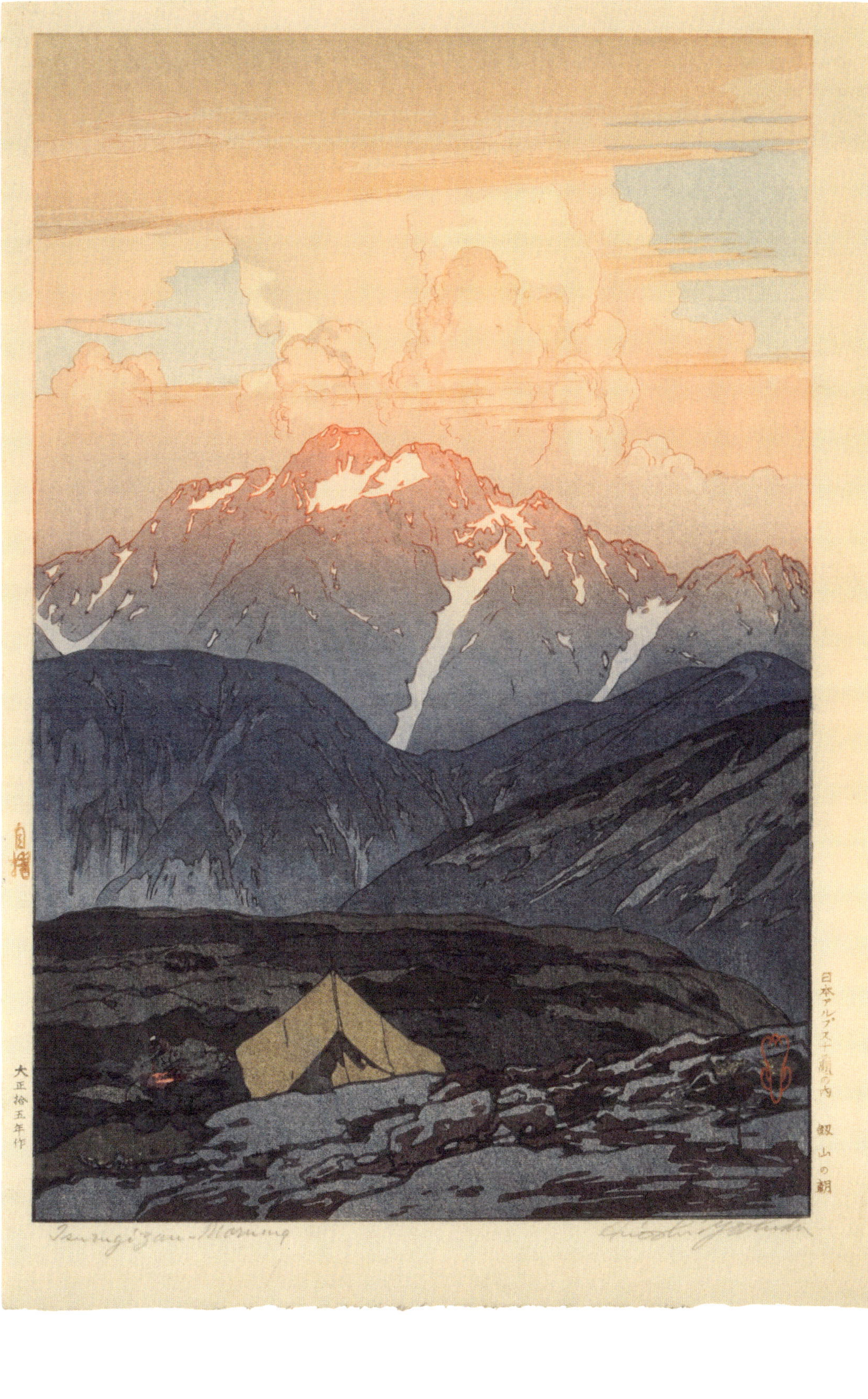

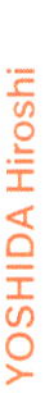

16 YOSHIDA Hiroshi

Morning at Mt Tsurugi, 1926. Woodblock print

well as those of the next, which included artists like Onchi, Hiratsuka Un'ichi (pp. 68–71), Inagaki Tomoo (pp. 72–75), Tokuriki Tomikichirō (pp. 196–201) and Munakata Shikō (pp. 104–7). Some *shin hanga* artists were not happy that they would be excluded[41] – they were modern too, after all – and in the end, *shin hanga* was represented in the exhibition with ten works by Hashiguchi Goyō, including *Woman at the Bath*.[42]

The fact that *ukiyo-e*, the 'origin' of the Japanese modern print, represented the majority of works in the show clearly indicates their continuing appeal abroad. Aware of this, the participating artists hoped for an equally positive reception of their creative prints 'by association'. As Hasegawa wrote: 'We thank France for the interest and sympathy it has always shown towards Japanese art and we hope that the French, who were the first to understand the art of Ukiyo-e, will also appreciate our contemporary prints.'[43]

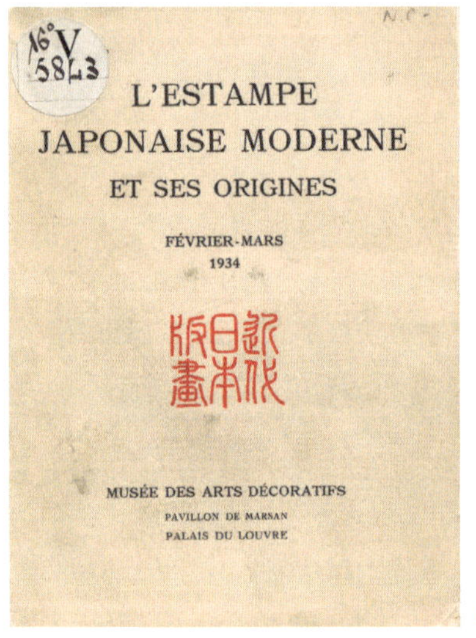

L'ESTAMPE
JAPONAISE MODERNE
ET SES ORIGINES
FÉVRIER-MARS
1934
MUSÉE DES ARTS DÉCORATIFS
PAVILLON DE MARSAN
PALAIS DU LOUVRE

17

À bientôt Paris, hello America

Following the Second World War, a new wave from the West swept over Japan. While the Meiji period had been predominantly marked by the influx of European culture, in the post-war period it was, not surprisingly, the United States that left an imprint. In fact, the American presence in post-war Japan came to play a significant role in the international appreciation of the modern Japanese print.

William Hartnett, a recreation director for American army personnel in Japan, was the first to 'discover' the work of Onchi Kōshirō and his fellow printmakers, and in 1946 he asked Onchi to put on an exhibition of *sōsaku hanga* prints.[44] Then came Oliver Statler (1915–2002), a civilian employee of the occupying forces, who was introduced to Onchi by his friend Hartnett. Statler and Onchi became friends, and through him, Statler was introduced to more print artists, from whom he bought prints not only for his own collection but also to sell to private clients and multiple American museums. Statler became perhaps the most significant collector and supporter of the contemporary printmakers during this period.[45] His deep interest in and research into contemporary Japanese printmaking resulted in the groundbreaking book *Modern Japanese Prints: An Art Reborn*, published in 1956 as the first focused on the subject. He also instigated the annual print shows of the College Women's Association of Japan (CWAJ),[46] the first of which opened on 22 October 1956. Forty artists and 91 prints were represented, including Azechi Umetarō (pp. 44–47), Munakata Shikō and Saitō Kiyoshi.[47] Statler would continue his work in supporting contemporary printmakers in Japan and remained involved with the CWAJ until his death.[48]

'For this is a living art'

Today, spurred on by a growing group of artists who have revived the neglected art of printmaking, hanga (block-print picture) art is beginning to bloom again. Most recent international recognition: a first prize at Venice's Biennale, awarded to the wild man of Japanese hanga artists, squat, myopic Shiko Munakata, 50, who also won a first prize in last year's São Paulo Bienal.[49]

Time, 1956

The 1950s witnessed print artists like Saitō and Munakata winning prizes at international exhibitions, catapulting the Japanese contemporary print to wider international acclaim and towards a recognition in Japan as a significant medium in contemporary art. In 1957, the International Biennial Exhibition of Prints in Tokyo was established as one of the earliest international art competitions in Japan. Co-hosted by the Tokyo National Museum of Modern Art and the *Yomiuri shimbun* newspaper, the first exhibition was held that year with more than 800 entries from 29 countries and 43 Japanese artists.[50]

However, with ever more international styles, print technologies and processes emerging, during the 1960s the tradition of *sōsaku hanga* shifted into decline, and the principle of 'self-carved, self-printed' as emphasised by Onchi began to seem 'old school'. The next generation who came of age in the post-war years – artists such as Ay-O (pp. 31–43), Kusama Yayoi (pp. 94–99), Ruth Asawa (pp. 26–29) and Teraoka Masami (pp. 189–95) – turned their attention to American culture and the avant-garde art scene, looking beyond their Japanese heritage. For these artists, printmaking formed only one aspect of a wider oeuvre, and they entered into collaborations with professional printers and publishers for the production of their prints, not unlike their *ukiyo-e* colleagues in the Edo period (fig. 18). Working with professional printing studios such as Stanley William Hayter's Atelier 17 in Paris, the Tamarind Lithography Workshop in Los Angeles and Okabe Tokuzo's print studio in Tokyo – in particular for silkscreens and lithographs – they joined the international print boom of the 1960s and '70s, popularising the print as a reproducible art medium.

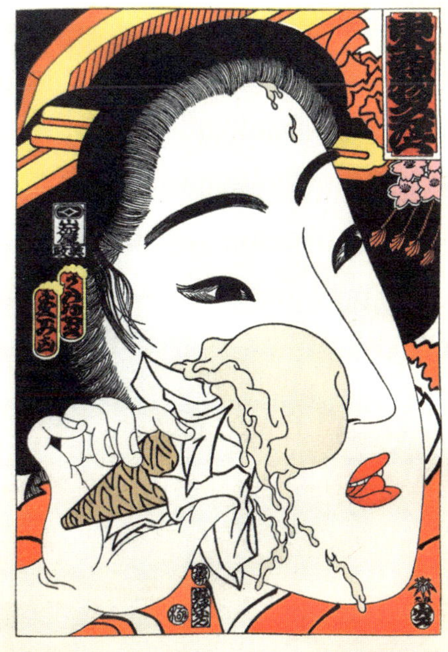

18

Today, only a few artists remain from this generation; even fewer are still active (fig. 19). New generations are finding their own paths within the realm of printmaking, the majority of whom are focused on the print as their main medium, and within woodblock printing there is an emphasis once again on self-carving and self-printing. Regardless of the technique, tradition, period or style, the idea of the print medium as equal to painting remains the same. The works of the 43 artists represented here – the oldest born in 1876 and the youngest in 1968 – stand as strong examples of this.

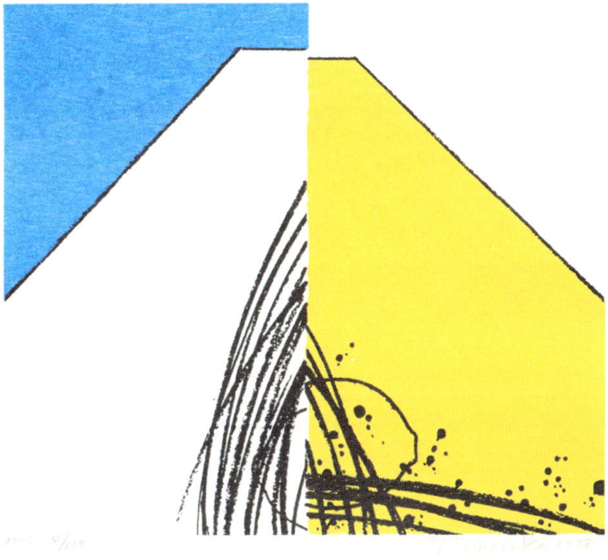

19

17 HASEGAWA Kiyoshi
From the catalogue for *L'estampe japonaise moderne et ses origines*, 1934
18 TERAOKA Masami
31 Flavours Invading Japan (Macadamia), 1978/2023. Relief print with lithograph and etching
19 FUNASAKA Yoshisuke
Untitled, 1998. Woodblock print

20 SHIOMI Nana

Even Monkeys Tea Bowl, 2024. Woodblock print

1 Shizuya Fujikake, 'Author's Note', in *Japanese Wood-Block Prints*, 2nd and revd edn (Tokyo: Japan Travel Bureau, 1949).

2 Fujikake, an acclaimed scholar of *ukiyo-e* prints, was to play an important role in the recognition of contemporary prints. Fujikake was also part of the major print exhibition organised in Paris by the Japan Print Association in 1934, discussed below.

3 See sections on Kasamatsu Shirō, pp. 76–81, Okuyama Gihachirō, pp. 124–29, and Tokuriki Tomikichirō, pp. 196–201.

4 See sections on Onchi Kōshirō, pp. 130–33, and Saitō Kiyoshi, pp. 138–45.

5 See Christine Guth, *Hokusai's Great Wave: Biography of a Global Icon* (Honolulu: University of Hawai'i Press, 2015), p. 30. In 2023, *The Great Wave* fetched the record price of $2.76 million at auction. Christie's New York, 'Japanese and Korean Art', 21 March 2023, lot 122.

6 Siegfried Bing, *Catalogue of Japanese Engravings: An Important Collection of Old Prints in Color Belonging to Mr S. Bing, Paris* (New York: American Art Association, 1894), p. 9.

7 The term Japonisme was first used by the art critic Philippe Burty in a series of articles on Japan in *La Renaissance littéraire et artistique*, May (pp. 25–26) and July (pp. 106–7) 1872.

8 From his shop at 19 rue Chauchat he sold Chinese and Japanese antiques and art, including *ukiyo-e*, expanding in 1881 to include 22 rue Provence around the corner. The previous year he had travelled to Japan, buying all that he could find, down to the most basic objects like combs and hairpins. Bing opened two other shops over the following years, at 13 rue Bleue and 19 rue Paix, selling both antiques and modern objects from China and Japan. See years 1881, pp. 837, 1030, 2120; 1882, p. 966; 1883, pp. 837, 1318, in *Annuaire-almanach du commerce, de l'industrie, de la magistrature et de l'administration*, Firmin-Didot, Paris.

9 See for example Chris Uhlenbeck, 'The Japanese Prints of Vincent van Gogh', in Chris Uhlenbeck, Louis van Tilborgh and Shigeru Oikawa, *Japanese Prints: The Collection of Vincent van Gogh* (London: Thames & Hudson, 2018), pp. 77–92.

10 Vincent van Gogh to Theo van Gogh, Arles, Sunday, 15 July 1888, letter 640, Van Gogh Museum, Amsterdam, https://vangoghletters.org/vg/letters.html.

11 As Japan first opened its ports to trade with the Americans, the United Kingdom, Russia, France and the Netherlands quickly followed suit, resulting in the so-called 'unequal treaties' that led to more countries pushing for trade deals. Among other things, the treaties gave Westerners extraterritorial rights and kept tariff rates low on Western goods imported into Japan. See for example Oliver R. Impey and Malcolm Fairley, eds, *Meiji no takara: Treasures of Imperial Japan – The Nasser D. Khalili Collection of Japanese Art*, vol. 1 (London: Kibo Foundation, 1995).

12 Despite Japan's self-imposed isolation, the country was never completely isolated, as it continued to carry out trade and cultural exchange with both Chinese and Dutch merchants via the little island of Dejima, in the bay of Nagasaki. See Donald Keene, *The Japanese Discovery of Europe, 1720–1830* (Stanford, CA: Stanford University Press, 1969), p. 13.

13 Colta Ives, *The Great Wave: The Influence of Japanese Woodcuts on French Prints*, exh. cat. (New York: Metropolitan Museum of Art, 1974), p. 11.

14 This was believed to be the way to establish Japan as a modern and civilised nation on a par with the Western powers and to potentially renegotiate the 'unequal treaties' of the 1850s and '60s.

15 The school's official programme stated: 'The technical Art School was established on November 6 as part of the main college. Its curriculum is to consist of painting and sculpture, painting involving instruction in drawing and oil painting, and sculpture involving instruction in the techniques for modeling the forms of various objects in plaster.' Quoted in Shūji Takashina and J. Thomas Rimer with Gerald D. Bolas, *Paris in Japan: The Japanese Encounter with European Painting* (Tokyo: Japan Foundation / St Louis, MO: Washington University in St Louis, 1987), p. 22.

16 See École Nationale Supérieure des Beaux-Arts, *Exposition de la gravure japonaise à l'École nationale des beaux-arts à Paris du 25 avril au 22 mai 1890*, exh. cat. (Paris: École Nationale des Beaux-Arts, 1890), cat. no. 476, p. 36.

17 See Segi Shinichi, 'Hayashi Tadamasa: Bridge between the Fine Arts of East and West', in *Japonisme in Art: An International Symposium* (Tokyo: Society for the Study of Japonisme, 1980), p. 169.

18 See Geneviève Aitken and Marianne Delafond, *Claude Monet's Collection of Japanese Prints* (Giverny: Éditions Claude Monet Giverny / Montreuil: Gourcuff Gradenigo, 2023).

19 Société de Peintres-Graveurs Français, *Troisième exposition, ouverte du 4 au 30 avril 1891*, exh. cat. (Paris: Galerie Durand-Ruel, 1891).

20 Jack Hillier, *The Japanese Print: A New Approach* (London: G. Bell & Sons, 1960), p. 168.

21 See for example Neil Harris, 'All the World a Melting Pot? Japan at American Fairs, 1876–1904', in *Mutual Images: Essays in American–Japanese Relations*, ed. Akira Iriye (Cambridge, MA: Harvard University Press, 1975), pp. 24–54. In 1905 Japan was also the victor in the Russo-Japanese War, begun in February the previous year.

22 The quotation in the subheading is from Oliver Statler, *Modern Japanese Prints: An Art Reborn* (Rutland, VT: Charles E. Tuttle, 1956), p. 181.

23 In March 2022, *Le repas frugal* set a world record for the price of a Picasso print when it fetched £6,014,500 at Christie's, London, also making it the most expensive print ever sold at auction. See 'Picasso's Prints: A Collecting Guide', www.christies.com, 23 February 2023.

24 For Degas, see Jill DeVonyar and Richard Kendall, *Degas and the Art of Japan*, exh. cat. (Reading, PA: Reading Public Museum, 2007); for Van Gogh, see Kate Bell, ed., *Van Gogh and Japan*, exh. cat. (Amsterdam: Van Gogh Museum, 2017); for Lautrec, see Ives, *The Great Wave*, pp. 79–95.

25 See for example Diana Widmaier, 'The Provenance of Picasso's Collection of Erotic Japanese Prints', in *Secret Images: Picasso and the Japanese Erotic Print*, exh. cat., Museu Picasso de Barcelona (London: Thames & Hudson, 2010), pp. 94–139.

26 Vincent van Gogh to Émile Bernard, Arles, Sunday, 18 March 1888, letter no. 587, Van Gogh Museum.

27 See for example the sections on Munakata Shikō, pp. 104–7, and Yayanagi Go, pp. 219–25.

28 Among the group's founding members was Yanagi Sōetsu, who later would become leader of the *mingei* (Japanese folk craft) movement and a significant influence on printmakers Munakata Shikō and Mori Yoshitoshi.

29 See Kōshirō Onchi, 'The Modern Japanese Print: An Internal History of the *Sosaku Hanga* Movement', *Ukiyo-e Art* (International Ukiyo-e Society), no. 11 (1965), p. 6.

30 The role Watanabe played was fundamental to the modern revival of the graphic medium in Japan. He also supported later generations of creative print artists, all the way up to his death in 1962, organising meetings in his print studio for young aspiring artists following the Second World War. See Funasaka Yoshisuke, pp. 57–63.

31 See Helen Merritt, *Modern Japanese Woodblock Prints: The Early Years* (Honolulu: University of Hawai'i Press, 1990), pp. 43–68.

32 Uncommon at the time, Watanabe also collaborated with Western print artists, including Friedrich 'Fritz' Capelari (1884–1950), Elizabeth Keith (1887–1956), Bertha Lum (1869–1954) and Charles Bartlett (1860–1940).

33 See the section on Yoshida Hiroshi, pp. 232–33.

34 Dorothy Blair, 'Foreword', in *Prints: Printed from a Photographic Reproduction of Two Exhibition Catalogues of Modern Japanese Prints Published by the Toledo Museum of Art in 1930 and 1936* (Toledo, OH: Toledo Museum of Art, 1997).

35 See also the section on Yamamoto Kanae, pp. 212–17.

36 Onchi, 'The Modern Japanese Print', p. 8.

37 See sections on Onchi Kōshirō, pp. 100–103, and Hiratsuka Un'ichi, pp. 68–71.

38 Onchi, 'The Modern Japanese Print', p. 3.

39 Ibid., p. 9.

40 Kiyoshi Hasegawa, *L'estampe japonaise moderne et ses origines: exposition organisée par la Société des peintres-graveurs japonais de Tokyo 'Nippon hanga kyokai'*, exh. cat. (Paris: Musée des Arts Décoratifs, 1934).

41 See Merritt, *Modern Japanese Woodblock Prints*, p. 147.

42 It was catalogued as *Femme nue, après le bain* (Nude Woman after Bathing) and dated 1915, Hasegawa, *L'estampe japonaise moderne et ses origines*, p. 67, cat. no. 392.

43 Société des Peintres-Graveurs Japonais, 'Introduction', in Hasegawa, *L'estampe japonaise moderne et ses origines*, p. 14.

44 Merritt, *Modern Japanese Woodblock Prints*, p. 152.

45 Introduction by James A. Michener in Statler, *Modern Japanese Prints*, p. xv.

46 The CWAJ is a non-profit organisation dedicated to education and run by volunteers since its founding in 1949. In 1951 the first travel grants were offered to nine students; the CWAJ Print Show became the main funder of the travel grants and scholarship programmes. This annual exhibition and sale of contemporary Japanese prints continues to this day and is the largest juried competition in Japan. It not only introduces high-quality Japanese print art but also offers opportunities for cultural exchange. The name College Women's Association of Japan was adopted officially in 1963 and by that time membership was extended to women of all nationalities. See for example CWAJ, *CWAJ Print Show: A 60-Year Journey, 1956–2015* (Tokyo: College Women's Association of Japan, 2015).

47 See *CWAJ Print Show: A 60-Year Journey*.

48 In 1960, Statler was also behind the Art Institute of Chicago's major exhibition *Modern Japanese Prints: Sōsaku hanga*, which was largely based on his personal collection. Statler also compiled the catalogue.

49 'Art: Japanese Print Revival', *Time*, 23 July 1956, https://time.com/archive/6803000/art-japanese-print-revival.

50 Merritt, *Modern Japanese Woodblock Prints*, p. 289. The quotation in the subheading is from Statler, *Modern Japanese Prints*, p. 181.

Artist Profiles

ASAWA, Ruth Aiko (1926–2013)

Medium:
Lithograph, monoprint and others

The excitement of printing has not left me, but I know it would take another lifetime to do it well.[1]

Ruth Asawa

As an artist recognised for her signature looped-wire biomorphic sculptures, based on a wire basketmaking technique she had learnt during a trip to Mexico in 1947 with Josef and Anni Albers, Ruth Asawa is rarely associated with printmaking. But during the course of just two months at the Tamarind Lithography Workshop in Los Angeles in 1965, Asawa created 54 lithographs. Based on original works by Asawa, they depict a range of eclectic motifs, including desert plants and flowers, portraits, nudes and patterns, often referencing the texture and form of her sculptures.

Born in California to Japanese immigrant parents, Asawa experienced the dark period of incarceration during the Second World War. In 1942–46, along with about 120,000 other people of Japanese descent, including the artist Isamu Noguchi (1904–1988), Asawa and most of her family were detained in incarceration camps by federal authorities. She was released in 1943, after sixteen months of incarceration, having gained admission to a teachers' college.

In 1946 Asawa enrolled at Black Mountain College, the progressive and experimental liberal arts college founded in North Carolina in 1933. She spent three years at the school, where she was taught by notable figures including the abstract painter and former Bauhaus educator Josef Albers (1888–1976) and the multidisciplinary designer R. Buckminster Fuller (1895–1983):

Teachers there were practicing artists, there was no separation between studying, performing the daily chores, and relating to many art forms. I … encountered great teachers who gave me enough stimulation to last me for the rest of my life – Josef Albers, painter, Buckminster Fuller, inventor, Max Dehn, the mathematician, and many others. Through them I came to understand the total commitment required if one must be an artist.[2]

It was Albers who recommended Asawa for the Tamarind fellowship, which he had participated in the year before. The Tamarind Lithography Workshop (today the Tamarind Institute) was founded in 1960 by the artist, entrepreneur and educator June Wayne (1918–2011) with the goal to save and revive traditional lithography printmaking. Taking up the eternal challenge to have printmaking accepted as an art form on a par with painting, Wayne saw the need for a place where artists could collaborate with printmakers to learn and gain from the technical process.[3] The establishment of the workshop helped contribute to a rising interest in printmaking among American collectors and artists during the 1960s.

Through art residencies and fellowships, the Tamarind Workshop hosted artists like Louise Nevelson (1899–1988), Matsumi Kanemitsu (1922–1992), Walasse Ting (1929–2010) and José Luis Cuevas (1934–2017), as well as master printmakers including Kinji Akagawa (b. 1940), Ernest de Soto (1923–2014), Irwin Hollander (1927–2018) and Kenneth E. Tyler (b. 1931), who afterwards set up workshops of their own. Tyler, for example, established several workshops throughout his career and collaborated with numerous

1 'Ruth Asawa's Little-Known Experiment with Printmaking', www.nga.gov/stories/ruth-asawa-experiment-with-printmaking.html, 11 May 2023.

2 'Black Mountain College', https://ruthasawa.com/life/black-mountain-college.

3 See Pat Gilmour, *Modern Prints* (London: Studio Vista, 1970), p. 122.

4 Ruth Asawa quoted in Tamara H. Schenkenberg, 'Life's Work', in *Ruth Asawa: Life's Work*, ed. Schenkenberg, exh. cat., Pulitzer Arts Foundation (St Louis, MO: Pulitzer Arts Foundation / New Haven, CT: Yale University Press, 2019), p. 11.

international artists, including Josef and Anni Albers (1899–1994), Roy Lichtenstein (1923–1997), Robert Rauschenberg (1925–2008) and Teraoka Masami (pp. 189–95).

A newcomer to the professional printmaking world, Asawa was already a successful sculptor and painter, having had an exhibition at the San Francisco Museum of Modern Art in 1954. She represented the USA at the São Paulo Biennial the following year and was included in the group show *Recent Sculpture USA* at the Museum of Modern Art, New York, in 1959. The San Francisco Museum of Modern Art, Museum of Modern Art in New York, Guggenheim Bilbao in Spain and Fondation Beyeler in Switzerland are hosting the first international posthumous Ruth Asawa retrospective in 2025–27.

Although Asawa is not known for her prints, she did experiment with many different forms of printmaking throughout her artistic career, including monoprints, mimeographs, serigraphs, photoelectric prints and relief prints. In this way, her work exists as a small part of a bigger modern printmaking history, with the medium connecting artists and printers, directly or indirectly, across countries and cultures.

Above everything be curious, learn all you can, and take a lifetime doing it.[4]

Ruth Asawa

Collections: Amon Carter Museum of American Art, Fort Worth; National Gallery of Art, Washington, DC; San Francisco Museum of Modern Art; Whitney Museum of American Art, New York.

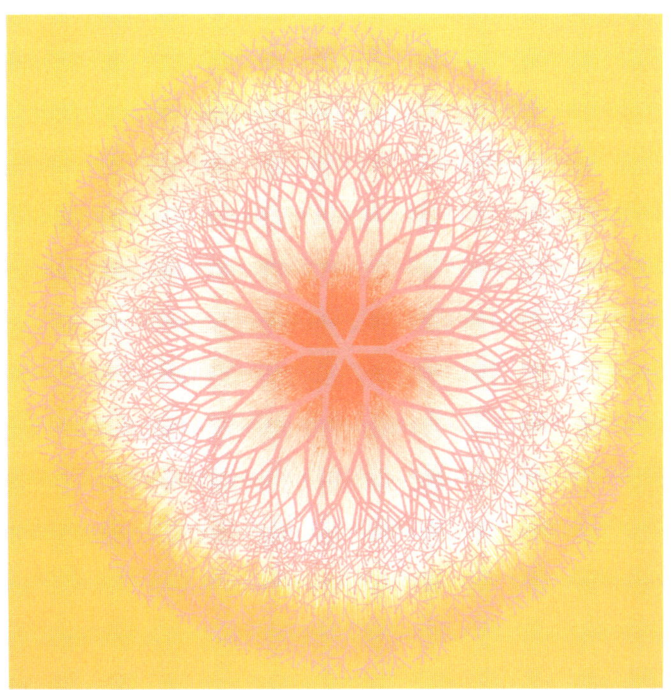

Desert Plant, 1965. Lithograph

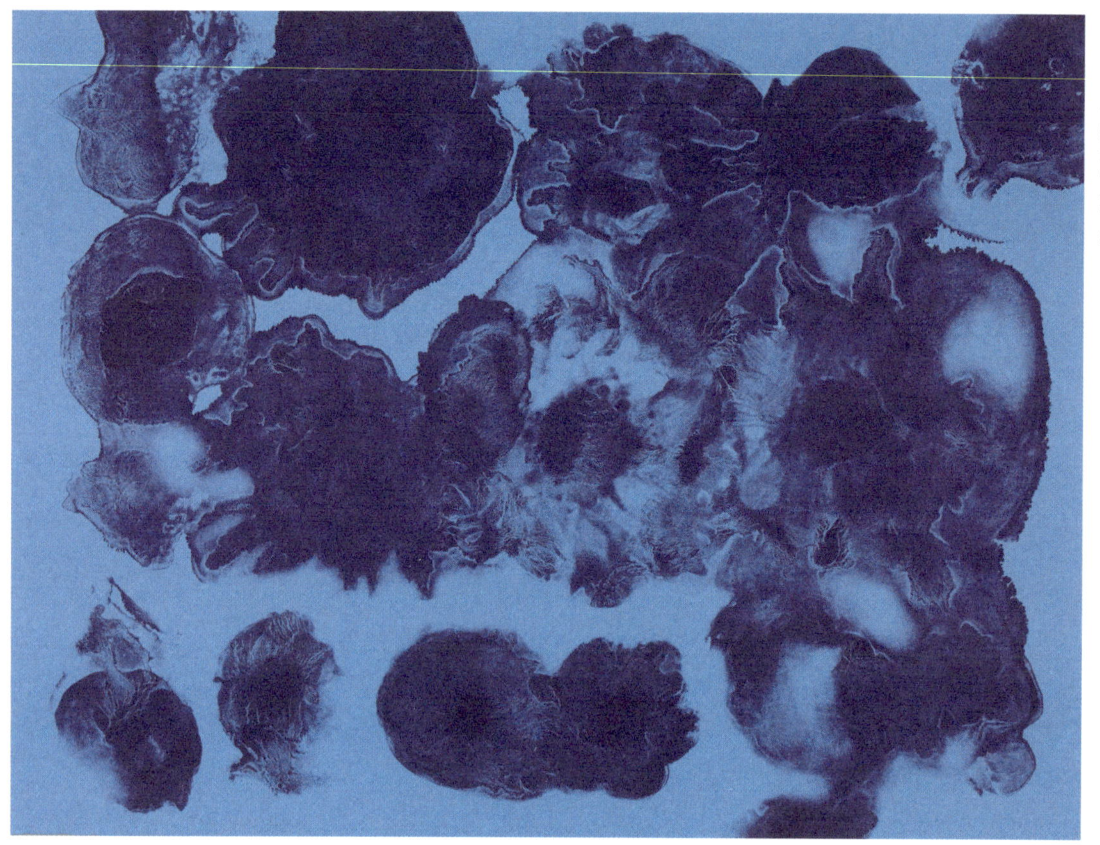

Untitled, 1965. Lithograph

Untitled, 1965. Lithograph

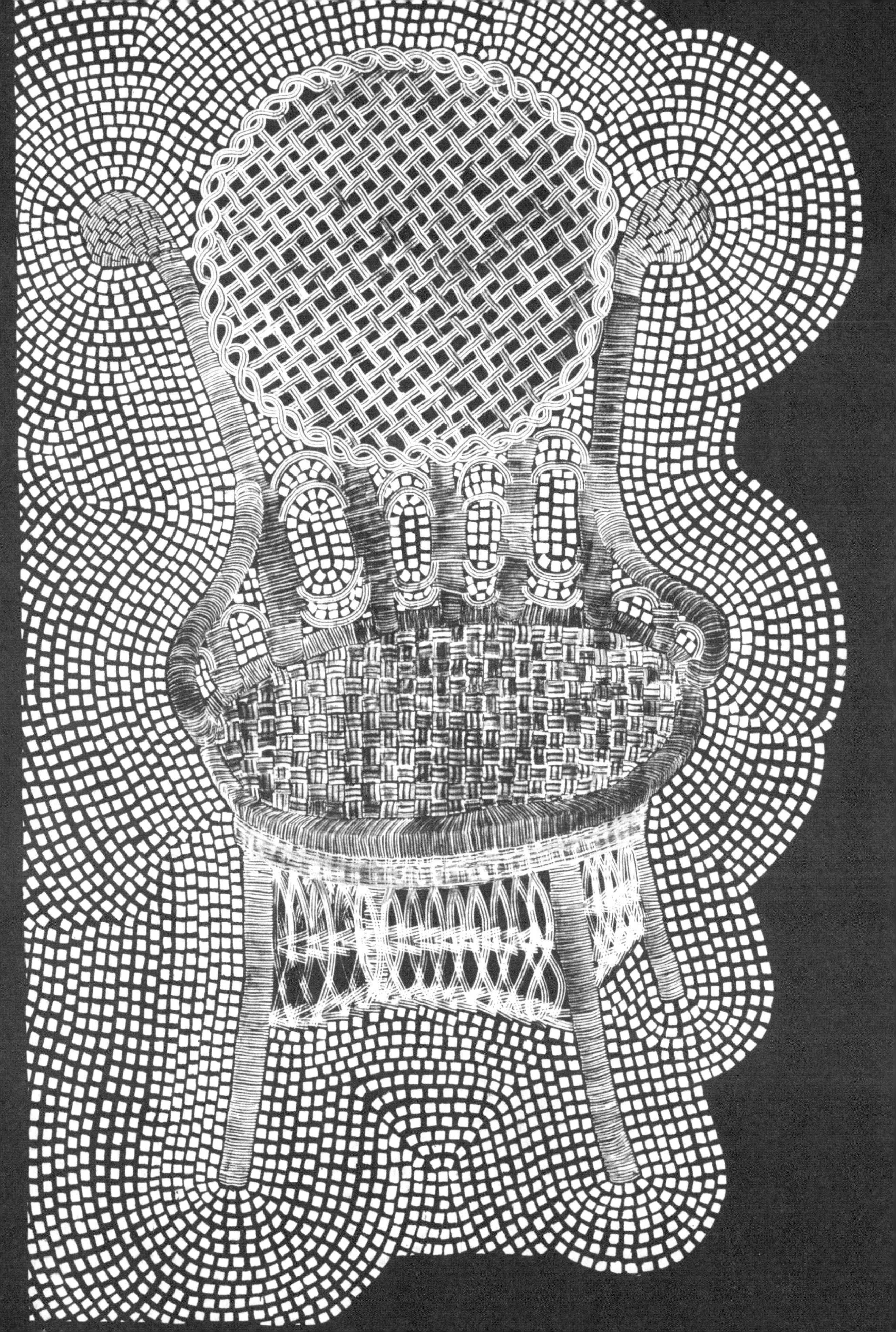

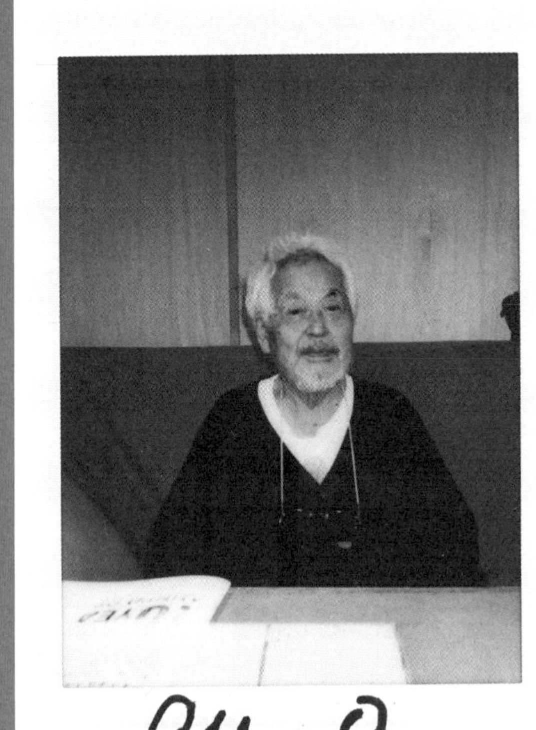
ay-O
2022

Ay-O (b.1931)

Medium:
Lithograph, silkscreen, stencil, woodblock

We know we can't turn back history. But we cannot pass up this marvelous lightness, benevolence, trust and love. New and amazing rebirths, including the trees and rocks, are all from love ... So my art only talks about these things.[1]

Ay-O, 1983

Having made the spectre of the rainbow his signature like a sort of modern-day King Midas, Ay-O has been known as the 'rainbow artist' since the 1960s, experimenting with a variety of modes of expression such as painting, printmaking, installations, environments and happenings. But according to Ay-O himself, he is not an artist.[2] From early on he fought against the concept, calling it 'a very stupid idea', as well as against the art establishment. Throughout his career, Ay-O's motivation has been to shock and move boundaries.

Born Iijima Takao in Ibaraki prefecture, Ay-O entered the art department of Tokyo University of Education in 1950. This was the same year that saw the American Abstract Expressionist Jackson Pollock's painting *Number 11, 1949* displayed in Tokyo at the annual Yomiuri Indépendant Exhibition, which made Ay-O think, 'I can do that, too.'

Ay-O took his artist name in 1953, while still a student. It derives from the word *ai*, meaning 'cloud', and *ō* from Jean-Paul Sartre's book *Nausea* (1938), in Japanese *Ōto*. In the beginning the artist would sign his work Ai-O, but he later changed it to Ay-O.[3] The name was likely inspired by his mentor Ei-Q (1911–1960), a Western-style painter turned avant-garde trailblazer who formed the multidisciplinary Democratic Artists' Association (Demokurāto Bijutsuka Kyōkai) in 1951, which Ay-O joined two years later.

In 1953, through Ei-Q, Ay-O met his patron Kubo Sadajirō (1909–1996), whose collection of works by artists such as Pablo Picasso, Paul Cézanne (1839–1906) and Fernand Léger (1881–1955) allowed Ay-O to study Western art up close. Equally important was Kubo's encouragement to work in the print medium, as he believed that it was 'an ideal form of art to be in the hands of the masses'.[4] This notion of the graphic medium's democratic nature echoes the earlier ideas of people like Yanagi Sōetsu (1889–1961), leader of the *mingei* movement, who emphasised that the original nature of (woodblock) prints was as an art for the many.[5]

As part of the wave of post-war artists who sought new inspiration outside Japan, Ay-O rejected Japanese art and culture, instead looking for chaos and colour in the West. Although Paris had been Ay-O's initial goal, by the time he graduated his enthusiasm for France had faded. This was replaced with an admiration for American art, specifically New York's avant-garde, with Pollock and his action paintings and Marcel Duchamp with his readymades foremost in his mind.

In 1958, at the age of 28 and encouraged by Ei-Q, he decided to move to New York. He did so with only $50, which he had bought on the Japanese black market. 'I am certain that May 19, 1958 was the first time I felt as though my heart was going to burst with excitement. This was both my birthday and the date I set to depart for America,' he later recalled.[6] Starting out with no real

1 First published in *Korekara dō naru: nihon, sekai, 21 seiki* [What Will Happen Next: Japan, the World, the 21st Century], ed. Iwanami Shoten Henshūbu (1983), quoted in *Ay-O: Rainbow 88*, exh. cat. (Karuizawa-machi: Karuizawa New Art Museum, 2019), p. 71.

2 Unless otherwise stated, this text is based on interviews conducted by the author with Ay-O in Tokyo, in the period October 2019 to May 2024.

3 Explained in *Ay-O: Rainbow 88*, p. 103.

4 Kubo Sadajirō quoted in Kazuko Todate, *Ay-O, 1950s–2010*, exh. cat. (Ibaraki: Tsukuba Museum of Art, 2010), p. 125.

5 See Munakata Shikō, pp. 104–7.

6 Ay-O, *Over the Rainbow: Retrospective, 1960–2006*, exh. cat., Fukui Fine Arts Museum and Miyazaki Prefectural Art Museum (Tokyo: Bijutsu Shuppan-sha, 2006), p. 153.

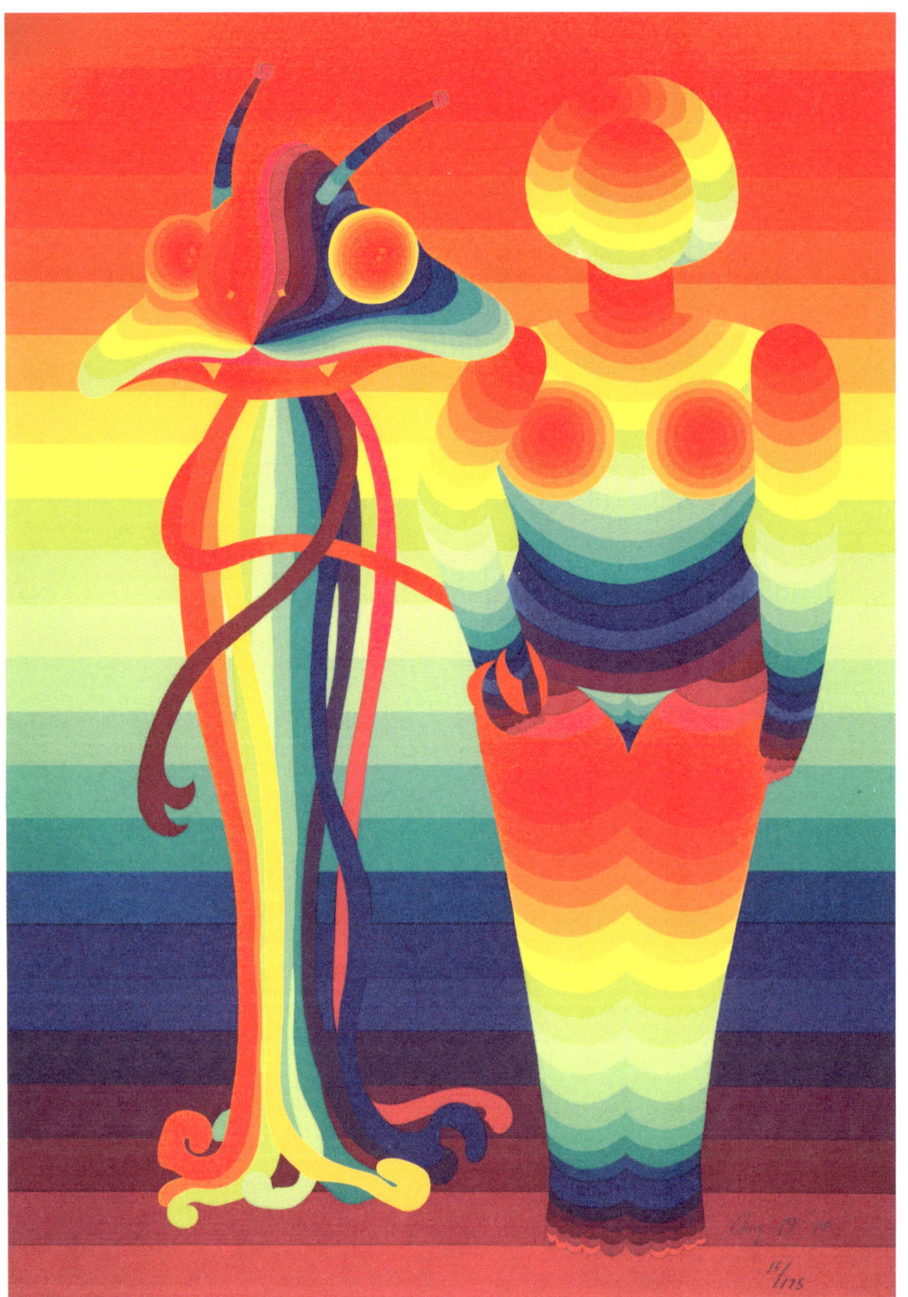

Well! Well! Well!, 1974. Silkscreen print

contacts, he worked in a restaurant and a souvenir shop, among other odd jobs, while pursuing art. For a good while he met continued resistance to – or rather, a lack of interest in – his Pollock-inspired action paintings at the galleries he visited, where he would show a note saying: 'My name is Ay-O. I am Japanese painter. Please look at my painting.'[7]

When Ay-O arrived in New York, Pollock had died two years previously. But he did meet Duchamp for the first time at the Alan Gallery. As Ay-O recalls, 'Because my English was not so good, I did not speak.' Yet he was happy.

Among the other people Ay-O encountered in New York was multimedia artist Yoko Ono (b. 1933): 'In those days, I met Yoko quite often. There were perhaps no other Japanese artists, except for me, who were searching for a new strange world like the one she saw.'[8] He also met Andy Warhol (1928–1987) and Isamu Noguchi, the latter of whom Ono brought to Ay-O's studio. It was also through an introduction by Ono that Ay-O met Lithuanian-born George Maciunas (1931–1978), the founder of the international interdisciplinary and experimental movement Fluxus, of which Ay-O became part.

Ay-O's first Fluxus 'environment' was *Tea House* (1961), a box painted black on the outside and red on the inside, which people could go inside to meditate: 'Since it was a small room with a certain atmospheric device than a work to look at, I explained to my new friends that this was called Atmosphere Art. I named it *Tea House*.'[9] The following year he had his first solo exhibition, *Ay-O First One Man Show in USA*, at Gordon's Fifth Avenue Gallery. The rainbow first appeared in Ay-O's oil paintings shortly after that show, when he started painting bands of different colours in gradation: 'My first work that appealed to the sense of sight was the rainbow spectrum piece that started in my empty studio after shipping my works to Gordon's Fifth Avenue Gallery.'[10] Ay-O's first 'rainbow exhibition' was held at the Smolin Gallery, New York, in 1964, titled *Rainbow Environment No. 1: Rainbow Room*.

A turning point came when he was chosen to exhibit as part of the Japanese pavilion at the 33rd Venice Biennale in 1966. 'In the fall of 1965, I received an announcement from [biennale] commissioner Sadajiro Kubo that I had been chosen to represent Japan in the Venice Biennale along with Toshinobu Onosato, Masuo Ikeda, and Morio Shinoda. I only had six months to prepare ... but I wanted to present a work that culminated everything that I had experienced then.'[11] At the time an active Fluxus member, Ay-O presented *Rainbow Environment No. 3: Tactile Room* in Venice, a tactile installation consisting of 65 rainbow-coloured 'finger boxes'. He invited the audience to interact with the work by putting a finger inside; a sign stated: 'Audience, please place finger here.'[12]

The installation proved popular among visitors, although the contents of some of the boxes became a problem (some contained iron nails). It was described by critic Lawrence Alloway as 'one of the first multi-sense art works to be seen in the Biennale ... and certainly a sign of many environmental displays to come'.[13] This led to his international acclaim as the 'rainbow artist', appearing in magazines like *Time and Life*.

In 1966 Ay-O also ventured into the graphic medium of silkscreen. Depicting his subjects in pure colours, and emphasising warm tones over cold, he

7 Ibid., p. 156.
8 Ay-O quoted ibid., p. 164.
9 Ibid., p. 161.
10 Ibid., p. 172.
11 Ibid., p. 173.
12 *Ay-O: Rainbow 88*, p. 11.
13 Lawrence Alloway, *The Venice Biennale, 1895–1968: From Salon to Goldfish Bowl* (New York: New York Graphic Society, 1968), p. 151.

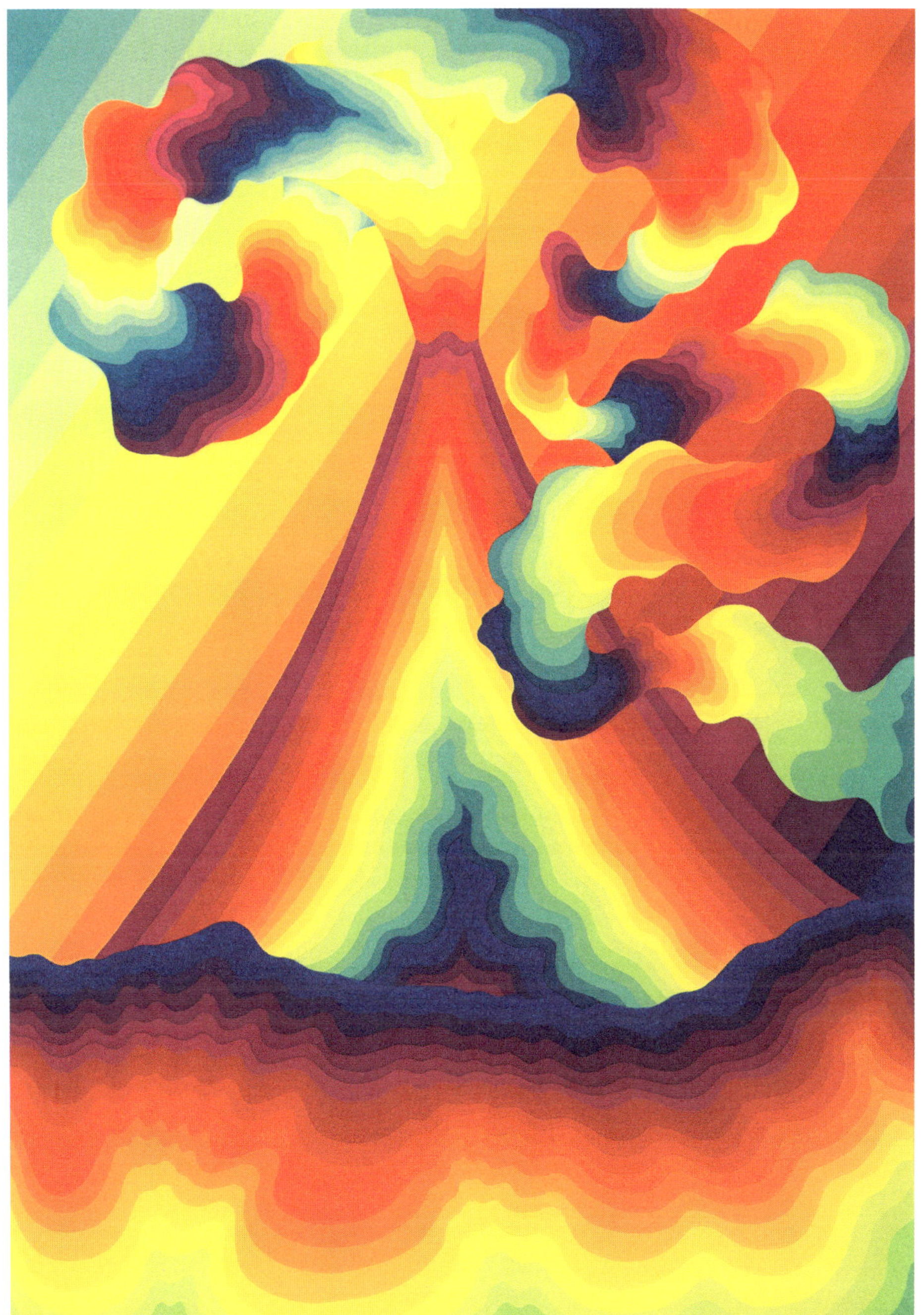

Rainbow Volcano, 1974. Silkscreen print

transformed them into his own language of lineless rainbow compositions in print. Ay-O rejected the use of lines, so that from the 1960s onwards his motifs came to exist only as colours.

Throughout his printing career, which has spanned almost seventy years, Ay-O has worked with the same two printers, both of whom he met via Kubo. Okabe Tokuzō (1932–2006), who had established the first screenprinting studio in Japan in 1964, made the first of Ay-O's silkscreen prints in 1966. They would work together until Okabe's death in 2006. In 1967 Ay-O also began collaborating with Sukeda Kenryō (b. 1941), with whom he continues to work to this day. Both printers played an important part in bringing Ay-O's concepts and ideas to life, working on more than one thousand prints. Working with 24 core colours, Ay-O would give Okabe and Sukeda only a few instructions to follow according to a colour system, such as '12 is lemon yellow, 20 is cobalt blue'. Having created the drawing, and with a rough idea of what he wanted, Ay-O would leave the colours in between for the printer to work with.[14] In this way, Ay-O himself is surprised by the finished result. He says of this process: 'Some people think that the artwork should be made by the artist and not be shared, but I wanted to change that idea. I wanted to involve other professional people to create the best artwork. I wanted to utilise the aspect of the traditional printmaking style of sharing,' referring to the old *hanmoto* system of *ukiyo-e* printmaking. Giving a 'cue' to his printers is also a reference to his Fluxus background, where it was common for artists to perform unpredictable actions according to a set of basic 'instructions'.[15]

Ay-O's subjects are eclectic, ranging from very Western motifs, such as in the work *Nashville Skyline* (1971), inspired by Bob Dylan's 1969 album, to quintessentially Japanese ones such as Mt Fuji and the Shinkansen (bullet train). But the artist also picks his subjects freely: 'If I see a cute horse in green fields and I like it, I will depict it,' he says with a laugh.

Taking a comical-ironic approach to gender, Ay-O produced several works during the 1970s playing with the idea of stereotypically 'male' and 'female' figures in various configurations, such as in *Well! Well! Well!*, which shows a phallic jellyfish and a woman holding 'hands' as part of the series *Rainbow Landscape* (1974). When Ay-O gave his friend and fellow printmaker Noda Tetsuya (pp. 117–23) the print *Mr and Mrs Rainbow B* (1971) as a wedding gift, in true Ay-O humour he had written the names so that it said 'Tetsuya' on the female figure and his wife's name, 'Dorit', on the male figure.

At times Ay-O has taken up classic Japanese subjects from woodblock prints, like sumo wrestlers and Mt Fuji, or he has borrowed from the erotic genre of *shunga*, such as in his print *Fingerbox* (1974), depicting an intimate Edo bath house scene. The title is clearly also a playful reference to his tactile 'finger boxes' from the 1960s. The most famous of his works in the *shunga* genre is *Depiction of the Ten Commandments, Rainbow Buddha*, also known as *Rainbow Hokusai* (1970). Based on a classic erotic woodblock print that Ay-O believed was by Hokusai but which was later identified as being by Keisai Eisen (1790–1848),[16] the work consists of 54 square silkscreen prints to be assembled like a puzzle. The story goes that while Ay-O was teaching at the University of Kentucky in 1968–69, he asked his friend Kubo to copy and send him two of his favourite *shunga* prints from his collection. To avoid trouble with the Japanese postal service because of the sexual content, Kubo cut them into several squares.[17] When Ay-O put the pieces back

14 See for example *Ay-O: Rainbow 88*, p. 40.
15 For more on Fluxus see ibid., pp. 119–26.
16 Thank you to Kit Brooks, Curator of Asian Art at Princeton University Art Museum, for sharing the source of the original print by Keisai Eisen.

together he was inspired to make a work of art as a puzzle, which would also function as an event piece (taking up to thirty minutes to assemble).

In 1970, *Rainbow Hokusai*, which was printed by Okabe, was shown in two versions, *Position A* and *B*, at the 7th International Biennial Exhibition of Prints in Tokyo, at which Ay-O won the prize offered by the Tokyo National Museum of Modern Art. Thirty-four Japanese artists participated with their prints that year, including Noda Tetsuya, Satō Ado (pp. 146–51), Funasake Yoshisuke (pp. 57–63), Yayanagi Go (pp. 219–25) and Kurosaki Akira (pp. 90–93). Among the US entrants was American composer and artist John Cage (1912–1992), who had a big impact on Ay-O and the Fluxus group. He was represented with the lithograph *Not Wanting to Say Anything about Marcel* (1969), a homage to Duchamp, who had died in 1968. Ay-O had also participated in the first print biennale in Tokyo in 1957, alongside other members of the Democratic Artists' Association, with etchings made from an etching press Kubo had sent Ei-Q.

From an anti-art 'rebel' to a leading figure in and exponent of the artistic exchange between Japan and the West, Ay-O has created his rainbow happenings, environments and silkscreen prints continuously since the 1960s. Perhaps he is best understood not as an artist but as an innovator. Either way, he does not care how he is perceived: 'The only reason I started making art was to destroy art. I just want to make fun things to make people happy,' he says.

Ay-O, now 94 years old, lives in Tokyo with his daughter and her family. In recent years he has begun producing rainbow ink paintings on paper, and in 2024 he returned to the print medium with new designs, which his lifelong printing partner Sukeda turns into silkscreen prints, following Ay-O's usual colour instructions. The new series is based on the hiragana syllabary, with each print representing a single character or syllable. So far, Ay-O has made eleven designs, with 37 more to go.[18]

In 2006 and 2010, two retrospective exhibitions spanning over fifty years of his creation of 'rainbows' were mounted in Japan. Ay-O was also included in the Museum of Modern Art exhibition *Tokyo 1955–1970: A New Avant-Garde* in 2013. In 2023 the National Museum of Asian Art in Washington, DC, presented the first Ay-O solo exhibition in a Western museum.

Collections: British Museum, London; Cincinnati Art Museum; Louisiana Museum of Modern Art, Humlebæk; Museum of Modern Art, New York; Tokyo National Museum of Modern Art.

17 As told to the author by Ay-O. The story is also published in *Ay-O: Rainbow 88*, pp. 40–41.

18 When the author visited Ay-O in April 2025, he was working on the titles for the remaining prints in the series.

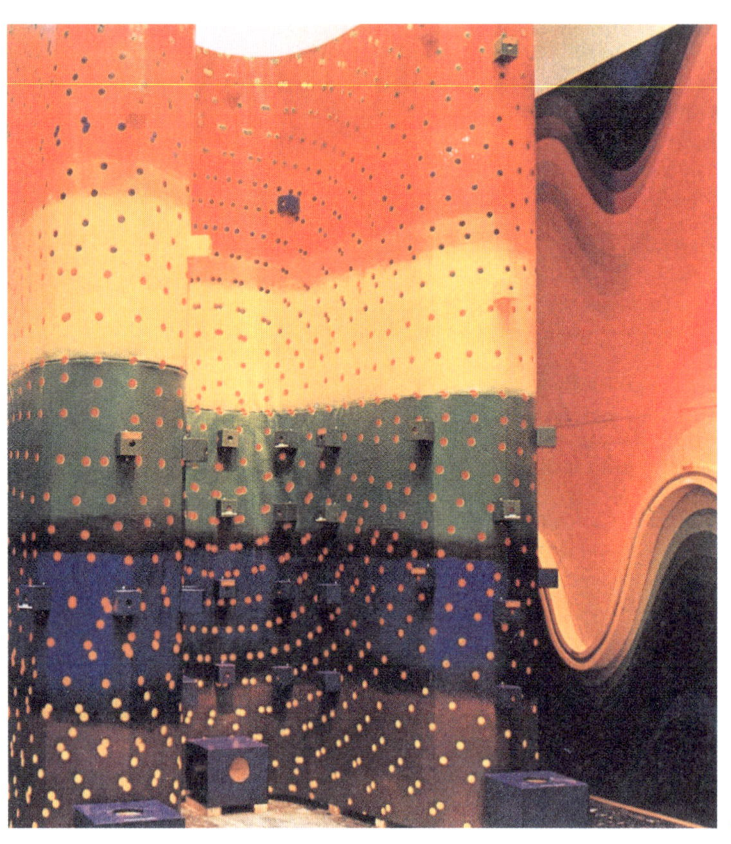

1

1 Ay-O — Installation view of *Rainbow Environment*, 1966, at the 33rd Venice Biennale
2 KEISAI Eisen — *Buddha*, c. early 19th century. Woodblock print
3 Ay-O — *Rainbow Hokusai, Position A*, 1970. Silkscreen print

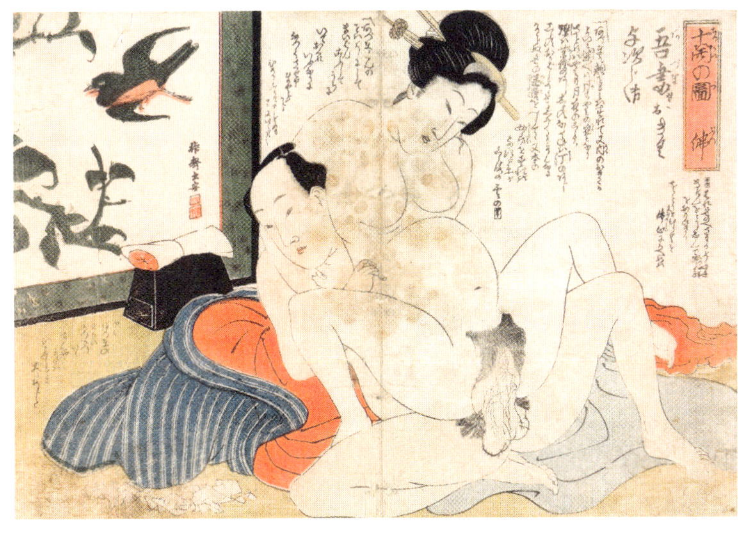

2

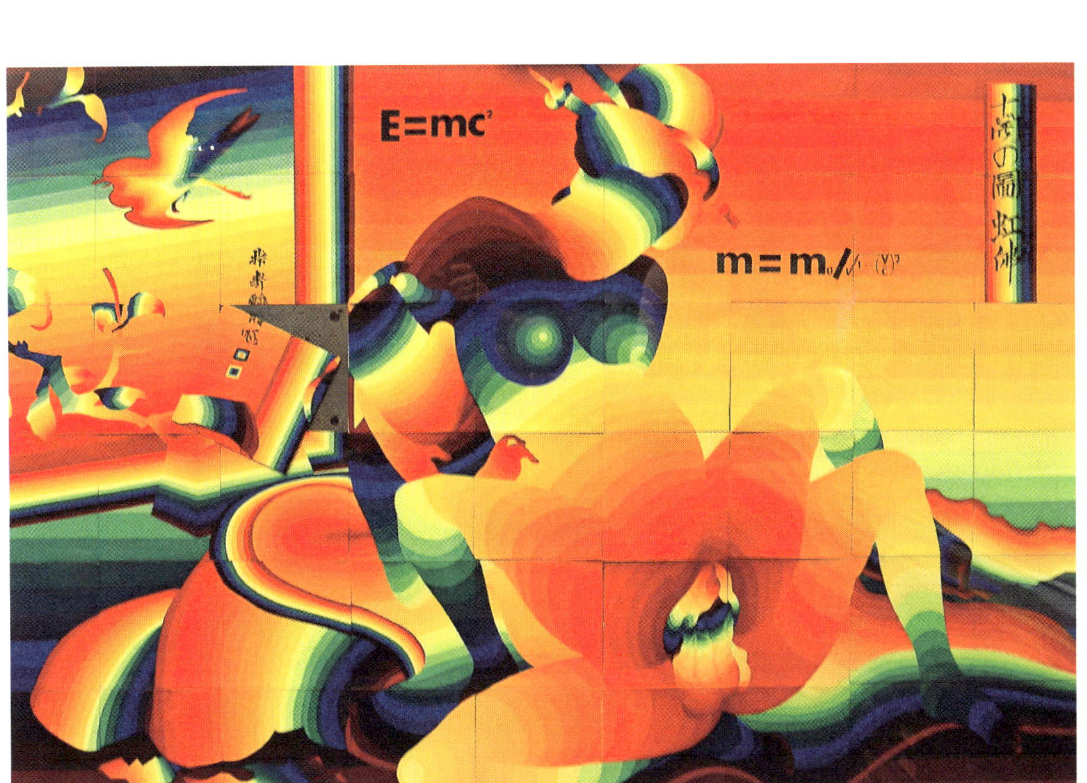

3

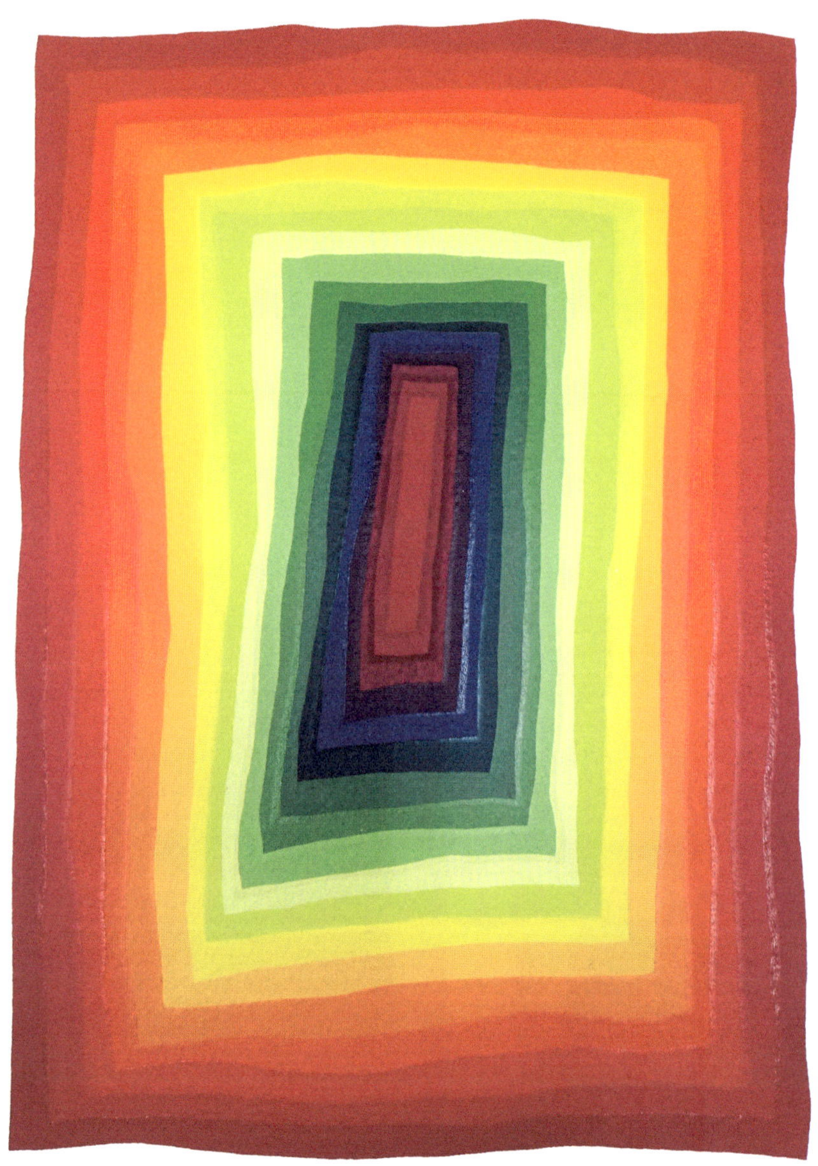

HO (ほ), 2024. Silkscreen print

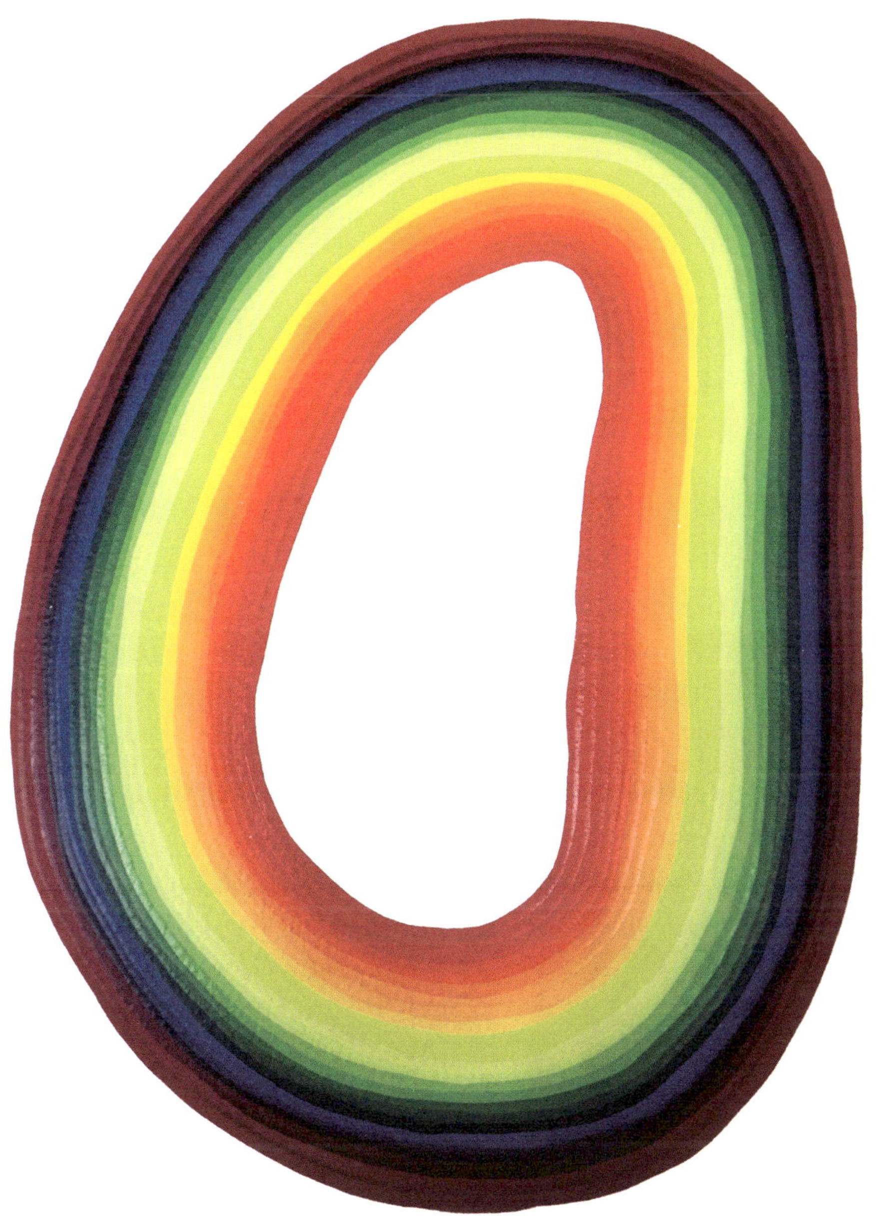

RU (る), 2024. Silkscreen print

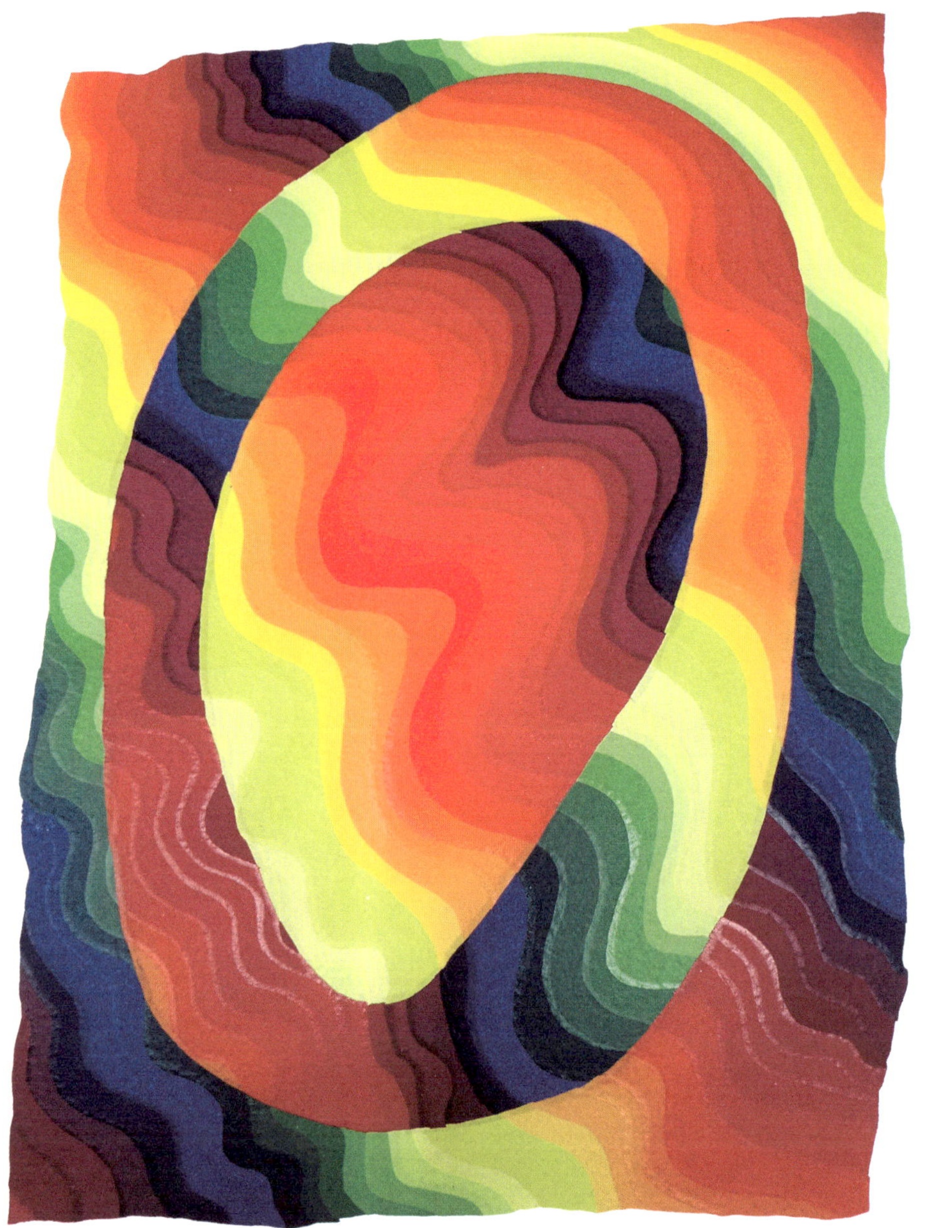

RI (רי), 2024. Silkscreen print

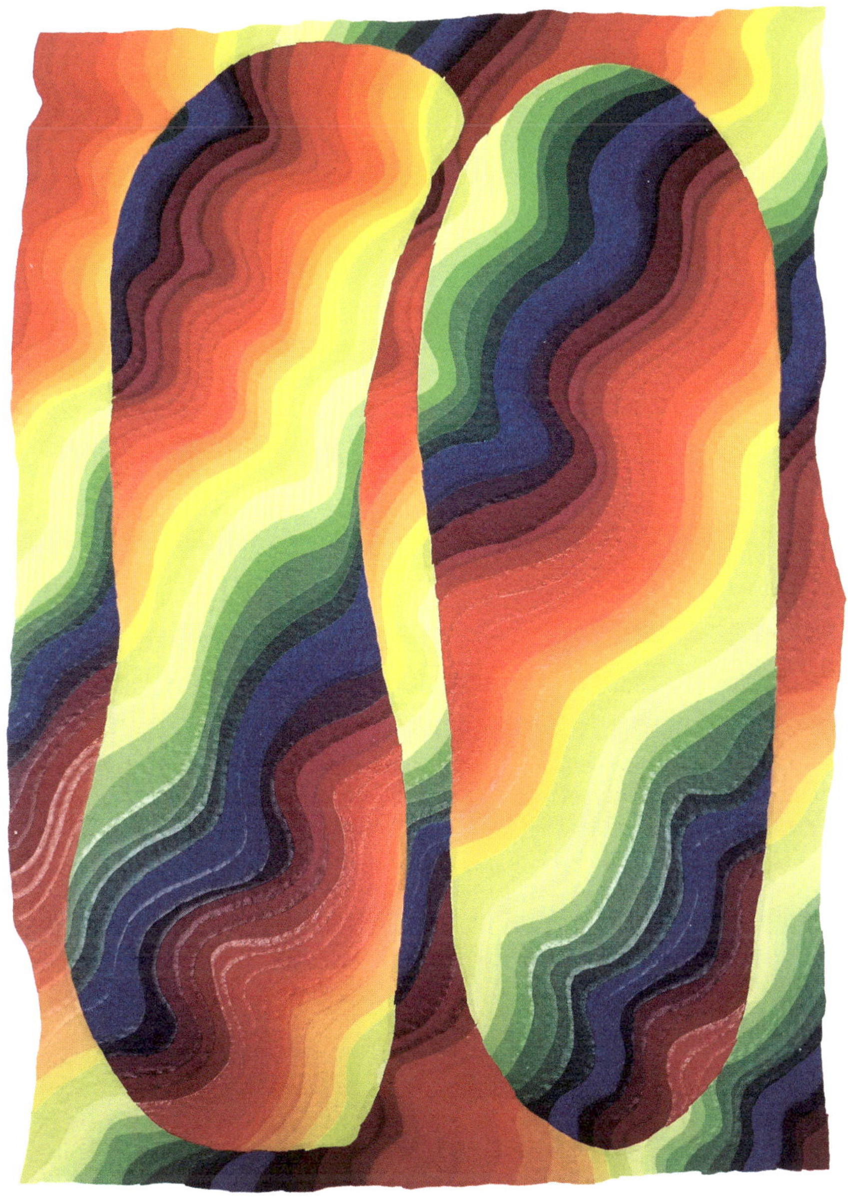

NU (ぬ), 2024. Silkscreen print

AZECHI Umetarō (1902–1999)

Medium:
Woodblock

Despite their repetitiousness, one never becomes bored with Azechi's prints. Their humour delights. They can be called primitive, but their primitiveness is the bold statement of a mature artist, not the accidental simplicity of a child.[1]

Frances Blakemore, 1975

Azechi Umetarō was born in rural Ehime prefecture on the southern Japanese island of Shikoku, the son of a poor farmer and amateur carver. His prints offer a nostalgic expression of the relationship between man and mountain: charming, bearded mountain men (*yama-otoko*), often holding a bird or climbing gear, portrayed in lonely mountains. Azechi's style is distinct and authentic – primitive, perhaps – rustic and bold, leaning towards Cubism and abstractionism.

Azechi studied Western art via correspondence courses from a school in Tokyo, and at nineteen years old he left home to try his luck in the capital. After a few detours and various jobs, he returned to Shikoku following the Kantō earthquake in 1923, which destroyed large parts of Tokyo. Azechi finally moved back to Tokyo in 1925 and began working at a government printing office, where he made prints by engraving on lead plates. Largely self-taught, his experiments with a nail or knife led him to the path of woodblock printing, when in 1926 he became a student of the *sōsaku hanga* artist Hiratsuka Un'ichi (pp. 68–71), who took him under his wing and became his mentor: 'Hiratsuka was kind. He invited me in, showed me his own work, and encouraged me about my lead-plate prints,' Azechi recalled.[2]

It was also Hiratsuka who encouraged Azechi to submit to the Japan Creative Print Association the following year and who managed to pass him occasional jobs as an artisan printer, which led Azechi to work for other important creative print artists like Onchi Kōshirō (pp. 130–33) and Maekawa Senpan (1888–1960), who would influence him as well: 'I'm grateful to Hiratsuka for his initial encouragement and his steady support all through the years. Maybe without him I wouldn't be an artist today. As for my work, the greatest influence was Onchi, and my simplified style today owes much to him.'[3]

Azechi's early prints from the 1920s and 1930s were generic landscapes and city scenes, but his great interest in mountain climbing brought him to his new subject: mountain scenes. With the mountain peaks as his focus, these prints usually show no humans and only a few trees, if any. Of them Azechi said: 'Most of my mountaineering friends don't like these prints. Their love for the mountains is very literal, and they strongly object that I change the forms of the peaks in my prints.'[4]

Azechi's next type of prints – 'rugged, simplified, idealized portraits of mountain men'[5] – became his trademark and led him to international recognition through their frequent inclusion in exhibitions in Japan and abroad. Azechi participated in the São Paulo Biennial in 1953 and 1957 and in the New York Museum of Modern Art's 1955 exhibition *Prints from Europe and Japan*, which included Azechi's *Mountain Guide B* (1953). The following year he showed at the first CWAJ exhibition, and did so for the next ten consecutive years. Azechi was also represented in an Art Institute of Chicago

1 Frances Blakemore, *Who's Who in Modern Japanese Prints* (New York and Tokyo: Weatherhill, 1975), p. 28.
2 Azechi Umetarō quoted in Oliver Statler, *Modern Japanese Prints: An Art Reborn* (Rutland, VT: Charles E. Tuttle Co., 1956), p. 138.
3 Ibid., p. 139.
4 Azechi Umetarō quoted in James Michener, *The Modern Japanese Print: An Appreciation* (Rutland, VT, and Tokyo: Charles E. Tuttle Co., 1968), p. 41.
5 Ibid.
6 Umetaro Azechi, *Japanese Woodblock Prints: Their Techniques and Appreciation* (Tokyo: Toto Shuppan, 1963), n.p.

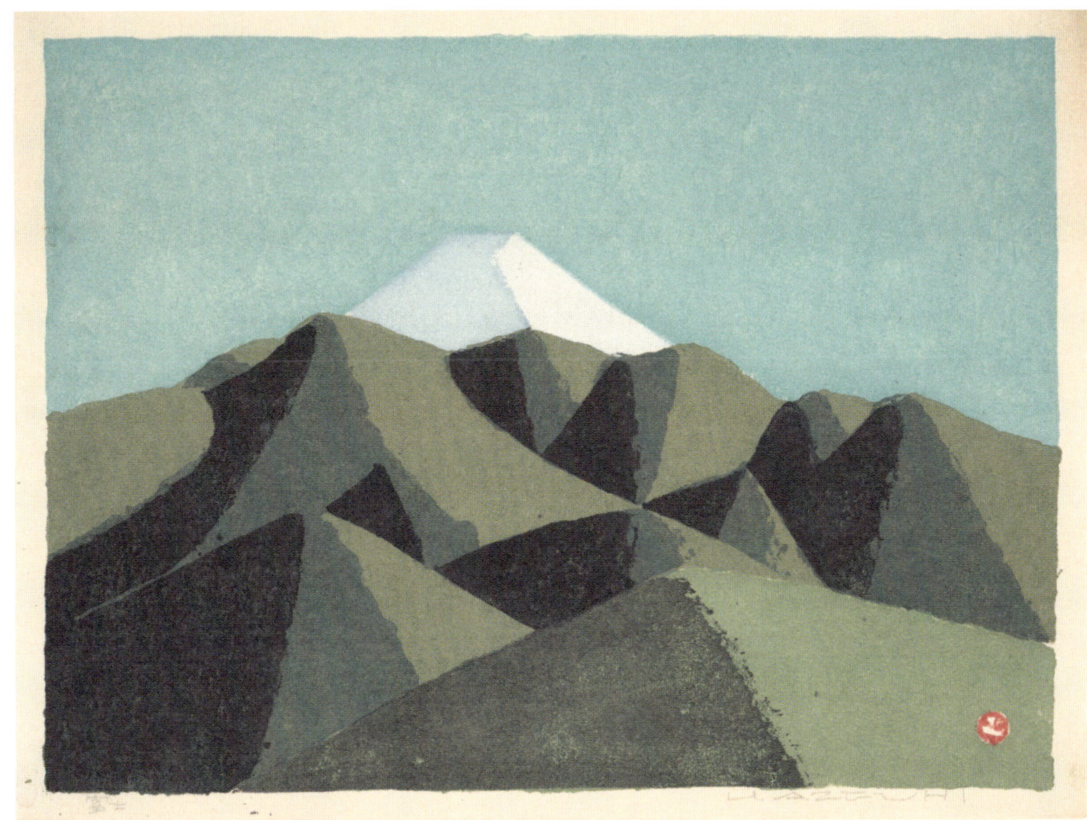

Fuji, 1951. Woodblock print

exhibition in 1960 with ten works, as well as at the Los Angeles County Museum of Art in the show *Contemporary Japanese Prints* in 1972.

Azechi worked to promote and teach printmaking, leading him to write the book *Japanese Woodblock Prints: Their Techniques and Appreciation* (1963), published in English, in which he stated: 'Although the famous *ukiyo-e* are a thing of the past, the reader will become aware that the unique traditional woodblock techniques which were evolved in Japan still live on in the "creative prints" of the present',[6] thereby cementing the connection between the traditional Japanese printmakers of Hokusai's era and the modern print movement of his own.

Collections: Art Institute of Chicago; Azechi Umetaro Memorial Museum, Uwajima; British Museum, London; Machida City Museum of Graphic Arts; Museum of Fine Arts, Boston; Museum of Modern Art, New York; National Museum of Modern Art, Tokyo.

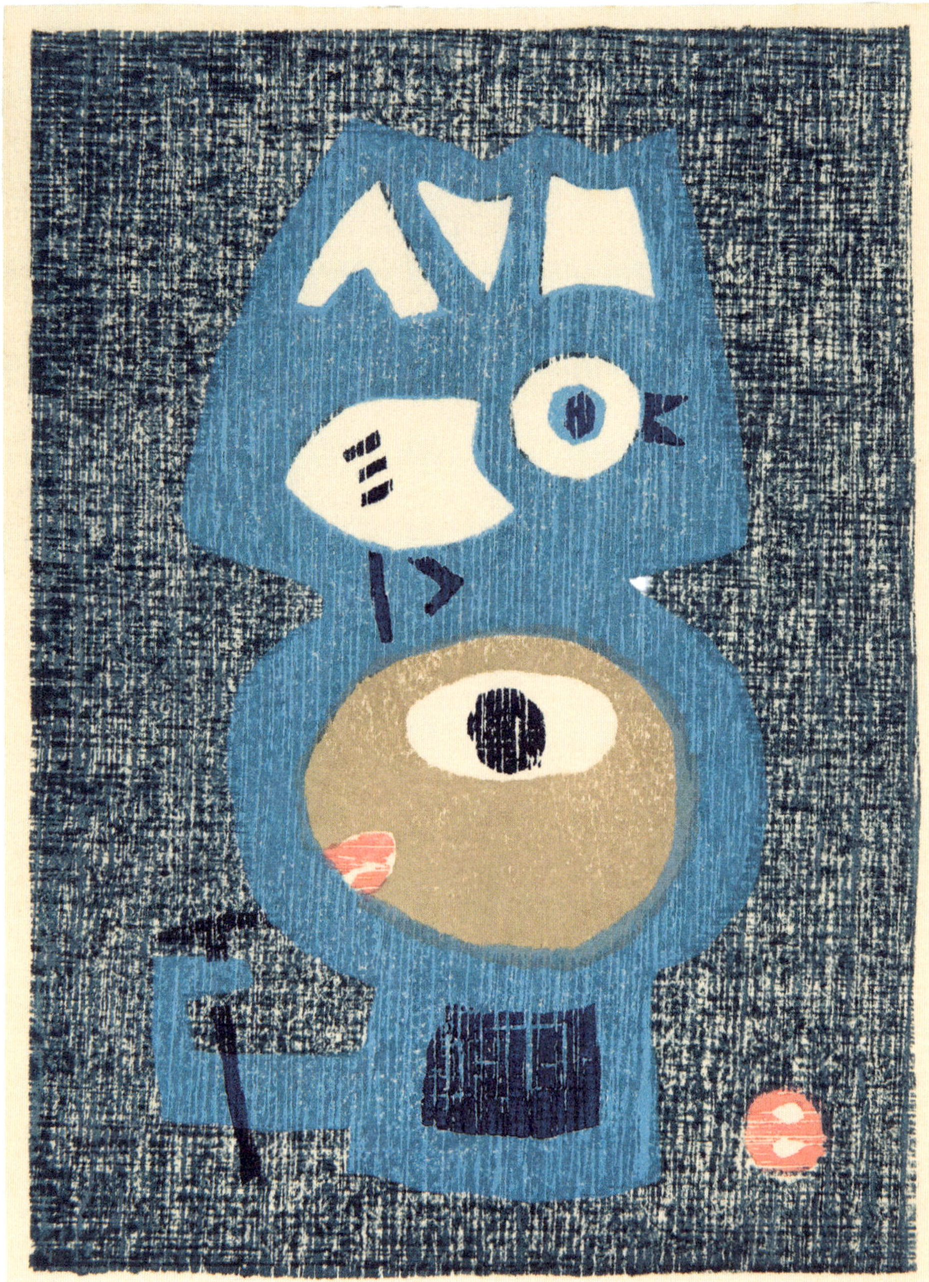

Bird and Pickle, c.1970s. Woodblock print

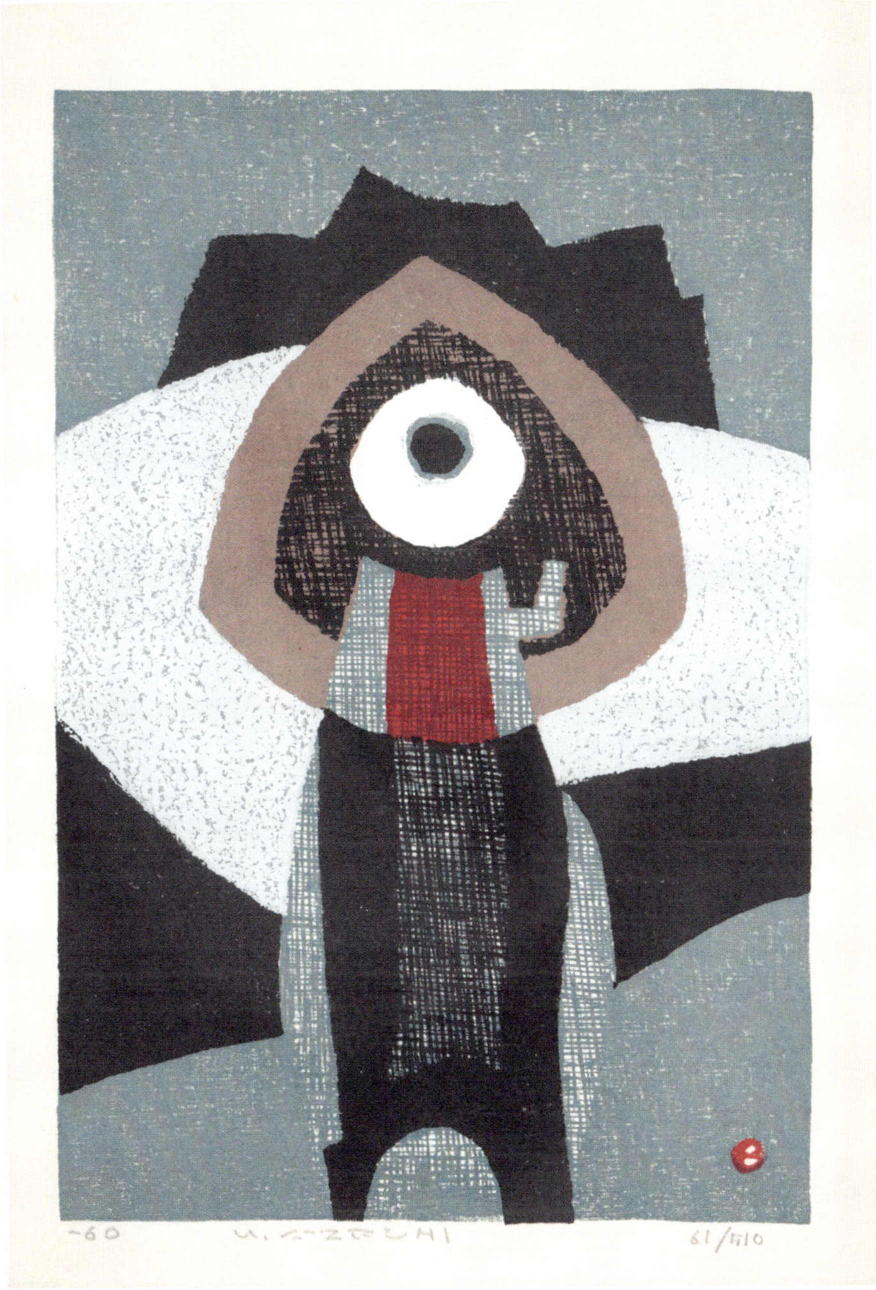

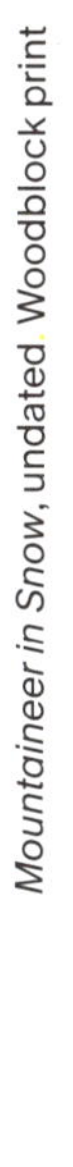

Mountaineer in Snow, undated, Woodblock print

FOUJITA
Léonard Tsuguharu (1886–1968)

Medium:
Etching, lithograph, woodblock and others

I was raised in Japan, but my painting grew up in France ...
So now I have two native countries. I'm an international person.
I feel nostalgia for two countries.[1]

Foujita, 1942

Foujita Tsuguharu, who took the Christian name Léonard after Leonardo da Vinci, was a living synthesis of East and West. Described in *Time* magazine in 1929 as 'wearing leopard skin trousers, grey suspenders, no shirt and a high silk hat',[2] in addition to his bluntly chopped pudding-bowl haircut, moustache, round glasses and hoop earrings, Foujita stood out as Frenchified to the Japanese. But in France he was considered 'exotic, original'[3] – and perhaps the chicest artist in 1920s Paris.

Born in the first half of the Meiji period, when Japan was undergoing rapid change, Foujita experienced how Western culture was favoured over Japanese, and how many young Japanese people went to the European capitals to study. And so did Foujita: after graduating in Western-style painting (*yōga*) from the Tokyo School of Fine Arts, in 1913 he left for Paris, where he would spend about half of his life.

After arriving in the 'City of Light', Foujita visited Pablo Picasso's studio. Being part of the École de Paris community of avant-garde artists who flocked to the French capital from around the world meant Foujita moved in the same circles as Picasso, Amedeo Modigliani (1884–1920), Diego Rivera (1886–1957) and Ossip Zadkine (1888–1967), as well as the dancer and singer Josephine Baker (1906–1975) and the painter and artists' model Kiki de Montparnasse (1901–1953). Foujita had his first solo exhibition of watercolours in 1917 at Galerie Chéron, and the following years saw him establishing himself in the Parisian art world and becoming a member of the Salon d'Automne in 1919.

Kiki posed for Foujita on several occasions, including in 1922 for the painting *Reclining Nude with Toile de Jouy*, which won him acclaim at the Salon d'Automne: 'The "great milk-white" skin depicted in delicately graceful lines in his portraits of nudes earned much esteem in Europe in those days.'[4] In portraying his nudes, Foujita was inspired by the classic *ukiyo-e* of his home country, especially the work of Kitagawa Utamaro (c. 1753–1806) and Suzuki Harunobu (c. 1725–1770) in their manner of depicting the human skin.[5]

Highly acclaimed for his paintings and drawings, especially his white nudes and depictions of cats, Foujita also worked in the graphic medium, like many of his contemporaries. In printmaking he used various techniques – lithography, etching, aquatint and woodblock – and collaborated with publishers such as Le Chien de Pique and Éditions Artistiques Apollo, as well as the Société de la Gravure sur Bois Originale (Society of Original Wood Engravers). The motifs are similar to those of his paintings and drawings: children, self-portraits, female nudes. Credited with popularising the 'artist and cat' archetype, he often portrayed his subjects in the company of a cat, his favourite animal and a symbol of luck in Japanese culture. 'The reason why I so much enjoy being friends with cats is that they have two different characters: a wild side and a domestic side,' he said.[6] In 1930 he produced *A Book of*

1 Foujita, *Foujita* (Paris: Éditions FAGE, 2018), p. 42.
2 'Art: Foujita's Return', *Time*, 5 August 1929, www.time.com/archive/6743194/art-foujitas-return.
3 Ibid.
4 Masaaki Ozaki, ed., *Léonard Foujita* (Tokyo: NHK Promotions Co. and Nihon Keizai Shimbun, 2006), p. 200.
5 Ibid., p. 188.
6 Ibid., p. 40.

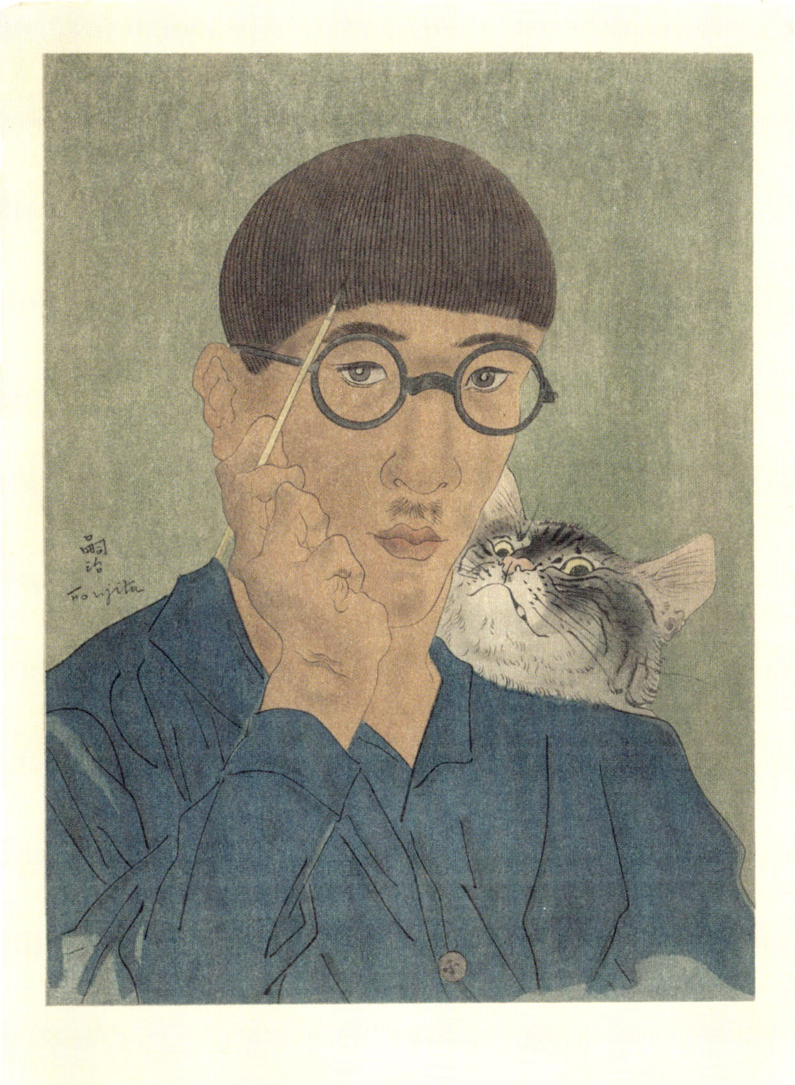

Self-Portrait with Cat, c.1920s. Woodblock print

Cats containing twenty etchings, published in New York by Covici Friede in an edition of 500. He continued to produce prints all the way into the final decade of his life.

Whether in prints, paintings or drawings, Foujita's work expressed a coming together of Eastern and Western aesthetics, a result of traditions and modernity meeting across cultures. Retrospective exhibitions were held at Pola Museum of Art in Hakone (2021); Tokyo Metropolitan Museum of Art and Musée Maillol in Paris (2018); and the National Museum of Modern Art, Tokyo (2006).

Collections: Art Institute of Chicago; Brooklyn Museum, New York; Centre Pompidou, Paris; Karuizawa Ando Museum of Art; Pola Museum of Art, Hakone.

Untitled (Reclining Nudes), undated. Etching and roulette

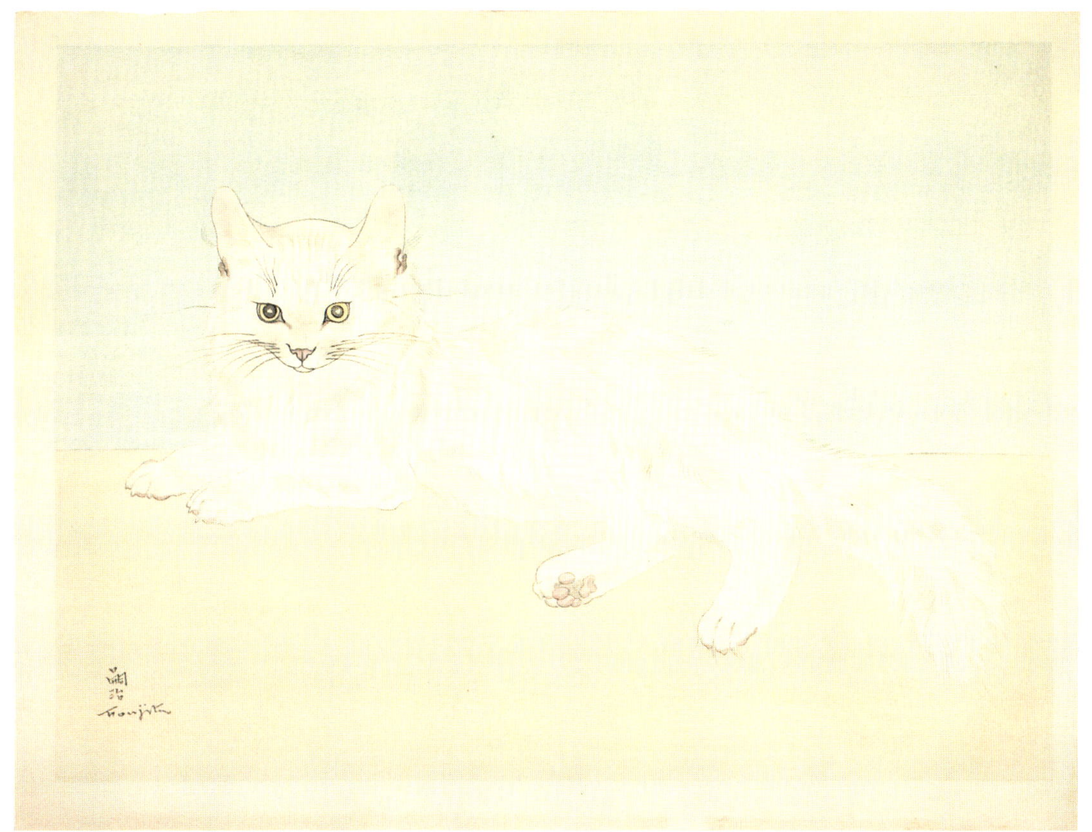

White Persian Cat, c.1929. Woodblock print

FUKITA Fumiaki (b.1926)

Medium:
Woodblock

Dots appear often in Fukita's prints – clustered dots, dots in a radial pattern, dots that pinpoint an explosion. However rendered, they seem to be a part of some exciting space phenomenon extending into infinity – into depths that might be measured in light years.[1]

Frances Blakemore, 1975

From the later generation of *sōsaku hanga* artists, Fukita Fumiaki, born in 1926, is now the oldest living member of the movement. He studied oil painting at Tokyo School of Fine Arts for one year and then turned to art education himself, teaching at an elementary school from 1947 to 1968.

Fukita became active as a printmaker in the 1950s, and in 1957 became associated with the Japan Print Association, which awarded him the Onchi Prize that year. A few years later, in 1960, he was represented in the significant *sōsaku hanga* exhibition held at the Art Institute of Chicago with two of his early woodblock prints from 1959, *Bird and Eye* and *Bird, Number 1*.[2]

In the 1960s, Fukita started creating woodblock prints of abstract geometric compositions that resemble something between constellations or galaxies and firework displays – a style that would become his trademark. Fukita's prints are often in bright blue tones, printed in oil-based inks using a press over water-based Japanese pigments, which are printed by hand. Throughout his career, he developed new woodblock techniques, such as combining relief and engraving methods.[3]

In 1968, Fukita became the first Professor of Printmaking in Japan, heading the printmaking department at Tama Art University in Tokyo for many years. He succeeded the highly acclaimed etcher Komai Tetsurō (1920–1976), who had won a prize along with Saitō Kiyoshi (pp.138–45) at the first São Paulo Biennial in 1951. By helping to lay the foundations of formal print education, Fukita was an influential figure for the younger generation of print artists. His students included Kawachi Seikō (b.1948) and Morozumi Osamu (b.1948), who was the first of the generation born after the Second World War to gain recognition in the woodblock medium, as well as Shiomi Nana (pp.161–67).

Fukita participated in numerous exhibitions and biennials, including the International Triennial of Original Colour Graphics in Grenchen, Switzerland, where he won an award (1958); the Northwest Printmakers International Exhibition in Seattle (1965), where he also won an award; the Lugano International Print Biennial (1967); the 8th International Exhibition of Graphic Arts, Ljubljana (1969); and the International Biennial Exhibition of Prints in Tokyo (1960–68). He participated in the São Paulo Biennial in 1967 with eight woodblock prints from the mid-1960s, winning a prize for *Two Figures in a Field* and *Breaking Stars*,[4] and becoming the third Japanese artist to win in the official print category following Munakata Shikō in 1955 and Hamaguchi Yōzō in 1957.[5]

Fukita has exhibited with the College Women's Association of Japan since its second show in 1957, and he was the cover artist for its catalogue in 1993. Apart from a few breaks, he has continued to contribute to the CWAJ show every year. A large retrospective exhibition was held in 2006 at the Setagaya

1 Frances Blakemore, *Who's Who in Modern Japanese Prints* (New York and Tokyo: Weatherhill, 1975), p.35.
2 *Japan's Modern Prints: Sōsaku Hanga*, exh. cat. (Chicago: Art Institute of Chicago, 1960), cat. nos. 252, 253.
3 Fukita's techniques are further explained in Gaston Petit and Amadio Arboleda, *Evolving Techniques in Japanese Woodblock Prints* (Tokyo, New York, San Francisco: Kodansha International, 1977), pp.22, 79 and *passim*.
4 'Japão', in *IX Bienal de São Paulo: Catálogo*, exh. cat. (Fundação Bienal de São Paulo, 1967), n.p.
5 'Os Premiados', in *XI Bienal de São Paulo: Catálogo*, exh. cat. (Fundação Bienal de São Paulo, 1971), pp.15–16.

Art Museum, Tokyo, and the Tokushima Modern Art Museum, located in the prefecture where Fukita was born. In 2013, the exhibition *Fukita Fumiaki's Woodblock Prints* was organised by Aioi Shinrin Museum of Art, Tokushima.

Collections: Art Institute of Chicago; British Museum, London; Carnegie Museum of Art, Pittsburgh; Museum of Modern Art, New York; National Museum of Modern Art, Tokyo; Setagaya Art Museum, Tokyo.

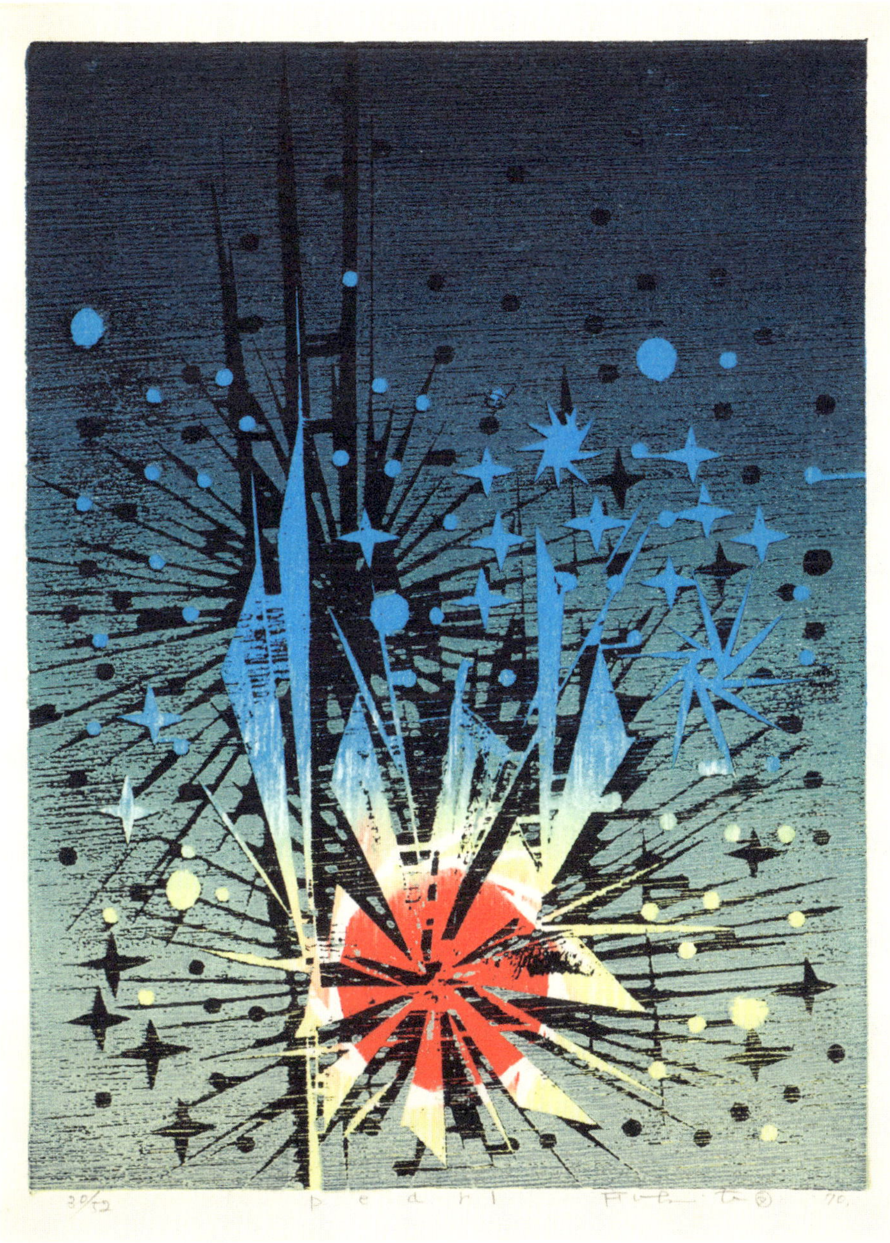

Pearl, 1970. Woodblock print

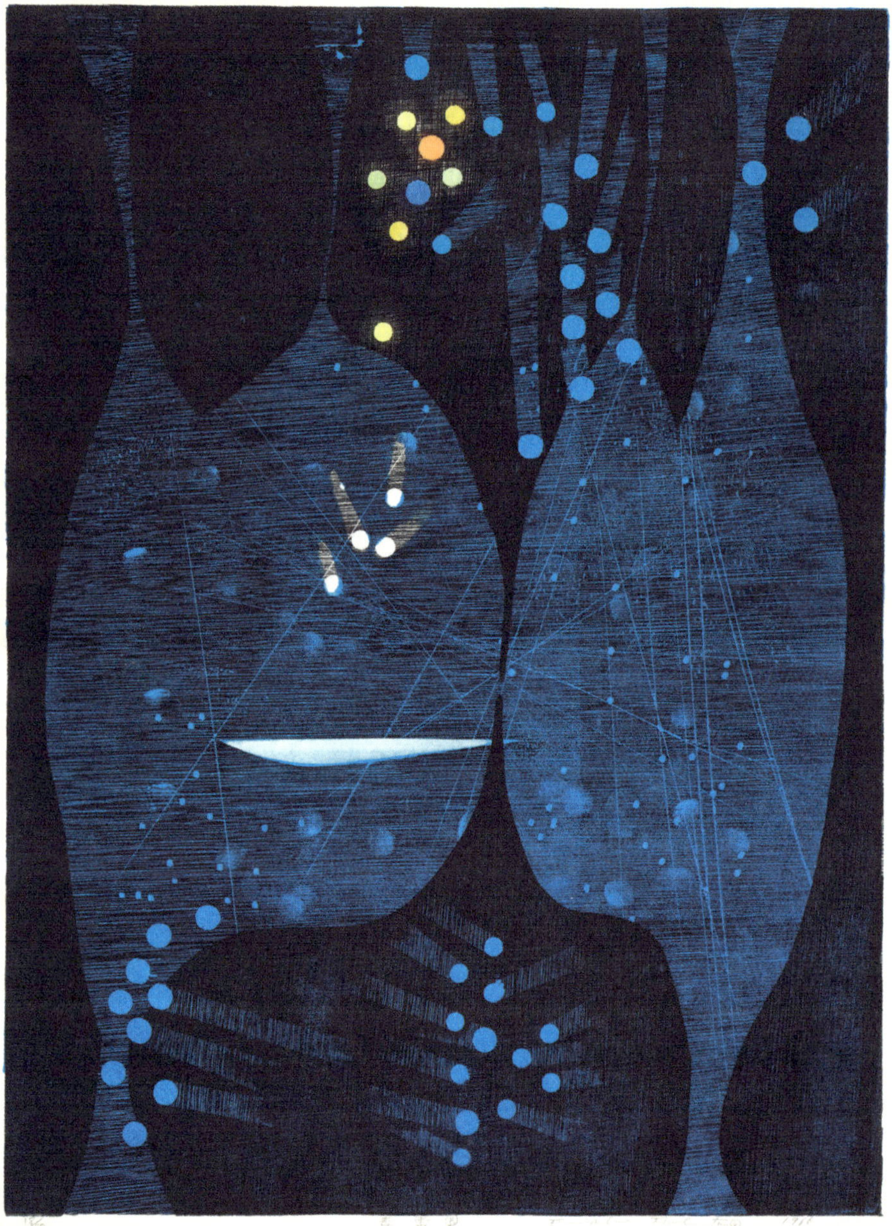

Thunder in Spring, 1966. Woodblock print

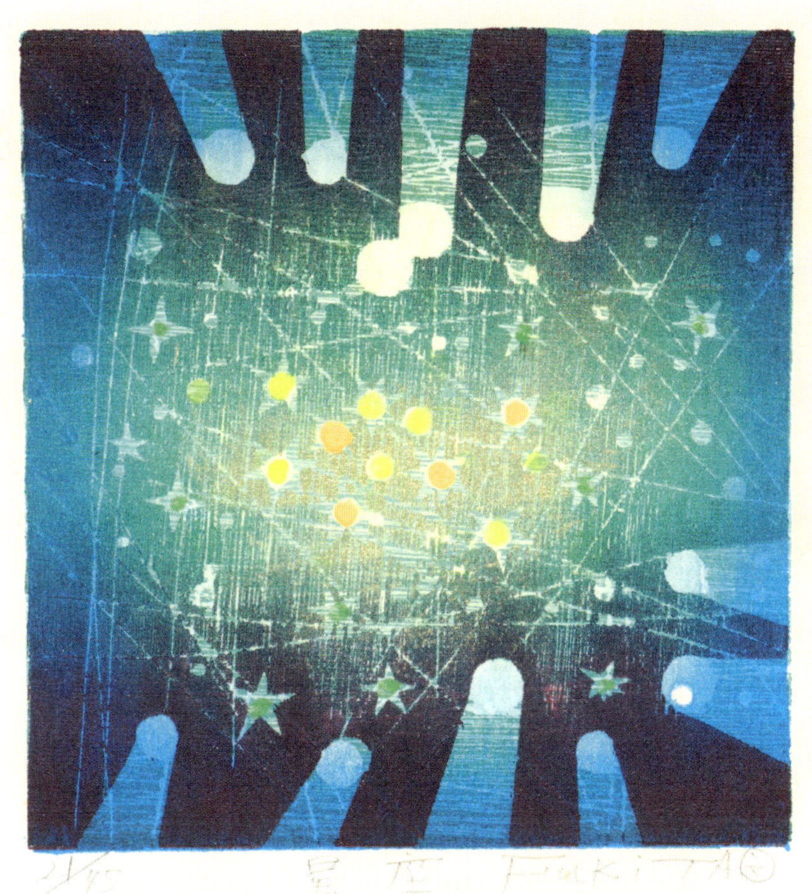

Constellation, 1974. Woodblock print

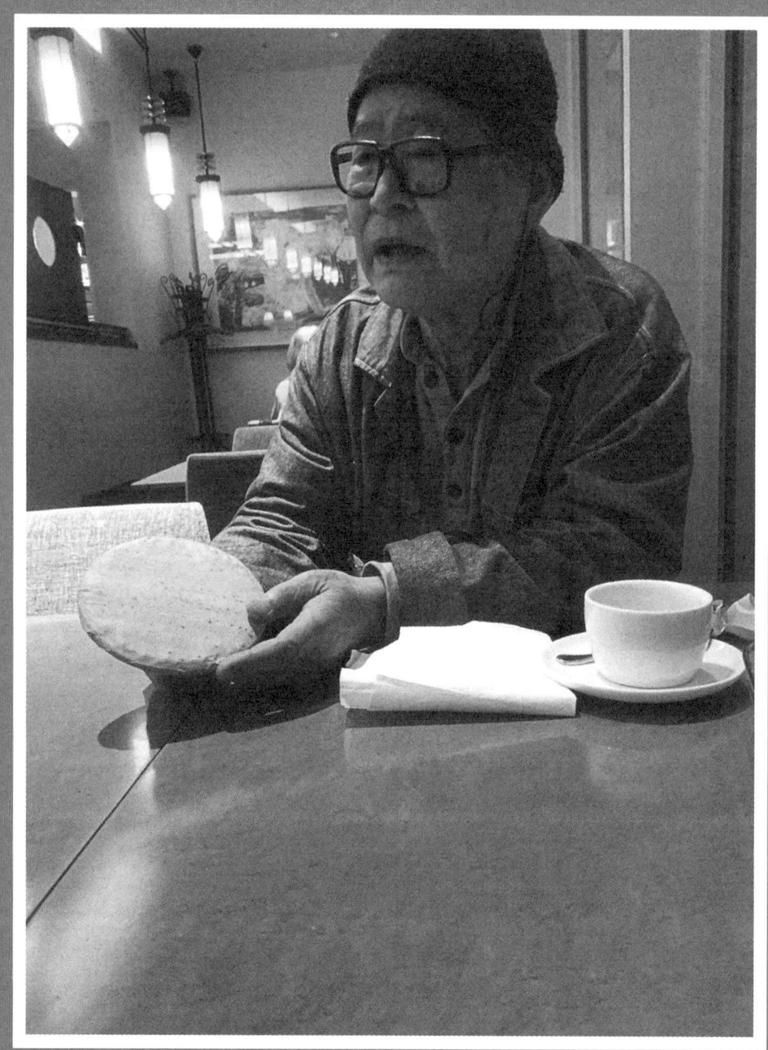

FUNASAKA Yoshisuke (b.1939)

Medium:
Silkscreen, woodblock and others

One hot summer day, I found some lemons on the counter in a café. While I was gazing at those lemons, I began to think that I could use the shape of lemons in my works as my special feature.[1]

Funasaka Yoshisuke

The lemon has been the trademark of Funasaka Yoshisuke since 1957 and has earned him the nickname 'Lemon Man'. Almost seventy years on, Funasaka continues to make woodblock prints with that specific fruit as his subject.

In two ongoing series, the lemon has been the focal point: *My Space and My Dimension*, mixed-media silkscreen and woodblock prints, and *Lemon, Black and White*, a series of six small-sized woodblocks. In the latter, the lemons appear either as a simple outline or as solid colours and in various sizes. Using the colours yellow, black and white, Funasaka depicts his subject in varying expressions and styles: geometric, abstract, patterned, multiple, singular. The lemon at times takes on a feminine character when Funasaka presents it as alluring body parts in a modern interpretation of the erotic *shunga* genre (see p.174). He even captures its tactility. Funasaka finds certain qualities in the fruit: 'I like the taste, I like the smell, I like the color – it represents freshness.'[2]

Funasaka's interest in woodblock printing emerged early, when making New Year's greeting cards as a young boy at school using the same woodblock printing technique as the traditional *ukiyo-e* artists of the Edo period. In junior high school, he submitted his work to a print competition run by the *Asahi shimbun* newspaper, and won a prize. One of the judges, Mutō Rokurō (1907–1995), a woodblock print artist known for landscapes, became Funasaka's mentor until his death.

The son of a watercolour painter, Funasaka graduated from the department of oil painting at Tama Art University, Tokyo, in 1962.[3] His teacher, Suematsu Masaki (1908–1997), who had returned from France after the war, introduced his students to contemporary French art, such as the abstractionism of the Salon de Mai (established in 1943), which had a great impact on Funasaka.

In the 1960s, Funasaka experimented with various printing techniques. While studying he worked in a linoleum store, and used the trimmings to make linocuts. He then searched for a new method and started experimenting with glue, using it to draw pictures on glass.[4] Even then, lemon shapes could be detected in his work. But the acclaim that the woodblock printmaker Munakata Shikō (pp.104–7) had gained both in Japan and abroad during the 1950s made Funasaka think that this medium would be the one to pursue: 'I think I was lucky to be able to decide which way to choose at the early age,' he reflected.[5]

Through an acquaintance of his mentor Mutō, Funasaka was recommended to visit the Watanabe print workshop if he wished to have a career in woodblock printing. Still run by the old *shin hanga* publisher Watanabe Shōzaburō, the workshop also encouraged young *sōsaku hanga* artists. Funasaka became part of the study group organised by Watanabe once a month on the workshop's second floor. The artists would discuss their work, exchange ideas and teach the younger artists; this continued until 1969. Funasaka was

1 *Funasaka Yoshisuke Print Exhibition, 1960–2010: My Space and My Dimension*, exh. cat. (Minokamo: Minokamo City Museum), 2011, p.15.
2 Funasaka Yoshisuke quoted in Frances Blakemore, *Who's Who in Modern Japanese Prints* (New York and Tokyo: Weatherhill, 1975), p.37.
3 In 1992–93 he returned to Tama Art University, this time as a lecturer teaching woodblock printmaking part-time.
4 *Funasaka Yoshisuke Print Exhibition*, p.15.
5 Funasaka Yoshisuke quoted ibid., p.15.

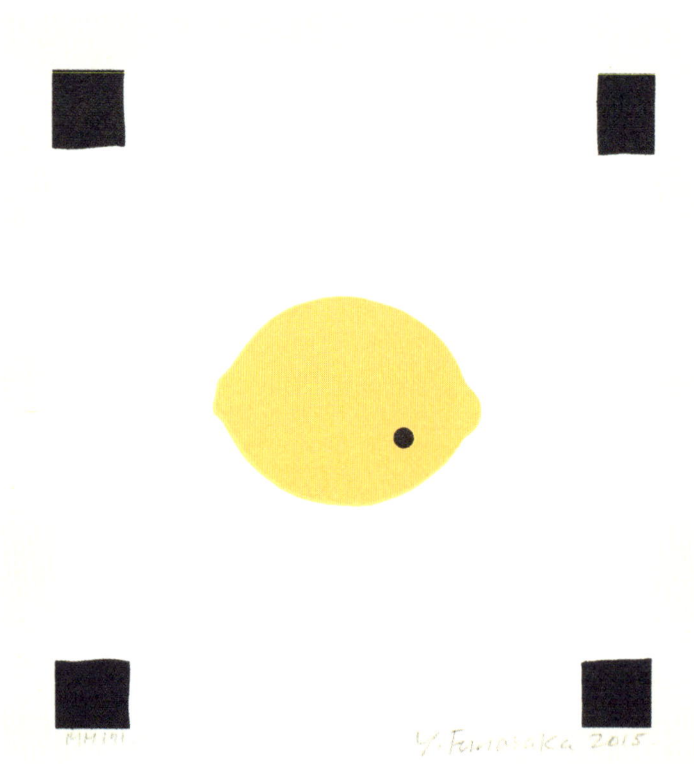

Lemon, Black and White, No.MM171, 2015. Woodblock print

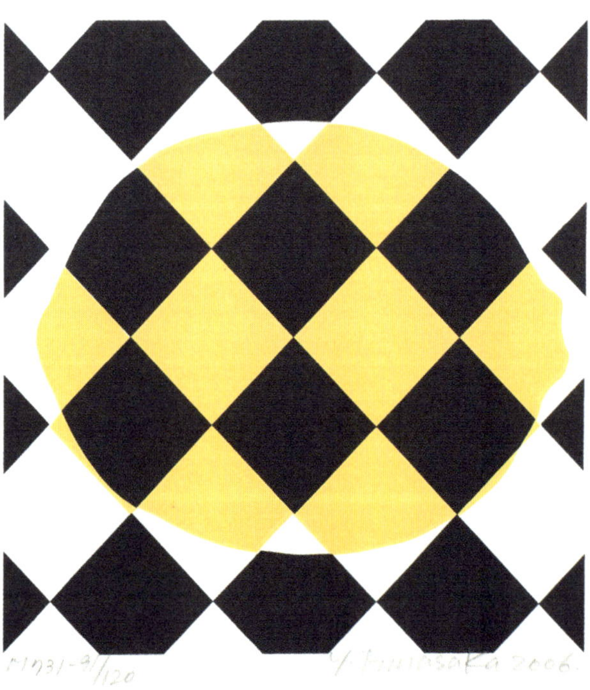

Lemon, Black and White, No.M731, 2006. Woodblock print

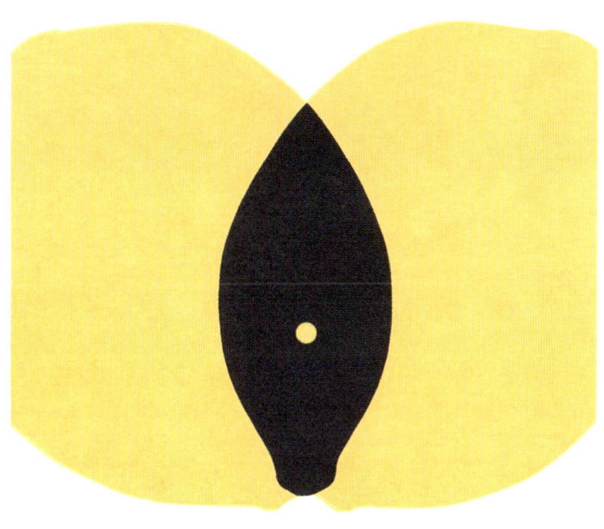

Lemon, Black and White, No. M741, 2007. Woodblock print

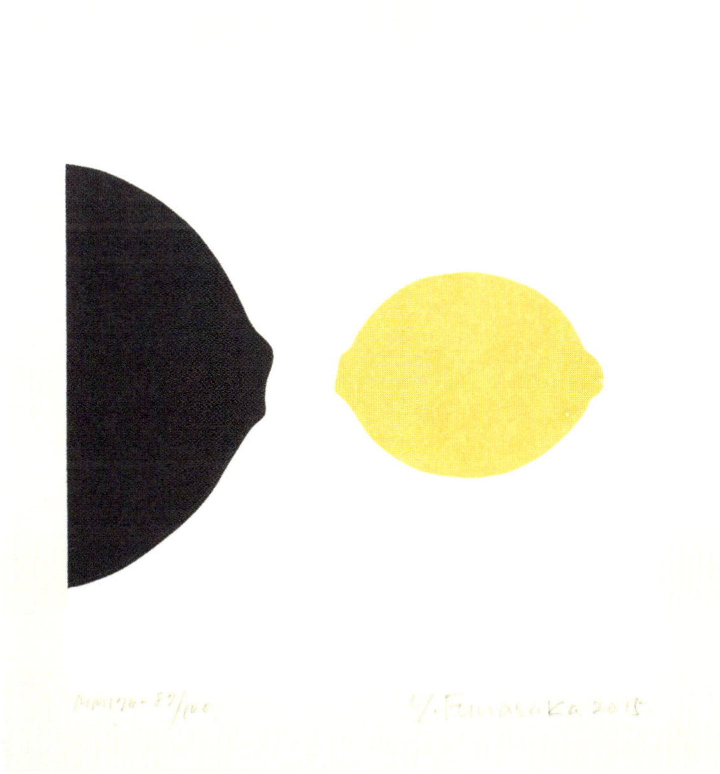

Lemon, Black and White, No. MM170, 2015. Woodblock print

also taught to make *baren*, the tool used by printers for centuries to rub the ink from the woodblock onto the paper in the traditional technique.[6] Funasaka continues to make *baren* today and has taught the method in workshops and on woodblock printing courses so that new generations may learn the old, almost forgotten craft. 'I believe it is desirable to study basic woodblock techniques, such as making a baren, carving the block and printing. It's never too late to move on to other printmaking techniques afterwards,' he has explained.[7] It was also at the Watanabe workshop that Funasaka met Ueno Makoto (1909–1980), who had studied printmak-ing for five years with Hiratsuka Un'ichi (pp. 68–71), and he encouraged Funasaka to submit his work to the Japan Print Association. In 1969 he became a member of the association.

While Funasaka printed his early work with woodblock processes – as he does today – around 1970 he developed his own, very distinctive technique to keep up with his editions, combining woodblock with silkscreen printing.[8] He would print the motifs, mostly lemons and other brightly coloured vertical shapes, with woodblock onto silkscreened paper: 'I had the wide blank space printed by silkscreen. I print the one-colour works or the many colours on one wood board ... by myself.'[9] He also used mica powder (*unmo*) to prevent the colours from fading and giving areas of the prints a satin-like texture; the material was also used by *ukiyo-e* artists to create glittering effects in the backgrounds of their prints.[10]

At the Tokyo International Biennial Exhibition of Prints in 1970 – the same year Ay-O won a prize for *Rainbow Hokusai* (p. 39) and Kurosaki Akira (pp. 90–93) for the woodblock print *Composition for the Darkness* – Funasaka was presented with an award by the National Museum of Modern Art, Kyoto, for his large-scale woodblock print *S7-1970*, one of two accepted to the biennale. This was a turning point in his career, and led to numerous group and solo exhibitions in Japan and abroad: at Gin Gallery, Tokyo (1972); the International Print Biennale, Kraków (1972, 1974, 1978, 1988); and the 7th International Triennial of Original Colour Graphics, Grenchen (1976), to mention just a few.

During 1976–77, Funasaka studied in the UK and the USA (at Western Michigan University) on a government fellowship from the Agency for Cultural Affairs. In London, where he spent eight months, he visited the Tate Gallery and saw works by the English Romantic painter J.M.W. Turner (1775–1851), which he later described as 'dynamic, with light, air, and arising steam'.[11] He had three exhibitions of his own while in the UK during 1977, among them at the London College of Printing.

Funasaka's aesthetics might appear more Western than Japanese, but his main technique is rooted in the age-old Japanese tradition of woodblock printing, and as one of the oldest Japanese artists working in the technique today, he is a significant link between the past and the present. He has exhibited with the CWAJ since 1968 and continues to do so today. In 2011, Minokamo City Museum in Gifu held the retrospective exhibition *Funasaka Yoshisuke Print Exhibition, 1960–2010: My Space and My Dimension*.

Collections: Bibliothèque National, Paris; British Museum, London; Cleveland Museum of Art; Los Angeles County Museum of Art; National Museum of Asian Art, Washington, DC; National Museum of Modern Art, Tokyo.

6 Information based on an interview between the author and Funasaka in Tokyo, October 2024.
7 Funasaka quoted in Furukawa Hideaki, 'The Fresh Originality of Yoshisuke Funasaka's Prints', in *Funasaka Yoshisuke Print Exhibition*, n.p.
8 Margaret K. Johnson and Dale K. Hilton, *Japanese Prints Today: Tradition with Innovation* (Tokyo: Shufunotomo Co., 1980), p. 62.
9 Funasaka quoted in *Funasaka Yoshisuke Print Exhibition*, p. 16.
10 Johnson and Hilton, *Japanese Prints Today*, p. 60.
11 Funasaka quoted in *Funasaka Yoshisuke Print Exhibition*, p. 16.

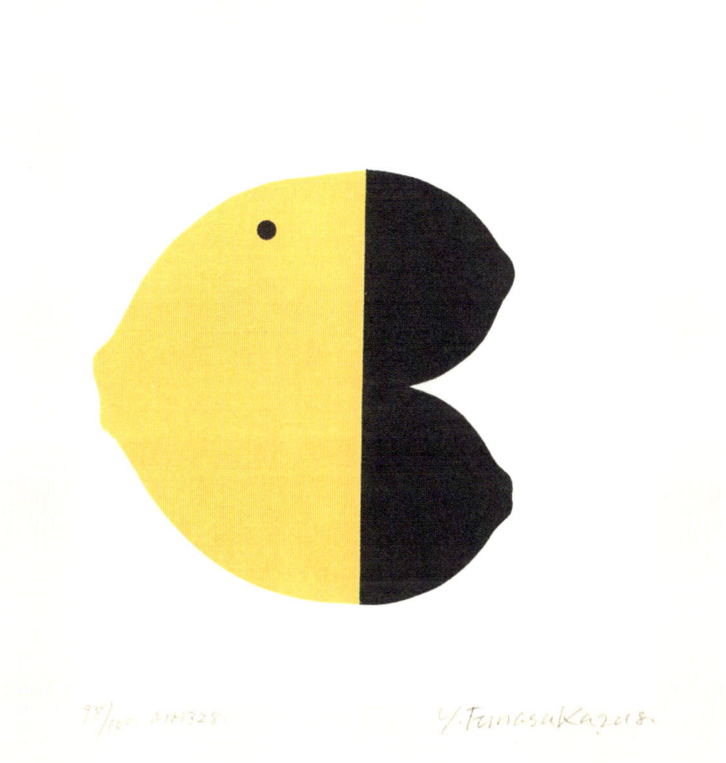

Lemon, Black and White, No. MM328, 2018. Woodblock print

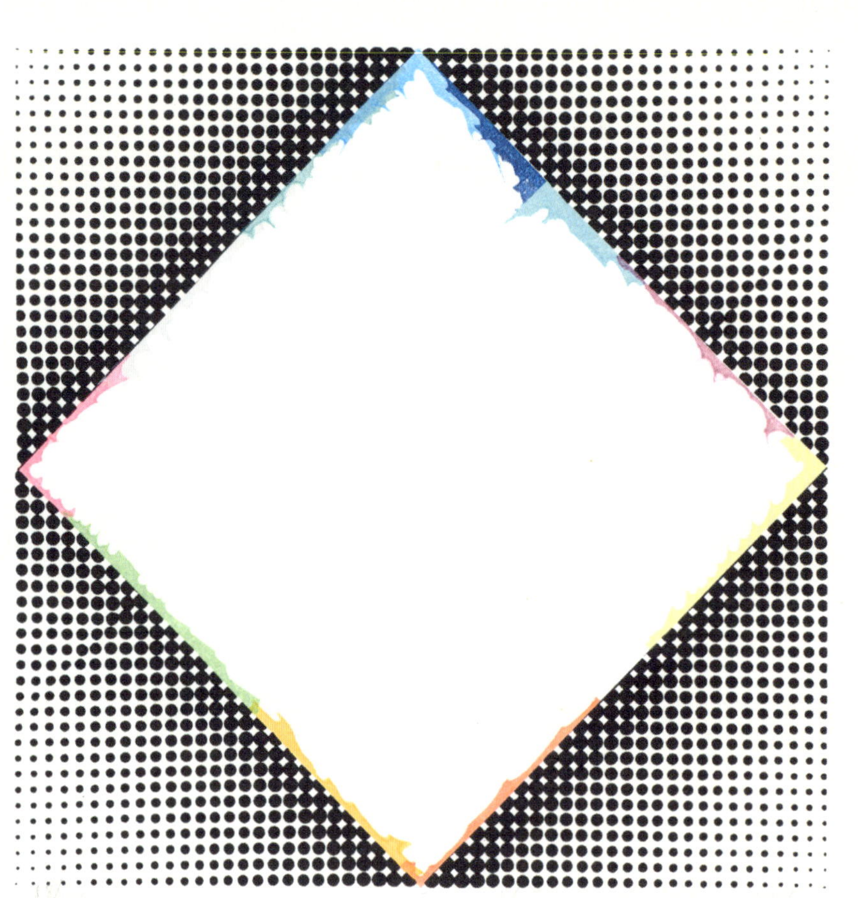

White Space No. 374, 1974. Woodblock and silkscreen print

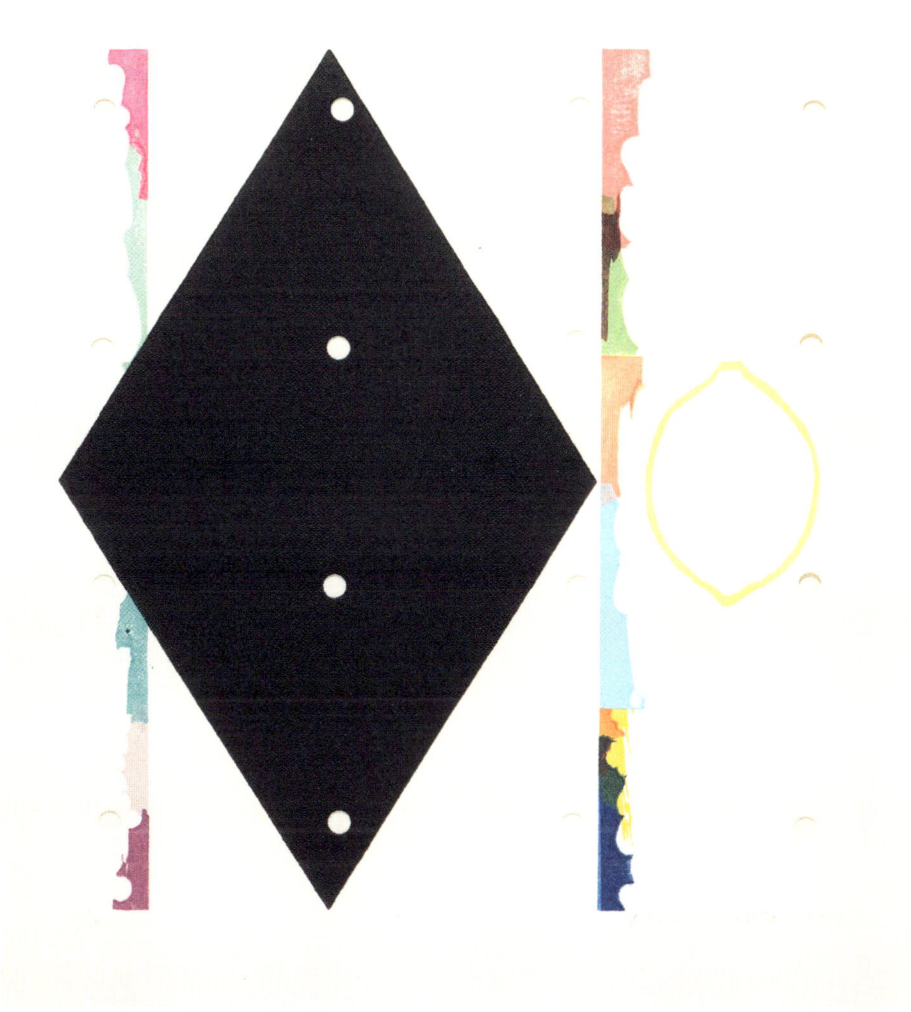

Untitled, 1971. Woodblock print

HAMAGUCHI Yōzō (1909–2000)

Medium:
Mezzotint

The mezzotints of Hamaguchi … stand apart from those engraved by previous masters, which were mainly reproductions of paintings rather than original designs conceived specifically for execution in mezzotint.[1]

Carol Wax, 1990

As the 'master of the colour mezzotint', Hamaguchi Yōzō was a pioneer in the field of graphic art and an accomplished printmaker. With his distinctive technique he created semi-surreal still-lifes of common everyday objects, vegetables, fruits and insects emerging from a mist into the light, tactile yet like dream visions.

Hamaguchi was born in Wakayama prefecture in 1909 into a family that ran a soy sauce production business (his father was the tenth-generation president of the Yamasa Corporation, a company that has been running since 1645). But Hamaguchi left the family business to pursue sculpture at Tokyo School of Fine Arts in 1927. However, in 1930 he also left university and moved to Paris to study oil painting, watercolour and copperplate printing. He made his first copperplate print, *Cat*, in 1937, and the following year he had his first solo show in Paris.[2]

Hamaguchi returned to Japan on the brink of the Second World War, working as an interpreter for the Japanese government. While in Japan, he had his first one-man show of copperplate prints at Formes Gallery in Tokyo. He returned to France in 1953, the year he also became a member of the Japan Print Association, giving his full attention to printmaking.

It was during his second 'Paris chapter', at the age of 46, that Hamaguchi developed an original copperplate engraving technique for producing colour mezzotints: 'In 1955, Hamaguchi was capable of over-printing four different mezzotint plates, inked in yellow, red, blue and black respectively, to create a full colour intaglio print.'[3] *Roofs of Paris* from 1956 is an early example of Hamaguchi's colour mezzotint process, with its subtle tonal qualities that became his trademark.

In 1955, Hamaguchi became a formal member of the Salon d'Automne and, following his success in developing the new technique, participated in several international art exhibitions. The year 1957, too, was an important one for Hamaguchi – he received the Tokyo National Museum of Modern Art Award at the first International Biennial Exhibition of Prints and participated with five mezzotints in the 4th São Paulo Biennial, where he became the second Japanese artist to be a prize-winner since the biennale's beginning in 1951.[4]

Hamaguchi exhibited at the Venice Biennale in 1960 with 22 mezzotints, including *Two Cherries* (1957). A year later, he received the Grand Prix at the 4th International Exhibition of Graphic Arts, Ljubljana; he also showed with the CWAJ in 1964–66. His work was featured in the book *Modern Prints* (1970) by Pat Gilmour and was part of the exhibition *Contemporary Japanese Prints* at Los Angeles County Museum of Art (1972). He designed the poster for the 1984 Winter Olympics in Sarajevo, and in 1985 Hamaguchi's first solo exhibition, which contained over 160 prints, was held at the National Museum of Art in Osaka.

1 Carol Wax in *Yozo Hamaguchi, Master of Mezzotint*, exh. cat., Tokyo Metropolitan Teien Art Museum (Tokyo: Mainichi Newspapers, 1990), p. 20.

2 Ibid., p. 196.

3 Dr Ad Stijnman in *Hamaguchi Yōzō*, exh. cat. (Tokyo: Musée Hamaguchi Yozo Yamasa Collection, 2022), p. 61.

4 See 'Os Premiados', in *XI Bienal de São Paulo: Catálogo* (Fundação Bienal de São Paulo, 1971), p. 15.

5 Minami Keiko, also a recognised print artist, studied etching with the artist Johnny Friedlaender and exhibited her first work in 1956.

An international artist who spent most of his adult life outside the country of his birth, having moved from France to San Francisco in 1981, Hamaguchi eventually returned to Japan in 1996, four years before his death. The Musée Hamaguchi Yozo was founded in Tokyo in 1998 by the Yamasa Corporation. The museum also shows works by Hamaguchi's wife, Minami Keiko (1911–2004), a true pioneer who was also a printmaker.[5] The Minneapolis Institute of Art held the exhibition *And more by more they dream their sleep: Mezzotints by Yōzō Hamaguchi* in 2024–25.

Collections: Fine Arts Museums of San Francisco; Harvard Art Museums, Cambridge, MA; Los Angeles County Museum of Art; Minneapolis Institute of Art; Musée Hamaguchi Yozo, Tokyo; Museum of Modern Art, New York; National Museum of Modern Art, Tokyo; Victoria and Albert Museum, London.

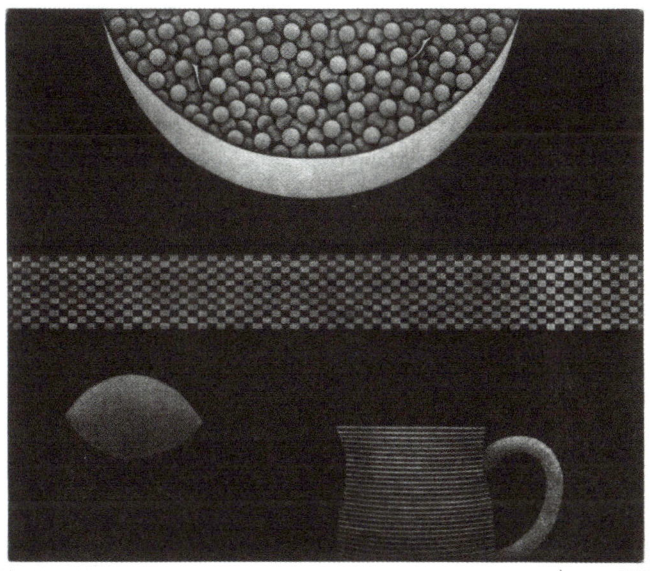

Pitcher, Grapes and Lemon, 1957. Mezzotint

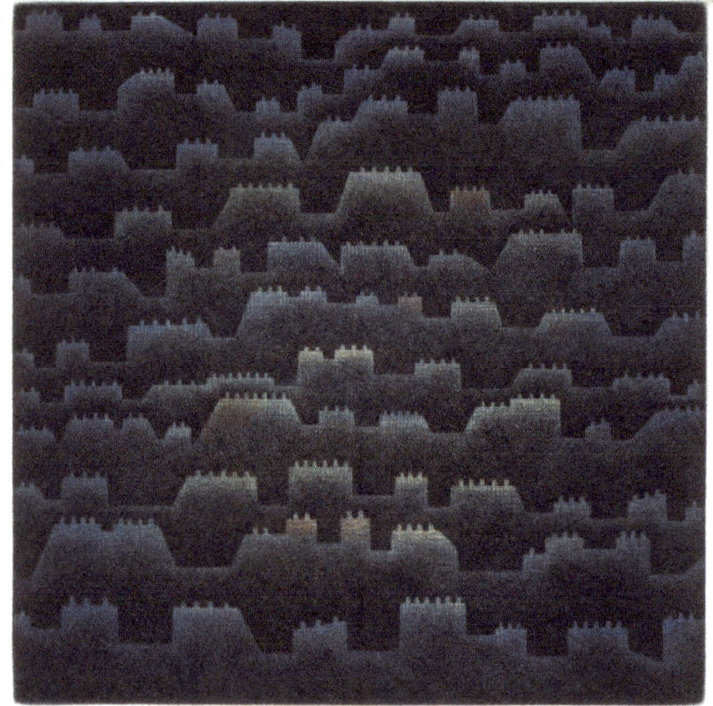

Roofs of Paris, 1956. Mezzotint

Fourteen Cherries, 1966. Mezzotint

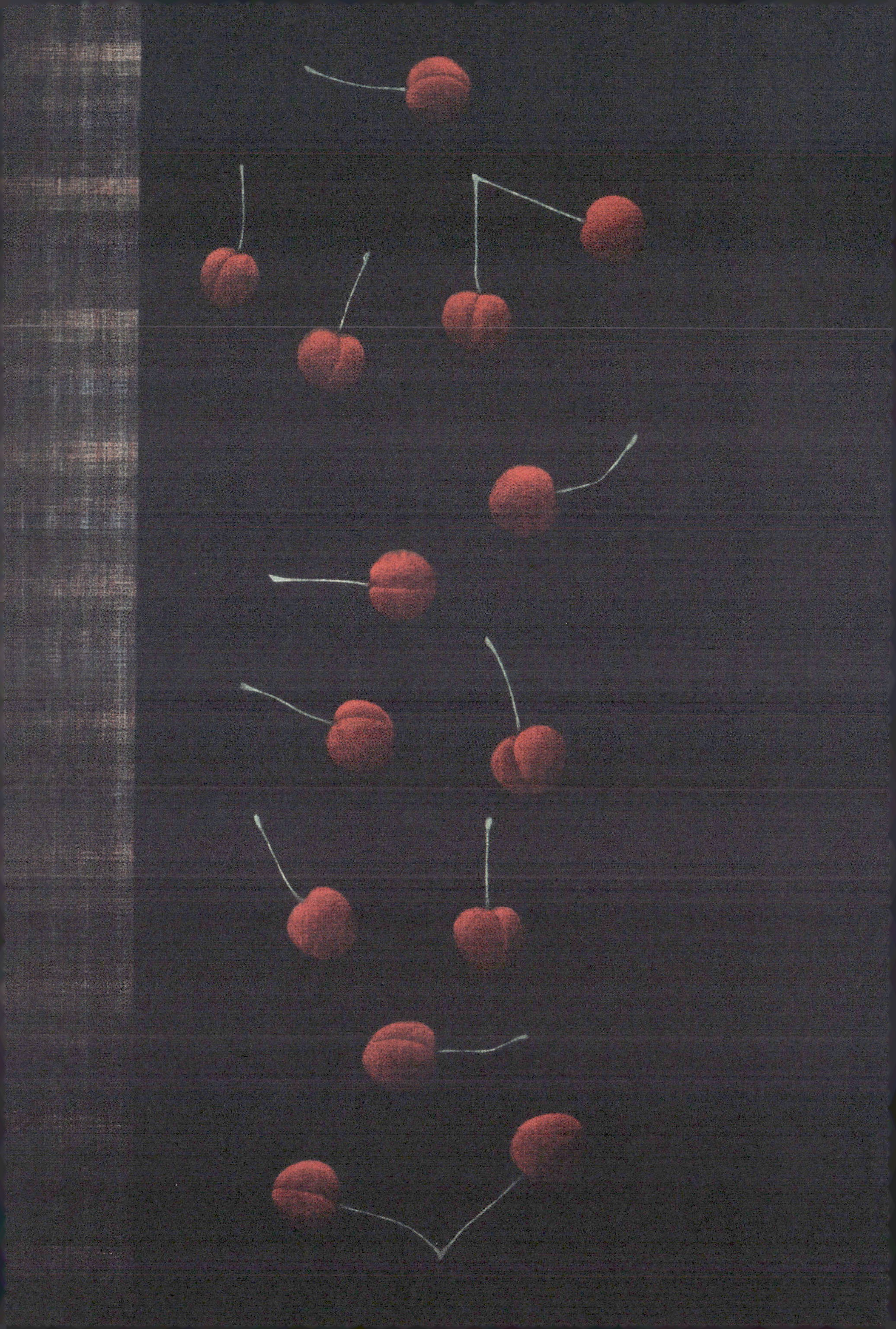

HIRATSUKA Un'ichi (1895–1997)

Medium:
Woodblock

I could never be the same once under the sway of the prints by Moronobu, or the Buddhist prints and paintings of the Heian era (794–1185).[1]

Hiratsuka Un'ichi, 1956

While Onchi Kōshirō (pp. 130–33) rejected classical Japanese art, Hiratsuka Un'ichi embraced it. While Onchi was the 'spiritual' leader of the *sōsaku hanga* movement, Hiratsuka was the 'practical' one – and the best trained carver of all the creative printmakers. 'My grandfather was an architect of houses and temples and there were always carpenters around our place, so I grew up with a feeling for wood and tools,' he told Oliver Statler.[2]

Hiratsuka took many younger artists under his wing. When the Tokyo School of Fine Arts finally opened a department for printmaking in 1935, it was Hiratsuka who taught the 56 students enrolled in the first woodblock printing class (until it was discontinued in 1944).[3] In 1950 he established the Hiratsuka Print Institute to continue to train print artists of the next generations.

Hiratsuka himself graduated from Matsue Commercial College and in 1913 took lessons in watercolour from Ishii Hakutei (1882–1958), a *yōga* painter and the publisher of Yamamoto Kanae's pioneering *sōsaku hanga* print *Fisherman* (1904, see p. 213). He encouraged Hiratsuka to study woodblock carving with the master carver Igami Bonkotsu (1877–1933), resulting in Hiratsuka mastering the traditional woodblock techniques of *ukiyo-e*. He showed his first prints in 1916.

While Hiratsuka's training was rooted in Japanese tradition, his early influences came from the Post-Impressionists through art and literary magazines such as *Myōjō* and *Shirakaba*.[4] In his work Hiratsuka combined Japanese tradition, especially the black-and-white Buddhist woodblock prints of the twelfth and thirteenth centuries (which Hiratsuka collected), with Western modernity: 'By working in black and white I am emphasizing the ink in traditional Japanese painting which should be combined with the expressive methods of European style.'[5] Black and white remained his preference and characteristic style throughout his career. 'To me black and white have always been the most beautiful colors,' he explained.[6]

In 1951, Hiratsuka was one of the 45 Japanese artists represented at the first São Paulo Biennial, which was a turning point for contemporary Japanese printmaking with the win of Saitō Kiyoshi's (pp. 138–45) and Komai Tetsurō's prints. Among the participants was also Hiratsuka's earlier student Munakata Shikō (pp. 104–7), whose work also borrowed from old Buddhist monochrome prints.

An example of Hiratsuka's monochrome work can be seen in his portrait of the American writer and philanthropist James A. Michener from 1957, in an interesting fusion of East and West. Michener is portrayed seated in front of a group of Japanese prints: a twelfth-century depiction of the Buddhist deity Bishamonten; a seventeenth-century print attributed to Hishikawa Moronobu (1618–1694), the earliest *ukiyo-e* master; an eighteenth-century *bijin* (beautiful woman) by Nishikawa Sukenobu (1671–1750); and, not least,

1 Hiratsuka Un'ichi quoted in Oliver Statler, *Modern Japanese Prints: An Art Reborn* (Rutland, VT: Charles E. Tuttle Co., 1956), p. 37.
2 Ibid., p. 36.
3 See Helen Merritt, *Modern Japanese Woodblock Prints: The Early Years* (Honolulu: University of Hawai'i Press, 1990), p. 149, and Statler, *Modern Japanese Prints*, p. 40.
4 See Statler, *Modern Japanese Prints*, pp. 36–38.
5 Hiratsuka Un'ichi quoted in Merritt, *Modern Japanese Woodblock Prints*, p. 209.
6 Hiratsuka quoted in Statler, *Modern Japanese Prints*, p. 37.
7 Identified in Alicia Volk, *Made in Japan: The Postwar Creative Print Movement*, exh. cat. (Milwaukee, WI: Milwaukee Art Museum, 2005), p. 5.

Bunraku Doll Yaeya Oshichi (1952) by Hiratsuka himself; the latter print has as a background another four prints by Utagawa Hiroshige (1797–1858).[7]

Hiratsuka's portrait bears a resemblance to Vincent van Gogh's portrait of Julien (Père) Tanguy from 1887, in which Van Gogh portrayed his patron in front of Japanese prints from his own collection. The portrait of Hiratsuka's patron Michener, depicted in a similar fashion, links the two eras of printmaking, culturally connected through *ukiyo-e*. Hiratsuka's contemporary Okuyama Gihachirō (pp. 124–29) made a woodblock print after that exact painting by Van Gogh around the same year as Hiratsuka did his portrait of Michener.

Hiratsuka showed with the College Women's Association in 1956–61, 1963–64 and 1967–68 and was represented at the International Biennial Exhibition of Prints in Tokyo in 1957 and 1960. He was also included in the 1960 exhibition on *sōsaku hanga* at the Art Institute of Chicago as well as the Los Angeles County Museum of Art exhibition on contemporary Japanese prints in 1972. He was one of the ten artists chosen for Michener's book *The Modern Japanese Print: An Appreciation*, first published in 1962.

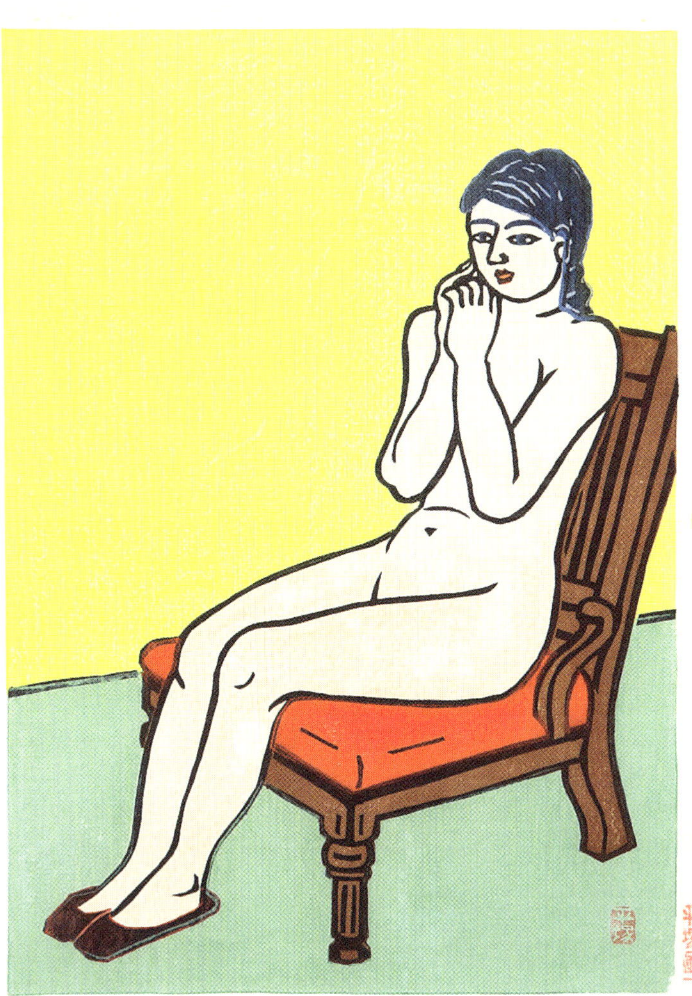

Nude on a Red Chair, 1939. Woodblock print

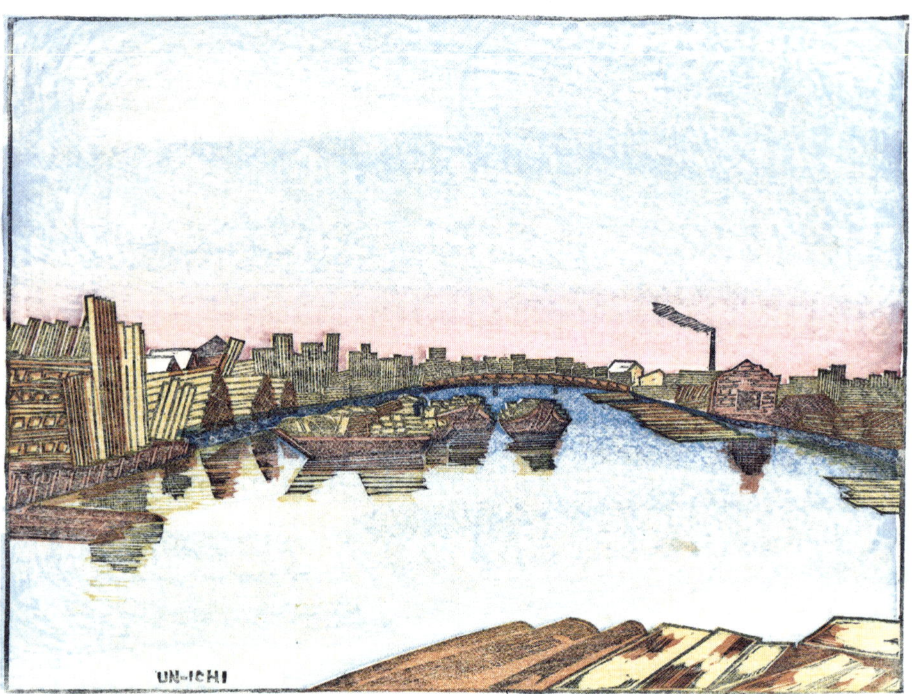

Fukagawa Timberyards, 1924. Woodblock print

That same year, Hiratsuka visited his daughter Keiko Hiratsuka Moore (1929–2020), also a woodblock print artist, who was living in Washington, DC. In the late 1950s, she had opened the Hiratsuka Nippon gallery on the ground floor of the building where she lived. Here she sold not only her father's works but also those of his students, such as Munakata and Azechi Umetarō (pp. 44–47).[8] Hiratsuka ended up staying in the United States for 33 years, producing and exhibiting prints. He ultimately returned to Japan in 1994, at almost 100 years old and with numerous young printmakers standing on his shoulders.

I am not a wood-print artist, I am an artist.[9]

Hiratsuka Un'ichi

Collections: Art Institute of Chicago; British Museum, London; Carnegie Museum of Art, Pittsburgh; Honolulu Museum of Art; Minneapolis Institute of Art; National Gallery of Art and Freer Gallery of Art, Washington, DC.

8 I would like to thank Hiratsuka's granddaughter Penelope Moore for sharing information about the family and Hiratsuka in particular.

9 Hiratsuka quoted in Statler, *Modern Japanese Prints*, p. 40.

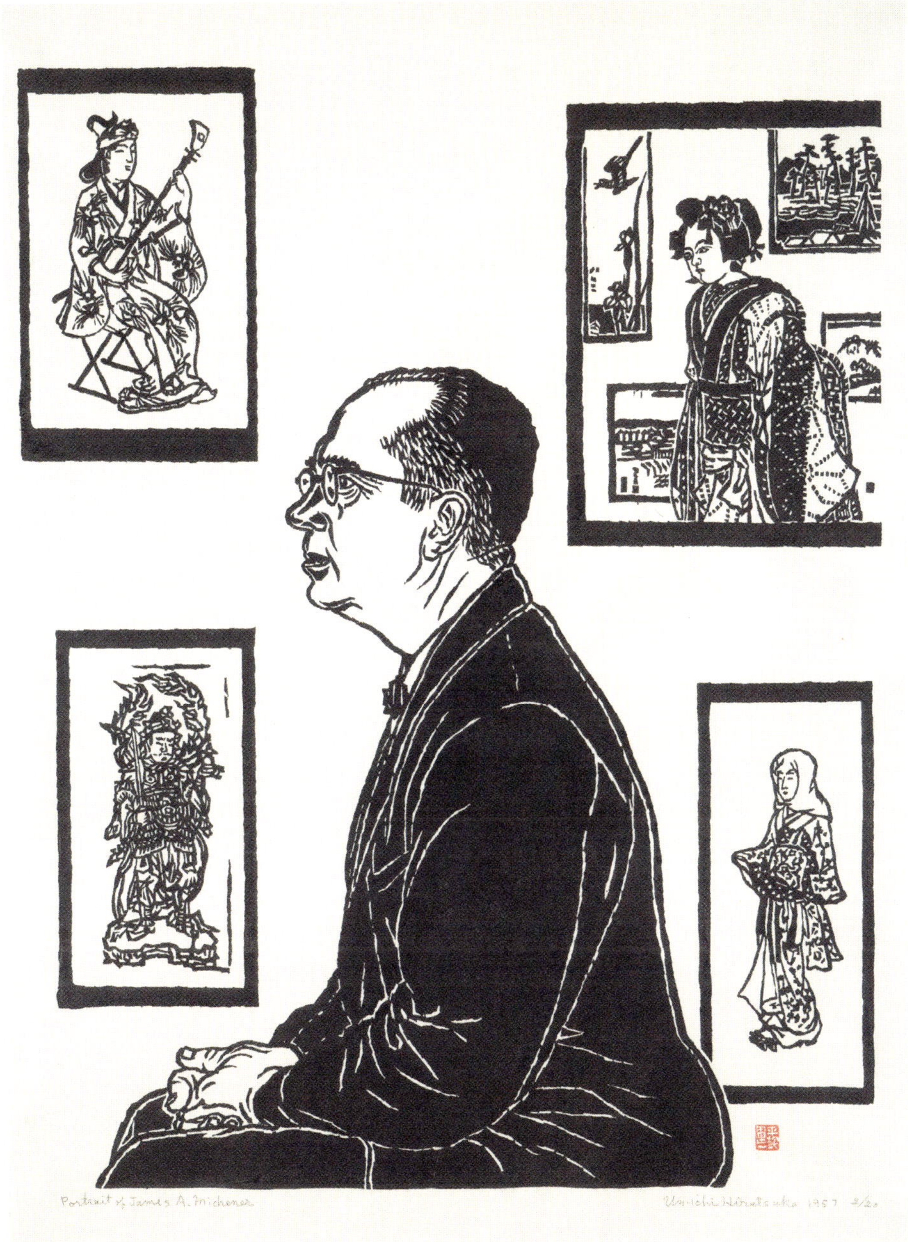

Portrait of James Michener, 1957. Woodblock print

INAGAKI Tomoo (1902–1980)

Medium:
Stencil, woodblock

'I like some qualities and reject others in Matisse and Picasso, but, above all, I was influenced by Onchi and Hiratsuka,' Inagaki Tomoo explained when he was interviewed by Oliver Statler in 1956 for the book that would help pave the way for many of the Japanese *sōsaku hanga* artists of the time.[1]

Inagaki was born in Tokyo and graduated from the Okura Commercial High School in 1923. His introduction to printmaking was through the magazine *Shi to hanga* (Poems and Hanga), published by Onchi Kōshirō (pp. 130–33) and Hiratsuka Un'ichi (pp. 68–71) in the early 1920s: 'I owe a great deal to *Poems and Hanga*,' Inagaki later recalled.[2] In 1924, he had a print accepted for publication and became a regular contributor, and he exhibited that year in the sixth Japan Creative Print Association show. Inagaki's early association with the *sōsaku hanga* movement led him to show four of his works at the Musée des Arts Décoratifs, Paris, when the first exhibition of modern Japanese prints was held there in 1934.

As with most print artists, Inagaki was not able to make a living only from printmaking. He taught commercial art at the Kyōhoku Commercial High School from 1935 to 1951 and then at the Japan Advertising Art School. He also established his own design business, Zuhansha, and had worked as a designer of ex libris and posters until the outbreak of the Second World War in 1939.

Inagaki's earlier works included landscapes, townscapes and still-lifes. He collaborated with a range of artists, including Onchi, Hiratsuka and Tokuriki Tomikichirō (pp. 196–201) on the print series *New Hundred Views of Japan* from the late 1930s to early 1940s. Just after the war, due to the shortage of good-quality wood and paper to print with, he turned to stencil prints, although woodblock was his main medium.[3]

Inagaki's work *Record of My Crop* (first published in 1949) was included in Statler's book and exhibited, along with two of his cat prints, at the first College Women's Association of Japan show in 1956. The same motif, showing one of Inagaki's wartime crops, was previously exhibited under the title *Pumpkins* as one of nine prints by Japanese artists in *Prints from Europe and Japan* at the Museum of Modern Art, New York, in 1955 (see p. 143).

Inagaki continued to participate in national and international exhibitions, including the CWAJ consecutively until 1968. In 1963, almost thirty years since his first exhibition in the city, he showed his work in Paris at an exhibition on contemporary Japanese prints at Galerie Epona and Musée Municipal d'Art et d'Histoire. His woodblock print of a mother cat with her kitten was used for the poster at both venues.

A cat lover, Inagaki turned his favourite subject into his trademark during the 1950s, joining a lineage of Japanese 'cat artists' that includes Utagawa Kuniyoshi (1798–1861), Foujita Tsuguharu (pp. 48–51) and Saitō Kiyoshi (pp. 138–45). Using stylised, graphic forms, typical of 1950s and 1960s aesthetics, he approached the subject with humour, such as in *Cat Mandala*, where a sacred Buddhist motif becomes a humoristic, semi-psychedelic cat trio.

1 Quoted in Oliver Statler, *Modern Japanese Prints: An Art Reborn* (Rutland, VT: Charles E. Tuttle Co., 1956), p. 164.
2 Ibid.
3 Ibid., p. 165.

Collections: Art Institute of Chicago; British Museum, London; Metropolitan Museum of Art, New York; Museum of Modern Art, New York.

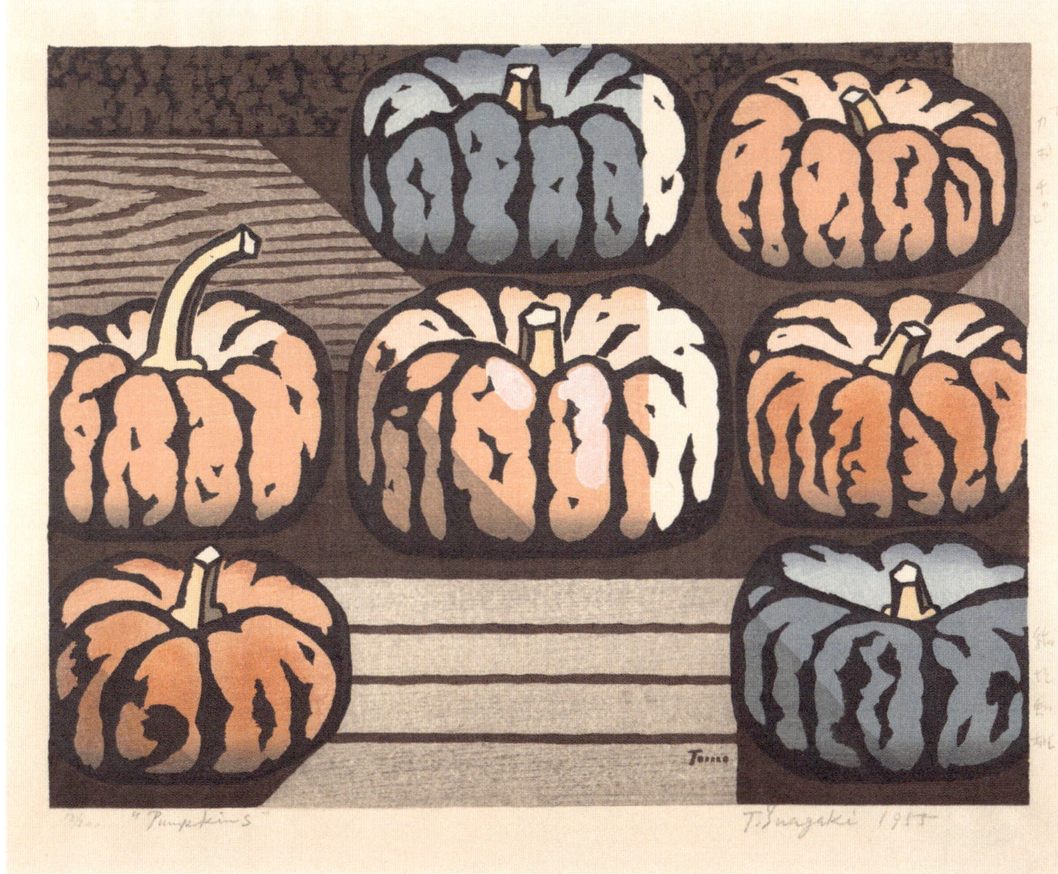

Pumpkins, 1955. Woodblock print

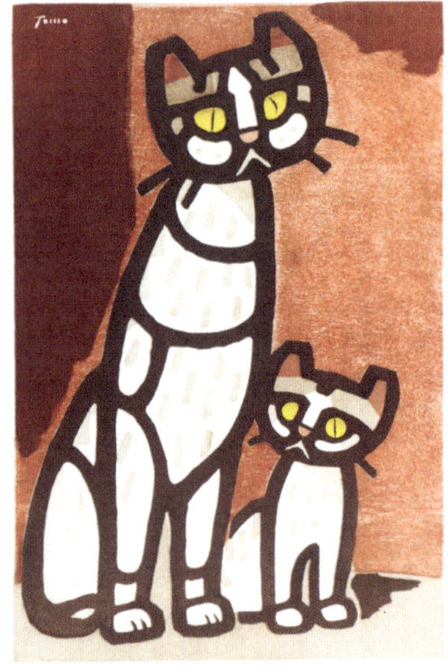

Poster for *100 Estampes japonaises contemporaines*, 1963. Lithograph

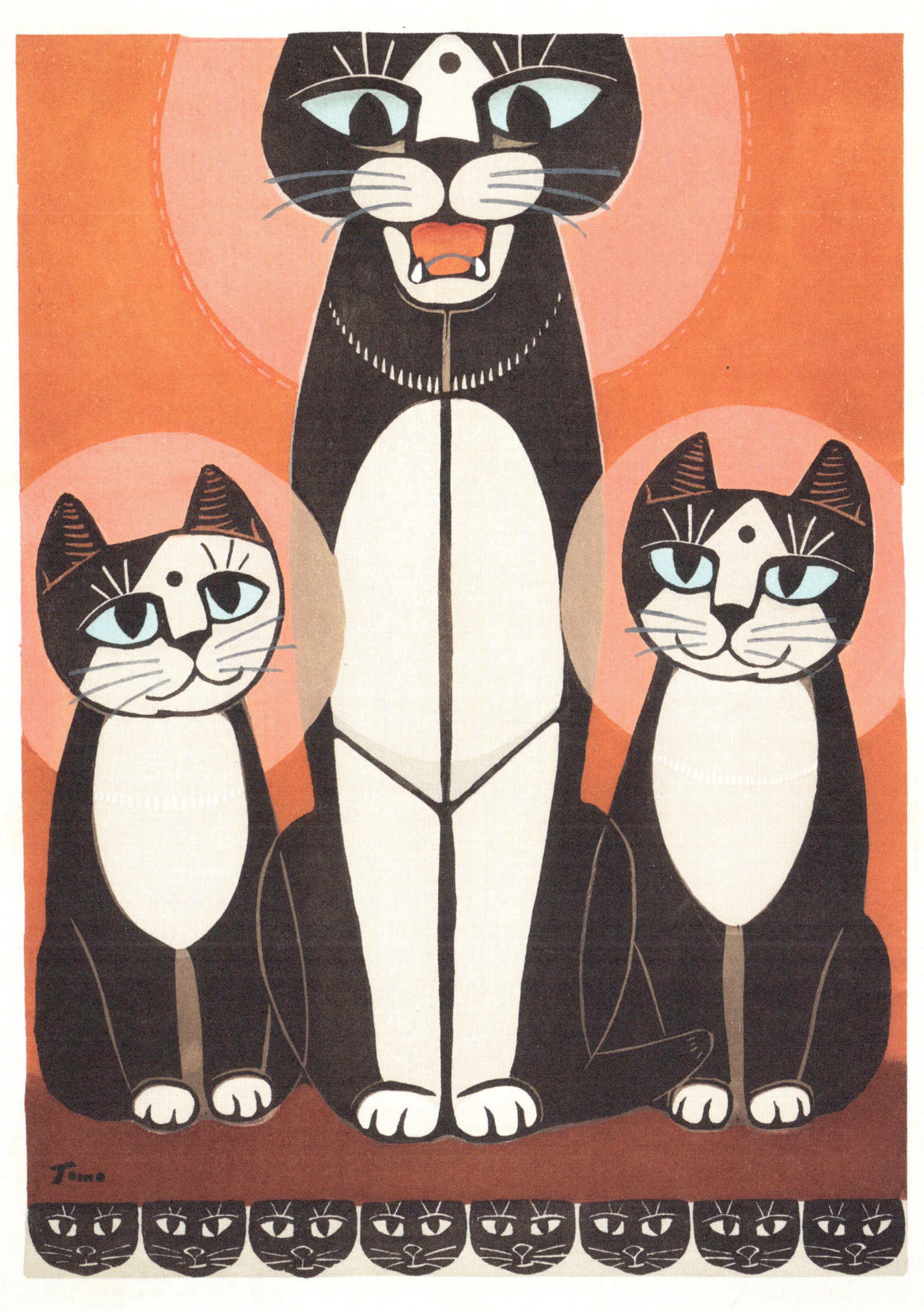

Cat Mandala, 1960s. Woodblock print

KASAMATSU Shirō (1898–1991)

Medium:
Woodblock

With an artistic career beginning in 1911 and continuing almost until the century's end, Kasamatsu Shirō was one of the few Japanese printmakers known for both his commercial *shin hanga* as well as his individualistic *sōsaku hanga* prints, creating close to three hundred works in his lifetime.

Born in Asakusa in Tokyo, Shirō began studying Western-style painting (*yōga*) when he was thirteen years old, focusing on landscapes. His teacher was Kaburaki Kiyokata (1878–1972), one of the leading artists of the *bijin-ga* ('pictures of beautiful women') genre, who himself had trained under Tsukioka Yoshitoshi (1839–1892), one of the last great *ukiyo-e* masters. Around the same time as Shirō, two other young aspiring artists studied with Kaburaki: Kawase Hasui and Itō Shinsui, both of whom would become leading exponents of the *shin hanga* movement.

It was Kaburaki who gave him the name Shirō. It was also he who encouraged Shirō to work with Watanabe Shōzaburō, the print publisher and man behind the *shin hanga* movement. After seeing Shirō's work at an exhibition, Watanabe commissioned the first print from him in 1919. This turned into a collaboration resulting in more than fifty prints. Unfortunately, the blocks for the early prints were lost when Watanabe's studio was destroyed during the Kantō earthquake that hit the Tokyo and Yokohama areas in 1923, but the collaboration between Watanabe and Shirō continued until the early 1940s.

In 1936, Shirō was one of the ten artists (including Kawase and Itō) who participated in the second of two *shin hanga* exhibitions held at the Toledo Museum of Art in Ohio. Like the first one in 1930, *Exhibition of Modern Japanese Prints*, it was organised in collaboration with the woodblock artist Yoshida Hiroshi (pp. 232–33). Shirō was represented with fourteen prints published by Watanabe in 1932–34, including his now famous *Hazy Evening on the Shore of Shinobazu Pond* (1932) and *Great Lantern at Asakusa Kannon Temple* (1934). Two of Shirō's other prints were purchased by the museum following the exhibition.[1]

After the Second World War, Shirō left Watanabe and started publishing *shin hanga* with Unsōdō. The publishing company, founded in Kyoto in 1891, had opened a Tokyo branch in 1918. From 1952 to 1959, Shirō created more than one hundred prints with Unsōdō of idyllic nature and temple scenes, animals and cityscapes, including the series *Eight Views of Tokyo* (1953). In 1959 he designed *Tokyo Tower*, depicting in its nightly glory the famous Tokyo landmark. Based on Paris's Eiffel Tower of 1889, the Tokyo version was completed in 1957 as then the tallest tower in Japan. The Tokyo Tower in Shirō's depiction is somewhat reminiscent of French artist Henri Rivière's series of colour lithographs *Thirty-six Views of the Eiffel Tower*, published in 1902. Rivière, who was a member of the Société des Amis de l'Art Japonais and a collector of *ukiyo-e*,[2] was himself inspired by the style of Japanese landscape prints, specifically Hokusai's famous series *Thirty-six Views of Mount Fuji* (c. 1830–32), from which he borrowed his series' title. Some fifty years apart, Shirō's and Rivière's designs are examples of a continuing exchange between Japanese and Western printmakers, connecting tradition and modernity across cultures.

From the mid-1950s, during the same period as he was producing *shin hanga* for Unsōdō, Shirō began to produce his own prints following the ideals of the *sōsaku hanga* movement: self-carved, self-printed and self-published,

1 'Shiro', cat. nos. 163–176: nos. 169 (acc. no. 1939.444) and 170 (acc. no. 1939.445) were acquired by the museum, according to the concordance in Dorothy Blair, *Modern Japanese Prints: Printed from a Photographic Reproduction of Two Exhibition Catalogues of Modern Japanese Prints Published by the Toledo Museum of Art in 1930 and 1936* (Toledo, OH: Toledo Museum of Art, 1997).

2 Henri Rivière's collection of *ukiyo-e* is now in the Bibliothèque Nationale de France.

3 Helen Merritt, *Modern Japanese Woodblock Prints: The Early Years* (Honolulu: University of Hawai'i Press, 1990), p. 68.

moving away from the traditional collaborative *hanmoto* system. This resulted in around eighty creative prints in the period 1955–65. One of his early prints from this time is *Sunset Glow* (1955), which clearly shows a personal and abstract expression, as well as a creative freedom in the carving, compared to the prints made in collaboration with artisans and publishers. Although not as commercially successful as his *shin hanga* designs during his lifetime, Shirō's creative prints are distinct and testify to an artist 'covering the whole range of modern woodblocks – from romantic landscapes produced by the *hanmoto* system to personal statements that are less refined in execution but charged with their own inner vitality'.[3]

A 1996 exhibition was held at the Yamanashi Prefectural Museum, titled *Mokuhan Nihon hyakkei: Kasamatsu Shirō mokuhanga ten* (Woodcuts of 100 Famous Views of Japan: Exhibition of Kasamatsu Shirō's Woodblock Prints). The Ōta Memorial Museum of Art exhibition *Kasamatsu Shirō: The Last Shin-hanga Print Artist* was held in Tokyo in 2021. This was followed by *Shirō Kasamatsu Woodblock Engraving Vol. 2* at Minami Alps City Museum of Art in 2023.

Shirō's daughter, Kasamatsu Mihoko (b. 1932), followed in her father's footsteps and became a printmaker as well, training under him. She also worked with woodblock, carving and printing herself, and depicting mainly nature and animals, especially owls and cats.

Collections: Art Institute of Chicago; British Museum, London; Honolulu Museum of Art; Minami Alps City Museum of Art; Museum of Contemporary Art, Los Angeles; National Museum of Modern Art, Tokyo; Toledo Museum of Art, Ohio.

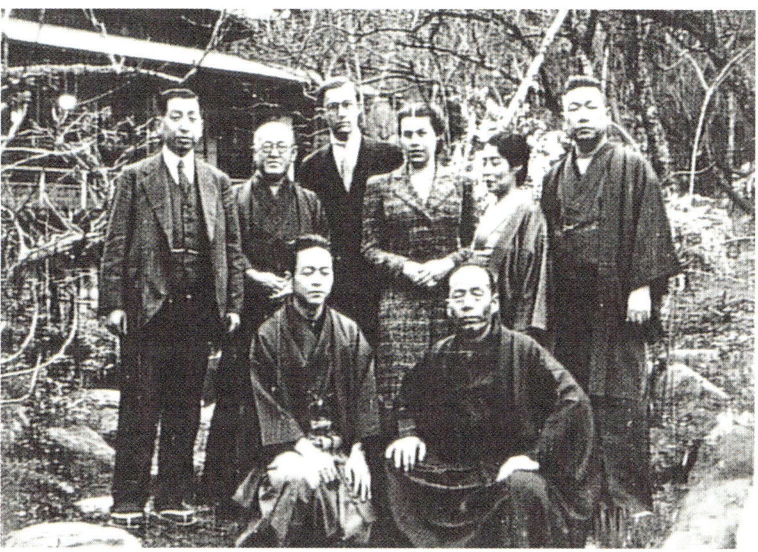

Group photograph in the garden at Itō Shinsui's home in Ikegami, 2 April 1940. Left to right, back row: Moriyama Tetsutarō (Watanabe's assistant), Kawase Hasui, Robert O. and Inge Muller, Itō Yoshiko and Itō Shinsui; front row: Kasamatsu Shirō and Watanabe Shōzaburō

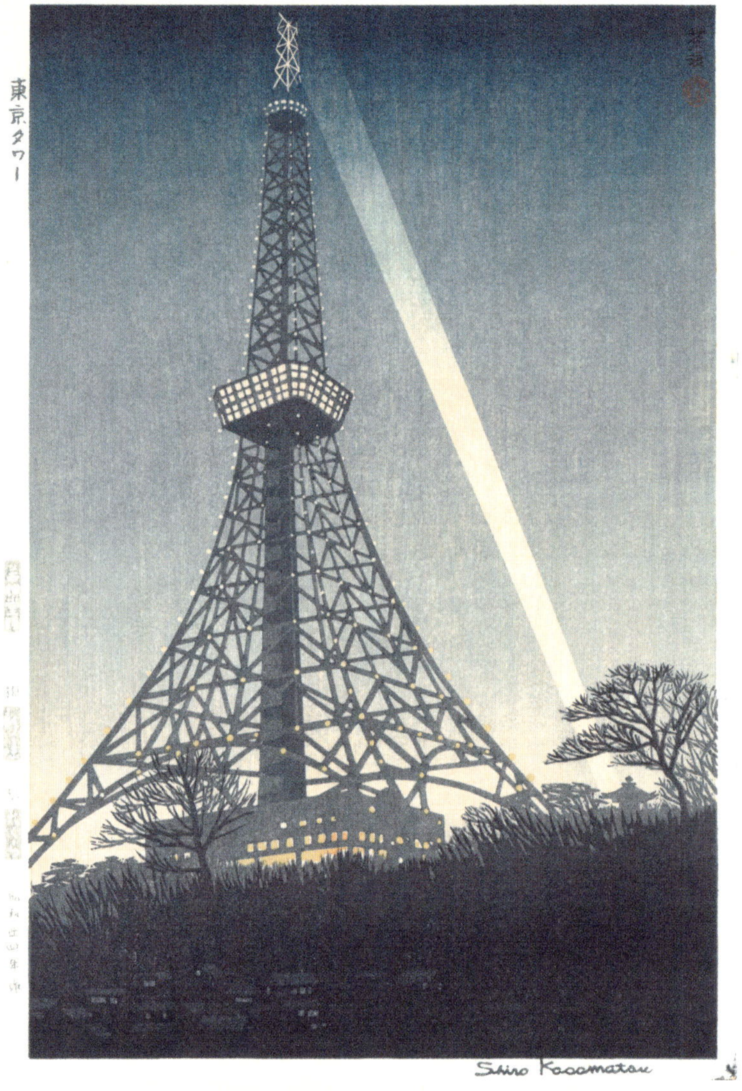

Tokyo Tower, 1959. Woodblock print

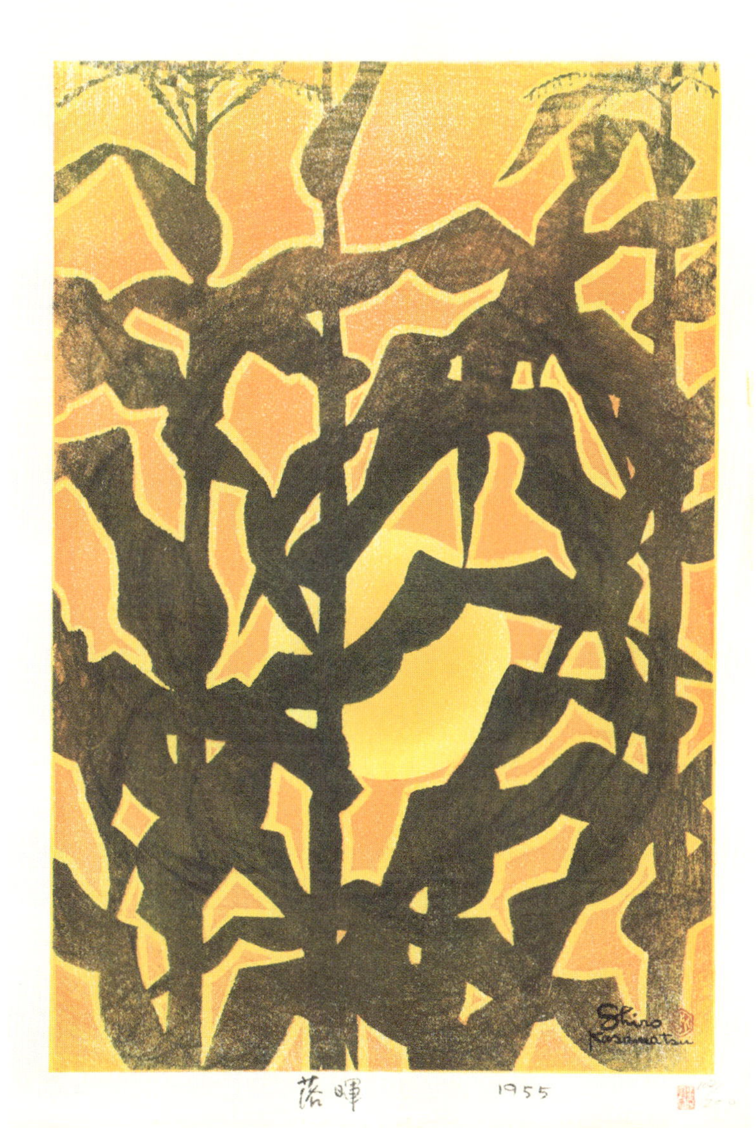

Sunset Glow, 1955. Woodblock print

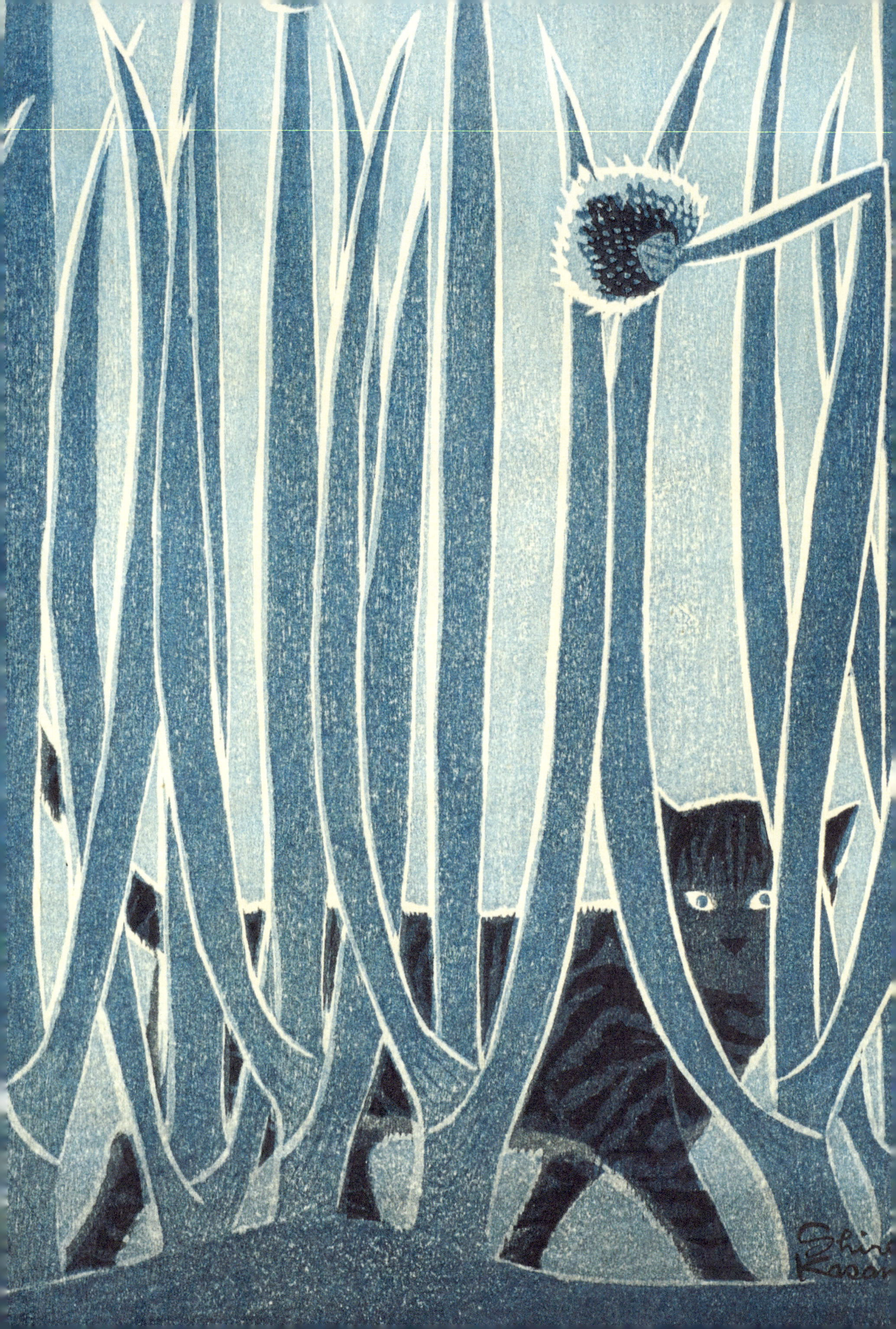

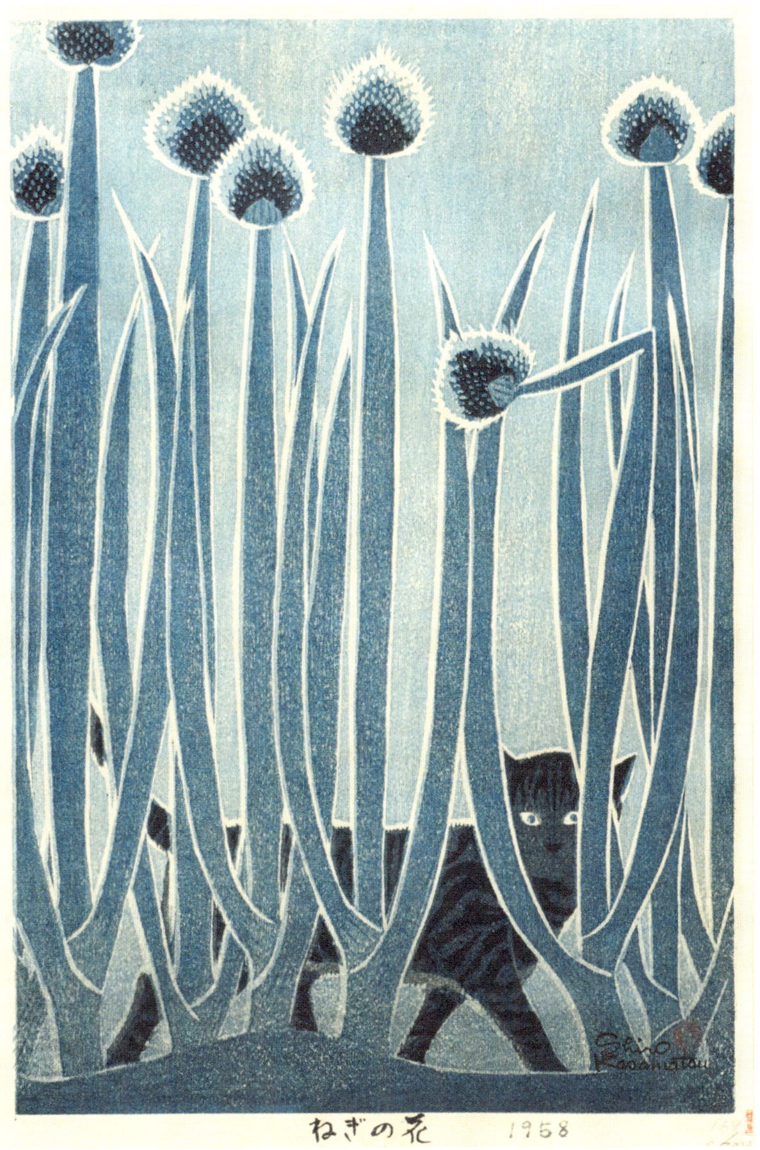

Onion Flowers, 1958. Woodblock print

KAWANO Kaoru (1916–1965)

Medium:
Silkscreen, woodblock

He was a man who ran through the ten years of the 1950s at full speed. It was a time when printmaking itself had not yet established its status as it has today. In Japan, there were a few people who bought prints as housewarming gifts for acquaintances, but it was still a time when people could not afford to buy them themselves and enjoy them. I remember feeling strangely excited when I saw my father's work on the wall of a Chinese restaurant in Ginza.[1]

Kobayashi Etsu
(Kawano Kaoru's eldest daughter)

A prolific and acclaimed printmaker in his day, Kawano Kaoru has been overshadowed in recent decades by his more famous contemporaries such as Saitō Kiyoshi (pp. 138–45). Kawano's career might have started much later than many of his fellow printmakers', and sadly ended early, but his works are still popular and celebrated among collectors today.

Kawano was born in Hokkaido and began his studies at the Kawabata Painting School in 1934. He was accepted to show with the Japan Print Association at its thirteenth exhibition in 1944, with his two woodblock prints *Solar Eclipse* and *Black Sun*. However, his career was put on hold by the war, as Kawano was drafted into the army in 1945; he was taken as a prisoner of war in Siberia, where he was interned for four years. As his daughter recalled: 'He did not like to talk much about his four years of Siberian internment. Stories of black bread and raisins, and the singing that would spontaneously arise when several people gathered, seemed like rather beautiful experiences to my child's mind, but later they became even more painful.'

Following his return from Siberia, Kawano began to exhibit again, first in 1949 with a silkscreen print. In 1956 he presented two woodblock prints, *Owls* and *Little Girl*, at the first College Women's Association of Japan show, in which he participated for the next ten years.

In his distinct 'naive' yet bold style, Kawano bridged traditional Japanese and Western modernist aesthetics, his prints at times semi-abstract in form and with only one or two colours on a dark background. The majority of his prints were portraits of children and birds, often together, while some subjects were related to traditional Japanese culture and religion, such as Buddhas and kokeshi dolls. Kawano played with textures, incorporating the grain patterns of the woodblock into the design, a feature also used by Saitō, with whom Kawano had a close friendship (the two artists lived only minutes from each other). It was also through Saitō that Kawano started to work for Nobarasha, a publishing company founded in 1929. Apart from Saitō, Munakata Shikō (pp. 104–7) also influenced Kawano.

During the 1950s and 1960s, Kawano also participated in several exhibitions in the United States, although he never travelled himself owing to poor health. He was represented at an exhibition of silkscreen prints in New York as well as in exhibitions in Chicago, the former Yugoslavia and other locations.[2] In 1962 he showed twenty works in a two-man exhibition with Saitō Kiyoshi at the Women's College Library in Minneapolis.

1 All quotes and much of the information on Kawano Kaoru are translated from the recollections of Kawano's eldest daughter, Kobayashi Etsu, published online: http://kaorukawano.jp/about/index.html.

2 Michiaki Kawakita, *Contemporary Japanese Prints*, trans. John Bester (Tokyo and Palo Alto, CA: Kodansha International, 1967), p. 180.

I don't need to be called an artist. I'm happy to be a printmaker.
As long as even one person likes my work, that's good enough.

Kawano Kaoru

Collections: Art Institute of Chicago; British Museum, London; Harvard Art Museums; Honolulu Museum of Art; Museum of Fine Arts, Boston.

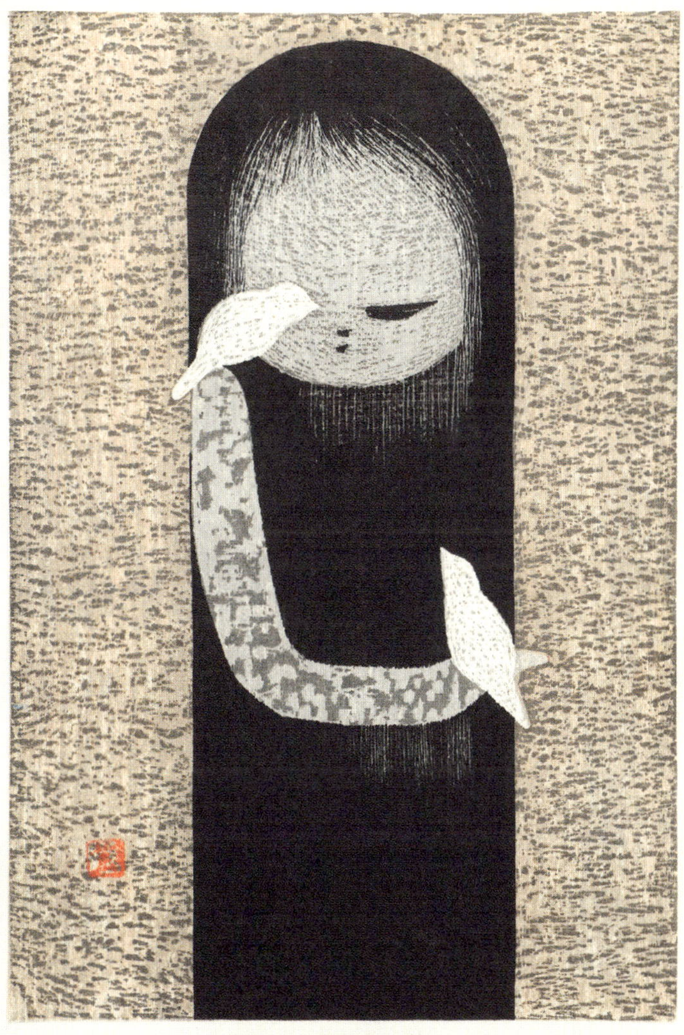

Small Birds, undated. Woodblock print

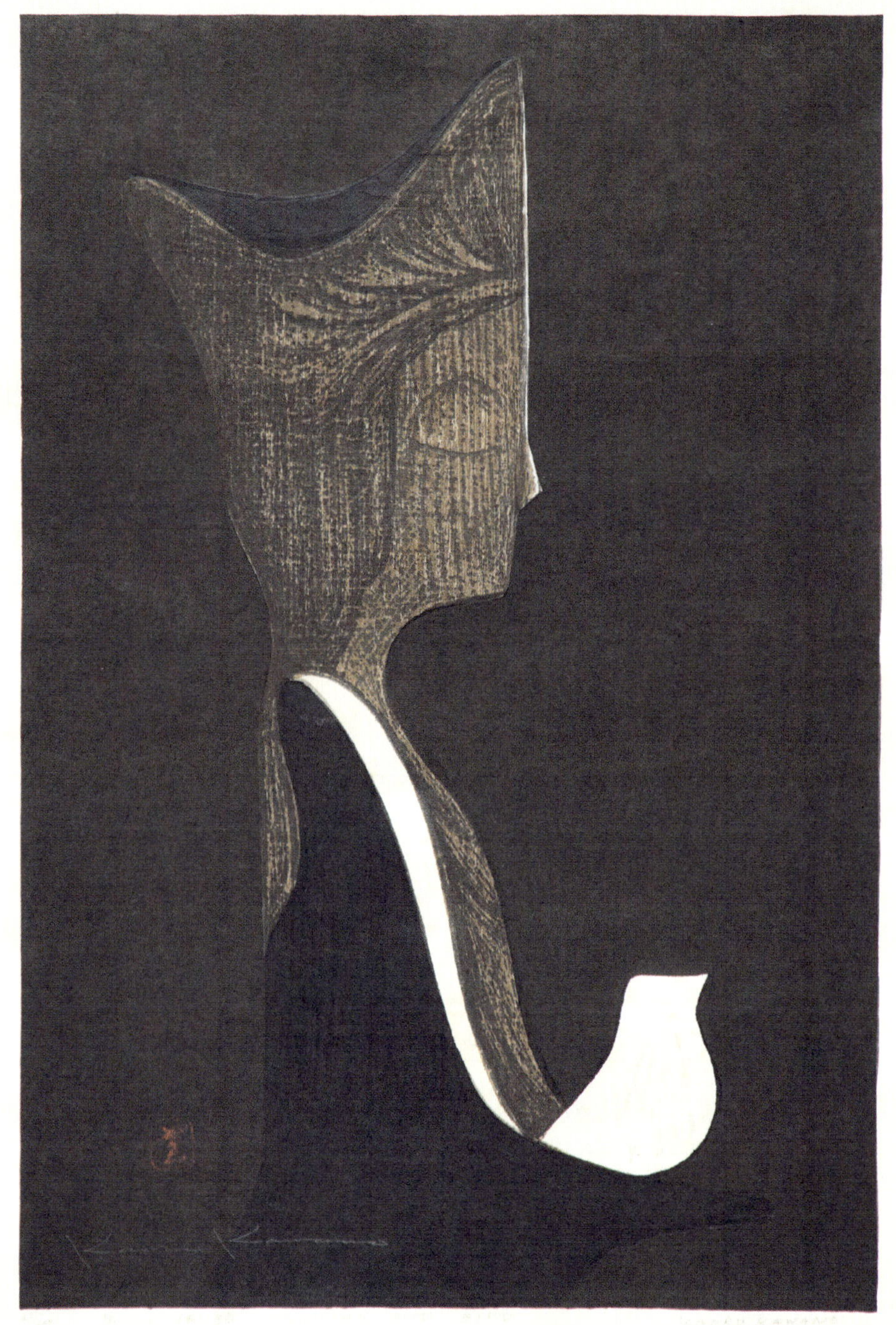

Buddha and Bird, undated. Woodblock print

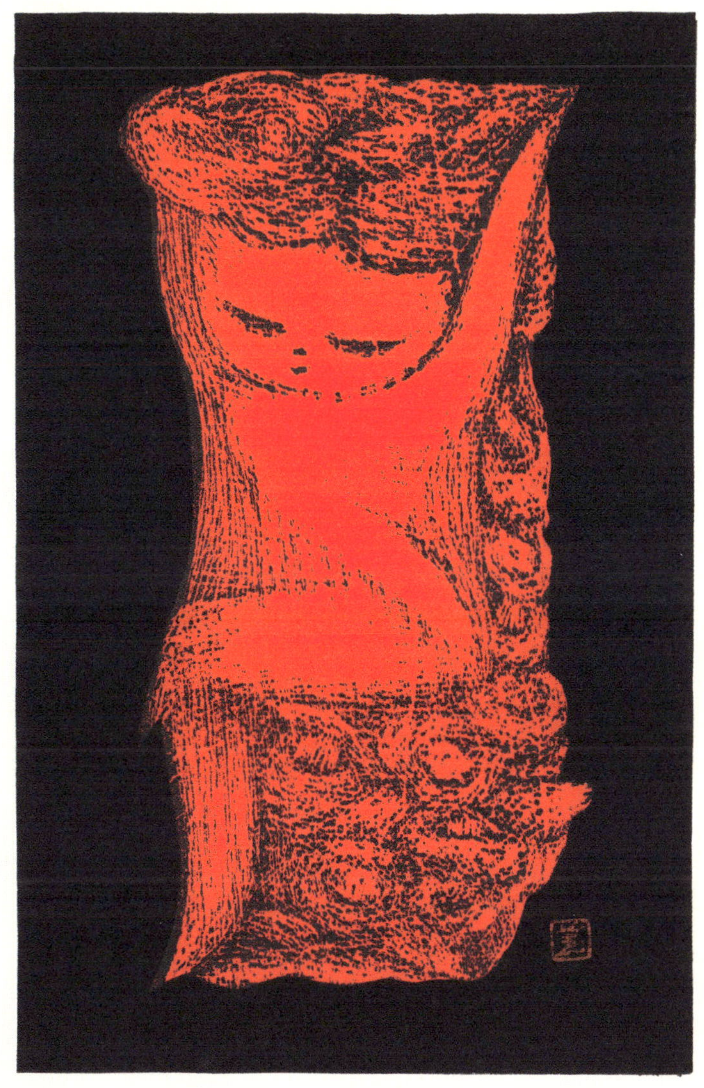

Flora (red), undated. Woodblock print

KINOSHITA Tomio (1923–2014)

Medium:
Stencil, woodblock

I am trying to express the sufferings of society, of man, of mankind, of all living beings. I am not too certain of my results: perhaps in the end I have produced mere 'prints'.[1]

Kinoshita Tomio, 1962

Originally an oil painter, Kinoshita Tomio was self-taught in printmaking, which he started in 1955, inspired by the work of the influential *sōsaku hanga* artist Hiratsuka Un'ichi (pp. 68–71). Having learned seal carving from his wife, carving became Kinoshita's favourite part of the process of creating a print. Kinoshita's technique and approach as a craftsman became his trademark, as observed by Gaston Petit and Amadio Arboleda in their book *Evolving Techniques in Japanese Woodblock Prints* (1977): 'Kinoshita Tomio creates a terrific impact in his works using a U-shaped gouge to produce lines in parallel.'[2] Seemingly leaning away from the Japanese tradition, Kinoshita's carving style was closer to that of European Old Masters like Lucas Cranach the Elder (c. 1472–1553) and Albrecht Dürer (1471–1528) in the 'methods of varying the width of lines in order to create depth and dimension'.[3]

While Kinoshita's first prints were copies of his own paintings and depictions of his birth town of Yokkaichi, a fishing village in Mie prefecture, his breakthrough came when he presented his new sculpture-like portrayals of masks or faces – often melancholic but always sympathetic – composed of carefully carved lines that stressed the feeling of wood. At the Japan Print Association exhibition in 1957, 'the hitherto unknown artist Kinoshita Tomio, then thirty-four years old, startled artistic Tokyo with a series of large prints consisting of stylized human heads depicted in a striking new manner.'[4] In 1958, Kinoshita won the Japan Print Association Prize, and from 1966 to 1994 he submitted works annually to its exhibitions.

James Michener wrote about Kinoshita as early as 1959 in his book *Japanese Prints: From the Early Masters to the Modern* and again in *The Modern Japanese Print: An Appreciation* (first published in 1962), where Kinoshita was one of ten print artists in focus. Testifying to Kinoshita's growing success not only in Japan but internationally, four of his prints were included in the Art Institute of Chicago's *sōsaku hanga* exhibition in 1960, including *Three Masks (Kamen 3)* from 1957 and *Masks, C* from 1959.[5]

Other international and national exhibitions and competitions included the Northwest Printmakers International Exhibition, where he won the Seattle Art Museum purchase award (1960), the Philadelphia International Prints Exhibition (1963) and the International Biennial Exhibition of Prints in Tokyo (1962, 1968). He was included in the exhibition *Images of a Changing World: Japanese Prints of the Twentieth Century* at the Portland Art Museum in 1983 and was chosen as the cover artist for the College Women's Association of Japan exhibition the following year.

It was during the 1980s that Kinoshita ceased making prints and stopped exhibiting, except for submissions to the Japan Print Association. For Kinoshita, printmaking was something he undertook without regard for commercial gain but for the simple pleasure. As Michener wrote: 'He wants to make prints only when he feels in the mood to tackle a piece of wood and carve something creative in it.'[6]

1 Kinoshita Tomio quoted in James A. Michener, *The Modern Japanese Print: An Appreciation* (Rutland: Charles E. Tuttle Co., 1968), p. 34.
2 Gaston Petit and Amadio Arboleda, *Evolving Techniques in Japanese Woodblock Prints* (Tokyo, New York, San Francisco: Kodansha International, 1977), p. 21.
3 Frances Blakemore, *Who's Who in Modern Japanese Prints* (New York and Tokyo: Weatherhill, 1975), p. 80.
4 Michener, *The Modern Japanese Print*, p. 32.
5 *Japan's Modern Prints: Sōsaku Hanga*, exh. cat. (Chicago: Art Institute of Chicago, 1960), catalogue nos. 243–44.
6 James Michener, *The Modern Japanese Print*, 1968, p. 33.

His woodblock and stencil print *Masks* (1957) was shown in New York as part of the Museum of Modern Art exhibition *Soldier, Spectre, Shaman: The Figure and the Second World War* in 2016. The Mie Prefectural Art Museum held an exhibition commemorating the 100th anniversary of Kinoshita's birth in 2023–24.

Collections: British Museum, London; Portland Art Museum; Cleveland Museum of Art; Mie Prefectural Art Museum, Tsu; Minneapolis Institute of Art; Museum of Modern Art, New York.

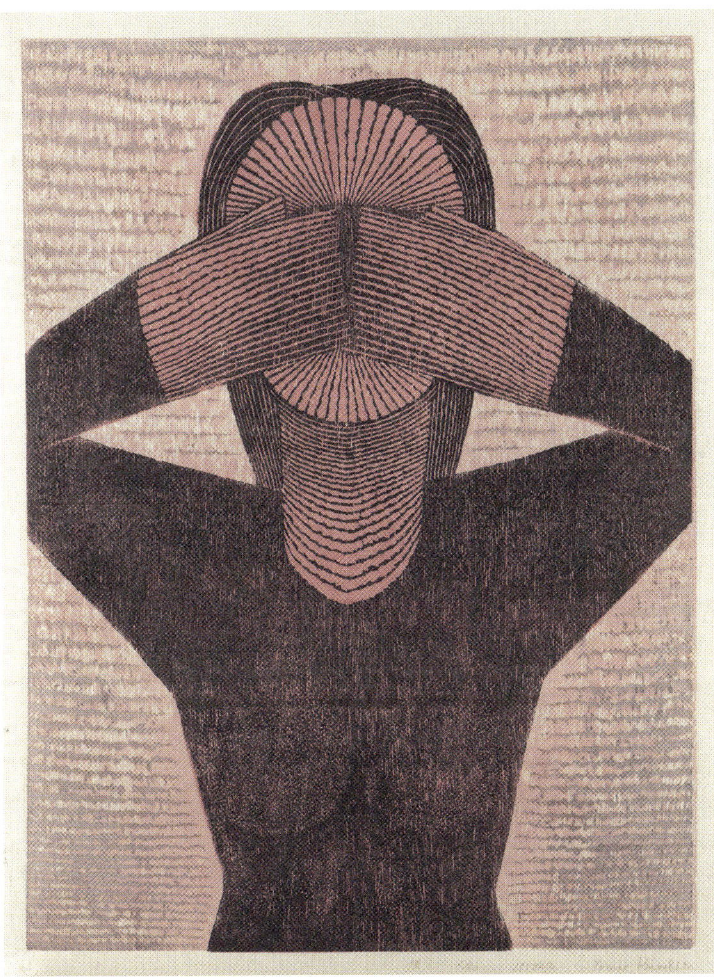

Alone, 1958. Woodblock print

Face, 1970. Woodblock print

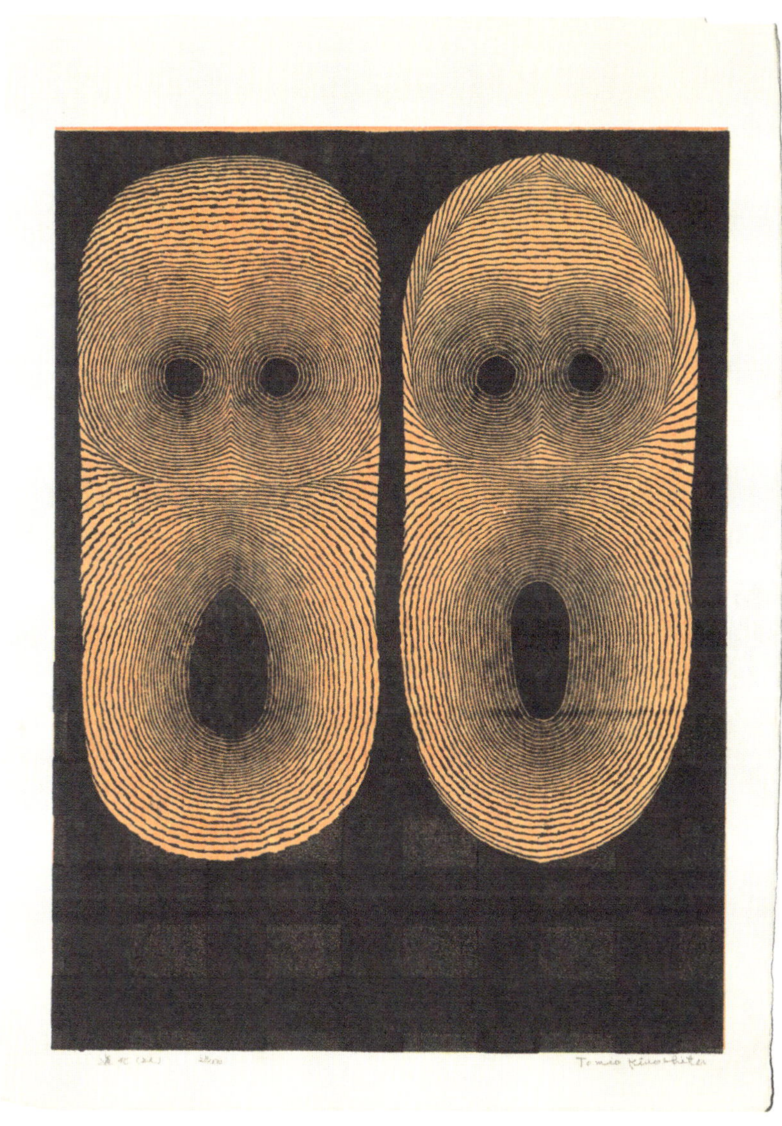

Clowns, 1965. Woodblock print

KUROSAKI Akira (1937–2019)

Medium:
Woodblock

The print boom of the 1960s, which continues into this decade, is represented by a diverse group of works. From abroad are examples of current Japanese printmaking.[1]

Recent Acquisitions, 1968–1973,
Museum of Modern Art, New York

The Museum of Modern Art exhibition *Recent Acquisitions, 1968–1973* included Kurosaki Akira's woodblock print *The Vermillion Darkness* (1970), which was displayed alongside works by major names like Josef Albers, Stanley William Hayter, Jackson Pollock and Roy Lichtenstein as well as contemporary Japanese artists including Satō Ado (pp. 146–51) and Noda Tetsuya (pp. 117–23). Ten prints by ten Japanese artists were presented in the exhibition, testifying to the variety in both style and technique in contemporary Japanese printmaking. The prints had been donated by Florene May Schoenborn, a MoMA trustee and important collector of modern art, including works by Pablo Picasso, Henri Matisse (1869–1954) and Alberto Giacometti (1901–1966).[2] Kurosaki was in well-established company.

Kurosaki was born in Manchuria (under Japanese colonial rule from 1932 to 1945) and after the end of the Second World War he returned with his family to Japan, like so many others. In 1962 Kurosaki graduated from Kyoto University of Industrial Arts, where he received a post as associate professor ten years later. His studies were followed by graduate work at Harvard University and the Hochschule für bildende Künste, Hamburg.

Kurosaki was fascinated by traditional Japanese printmaking and while a student amassed a small collection of *ukiyo-e*.[3] His work was technically unusual in that he combined the idea of the modern print artist working independently with the traditional collaborative *hanmoto* system of the *ukiyo-e* artists. From 1965 he would seek advice from professional craftsmen, with whom he would collaborate on the cutting of the blocks and most of the printing.[4] His precision and intensely saturated hues, normally associated with silkscreen prints, became his trademark.

It was during the late 1960s and 1970s that Kurosaki's career as a print artist took off and he started to exhibit both in Japan and abroad, including print biennales in Tokyo, Maastricht, Kraków, Ljubljana, Paris and Fredrikstad, through which he became known to an international audience. In 1969 he became a member of the Japan Print Association.

At the seventh International Biennial Exhibition of Prints in Tokyo in 1970, Kurosaki was awarded the Minister of Education Award for his woodblock print *Composition of the Darkness* (1970). Other participants at that year's biennale included Roy Lichtenstein, Ay-O (pp. 31–43) and Yayanagi Go (pp. 219–25) with their bright lithographs and silkscreen prints. In a period dominated by Pop art, Kurosaki's semi-surreal and dark dreamscapes offered a calm escape of mysticism and solitude. In 1972, for the exhibition *Contemporary Japanese Prints*, the Los Angeles County Museum of Art described Kurosaki's work: 'round and rectangular forms are modeled with dramatic shading and treated in sharp perspective. These features, together with the deep reds and blacks, create inner spaces of mysterious portent.'[5]

1 Museum of Modern Art, *Recent Acquisitions, 1968–1973: Prints and Illustrated Books*, press release, 19 June 1973, www.moma.org/calendar/exhibitions/1754.

2 Carol Vogel, '32 Works of Art by Masters Left to Met and the Modern', *New York Times*, 25 November 1996, and press release, 'The Museum of Modern Art Receives Major Gift from the Late Florene May Schoenborn', 25 November 1996, www.moma.org/research/archives/press-archives.

3 Thank you to Monica Bethe for sharing this information.

4 Gaston Petit, *44 Modern Japanese Print Artists*, 2 vols (Tokyo, New York, San Francisco: Kodansha International, 1973), p. 194.

5 George Kuwayama, *Contemporary Japanese Prints*, exh. cat. (Los Angeles: Los Angeles County Museum of Art, 1973), p. 118.

The years 1973–74 also saw Kurosaki study abroad under a Japanese government scholarship through the Agency for Cultural Affairs. In 1978 he worked as a guest lecturer at Washington University, Seattle, and after a long period of working and living outside Japan he returned to Kyoto and started teaching in the department of printmaking at Kyoto Seika University. One of his students was Shibata Yasu (b. 1968), who would become a successful print artist in his own right but also a printer collaborating with artists such as Nara Yoshitomo (pp. 112–15) and Teraoka Masami (pp. 189–95).

Collections: British Museum, London; Museum of Modern Art, New York; National Museum of Modern Art, Tokyo; Victoria and Albert Museum, London.

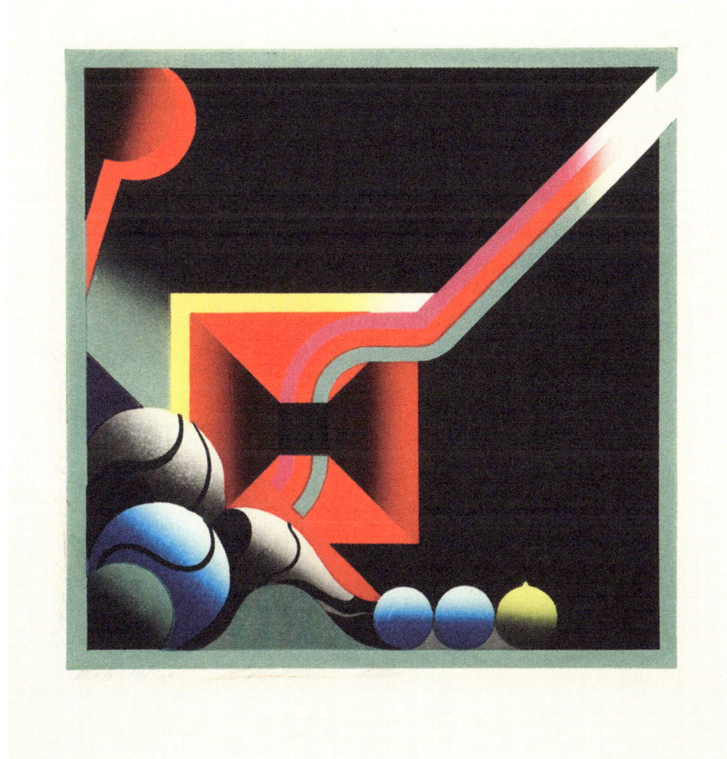

Mysterious Night, 1972. Woodblock print

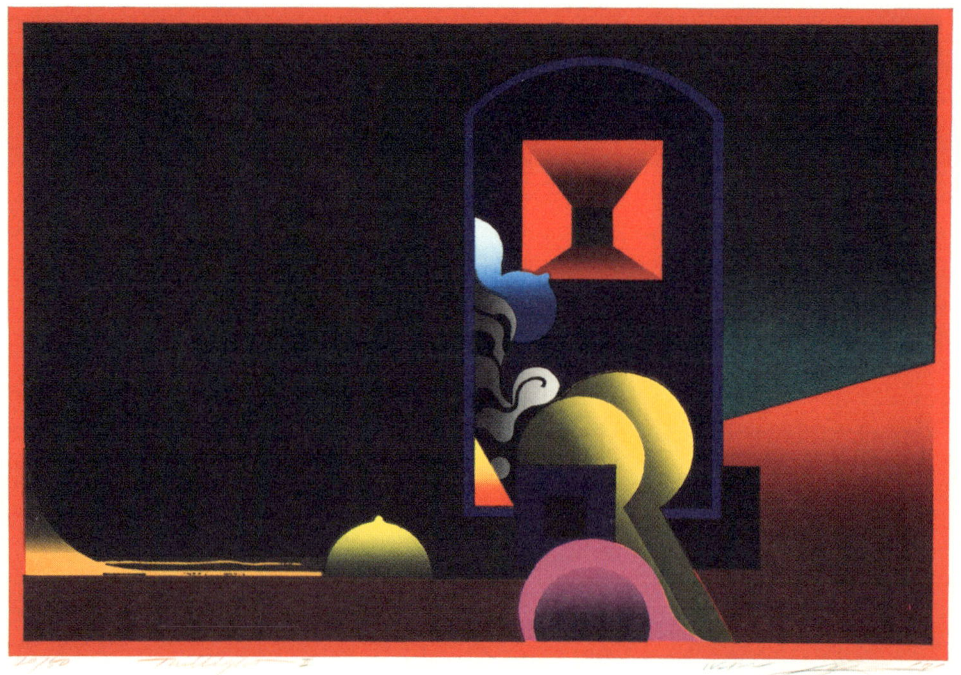

Twilight II, 1971. Woodblock print

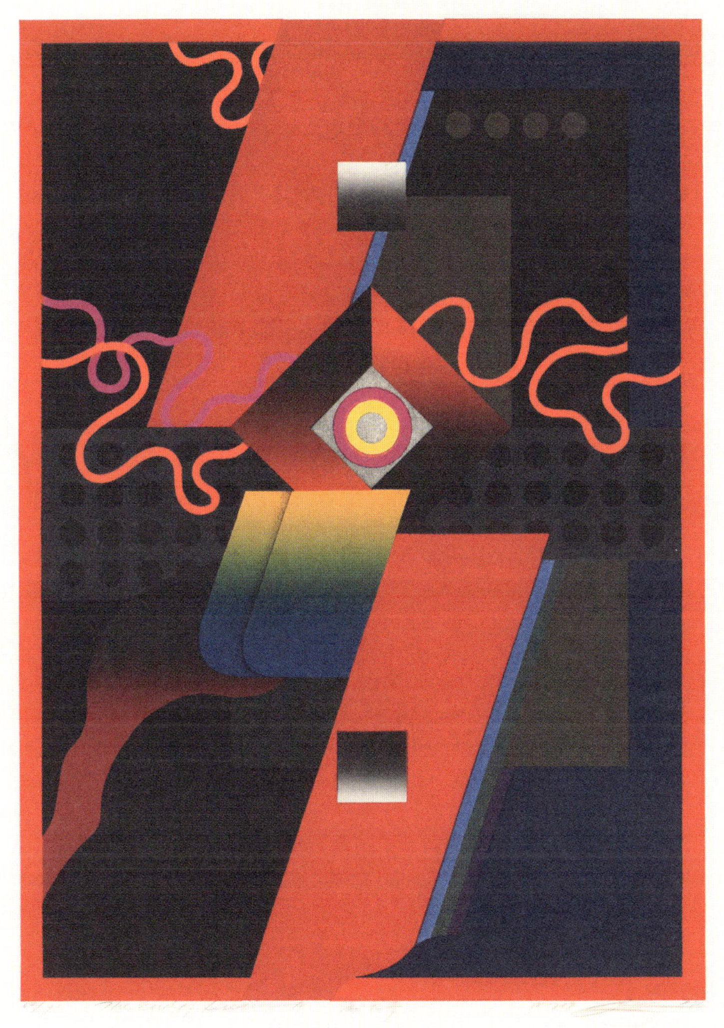

The End of Dream A, W-209, 1976. Woodblock print

KUSAMA Yayoi (b. 1929)

Medium:
Etching, lithograph, silkscreen, woodblock

I have been making prints ever since I was captivated by their allure, and am constantly overwhelmed by the brilliance arising from within the process of making them … I create prints with all my heart for people who love them. I wish to make countless duplicates of the same visual field and spread them across the world.[1]

Kusama Yayoi, 2005

Kusama Yayoi is one of the most significant Japanese multidisciplinary artists working today, associated with her iconic pumpkins, repetitive polka dots, net patterns and 'Infinity Mirror Rooms', as well as the cutting-edge, provocative happenings of her early career. But Kusama's work in the print medium, whose nature of repetition seems a perfect match for that of her aesthetic practice, is a significant part of her oeuvre.

In 1948, Kusama studied Japanese-style painting (*nihonga*) at the Kyoto City Senior High School of Art. However, she was interested in contemporary Western art, like many Japanese artists of her generation who looked towards New York's avant-garde scene in the late 1950s and 1960s. After seeing the work of the American painter Georgia O'Keeffe (1887–1986) in a book in 1955, Kusama wrote to the artist, who advised her to go to New York to become an artist. So Kusama decided to leave Japan.[2]

With no connections to the art world, in June 1958, 29-year-old Kusama arrived in New York – coincidentally, the same year as Ay-O (pp. 31–43). Her entry onto the international art scene was to be both a pioneering and a lonely one, with Kusama often standing in the shadow of her male contemporaries, despite many of her ideas and her work being ahead of its time.[3]

Kusama used the print medium for its repetitive quality in her first installation at the Gertrude Stein Gallery. *Aggregation: One Thousand Boats Show*, which opened in December 1963, was a room-sized installation consisting of a white boat covered with phallic protrusions of fabric – she had found the boat in a junkyard with her friend and fellow artist Donald Judd (1928–1994).[4] Pasted on the walls were black-and-white posters depicting the same boat 999 times. Kusama's use of repetition of and in an artwork predated that of Andy Warhol, who had his screenprinted *Cow Wallpaper* exhibited at the renowned Leo Castelli Gallery in New York in 1966.

That same year, at the 33rd Venice Biennale, Kusama staged a guerilla happening in front of the Italian pavilion. In her *Narcissus Garden*, consisting of 1,500 mirrored plastic balls laid out on the ground, Kusama, dressed in either a kimono or a red leotard, greeted visitors, who could buy her balls for the price of $2. While the four other Japanese artists were officially invited to show at the Japanese pavilion – including Ay-O, who gained acclaim for his *Rainbow Environment No. 3* (see p. 38) – Kusama had not received an official invitation. Although the committee had given her permission to exhibit, she was eventually asked to stop her performance, and not until almost thirty years later, in 1993, was she asked to officially represent Japan.[5]

Kusama began making and exhibiting her first stand-alone prints in 1979, following her move from New York to Japan in 1973. Experimenting with a variety of techniques, such as silkscreen, etching, lithography and woodblock

1 Yayoi Kusama, *All Prints of KUSAMA YAYOI 1979–2004* (Tokyo: Abe Publishing, 2005), p. 5.
2 See Stephanie Rosenthal, ed., *Yayoi Kusama: A Retrospective*, exh. cat., Gropius Bau, Berlin (London: Prestel, 2021), p. 8.
3 See Thomas Frick, ed., *Love Forever: Yayoi Kusama, 1958–1968*, exh. cat. (Los Angeles: Los Angeles County Museum of Art, 1998), p. 8.
4 For more on Judd and Kusama, see Rosenthal, ed., *Yayoi Kusama*, p. 92.
5 On her 1966 performance, see ibid., p. 161. Her show in 1993 was the first single-artist exhibition ever shown in the Japanese pavilion, and the first of a female artist. See, for example, Frick, ed., *Love Forever*, p. 8.

printing, Kusama has created vivid prints composed of her distinct polka dots and nets. Many of the motifs are also recognisable from her paintings: pumpkins, flowers, shoes, hats, fruit, butterflies, and sometimes a subject as traditionally Japanese as Mt Fuji.

Among her print collaborators was master printer Okabe Tokuzō, who set up the first silkscreen printing studio in Japan in 1964. Artists such as Ay-O, Satō Ado (pp. 146–51), Onosato Toshinobu (pp. 134–37), Teraoka Masami (pp. 189–95) and Nam June Paik (1932–2006) all worked with Okabe, who was offering silkscreen printing to order. In 1984, Kusama began working on etchings and lithographs with Kimura Kihachi (1934–2014), a master printer who also collaborated on prints with another prominent female artist, Shinoda Tōkō (pp. 152–53).

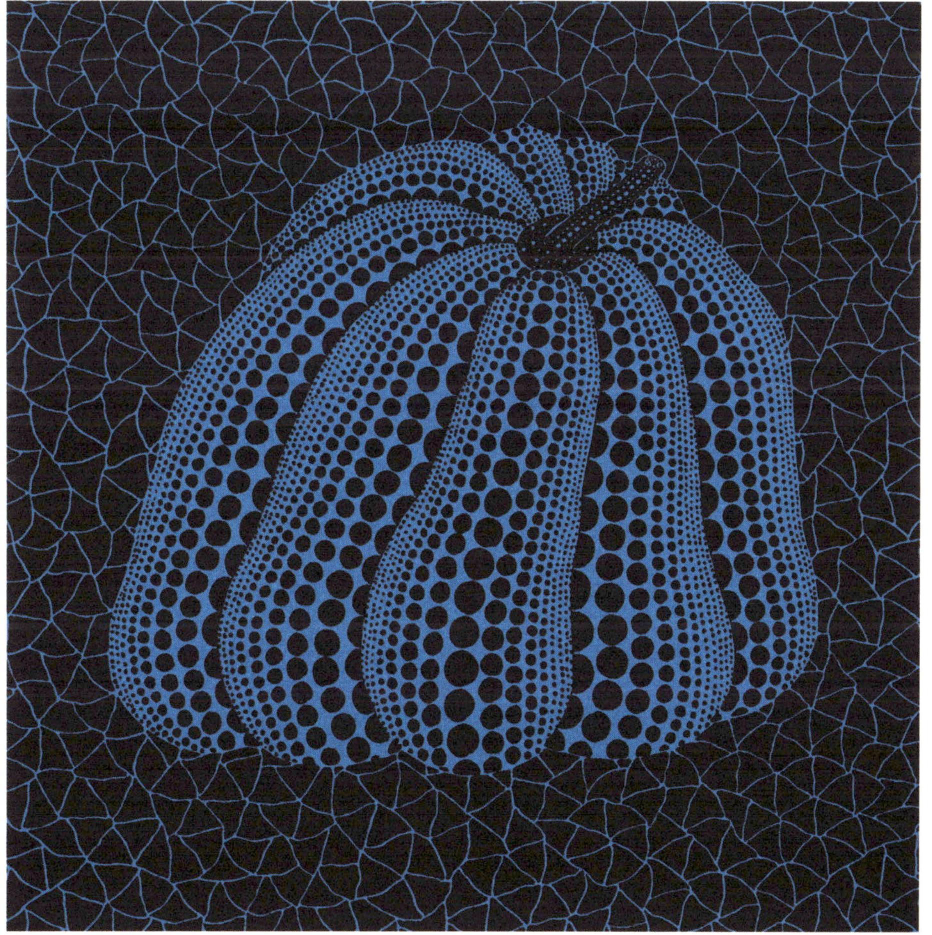

Pumpkin (BSQ), 1998. Silkscreen print

Kusama has continued to expand her printmaking oeuvre, producing a series of traditional woodblock prints of Japan's sacred mountain, *Mt Fuji in Seven Colours*, in collaboration with the Adachi Institute of Woodcut Prints, Tokyo, in 2014. Her serial view of Fuji consists of seven prints in seven colour versions, each accompanied by a poetic title:

Orange:	'When life boundlessly flares up to the universe'
Blue:	'Where the universe and human life are'
Green:	'All about Mt Fuji that I have loved my whole life'
Pink:	'All things full of kindness touched my heart'
Red:	'Mt Fuji, I love'
Yellow:	'My life shining forever, this human love shall not perish even after billions of light years'
Black:	'Where our soul sets in, this dark mountain embraces all with love'

Kusama's signature polka dots – 14,685 of them – make up the sky behind Mt Fuji. The woodblock prints were carved by Chikura Kishi and printed by Yoshio Kyoso of the Adachi Institute. The prints are based on a painting that Kusama made following her first encounter with the mountain at close range. In 1983, Kusama had already taken up the classic subject in the screen-print *Mt Fuji*. With this series of contemporary woodblock prints, Kusama follows in a long line of Japanese printmakers working in the traditional *moku hanga* technique who have paid homage to Japan's iconic mountain, among them Hokusai and Hiroshige in the 1830s and '40s, Yoshida Hiroshi (pp. 232–33) in the 1920s and '30s, Tokuriki Tomikichirō (pp. 196–201) in the 1940s, Munakata Shikō (pp. 104–7) in the 1950s and Ay-O in the 1970s.

An exhibition solely dedicated to Kusama's prints, *Kusama Print Works: Repetition and Proliferation*, was held at the Kyoto City Kyocera Museum of Art in 2025.

Collections: Fukuoka Art Museum; Matsumoto City Museum of Art.

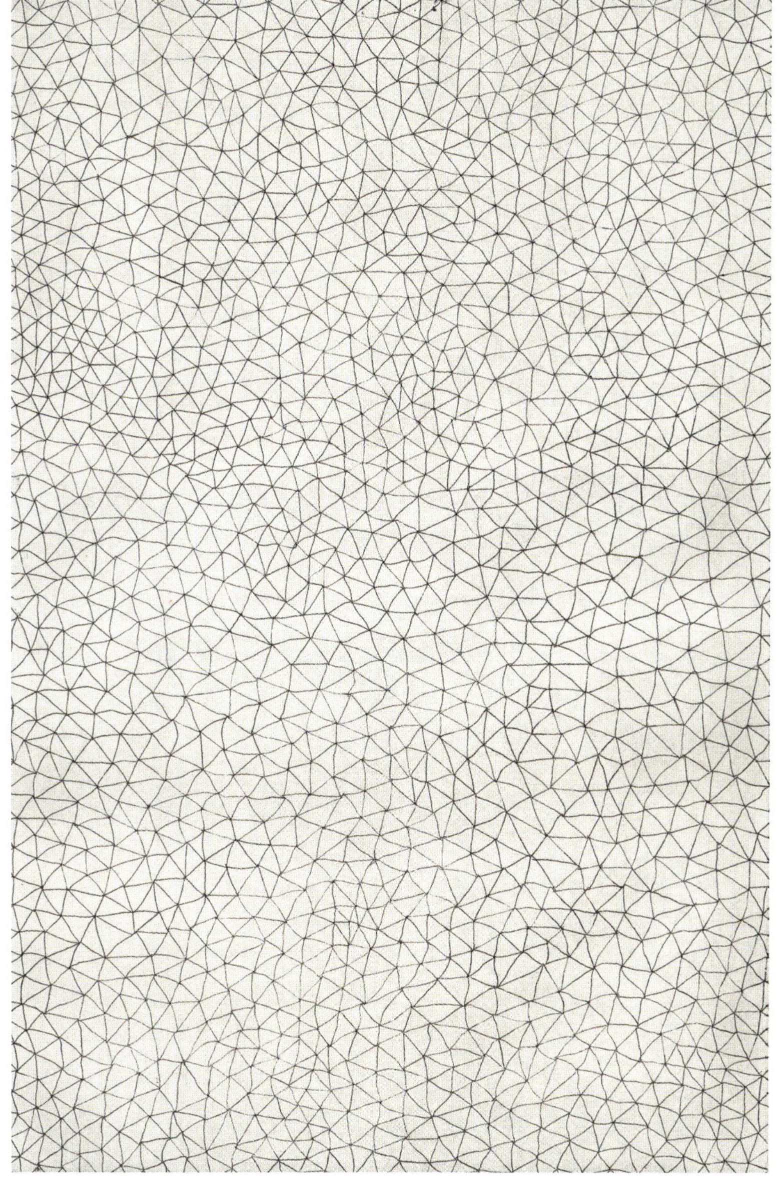

Infinity Nets (A · B), 1994. Etching

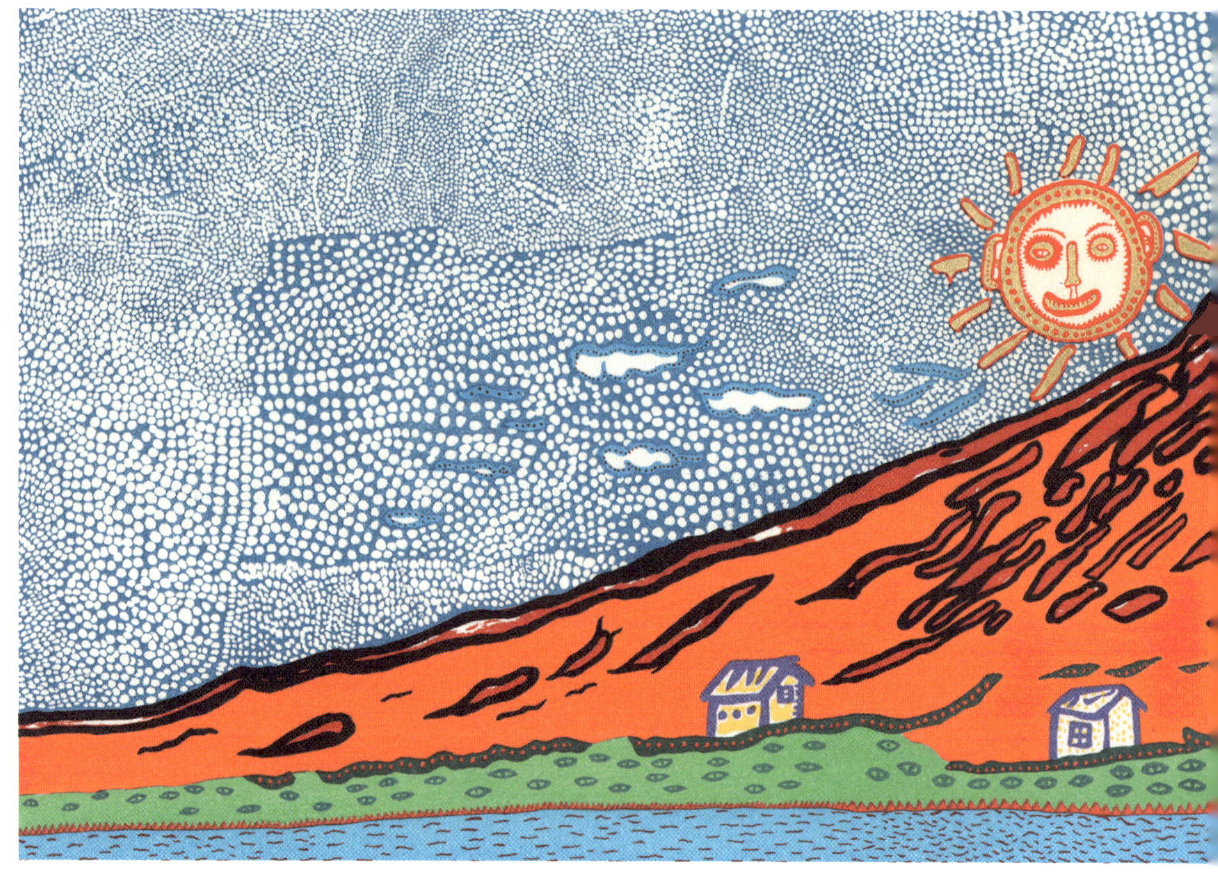

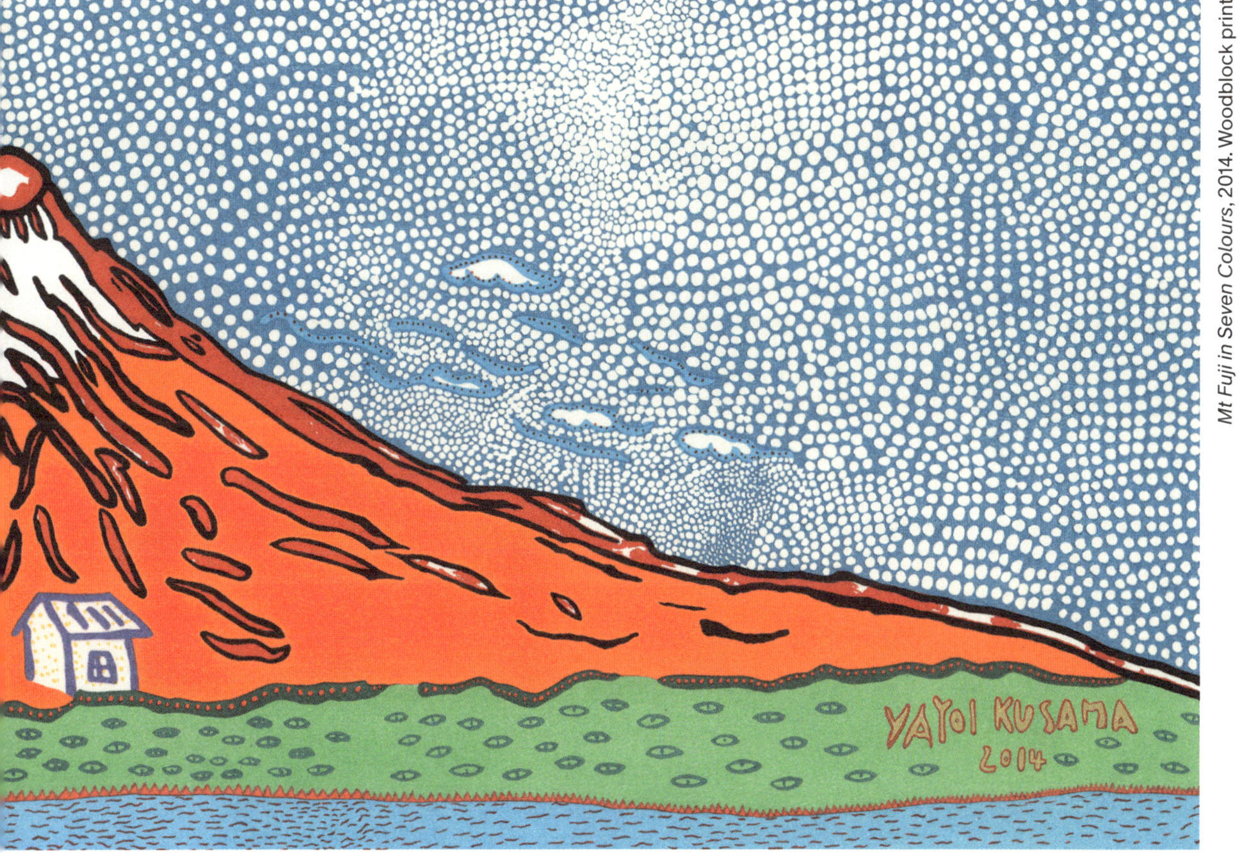

Mt Fuji in Seven Colours, 2014. Woodblock print

MORI Yoshitoshi (1898–1992)

Medium:
Stencil, woodblock

When Mori Yoshitoshi was eight years old, his grandfather – whose Tokyo wholesale fish market Nishigen had gone bankrupt a few years prior – died by *seppuku*, the ritualistic suicide traditionally reserved for the samurai. It was young Mori who discovered his grandfather's body.[1]

Born during the Meiji period, Mori grew up at a time of confusing transition from old to new Japan, with the traditional ways becoming something of the past. While victory over China in the first Sino-Japanese War (1894–95) established Japan as a modern military nation, many of the old aspects of Japanese society, including its arts and crafts, were clinging on for survival. It was in this context that Mori became an artist specialising in *kappazuri* (stencil printing), a technique associated with traditional kimono textiles.

In 1915, Mori studied painting and illustration under *shin hanga* artist Yamakawa Shūhō (1898–1944), born the same year as Mori. His father, Yamakawa Seihō, a textile artist, taught Mori the craft of *yūzen* dyeing, a paste-resist dyeing technique established at the end of the seventeenth century.

By 1925, after serving in the army in Korea and having graduated in Western-style painting (*yōga*) from the Kawabata Painting School, Mori set up his own workshop. He would work for thirty years as a designer and dyer of kimono textiles. In 1938 his textile work brought him in touch with the *mingei* (folk craft) movement and its founder, Yanagi Sōetsu. Mori would often visit the Japan Folk Crafts Museum (Nihon Mingei-kan) in Tokyo, which had been established in 1936 with Yanagi as its president. Through Yanagi, Mori also met the print artists Munakata Shikō (pp. 104–7) and Sasajima Kihei (1906–1993) and *mingei* textile designer Serizawa Keisuke (1895–1984).

It was alongside Serizawa that Mori began experimenting with stencil printing, applying the method to paper, rather than textile, to create expressive and vibrant motifs of traditional Japan.[2] His distinctive prints portray dynamic kabuki actors and beautiful women (*bijin*), Buddhist iconography, scenes from Japanese history as well as festivals, markets and townscapes. Encouraged by Yanagi, Mori entered a print in the Japan Print Academy (Nihon Banga-in) exhibition, organised by Munakata in 1954.

Mori participated in numerous national and international exhibitions, including the International Biennial Exhibition of Prints in Tokyo (1957 and 1966) and several CWAJ shows (1963–68, 1970, 1977 and others), and won an award at the Tuttle Company Contemporary Japanese Art Exhibition (1960).

Although Mori did not begin his career as a printmaker until late in life, he chose to pursue printmaking full-time in 1960, quickly becoming one of the leading exponents of the modern print movement, being involved in both *mingei* and *sōsaku hanga*. Working in a medium traditional to Japan, Mori was instrumental in bringing it to an international audience as well as into the modern era. In 1985 a major exhibition of his work was held at the National Museum of Ethnology, Leiden.

Collections: Art Institute of Chicago; Berlin National Museum; British Museum, London; Los Angeles County Museum of Art; Museum of Fine Arts, Boston; Museum of Modern Art, Tokyo.

1 See Abe Setsuko et al., *Mori Yoshitoshi: Kappa-ban*, exh. cat., Ginza Matsuzakaya, Tokyo, and National Museum of Ethnology, Leiden (Tokyo: Mori Yoshitoshi-ten Jikko Iinkai, 1985).

2 The method is described in detail in Margaret K. Johnson and Dale K. Hilton, *Japanese Prints Today: Tradition with Innovation* (Tokyo: Shufunotomo Co., 1980), pp. 58–59.

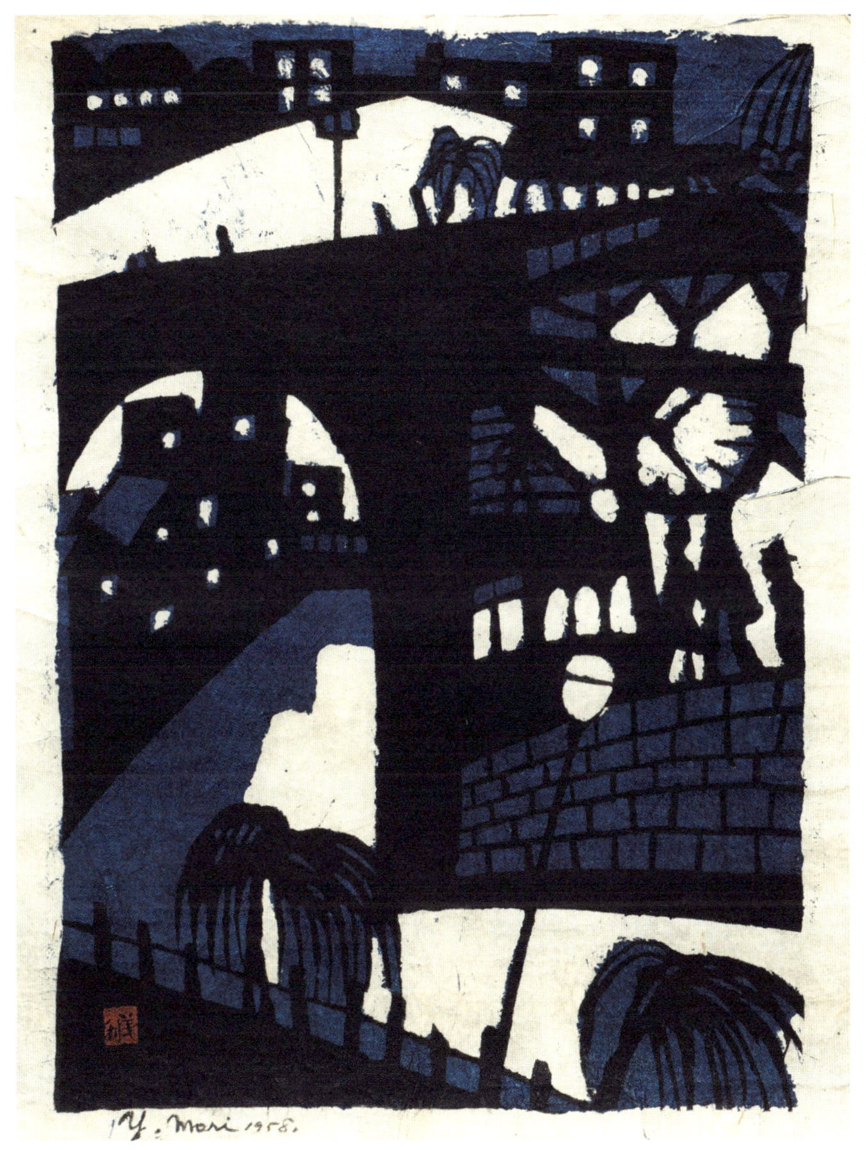

Cityscape, 1958. Stencil print

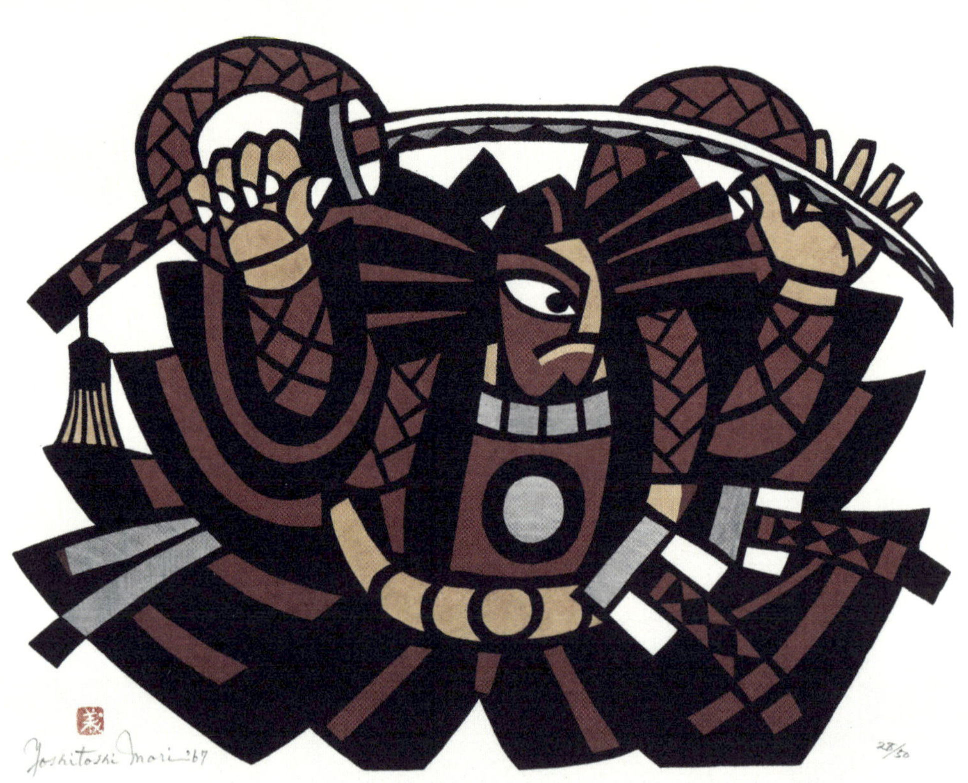

Kabuki C: Shibaraku (Just a Moment), 1967. Stencil print

Geisha, 1970. Woodblock print

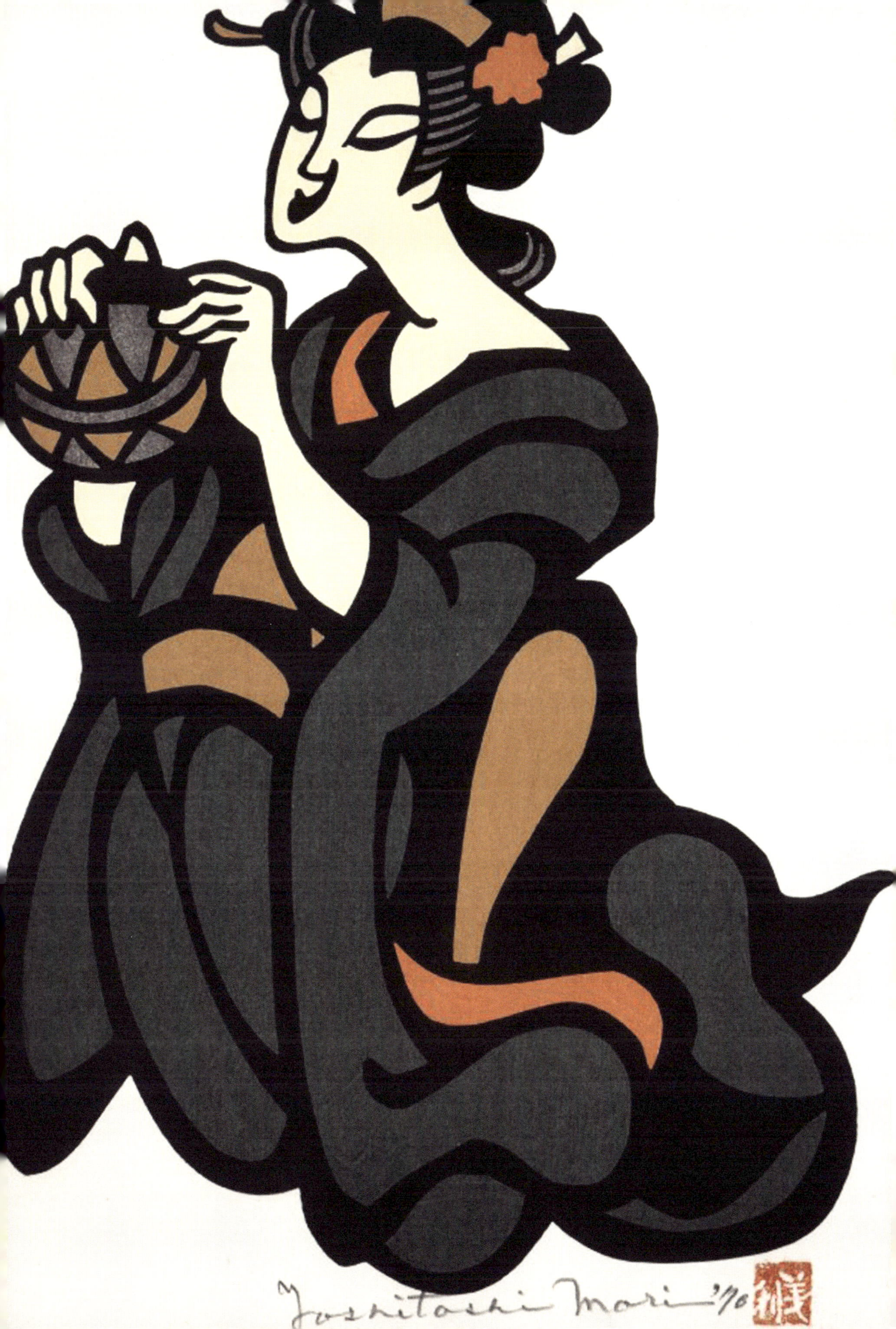
Yoshitoshi Mori '70

MUNAKATA Shikō (1903–1975)

Medium:
Woodblock

Fellow artists like to say that 'Munakata is kamigakari – obsessed with God,' and at work Munakata vividly demonstrates why. Kneeling before his low work table with his broad rump in the air, he first squints nearsightedly at a sumi (black-ink) drawing he has pasted to a block of Judas-tree wood. Suddenly he seizes his chisel and, in a fury of motion, starts jabbing at the block, banging away with the mallet as the chips fly in all directions.[1]

Time, 1956

With his impressive international wins in the printmaking divisions at the 3rd São Paulo Biennial (1955) and at the 28th Venice Biennale (1956), Munakata Shikō – spontaneous, wild-natured and extremely short-sighted – not only put himself on the international art map but helped pave the way for contemporary printmaking in Japan.

The series *Two Bodhisattvas and Ten Great Disciples of Sakyamuni* (1939) – large, monochrome woodblock prints of bold and expressive compositions with the figures touching the sides, combined with the use of traditional Buddhist subject matter – is representative of Munakata's trademark style. 'My work is based on Zen Buddhism. Others treat black as black ink. To me it is life itself,' he told Oliver Statler in the 1950s.[2] It was works from this series – which had already won him acclaim in Japan with the Saburi award in 1940 – that secured him the top prizes in 1955 and 1956.[3]

Born in Aomori in the Tōhoku region of Japan, at the age of 21 Munakata moved from his birth town to Tokyo to make a career as a painter. It was a reproduction of Vincent van Gogh's *Sunflowers* in the magazine *Shirakaba* that moved Munakata to such an extent that he made up his mind to become an artist.[4] Not formally trained, he continued to submit oil paintings to various exhibitions during the 1920s and had one accepted for the first time in 1925. But Munakata started to feel that the medium was too foreign, given its strong association with the canon of Western art history, and his interest turned to woodblock printing. Since he had studied wood sculpture while in Aomori, working with a chisel was somewhat familiar to him.[5]

Through the artist Shimozawa Kihachirō (1901–1986), whom Munakata knew from home, he was introduced to the circle of Hiratsuka Un'ichi (pp. 68–71) in 1928. He started learning the medium of woodblock from Hiratsuka, and the following year Munakata participated in the Japan Creative Print Association exhibition.

A turning point came in 1936, when Munakata met philosopher and art critic Yanagi Sōetsu, the leading figure of the *mingei* (folk craft) movement. As a counter-reaction to Japan's ongoing Westernisation and industrialisation, Yanagi believed in see(k)ing beauty in everyday ordinary and utilitarian objects by 'unknown craftsmen' of the pre-industrial period. Emphasising the importance of traditional craftmanship for and by the common people, he wrote in 1939: 'In this sense, art is an individual endeavour while woodblock prints are communal. Woodblock prints seek a wide audience; they do not shun the common people.'[6] Yanagi believed that woodblock prints should be seen as utilitarian 'handicraft' to understand their true meaning, not as 'art'. Yanagi, who referred to Munakata as 'the bear cub', would

1 'Art: Japanese Print Revival', *Time*, 23 July 1956, https://time.com/archive/6803000/art-japanese-print-revival.
2 Quoted in Oliver Statler, *Modern Japanese Prints: An Art Reborn* (Rutland, VT: Charles E. Tuttle Co., 1956), p. 80.
3 The original blocks for the two bodhisattvas were destroyed during the war, and Munakata recarved them in 1948. See Yanagi Sōri, ed., *The Woodblock and the Artist: The Life and Work of Shiko Munakata*, exh. cat., Hayward Gallery, London (Tokyo: Kodansha International and Japan Folk Crafts Museum / London: South Bank Centre, 1991), p. 65.
4 Hanai Hisaho et al., *The Making of Shiko: Celebrating the 120th Anniversary of the Artist's Birth*, exh. cat., National Museum of Modern Art, Tokyo (Tokyo: NHK Promotions, 2023), p. 25.
5 Yanagi, ed., *The Woodblock and the Artist*, p. 13.
6 Sōetsu Yanagi, *Selected Essays on Japanese Folk Crafts*, trans. Michael Brase (Tokyo: Japan Publishing Industry Foundation for Culture, 2020), p. 159.
7 Yanagi Sōri in *The Woodblock and the Artist*, p. 9.
8 Statler, *Modern Japanese Prints*, pp. 80–81.
9 Munakata Shikō quoted in Yanagi, ed., *The Woodblock and the Artist*, p. 138.
10 Museum of Modern Art, New York, *Contemporary Painters and Sculptors as Printmakers*, master checklist, 1964, www.moma.org/calendar/exhibitions/2766.
11 Munakata quoted in Statler, *Modern Japanese Prints*, p. 84.

become a key adviser and supporter of Munakata, buying his prints for the newly established Japan Folk Crafts Museum (Nihon Mingei-kan) in Tokyo.[7]

As Munakata became closely associated with the *mingei* movement, it led him further away from *sōsaku hanga*'s aim of self-expression. In line with *mingei*, Munakata rejected the 'ideal of the artist': 'Too many artists have too much of self in their work,' he stated.[8] More important to Munakata was honesty of expression, as could be found in the classical Buddhist woodblock prints made by artisans. In this spirit, Munakata also preferred the old expression *ita-ga* (block picture) to describe his prints rather than *sōsaku hanga* (creative print), as *ita-ga* emphasised the importance of the block rather than the process: he believed 'it is from the indirect medium of the block itself that a secret, unintended beauty comes forth.'[9]

Paradoxically, Munakata, having made a name for himself both in Japan and abroad during the 1950s, continued to be and still is one of the most celebrated twentieth-century Japanese artists. An exhibition dedicated solely to him was organised at the Cleveland Museum of Art in 1960, and Munakata was also represented in the Chicago Institute of Art's exhibition *Japan's Modern Prints: Sōsaku Hanga* that same year. He was one of three Japanese artists shown in the exhibition *Contemporary Painters and Sculptors as Printmakers* at the Museum of Modern Art, New York, in 1964, which featured renowned international artists working in the print medium including Josef Albers, Alberto Giacometti, Pablo Picasso and Robert Rauschenberg.[10] In 1983, when MoMA organised another print exhibition, *Prints from Blocks: Gauguin to Now*, Munakata was again represented as one of only two Japanese artists (the other being Onchi Kōshirō; pp. 130–33). The print *Hara: A Line at the Foot of Mt Fuji* (1963), Munakata's monochromatic interpretation of Japan's ancient mountain, was shown alongside works by artists like Félix Vallotton (1865–1925), Emil Nolde (1867–1956), Paul Gauguin (1848–1903), Wassily Kandinsky (1866–1944) and Edvard Munch (1863–1944), testifying to Munakata's place among acclaimed and widely known Western artists.

In 1975, the year of his death, the Munakata Shikō Memorial Museum of Art opened in his home town of Aomori. The National Museum of Modern Art, Tokyo, commemorated the 120th anniversary of Munakata's birth with the major retrospective *The Making of Munakata* in collaboration with Toyama Prefectural Museum of Art and Design and Aomori Museum of Art in 2023.

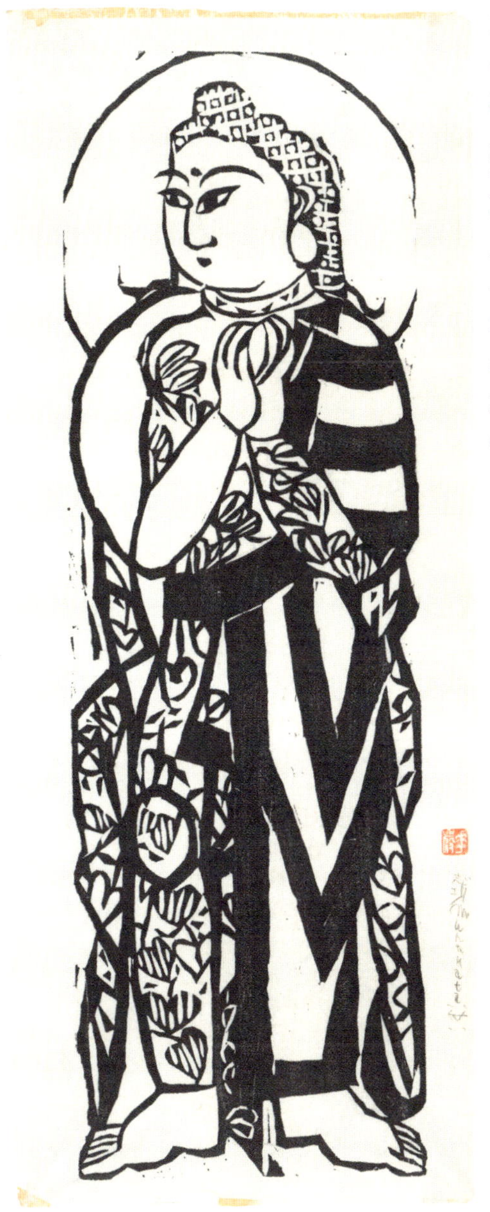

Bodhisattva Manjusri, undated. Woodblock print

Collections: Art Institute of Chicago; British Museum, London; Munakata Shikō Memorial Museum of Art, Aomori; Museum of Modern Art, New York; National Museum of Modern Art, Tokyo.

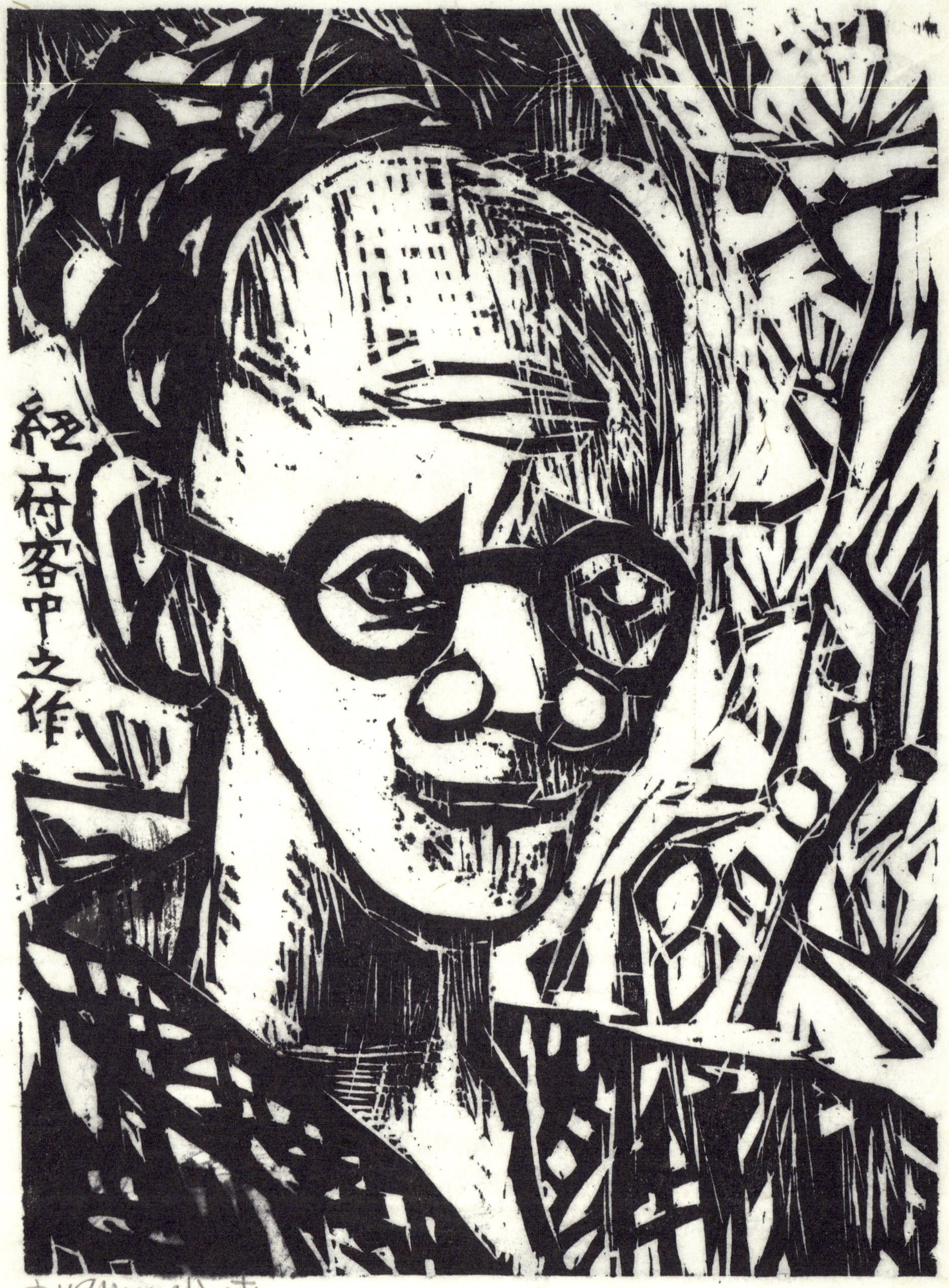
紐府客中之作

Self-Portrait, 1959. Woodblock print

My work must not be of the mind,
not of the fingertips, but of the heart.[11]

Munakata Shikō, 1956

Hara: A Straight Line at the Foot of Mt Fuji, no. 14, 1963. Woodblock print

NAGAI Kazumasa (b.1929)

Medium:
Etching, lithograph, silkscreen, woodblock, zinc relief

Kazumasa Nagai is a noted graphic designer as well as an excellent print artist, very active at present. The relationship between the design and the print has become one of the current problems in this field in which he is a central figure.[1]

Ogura Tadao,
Japanese curator at the São Paulo Biennial, 1971

Nagai Kazumasa is mostly recognised today for his iconic graphic design work for Nikon (1960), the Sapporo Winter Olympic Games (1966), Asahi beer (1960s–'80s), Bloomingdale's (1985) and Japan Railways (1987), to mention only a few of his prominent commissions. However, Nagai has made a career as a print artist as well. At the Saõ Paulo Biennial in 1971 he represented Japan with ten silkscreen prints, together with seven other Japanese artists including Ay-O (pp. 31–43), Yayanagi Go (pp. 219–25) and Noda Tetsuya (pp. 117–23).

As a young man, Nagai had enrolled in the department of sculpture at Tokyo University of the Arts but decided to leave in 1951 and return to his home town of Osaka. Here he was offered a position in charge of advertising at the textile manufacturing company Daiwabo, and so his career in graphic design began.

The following year, Nagai founded the A-Club with graphic designer Tanaka Ikkō (1930–2002) and two others, organising study meetings and training sessions for local designers, and in 1953 he joined the JAAC (Japan Advertising Artists Club). He was a founding member of Tokyo's Nippon Design Center in 1959, a creative organisation established by 'Japan's top designers, copywriters, and photographers ... as a creative organization aiming to further develop and improve the quality of advertising design in Japan'.[2]

In 1964, along with Tanaka and graphic designer Yamashiro Ryūichi (1920–1997), Nagai participated in documenta III in Kassel alongside acclaimed artists like Robert Rauschenberg, Victor Vasarely (1906–1997) and Isamu Noguchi. Three of his designs appeared on the cover of *Life* magazine's Science Library series, including his psychedelic interpretation of *The Cell*, promoting the 1966 Japanese edition of John E. Pfeiffer's book. That year, Nagai won the design competition to create the official emblems of the Sapporo Winter Olympics; he would do the same in 1972 for Expo '75, held in Okinawa. The following year, he was part of organising the exhibition *Graphic Image* '73 as a creative outlet for fellow graphic designers following the dissolution of the JAAC in 1970.[3] The exhibition was held at the Tokyo Central Museum of Arts, with artists Yokoo Tadanori (pp. 226–31) and Sugaï Kumi (pp. 168–71) also participating.

For the 7th Tokyo International Biennial of Prints in 1970, Nagai designed the exhibition poster and catalogue. This was the biennial at which Ay-O, Funasaka Yoshisuke (pp. 57–63) and Kurosaki Akira (pp. 90–93) won prizes among the Japanese print artists. Nagai's design – worthy of a prize itself – reflects his personal aesthetic with abstract geometric shapes and detailed, colourful patterns. In 1972, Nagai himself was represented in the museum exhibition *Contemporary Japanese Artists* at the Los Angeles County Museum of Art, with two of his zinc relief prints showing his use of three-dimensional graphic effects. In her book *Who's Who in Modern Japanese*

1 *XI Bienal de São Paulo: Catálogo* (Fundação Bienal de São Paulo, 1971), p. 135.
2 'History', Nippon Design Center, www.ndc.co.jp/en/about/history.
3 See 'Introduction', in *Graphic Image* '73, exh. cat. (Tokyo: Tokyo Central Museum of Arts, 1973), n.p.

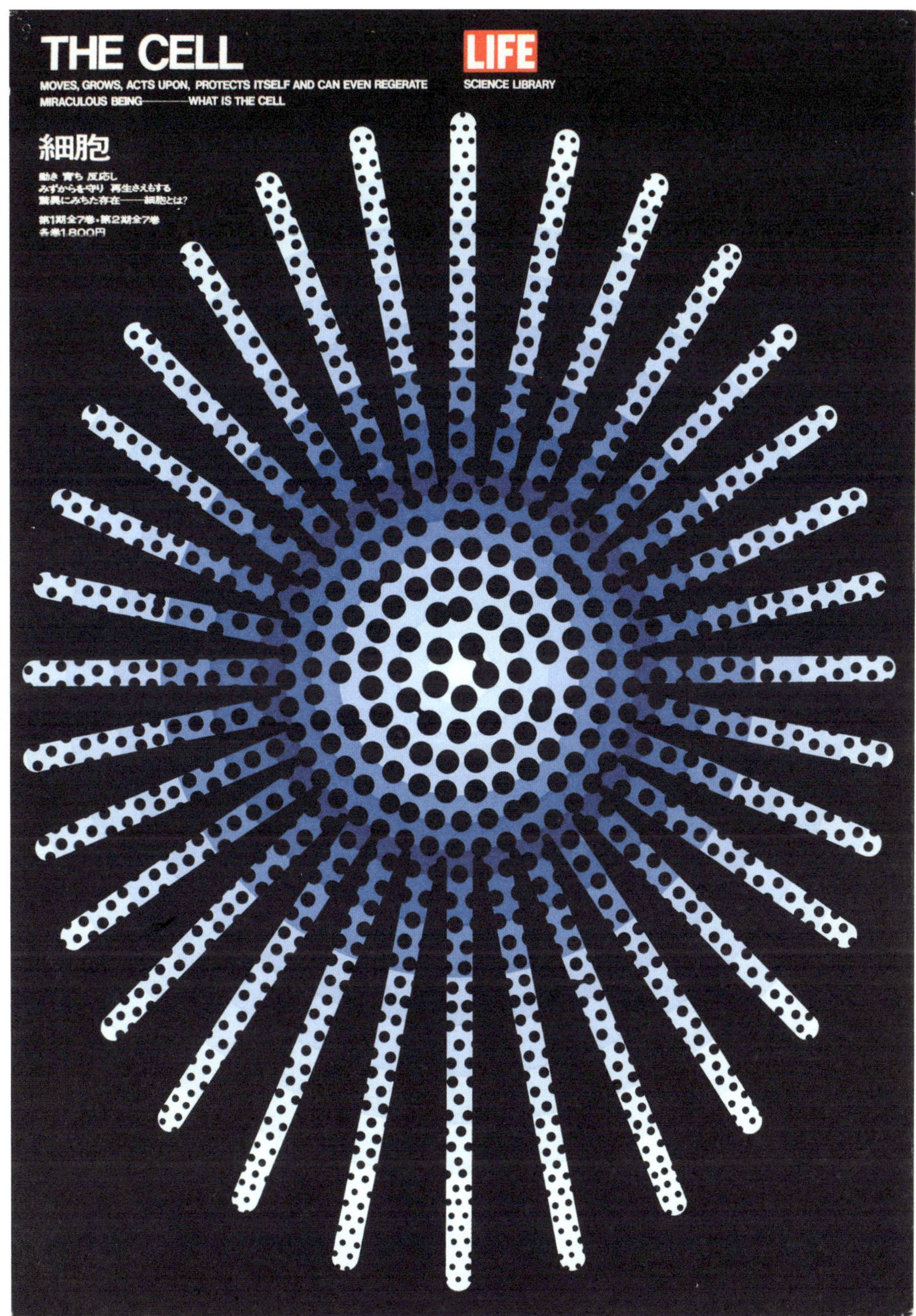

Poster for *The Cell*, 1966. Silkscreen print

Prints (1975), Frances Blakemore focused on this line of Nagai's work, describing him as 'a print artist who confines himself to the color white'.[4] Far from confined to white, however, Nagai's 1960s and '70s silkscreens of bold, colourful psychedelic abstractions, as well as his later lithographs and woodblock prints, stand as a stark contrast to his pure, monochrome zinc reliefs.

During his long, prolific career as a commercial graphic designer, Nagai has moved effortlessly between the spheres of art and design, with his work finding its way into museum collections and exhibitions. Creating numerous posters, cover designs and corporate logos as Japan's advertising industry expanded during the 1960s and '70s, Nagai was part of a generation who led the way for the graphic medium to be considered not only commercial art but also fine art.

> *Japan has emerged in the forefront of graphic design, producing some of the most exuberant, inventive, and fascinating posters in the world. The country's mastery of the poster form combines the legacy of its venerable printmaking tradition with the distinctive artistic sensibility of its designers.*[5]
>
> *Recent Japanese Posters from the Collection,* Museum of Modern Art, New York, 1989

Collections: British Museum, London; Los Angeles County Museum of Art; Museum of Contemporary Art, Tokyo; Museum of Modern Art, New York; National Crafts Museum, Kanazawa.

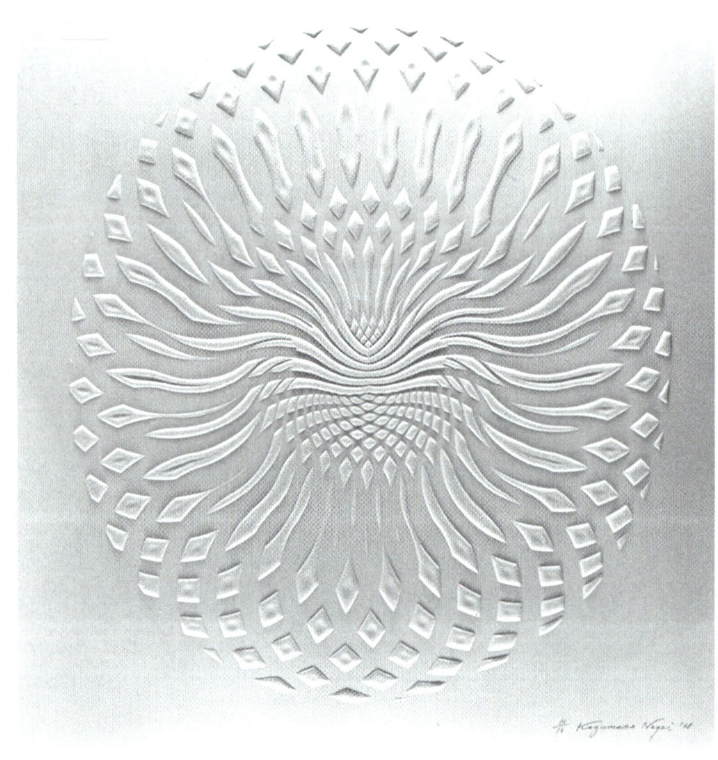

Untitled, 1968. Zinc relief print

4 Frances Blakemore, *Who's Who in Modern Japanese Prints* (New York and Tokyo: Weatherhill, 1975), p. 127.
5 Museum of Modern Art, New York, *Recent Japanese Posters from the Collection*, press release, 1989, p. 1, www.moma.org/calendar/exhibitions/1739.

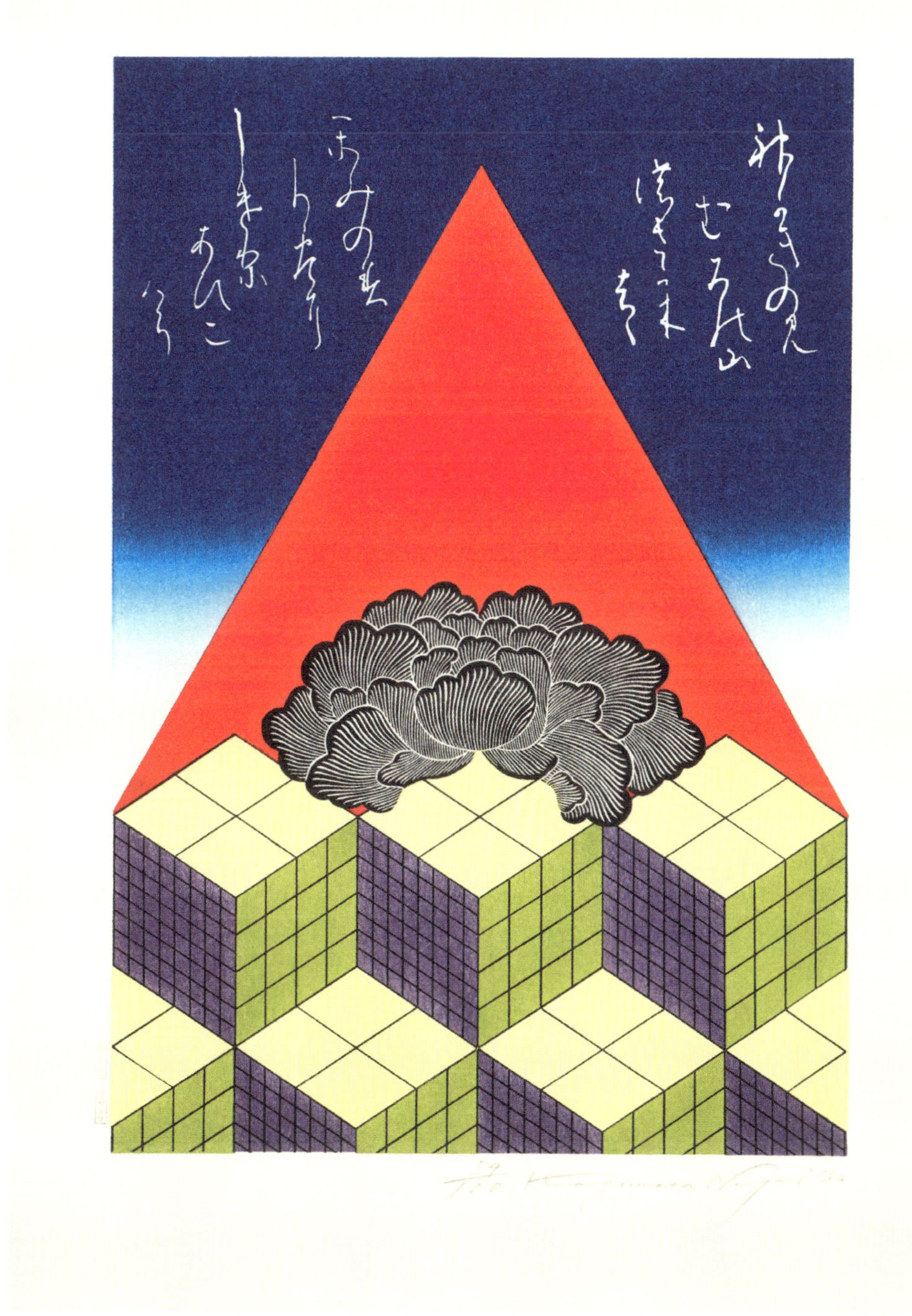

Untitled, 1982. Woodblock print

NARA Yoshitomo (b. 1959)

Medium:
Etching, lithograph, silkscreen, woodblock and others

If Hokusai had been around to enjoy Nara Yoshitomo's twenty-first-century interpretations of his famous Edo-period landscapes, who knows what he would have said. Perhaps, knowing Hokusai's creative mind and the sense of humour expressed in many of his works, he would have appreciated Nara's cute, uncanny 'big-headed' children expressing an inner world of personal memories. Two artists, almost two hundred years apart, with two distinctive and bold graphic styles that both brought Japan onto the international art scene.

Born in Aomori prefecture, Nara graduated from Aichi University of the Arts in 1987 and moved to Germany the following year, where he studied at the Kunstakademie Düsseldorf. One of the most celebrated of contemporary Japanese artists, he works in various media, from painting and drawing to ceramics, sculpture and print. During the 1990s, Nara began producing prints incorporating a wide range of techniques: etching, aquatint, engraving, photogravure, woodblock, silkscreen, lithography and drypoint.[1]

In 1999, he produced a series of prints titled *In the Floating World*, a reference to the traditional prints of the Edo period. Consisting of sixteen motifs borrowed from woodblock prints by *ukiyo-e* artists Hokusai, Hiroshige, Sharaku and Utamaro, Nara's series is a hybrid of classic Edo-period 'pop art' and the artist's distinctive creative world. In *White Fujiyama Ski Gelände*, a little girl in a pink dress is using snow-covered Mt Fuji as a ski slope, a take on Hokusai's famous image 'Red Fuji' (*South Wind, Clear Sky*) from the series *Thirty-six Views of Mount Fuji* (c. 1830–32). In another, titled *Ocean Child*, a giant child with a cute bob and red dress is 'taking a dip' in Hiroshige's *The Whirlpools of Awa*. In a third, *Fuck 'bout Everything*, two of Utamaro's characteristic courtesans are being threatened by a small girl with a knife.

Adapting another of Utamaro's motifs, *Mirror* is based on a print from circa 1790–95. It portrays the famous waitress Naniwa Okita of the Naniwaya teahouse, near Sensō-ji temple in Edo, who was a celebrated beauty at the time and a popular subject among *ukiyo-e* artists. Utamaro portrayed Okita in several of his prints. In his contemporary interpretation of the classic subject, Nara has transformed Okita's mirror reflection into an uncanny-*kawaii* version of Okita, who is not looking back as in Utamaro's original print but instead has her eyes closed, accompanied by the words: *Mask in the mirror!*

Technically, Nara's *In the Floating World* works are not woodblock prints: the artist has painted on reproduction woodblock prints of famous *ukiyo-e* motifs and then copied these using a Fuji Xerox machine to make editions of fifty. But Nara has also worked in the woodblock medium, as can be seen for example in *Life is Only One* (2010), and has collaborated with Pace Prints' master printer Shibata Yasuyuki (b. 1968) for over twelve years. Shibata, who studied printmaking under Kurosaki Akira (pp. 90–93), also worked as a printer at Tyler Graphics, where he printed for Teraoka Masami (pp. 189–95). Using the old *hanmoto* collaborative system of an artist, woodcutter, printer and publisher, Nara and Shibata created more than thirty woodblock prints together. Shibata, however, does both the carving and printing. He uses water-based pigment and usually prints with a *baren*, the traditional Japanese printing tool used to apply pressure to the block; sometimes a hydraulic press is also used for large areas.[2]

1 See Noriko Miyamura and Shinko Suzuki, eds, *Yoshitomo Nara: The Complete Works*, vol. 1: *Paintings, Sculptures, Editions, Photographs, 1984–2010* (Tokyo: Bijutsu Shuppan-sha, 2011), pp. 316–19.

2 With many thanks to Shibata Yasuyuki for explaining the technical process in detail.

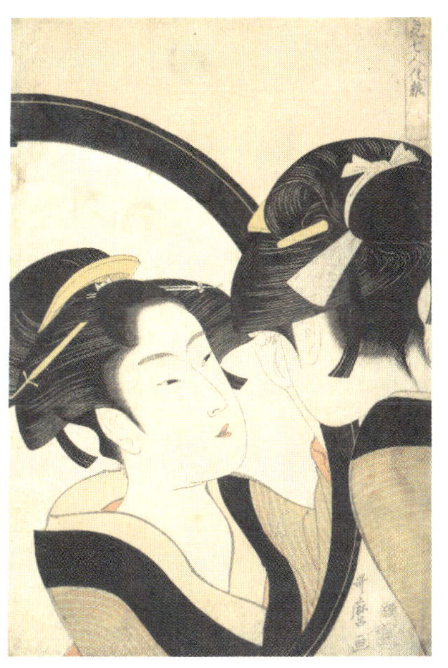

1

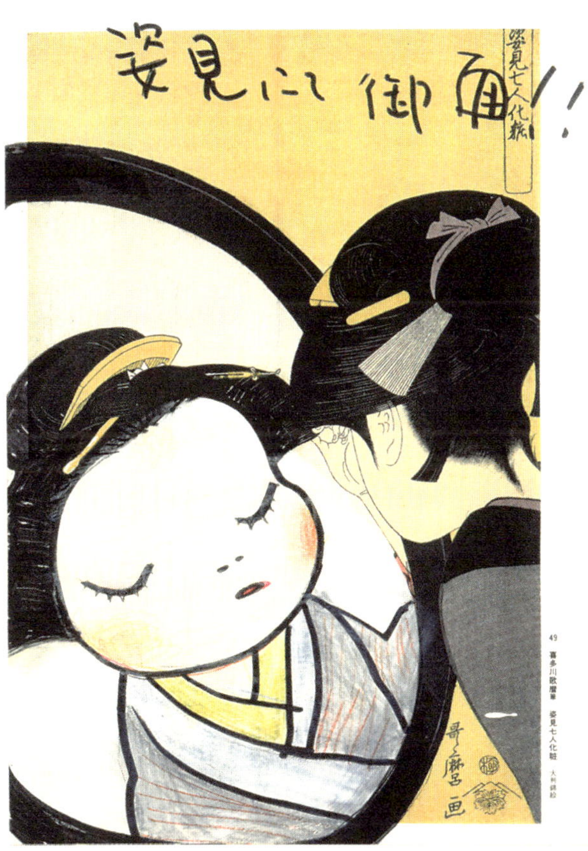

2

1 KITAGAWA Utamaro — *Naniwa Okita Admiring Herself in a Mirror*, c. 1790–95. Woodblock print
2 NARA Yoshitomo — *Mirror*, 1999. Fuji Xerox copy

Whether through his technical or stylistic approach, Nara manages to connect the old world of Hokusai and his Edo contemporaries to today's neo-Pop art. Nara has had close to forty solo exhibitions worldwide, including at the Guggenheim Museum Bilbao (2024), Los Angeles County Museum of Art (2021–22) and the Hayward Gallery, London (2025).

Collections: Aomori Museum of Art; Machida City Museum of Graphic Arts, Tokyo; Museum of Modern Art, New York.

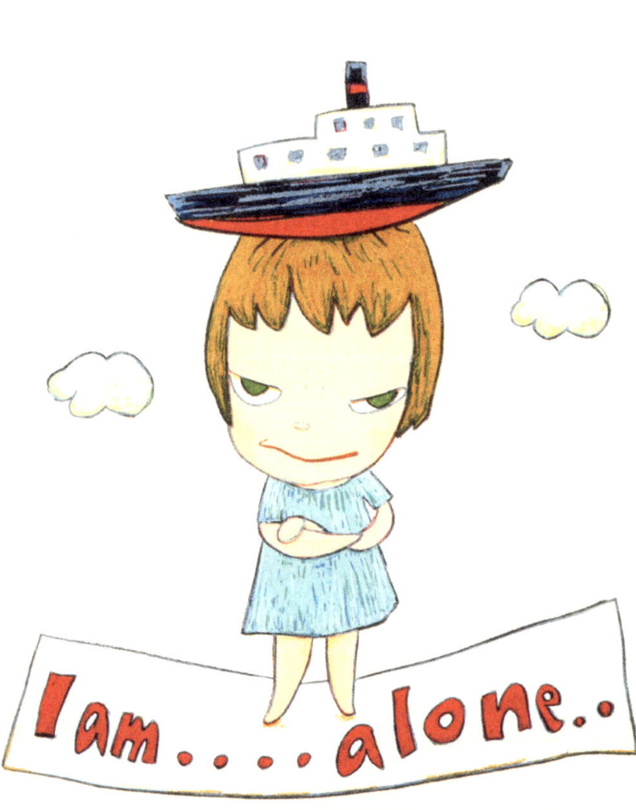

I Am Alone..., 2003. Lithograph

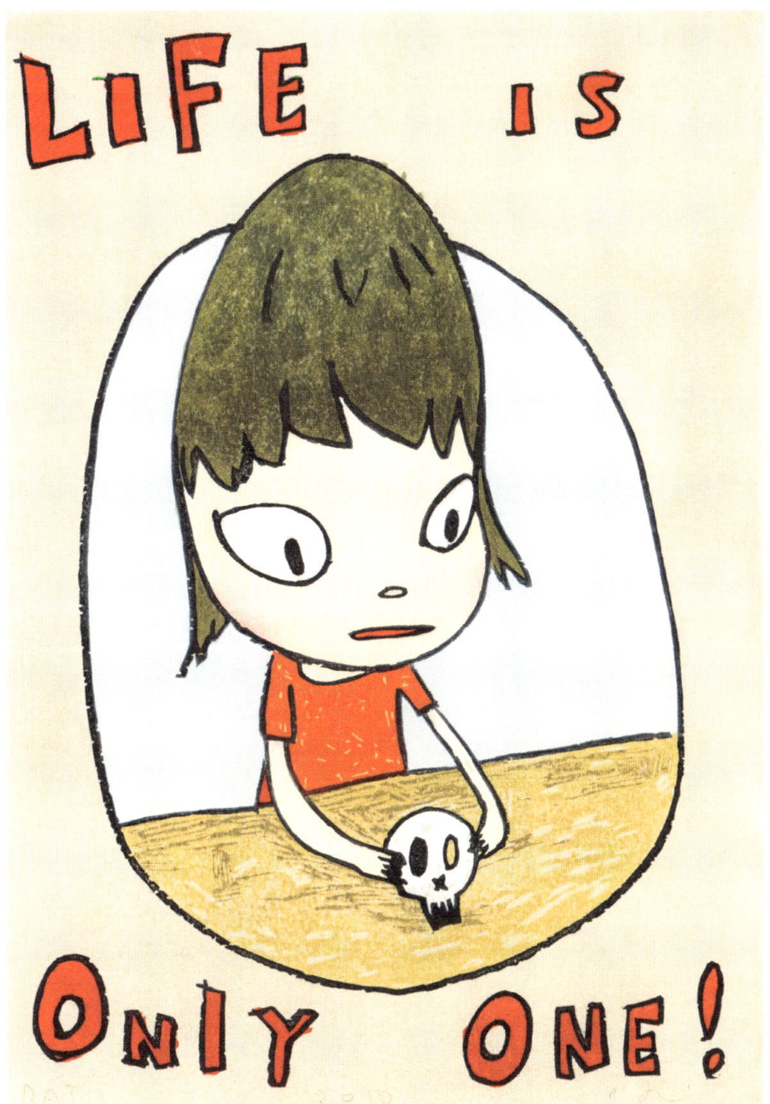

Life is Only One, 2010. Woodblock print

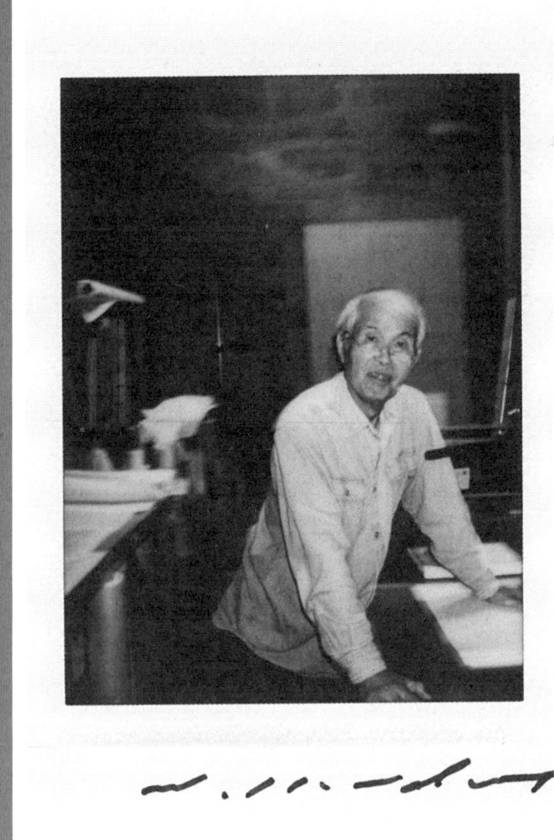

NODA Tetsuya (b. 1940)

Medium:
Lithograph, silkscreen, woodblock

The highly personal works of Noda reveal the circumstances of his life and his emotions ... He utilizes photography to capture his feelings about his surroundings and to record his experiences and then incorporates these photographs into his prints using silkscreen techniques.[1]

George Kuwayama, 1972

Noda Tetsuya studied oil painting at Tokyo University of the Arts, partly inspired by his uncle, the Japanese American modernist painter Noda (Benjamin) Hideo (1908–1939). Oil painting was the chosen medium for many young artists at the time, since it was believed this was the way to become an artist. But Tetsuya realised that the more he painted in oil, the more he tended to imitate not just the technique but also the subjects of the Western tradition. He resolved that 'it was not enough just to follow Western expressions. I had to look at myself and my surroundings to find my own expression.'[2]

As a second subject he took up printmaking, both etching and woodblock. The latter technique was the one he found the most familiar, as he had made woodblock prints as a child in school as part of the custom of exchanging woodblock prints as New Year's cards. He completed an additional two years of study under the acclaimed *sōsaku hanga* artist Ono Tadashige (1909–1990), training in traditional Japanese woodblock print technique as well as learning from Ono his creative technique known as *inkoku tashoku-zuri mokuhan*, or 'colour negative woodblock printing', which allowed him to make a colour print with only one block, as he would begin printing with the darker colours first. But Ono was also a scholar, and so his students learned about the history of *ukiyo-e*, and he invited different artisans every year to teach traditional woodblock printing. It was *ukiyo-e* that made Tetsuya interested in and focused on technique.

While becoming more serious about making woodblock prints, Tetsuya was still looking for his own distinct style. He recalls: 'When looking for my own expression, I remembered an assignment in primary school. We had to keep a picture diary during the summer holidays. I remember that I was drawing quite honestly what had happened to me day by day. This is one of the reasons why the idea of choosing subjects from my daily life came to me – by recording them with my camera.'

Photography had first become Tetsuya's hobby while a primary school student, when in order to get a small camera, he collected points from a sweet store: 'It meant that I had to eat a lot of candy,' he recalls, laughing. 'Especially when I was a student at university, Japan was very famous for producing cameras, and I also bought a good camera at that time. I thought it was a good idea to combine a photographic image with my woodblock print.' To combine his photographs with the traditional woodblock printing technique, Tetsuya tried standard silkscreen printing. A classmate at university, who was also working at a primary school, told him about the mimeograph scanning machine at his school – a standard object in most offices at the time as the cheapest way to make copies – which could be used to transfer the images.

Tetsuya discovered that his university also had one of the scanning machines, which he was kindly allowed access to although it was frequently in use. The

1 George Kuwayama, *Contemporary Japanese Prints* (Los Angeles: Los Angeles County Museum of Art, 1972), p. 106.

2 Information and quotes are based on an interview with Noda Tetsuya in Tokyo, October 2022, and email correspondence, spring 2025.

electric mimeograph would become a unique tool in Tetsuya's printmaking approach by allowing him to create a stencil from a photographic image that could then be attached to a silkscreen, combined with a woodblock print. He explains: 'I take a photograph, which I alter by drawing on it, then run it through an electric mimeograph machine, which makes a perforated stencil of the photographic image. Using this stencil, I print it with a roller onto Japanese paper [*washi*] with colour woodblock for the background.'

During the late 1960s, Noda began his now lifelong project: a visual diary in a series of multimedia prints. *Diary* is based on Tetsuya and his family's everyday life experiences and events, and he has created more than five hundred mixed-media prints in the series so far. Nostalgic in feel, these subdued images appear as soft, hazy memories. 'The print is a medium to express something,' Tetsuya explains. 'Modern prints lack depth with their main emphasis on decorative design, rather than meaning.' His series stands out as a personal recording of private matters, feelings and events. 'Andy Warhol used photographs of Marilyn Monroe and Jacqueline Onassis, but notice that the subjects are famous people, and the photographs themselves had already appeared dozens of times in the mass media. I never use photos taken by other people. My photos are all my own.'[3]

While the techniques of many modern print artists were creative rather than technical, Noda's must be described as both. The hybrid nature of his works by the combined processes of photography, woodblock and silkscreen printing was pioneering at the time. In the 1960s the use of photography in Japanese printmaking was unusual, while in the USA it was towards the end of that same decade that photorealism developed, with a focus on portraits and landscapes.

In 1968, at the age of 28, Tetsuya participated for the first time in the Tokyo International Biennial Exhibition of Prints with *August 22nd '68* and *Sept. 11th '68*, two family portraits, one depicting Tetsuya's Japanese family, the other his future family-in-law. He won the grand prize. The work was highlighted in Pat Gilmour's book *Modern Prints* (1970) as 'a hybrid image by Tetsuya Noda ... a posed family snapshot enlarged by photo-screen, with its members sitting inscrutably on a sofa exquisitely printed by traditional wood-block'.[4] Interestingly, as Gilmour pointed out, all three main prize-winners at the 1st British International Print Biennale, held in Bradford that same year, also made creative use of photographic techniques.

At the same biennial two years later, Tetsuya participated with another of his mixed-media prints, *Diary: May 8th '70, in New York*. This time, Tetsuya had documented what would turn out to be a historic event: the 'Hard Hat Riot' that took place in New York on that date, which saw construction workers attack a student demonstration against the Vietnam War and recent Kent State University shootings. 'When walking along the streets near Federal Hall I encountered the construction workers raising the American flag [and] storm the students' protests against the Vietnam War while the police officers got into them,' Tetsuya recounts. Tetsuya's 'documentary' work would have complemented French artist Gérard Fromanger's silkscreen printed *Album The Red*, created in response to the student protests of 1968, while standing in stark contrast to Tetsuya's friend Ay-O's brightly coloured and humorous silkscreen *Rainbow Hokusai*, for which he won a prize (p. 39).[5]

3 Tetsuya Noda, *The Works, 1964–1978* (Tokyo: Fuji Television Gallery, 1978), pp. 16–17.

4 See Pat Gilmour, *Modern Prints* (London: Studio Vista, 1970), pp. 87–88.

5 An unlikely pair, Tetsuya and Ay-O later exhibited together in two-man shows, including in 2009 and 2018 at Gallery Goto, Tokyo.

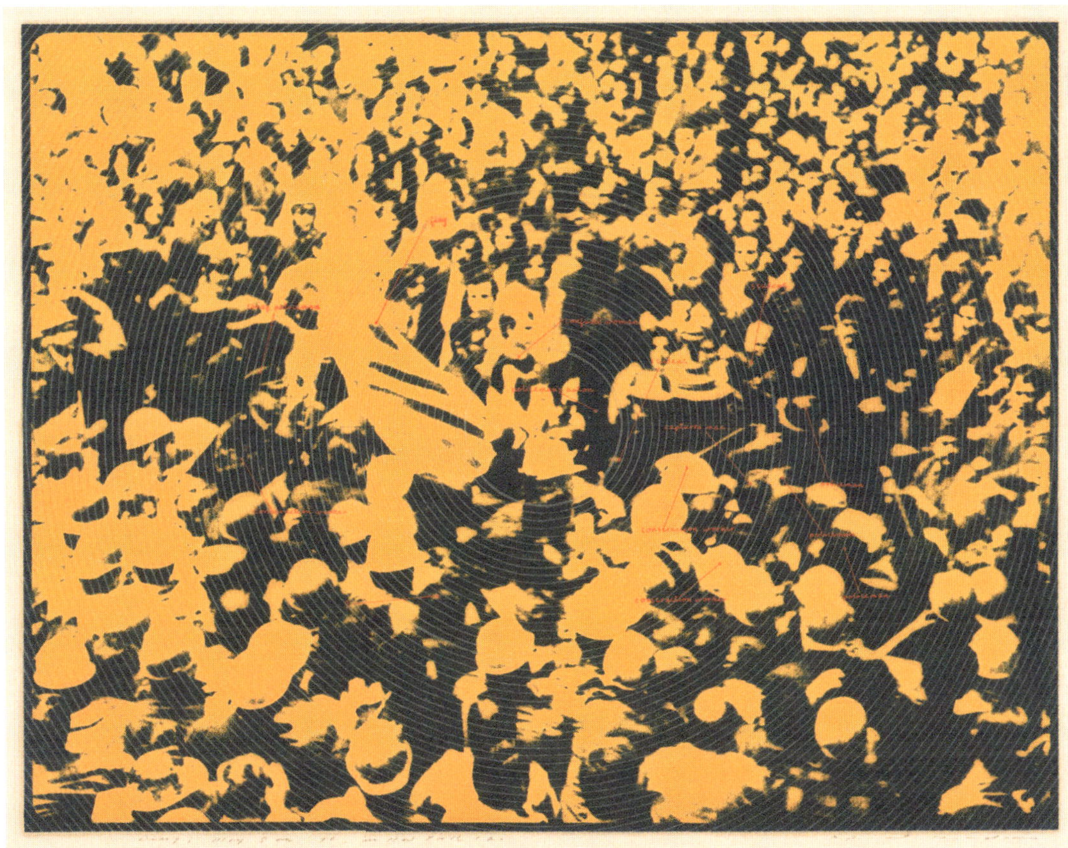

Diary: May 8th '70 in New York (a), 1970. Woodblock and silkscreen print

At the São Paulo Biennial in 1971, Tetsuya was one of seven young Japanese artists represented, including Yayanagi Go (pp. 219–25) and Nagai Kazumasa (pp. 108–11). Ogura Tadao, who curated the Japanese section, wrote of Tetsuya: 'Applying the technique of the phototype process, Tetsuya Noda has expressed his unique vision of men and society under the title of "diary" in which he draws from his own daily life. His original view of the world seen through sharp, observing eyes, and the objective image by photograph which fixes an actual scene on a plate create a personal vision through which some symbolic image of our time can be seen.'[6]

Tetsuya's portrait of the British Pop artist Allen Jones (b. 1937), *March 19 '70*, was included in the 1973 exhibition *Recent Acquisitions, 1968–1973* at the Museum of Modern Art, New York. Among other artists represented were Jasper Johns (b. 1930) with his lithograph *Decoy* (1971) and Robert Rauschenberg with *Skygarden* (1969), which combines silkscreen and lithograph.[7] Tetsuya admired both artists, in particular Johns: 'He is so very conscious about everyday life,' he has said.[8] For *Decoy*, Johns also made use of overprinting, using a lithography press rather than a mimeograph like Tetsuya.

From 1977 to 2006 Noda headed the printmaking department at Tokyo University of the Arts, from where he himself had graduated. As a teacher he emphasised the importance of the traditional Japanese printmaking techniques for the next generation to understand and appreciate.

Tetsuya has had numerous shows in Japan and abroad. He began exhibiting with the College Women's Association of Japan in 1969, which he continues to do today. He participated in the Ljubljana Biennale of Graphic Arts in 1977 and 1987 – at which he won the Grand Prize and Grand Prize of Honour, respectively – and the Norwegian International Print Biennial in 1987, also winning the Grand Prize. A retrospective exhibition, *Days in a Life: The Art of Tetsuya Noda*, was held at the Asian Art Museum, San Francisco, in 2004–5, followed by *Noda Tetsuya's Diary* at the British Museum, London, in 2014 and *Noda Tetsuya: Negotiating Memory* at the Art Institute of Chicago in 2020. Tetsuya – one of the humblest and most smiling of artists – lives in Tokyo with his wife, Dorit, and continues to make prints in his large studio, where a mimeograph machine can also be found.

My work is my diary. It is about my personal, private matters, feelings or concerns of my daily life, close at hand. So, I sometimes wonder how much sense it would make to other people. But as a human being living at present, I am also leading a rather common or ordinary life, and I think that it could be of some interest to others – with whom I wish to share my interest and concerns.

Noda Tetsuya

Collections: Art Institute of Chicago; Asian Art Museum, San Francisco; British Museum, London; National Museum of Modern Art, Kyoto; National Museum of Modern Art, Tokyo; Portland Art Museum.

6 Ogura Tadao in 'Japão', in *XI Bienal de São Paulo: Catálogo* (Fundação Bienal de São Paulo, 1971), p. 130.

7 Museum of Modern Art, New York, *Recent Acquisitions, 1968–1973: Prints and Illustrated Books*, master checklist, 1973, www.moma.org/calendar/exhibitions/1754.

8 Noda Tetsuya quoted in Robert Flynn Johnson, *Anonymous: Enigmatic Images from Unknown Photographers* (London: Thames & Hudson, 2004), p. 14.

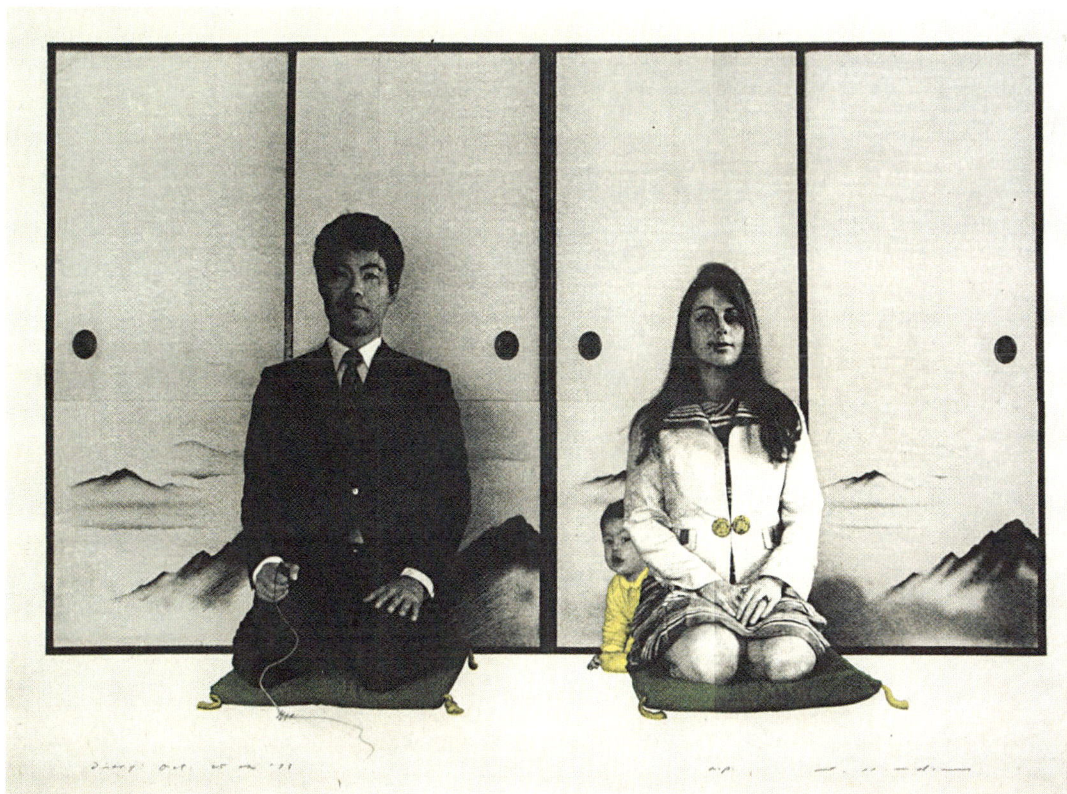

Diary: Oct. 25th '73, 1973. Woodblock and silkscreen print

'This shows my son on his first year's birthday, sitting between his parents in our Japanese-style room. I wanted him to sit properly, but it was too difficult for him to do so at that time. I rarely wore a suit and tie, but for this occasion I preferred it to be formal.'

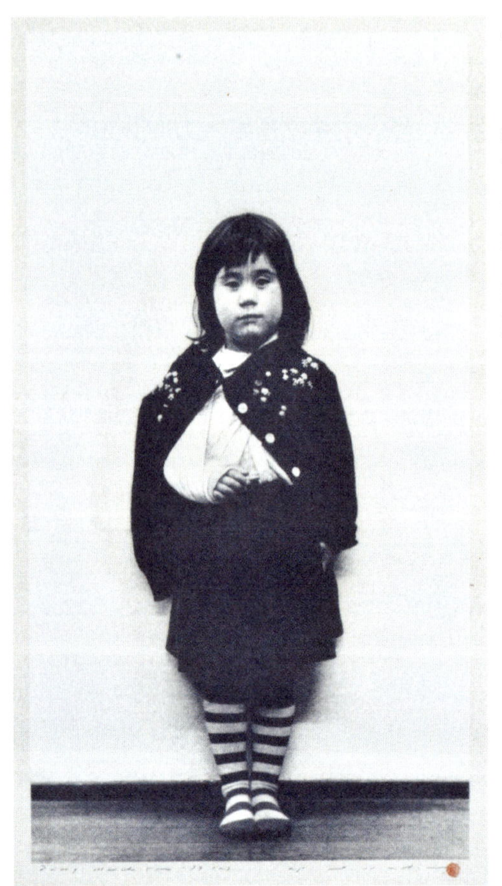

Diary: Mar. 5th '79 (a), 1979. Woodblock and silkscreen print

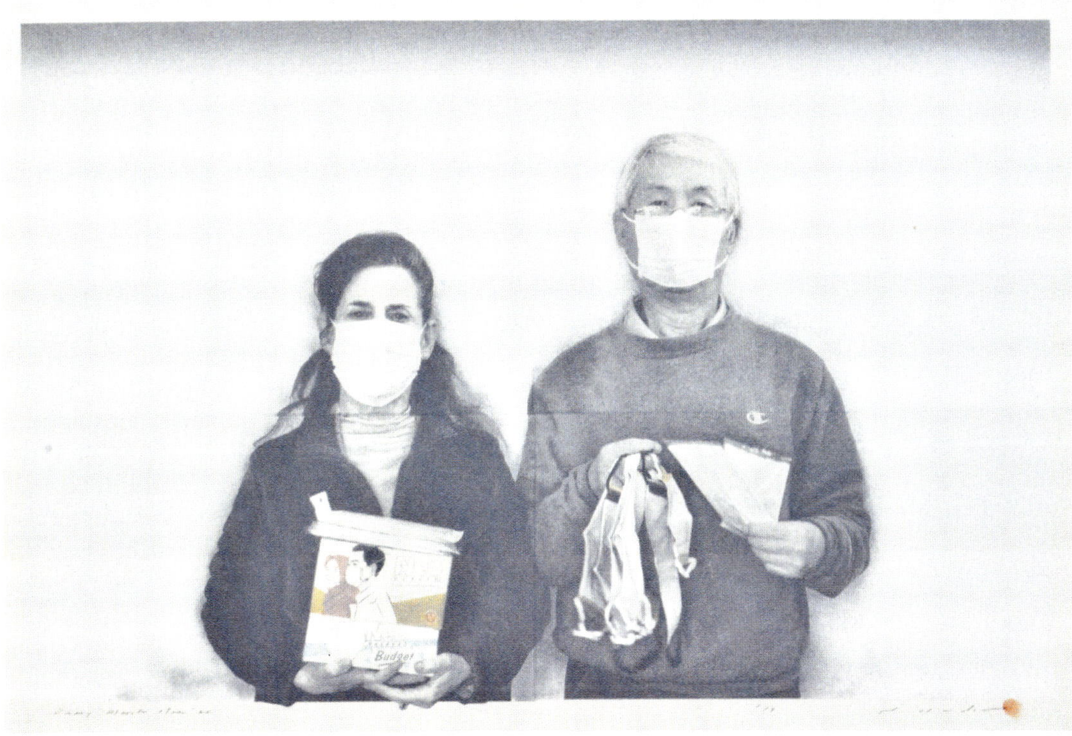

Diary: Mar. 13th '20, 1920. Woodblock and silkscreen print

OKUYAMA Gihachirō (1907–1981)

Medium:
Lithograph, woodblock

If one modern print artist connected the old world of printmaking and print advertising with that of the new, it was Okuyama Gihachirō. A few decades before graphic designers such as Nagai Kazumasa (pp. 108–11) and Yokoo Tadanori (pp. 226–31) rocked the world of Japanese advertisements with their silkscreens and Pop art aesthetics, Okuyama combined poster design and woodblock printing, thereby continuing the tradition of producing advertisements begun by the *ukiyo-e* artists in the Edo period. Furthermore, Okuyama was a prolific artist active in both the *shin hanga* and the *sōsaku hanga* movements and created more than a thousand designs throughout his career.

Okuyama first tried his hand at printmaking at the age of thirteen, when he moved to Tokyo from his home town of Sagae in Yamagata prefecture. In 1924 he entered the Kawabata Painting School, founded by Kawabata Gyokushō (1842–1913) in 1909, and the following year the *sōsaku hanga* artist Kōsaka Gajin (1877–1953) started teaching him.

After he had his print *The Little Match Girl* (after the story by Hans Christian Andersen) accepted to the 8th Japan Creative Print Association exhibition in 1928, Okuyama's path as a professional printmaker began. That same year he also started working part-time as a commercial designer, creating woodblock print and lithographic posters and advertisements for Nikke, the Japan Wool Textile Company. The prints were expressive, their bold, dynamic compositions pointing to both Constructivism and German Expressionism. Later Okuyama collaborated with companies such as Nikka Whisky, Tamaoki Pharmaceuticals and Kimura Coffee; to this day his designs remain modern and cutting edge in their expressive graphic abstraction.

In 1941, Okuyama gave up designing advertisements and entered a collaboration with an engraver and printer to produce *shin hanga* woodblock prints. Immediately after the war he started the Japan Print Institute (Nihon Hanga Kenkyūsho), where he would make and sell reprints of the old *ukiyo-e* masters' work, such as Utagawa Hiroshige's *Fifty-three Stations of the Tōkaidō*, originally published in 1848–49. In 1954 Okuyama established the studio Okuyama Hanga Kōbō, where he designed, carved and printed his own designs. Mostly known today for his monochrome woodblock prints of traditional landscapes, temple gardens and snowscapes, which he began making in the 1950s, Okuyama also produced a series of woodblock prints after works by Vincent van Gogh and Henri de Toulouse-Lautrec. These were exhibited in Tokyo in 1957. One was based on Van Gogh's 1887 *Portrait of Père Tanguy*. This was one of three portraits that Van Gogh made of the art dealer and patron Julien Tanguy; here, he is depicted in front of a group of *ukiyo-e* from Van Gogh's own collection, including prints by Hiroshige and Utagawa Kunisada (1786–1865).

Okuyama's woodblock print based on Van Gogh's portrait is a compelling comment on the role of Japanese prints in the nineteenth and twentieth centuries. Van Gogh, who was a keen *ukiyo-e* collector and an admirer of Japan,[1] made a clear statement in his painting on the importance, to him, of Japanese art and *ukiyo-e* specifically. In turn, Okuyama's print can be seen as a homage to Van Gogh, who left a big impression on his generation of artists: the cross-cultural artistic exchange coming full circle.

Okuyama's son, Okuyama Gijin (Yoshito) (1934–2020), trained under his father as well as Sakakura Seijiro, who also printed for *shin hanga* artist

1 See Louis van Tilborgh et al., *Van Gogh and Japan*, exh. cat. (Amsterdam: Van Gogh Museum, 2017).

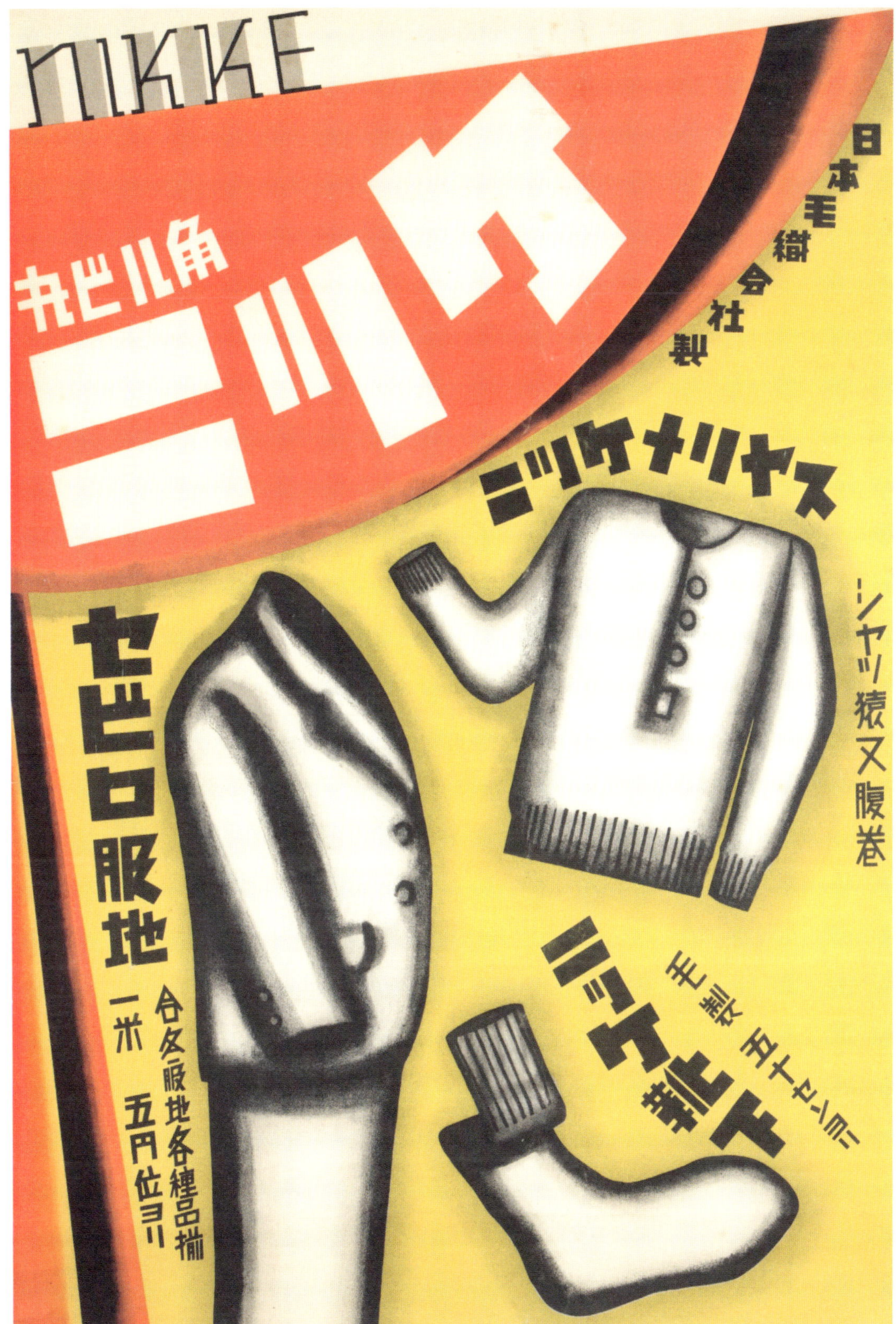

Nikke, c. 1930. Lithograph

Kawase Hasui. Gijin took over the studio after Okuyama retired in 1973. Gijin produced around fifty woodblock prints, many in the trademark monochrome style of his father.

In 1999, the Matsudo Museum in Chiba prefecture held a retrospective exhibition, *Okuyama Gihachirō: Woodblock Prints of Creativity and Tradition.*

Collections: British Museum, London; Cleveland Museum of Art; Matsudo Museum; National Museum of Modern Art, Tokyo; Seattle Art Museum; Victoria and Albert Museum, London.

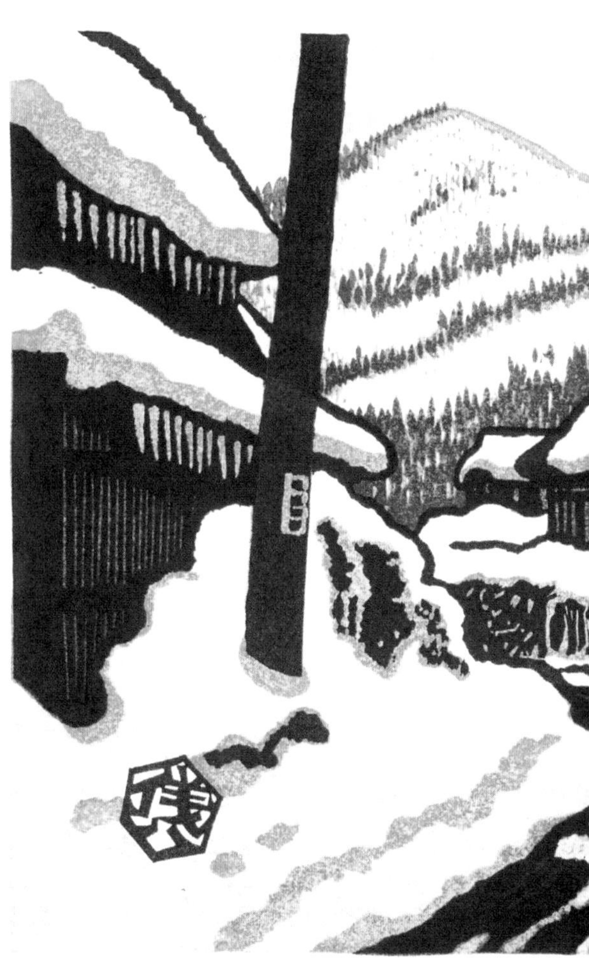

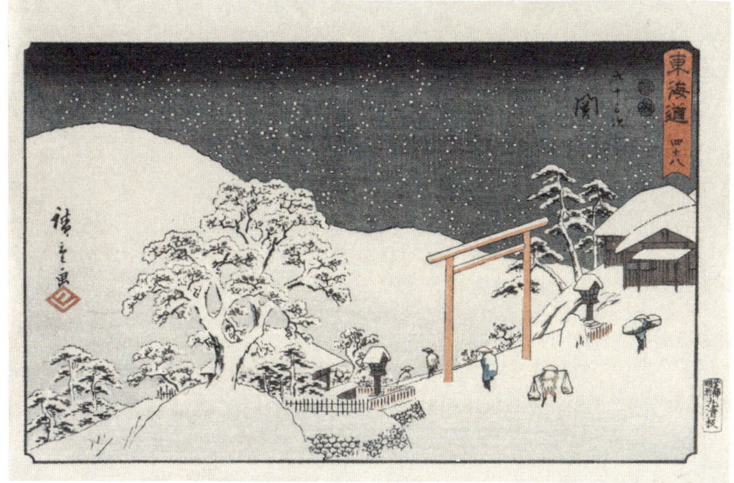

UTAGAWA Hiroshige

Seki, c. 1848–49. Woodblock print

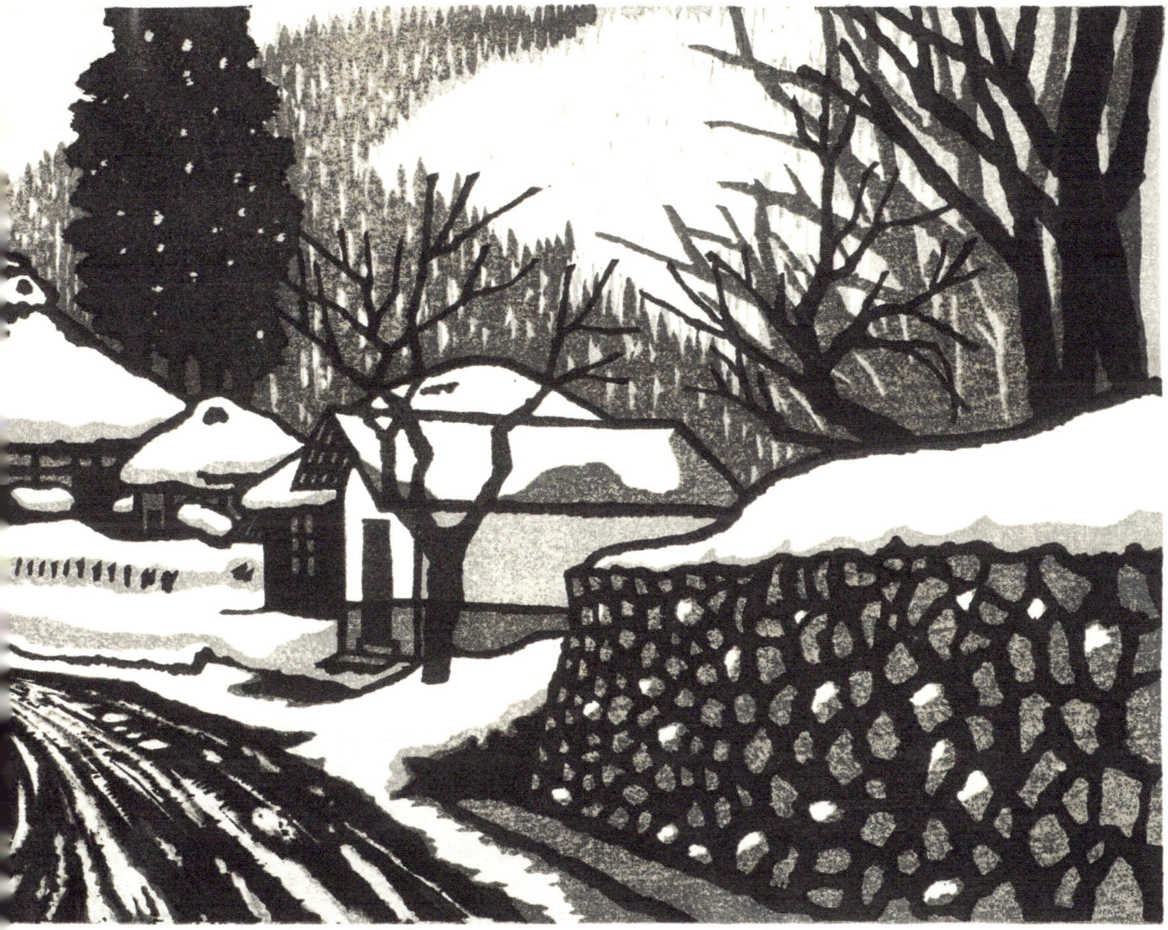

Snow Scene in Yamagata, c. 1950s–'60s. Woodblock print

OKUYAMA Gihachirō

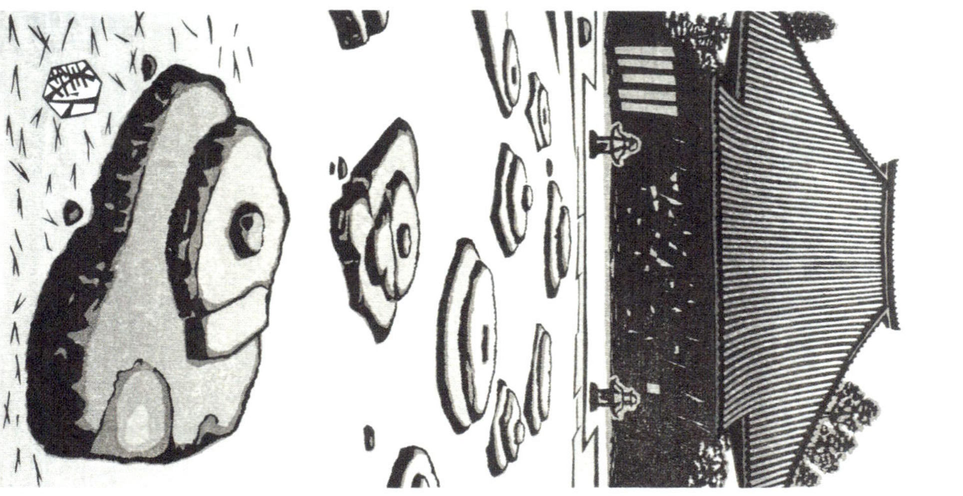

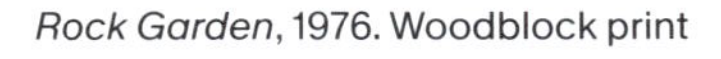

Rock Garden, 1976. Woodblock print

Landscape with Moon, 1954. Woodblock print

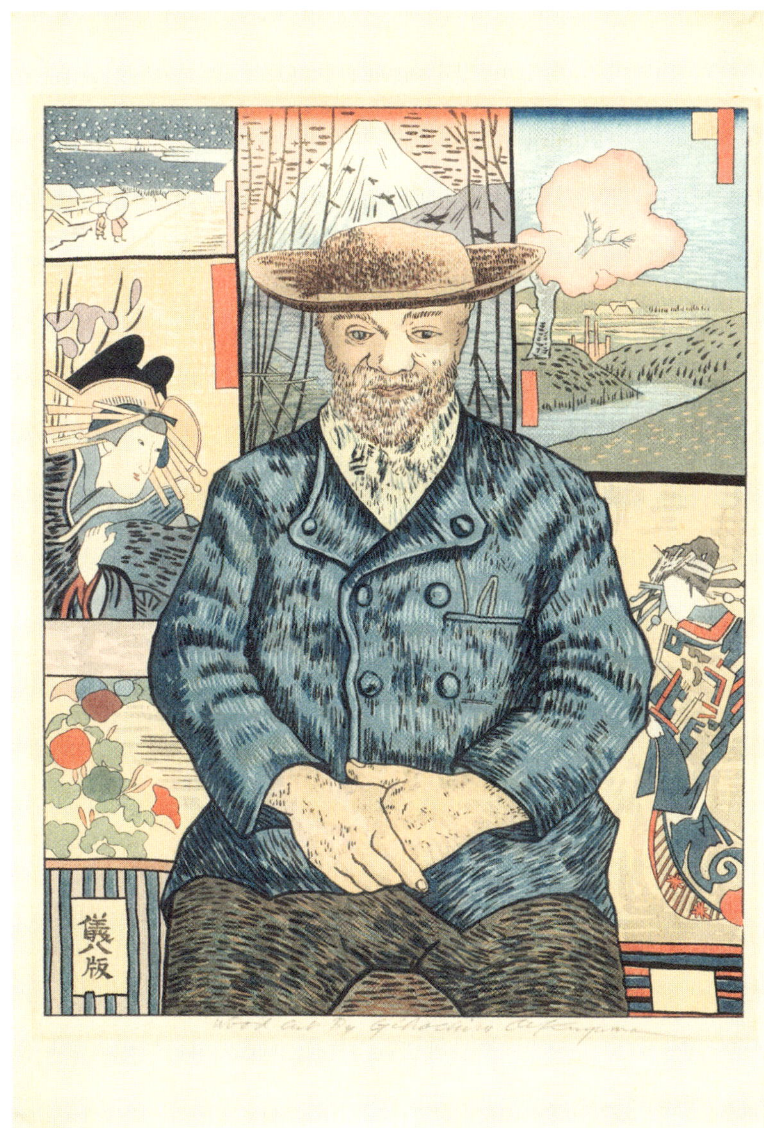

Le Père Tanguy (Old Man Tanguy – Van Gogh), c.1950s. Woodblock print

ONCHI Kōshirō (1891–1955)

Medium:
Cardboard, paper, woodblock and others

At first we were simply ignored ... And then, when we couldn't be ignored, we were ridiculed. All the shows were run by oil painters. If we were allowed to submit our work, it was hung on some remote wall and judged in the same category as the oils, by a jury composed of oil painters. Of course we got nowhere.[1]

Onchi Kōshirō, 1956

Often described as the 'father of the *sōsaku hanga* movement', Onchi Kōshirō – book designer, poet, writer and printmaker – took over the 'leadership' of the creative print movement after Yamamoto Kanae (pp. 212–17). Onchi, alongside Hiratsuka Un'ichi (pp. 68–71), became instrumental in teaching, promoting, organising and supporting the new generation of artists 'to whom printmaking was a career and not a bypath'.[2]

In 1909, with the reluctant permission of his father, Onchi had taken up Western art studies at the Hakuba-kai (White Horse Society). It was here that he became familiar with the work of painter and print artist Takehisa Yumeji (1884–1934), an influential figure in twentieth-century Japanese graphic design. Yumeji would go on to play an important role in Onchi's artistic career, among other things encouraging Onchi to attend the Tokyo School of Fine Arts, where he studied oil painting and later sculpture.

Yumeji most likely influenced Onchi's decision to make prints, while Yamamoto and the group around the magazine *Hōsun* (see p. 212) had an impact too. However, it was Western art that really took hold of Onchi: 'I was especially impressed by Munch's expression of human feeling, not his form but his content.'[3] Both Edvard Munch and Wassily Kandinsky, whose work was being reproduced in Tokyo avant-garde magazines such as *Shirakaba*, led Onchi towards abstract art. He became a pioneer of new printing techniques and experimented in the use of materials, which would influence artists of the next generations. Besides the conventional wood, Onchi also printed with paper, cardboard, string, leaves, textiles and even the rubber heel of a shoe.[4]

Onchi saw many *sōsaku hanga* artists through the war years with his generosity and kindness. Through the students whom Onchi frequently invited to his house in Tokyo, he established the Ichimoku-kai (First Thursday Society) in 1939, a 'support group' for artists, who met on the first Thursday of the month, and it continued to operate until the 1950s.[5]

Onchi participated as one of the 45 Japanese artists, including his fellow printmakers Hiratsuka, Saitō Kiyoshi (pp. 138–45) and Munakata Shikō (pp. 104–7), in the first international exhibition that Japan took part in following the war: the first São Paulo Biennial in 1951 (and again in 1955), experiencing the post-war boom for creative prints before his death. Onchi was also represented in the Art Institute of Chicago's exhibition *Japan's Modern Prints: Sōsaku Hanga* (1960), and the Achenbach Foundation for Graphic Arts in San Francisco held the first solo exhibition of his work abroad, *Koshiro Onchi (1891–1955): Woodcuts*, in 1964. He was included in *Contemporary Japanese Prints* at Los Angeles County Museum of Art in 1972.

Onchi was a 'superb abstractionist, who will ultimately stand beside European artists', as James Michener noted in 1962.[6] When the Museum of

1 Onchi Kōshirō quoted in Oliver Statler, *Modern Japanese Prints: An Art Reborn* (Rutland, VT: Charles E. Tuttle Co., 1956), p. 23.
2 Ibid., p. 21.
3 Quoted ibid., p. 23.
4 Margaret O. Gentles, 'Modern Japanese Prints', *Art Institute of Chicago Quarterly* 53, no. 1 (February 1959), p. 16.
5 For more on the First Thursday Society see Lawrence Smith, *Japanese Prints during the Allied Occupation, 1945–1952: Onchi Kōshirō, Ernst Hacker and the First Thursday Society* (London: British Museum Press, 2002), pp. 31–36.
6 James A. Michener, *The Modern Japanese Print: An Appreciation* (Rutland, VT, and Tokyo: Charles E. Tuttle Co., 1968), p. 11.
7 Museum of Modern Art, New York, *Prints from Blocks: Gauguin to Now*, press release, 1983, www.moma.org/calendar/exhibitions/1713.
8 Ibid., p. 3.

Modern Art organised the exhibition *Prints from Blocks: Gauguin to Now* in 1983, Onchi's work was shown alongside prints by artists like Pablo Picasso, Emil Nolde, Leonard Baskin (1922–2000), Paul Gauguin, Wassily Kandinsky and Edvard Munch.[7] The exhibition illustrated the significant connection between nineteenth-century European artists like Gauguin and Munch, whose prints owed much to *ukiyo-e*, and the Japanese creative print artists who in turn were influenced by them. As the museum wrote at the time: 'Some artists in Japan, influenced by European abstraction, produced images that coupled a traditional understanding of the medium with assimilated European forms.'[8] In the post-war print revival that took place simultaneously in Japan and the West, the cross-cultural exchanges seemed to have come full circle.

Collections: British Museum, London; Harvard Art Museums, Cambridge, MA; Museum of Fine Arts, Boston; Museum of Modern Art, New York; National Museum of Modern Art, Kyoto; National Museum of Modern Art, Tokyo.

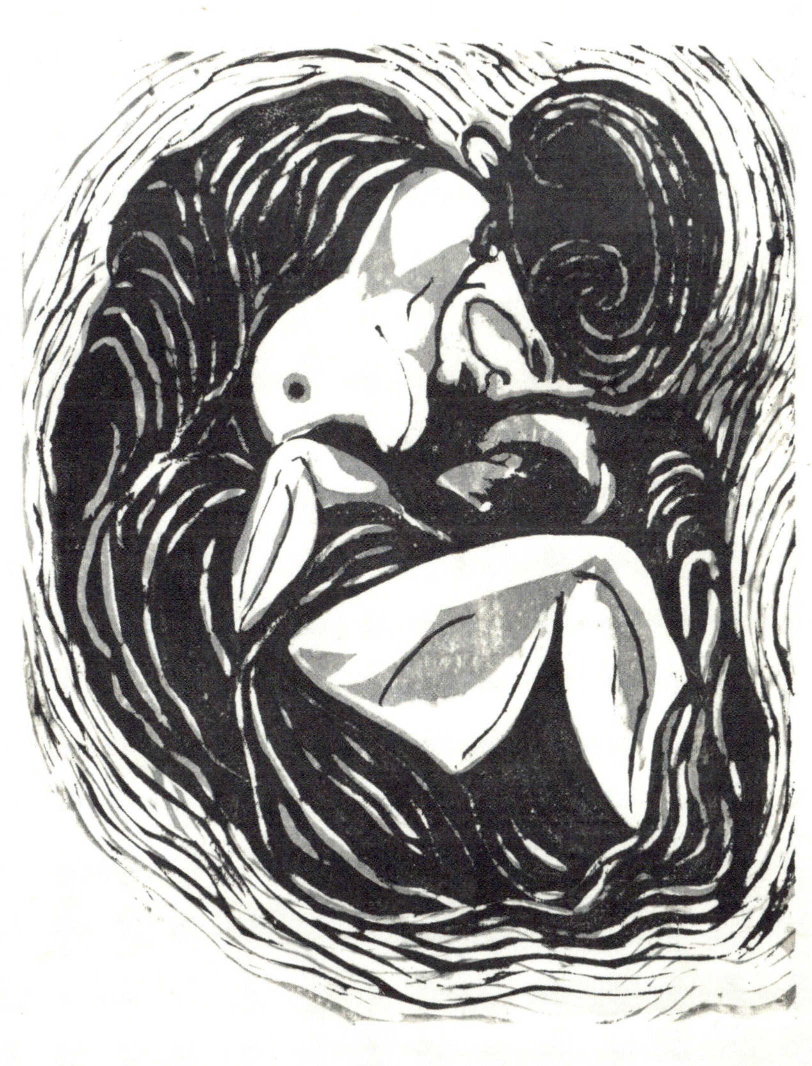

Mother and Child, c. 1915–55. Woodblock print

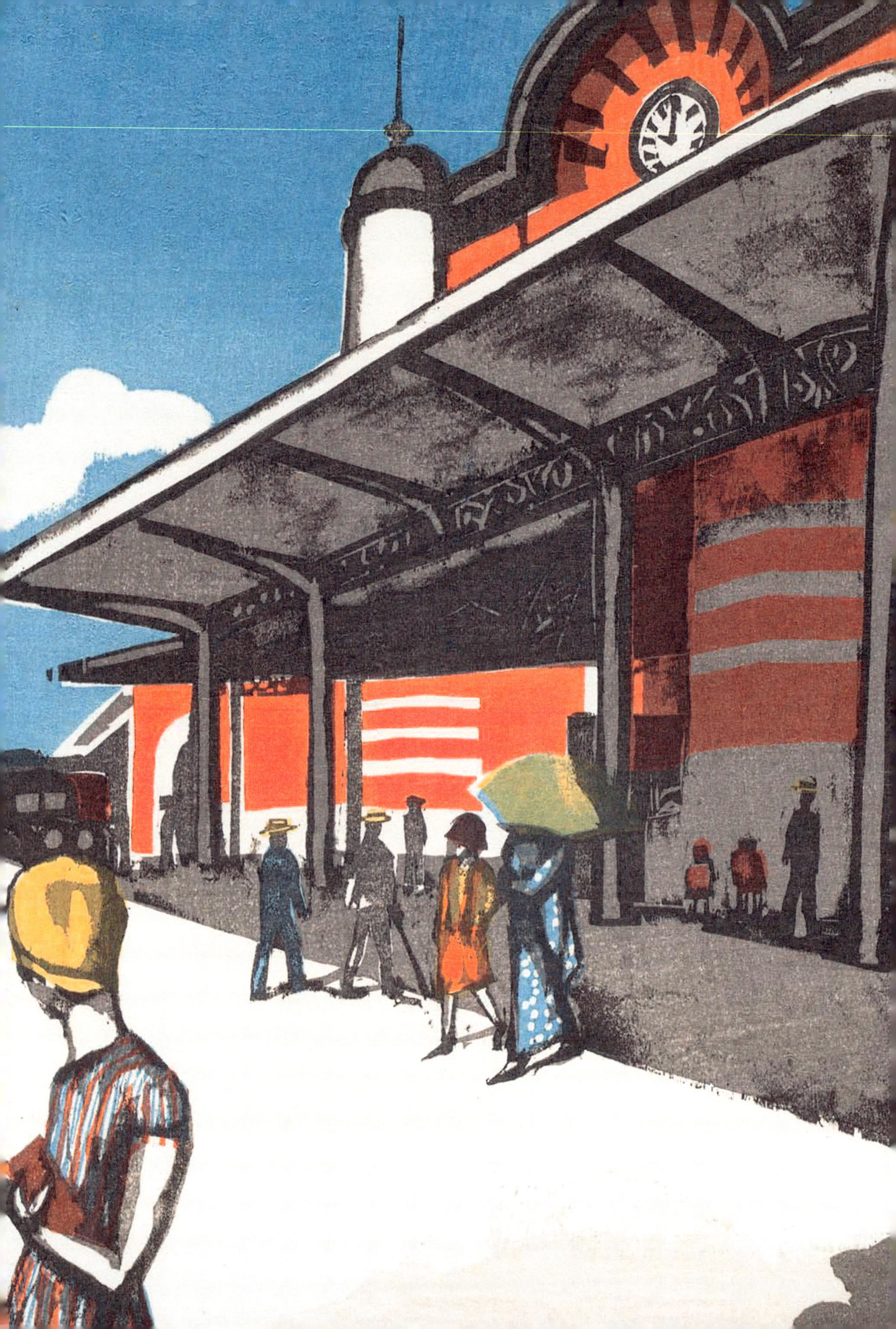

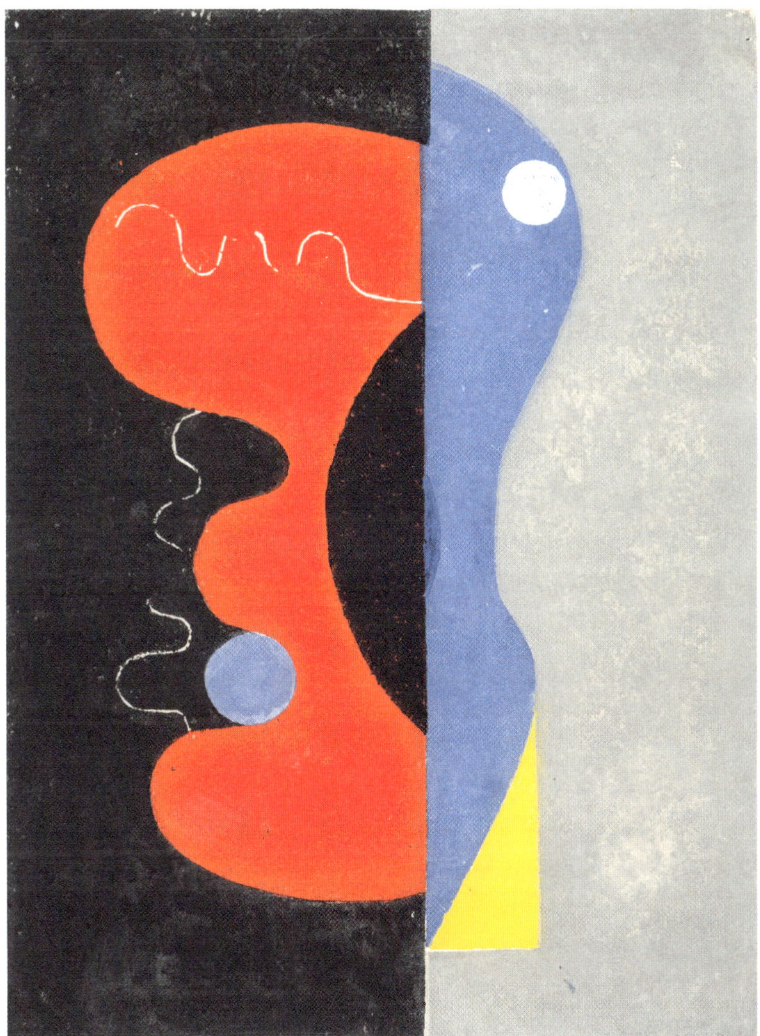

Lyric No. 23, 1955. Woodblock print

Tokyo Station, 1945. Woodblock print

ONOSATO Toshinobu (1912–1986)

Medium:
Lithograph, silkscreen

Circles within squares within triangles. Geometric shapes abstractly intertwined in bright yellow, orange and blue patterns – a mere optical illusion or a psychedelic trip? Onosato Toshinobu's circle-filled works mirror the essence of 1960s Op art aesthetics; however, his fascination with circles and squares was a scientific one, stemming from his background as an engineer, and can perhaps be appreciated more as a method than as a theme.

Born in Nagano prefecture, Onosato first studied to become an engineer but changed his mind and decided to become an artist instead. From 1932 he studied painting under Tsuda Seifū (1880–1978), whose abstract pattern designs likely had an influence on Onosato's later work.[1] In 1935 Onosato won first prize at the Nika Association Exhibition and in 1937 participated in the founding of the Free Artists' Association (Jiyū Bijutsu-ka Kyōkai), which he would remain part of for almost twenty years.

During the war, Onosato was conscripted into the army and survived three years in internment in Siberia before returning to Japan in 1948. Naturally marked by this experience, not long after he altered the spelling of his artist name, Onosato Toshinobu, from kanji to katakana[2] and developed his own unique painting style. Continuing to pursue a career as an abstract painter – influences included Paul Cézanne and later Wassily Kandinsky and Piet Mondrian (1872–1944) – Onosato's abstraction evolved all the more.

In 1955 he arrived at the idea of arranging equal-sized circles at regular intervals, and three years later Onosato turned to printmaking, beginning with lithography. During the 1960s he moved to silkscreen printing, duplicating the themes of his paintings. Collaborating with a printer, Onosato would execute an oil painting specifically for the purpose of having the printer reproduce its exact measurements onto the silkscreen frames.[3]

Onosato quickly gained national and international recognition with his vibrant, scientifically oriented designs; he had several solo exhibitions in Tokyo during the 1950s as well as one at Gres Gallery in Washington, DC, in 1961. In 1964 he was awarded a Guggenheim Fellowship and exhibited in the Guggenheim International Prize Exhibition, and was invited to participate in the Venice Biennale that same year, with five oil paintings 'in a "geometric abstract style" with squares painted in bright colors filling the entire picture plane like a mosaic, from which large circular forms appeared to emerge'.[4] He was invited back in 1966 with twenty paintings, again with his trademark circles and lines in bright colours, alongside fellow artists Ikeda Masuo (1934–1997), Shinoda Morio (b. 1931) and Ay-O (pp. 31–43).

Also in 1966, Onosato was included in the exhibition *The New Japanese Painting and Sculpture* at the Museum of Modern Art, New York, at the time the largest American exhibition of contemporary Japanese artists: 46 in total, highlighting artistic movements in modern Japan. For Onosato, it placed him at the forefront in terms of visibility among international museums and collectors. Of the four paintings of his that were displayed, two were on loan from Mr and Mrs John D. Rockefeller III.[5]

He was represented with two silkscreen prints at the Tokyo International Biennial Exhibition of Prints in 1970, in which Satō Ado (pp. 146–51), Kurosaki Akira (pp. 90–93), Noda Tetsuya (pp. 117–23), Ay-O and other

1 Nerima Art Museum, Katsuhiko Yokoyama (eds.), *Onosato Toshinobu* (Tokyo: Nerima Art Museum Publishing, 1989).

2 Kanji is the script derived from Chinese characters. Katakana is a syllabic form often used for rendering foreign language words.

3 See Gaston Petit, *44 Modern Japanese Print Artists*, 2 vols (Tokyo, New York, San Francisco: Kodansha International, 1973), p. 89.

4 '1964: Yoshishige Saito, Toshinobu Onosato, Hisao Domoto, Tomonori Toyofuku', Japan Pavilion Official Website, La Biennale di Venezia, https://venezia-biennale-japan.jpf.go.jp/e/art/1964.

5 Museum of Modern Art, New York, *The New Japanese Painting and Sculpture*, 1966, master checklist, p. 114, www.moma.org/calendar/exhibitions/2584.

Japanese contemporaries also participated. In 1992 the Toshinobu Onosato Museum was built in Kiryu, Gunma prefecture.

Collections: British Museum, London; Los Angeles County Museum of Art; Metropolitan Museum of Art, New York; Museum of Modern Art, New York; National Museum of Modern Art, Tokyo; Toshinobu Onosato Museum, Kiryu.

Installation view of the exhibition *The New Japanese Painting and Sculpture*, 19 October 1966 – 2 January 1967, Museum of Modern Art, New York, showing works by Onosato Toshinobu

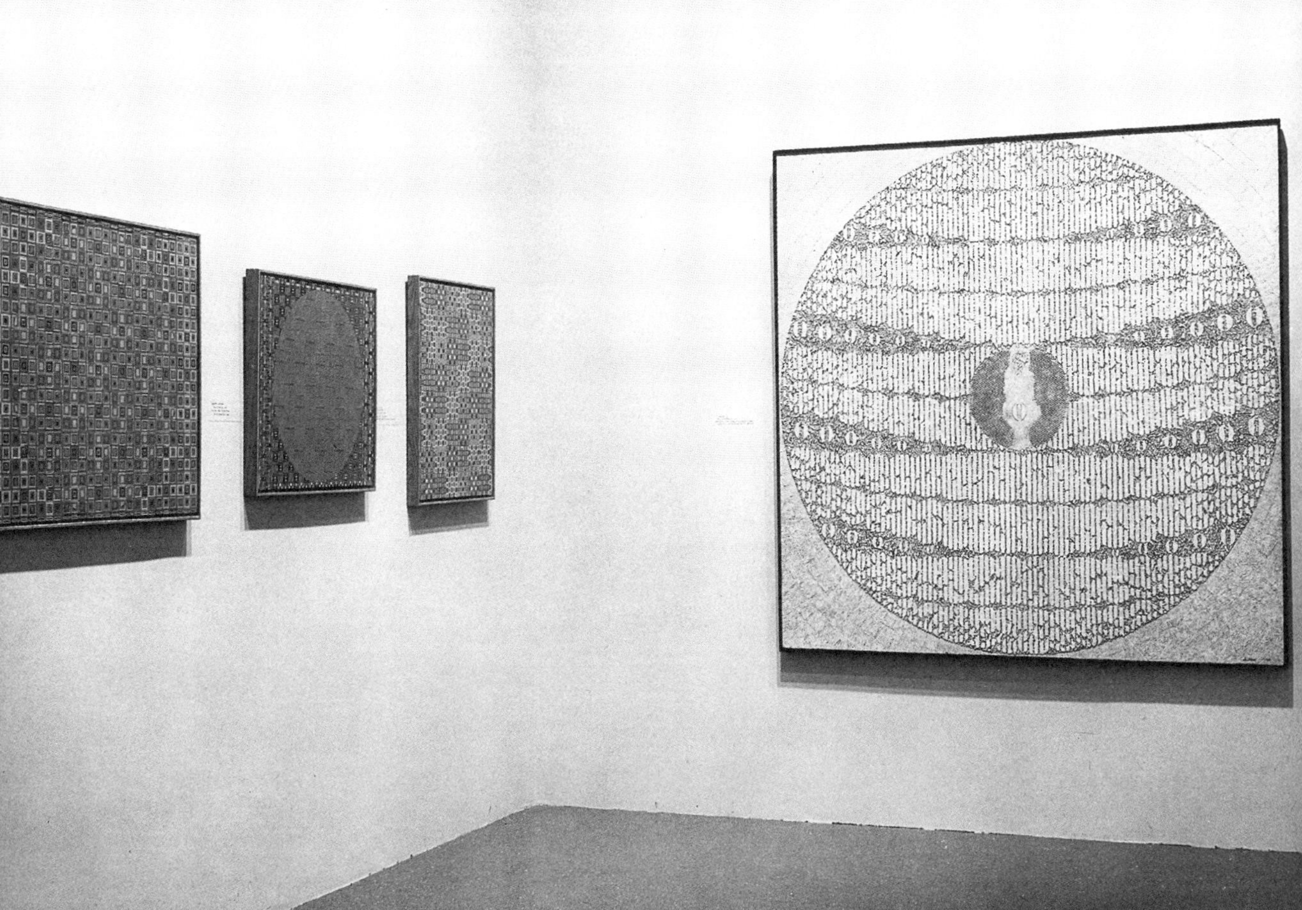

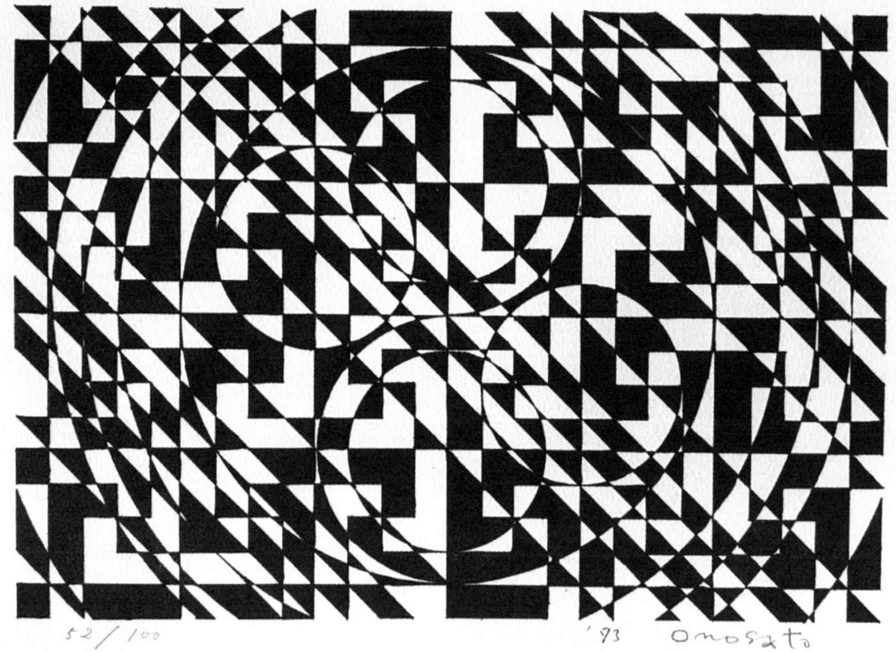

Lithograph B, 1973. Lithograph

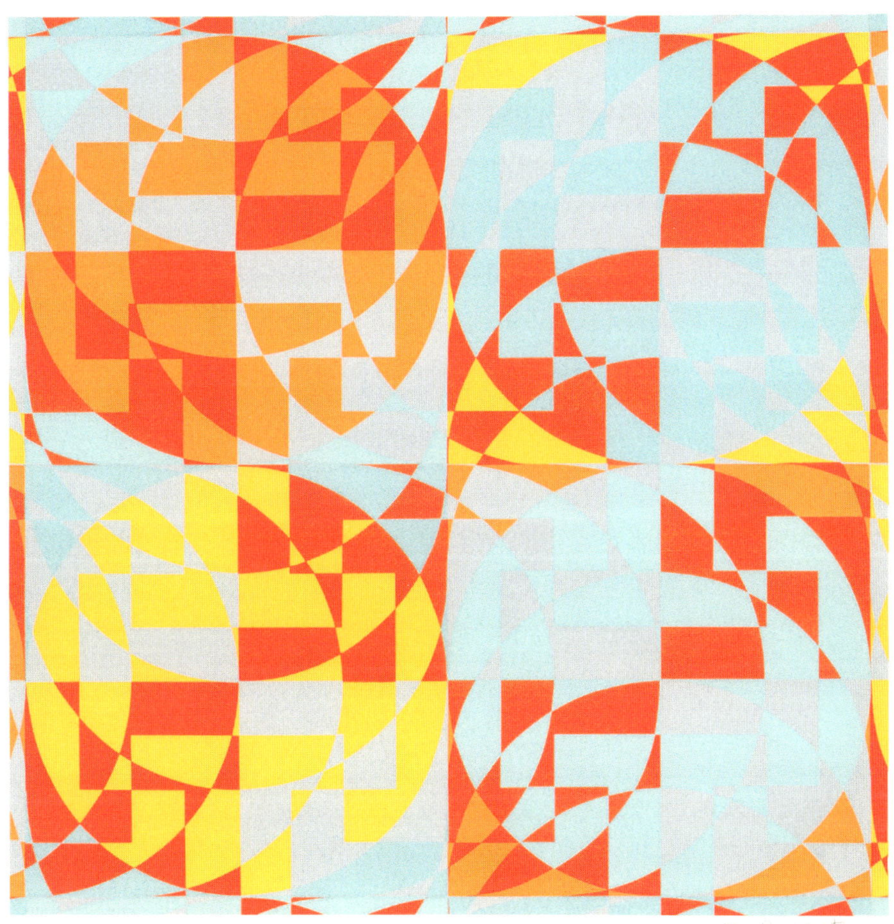

71-K, 1971. Silkscreen print

SAITŌ Kiyoshi (1907–1997)

Medium:
Woodblock

When interviewed by Oliver Statler for the book *Modern Japanese Prints: An Art Reborn* (1956), Saitō Kiyoshi described his first reaction to the work of early *ukiyo-e* artist Suzuki Haranobu (c. 1725–1770): 'I was nauseated. It was only through Gauguin that I began to appreciate the qualities of ukiyo-e, and still I feel closer to Gauguin than ukiyo-e.'[1]

Saitō, one of Japan's most renowned and prolific modern print artists, was self-taught as a painter and later in printmaking. After seeing prints by the noted *yōga* painter Yasui Sōtarō (1888–1955), he became inspired to make his own, and he produced his first prints, *Girl* and *Seated Child*, in 1936. Both were accepted by the Japan Print Association that same year.[2] Soon followed his *Winter in Aizu* series (1938–40), depicting his home region, which he visited in 1937 for the first time in 26 years. He continued to work on this series all the way up to 1996.[3]

Like many other printmakers, Saitō worked as a graphic designer to make a living, first for the *Asahi shimbun* newspaper from 1944 and then the Tokyo National Museum starting in 1947. In 1944 Saitō also met Onchi Kōshirō (pp. 130–33), who invited him to join the First Thursday Society, a group of artists who would meet monthly at Onchi's house. Saitō further exhibited prints from *Winter in Aizu* at the Japan Print Association exhibition. In 1949 he received first prize for *Milk* at the Salon du Printemps exhibition in Tokyo.

Like the majority of his contemporaries, Saitō was influenced by European art, especially the work of Odilon Redon (1840–1916), Edvard Munch and Paul Gauguin, whose work he had seen in magazines: 'From the moment I first saw their work I've been attracted by their romanticism, their exoticism, and their mysticism,' he explained.[4] Piet Mondrian's grid-based compositions influenced Saitō in his depictions of architecture and garden structures. In woodblock printing, Saitō would also find a source of inspiration in the textures of the various woods, incorporating the grain patterns from the boards into his figurative compositions.[5]

At the first São Paulo Biennial in 1951, Saitō and Komai Tetsurō were awarded the Expatriates Prize. This was a turning point not only for Saitō himself, who won for his woodblock print *Steady Gaze (Flower)*,[6] but for Japanese printmaking in general. The prints were favoured over oil painting or sculpture, which shocked the Japanese art world: 'The Japanese still condescend to us, but it was even worse before Komai and I won prizes at the Brazil show in 1951,' Saitō recollected.[7]

Following his success in São Paulo, Saitō's commercial appeal grew, especially in the USA. Apart from exhibitions, this was manifested in several of his prints being published in magazines, such as the covers for *Holiday* in 1961, which featured one of his *Bunraku* puppet prints, and *Time* in 1967 and 1977, with Saitō's portraits of Japan's prime ministers Eisaku Satō and Fukuda Takeo. Saitō's print *Steady Gaze (Cat)* had already been published in *Time* in 1951 and became a collector's item: 'Suddenly my gallery was swamped with orders for *Cat* from around the world. In no time at all, the print disappeared from Japan,' Saitō remembered.[8] At the time, one of the prints was quoted by a Manhattan dealer at $1,500. Saitō's original price was $16.60.[9]

Besides many portraits of cats, Saitō's motifs ranged from scenes of Buddhist statues, temples and gardens in Kyoto, Nara and Kamakura, to female

1 Oliver Statler, *Modern Japanese Prints: An Art Reborn* (Rutland, VT: Charles E. Tuttle Co., 1956), p. 54.
2 See Rhiannon Paget, *Saitō Kiyoshi: Graphic Awakening*, exh. cat., John and Mable Ringling Museum of Art, Sarasota, FL (New York: Scala Arts Publishers, 2021), p. 205.
3 Ibid., p. 72.
4 Statler, *Modern Japanese Prints*, p. 54.
5 Gaston Petit and Amadio Arboleda, *Evolving Techniques in Japanese Woodblock Prints* (Tokyo, New York, San Francisco: Kodansha International, 1977), p. 56.
6 This is referred to as *Staring* in Statler, *Modern Japanese Prints*, p. 55.
7 Saitō Kiyoshi quoted ibid.
8 Saitō Kiyoshi quoted in 'A Letter from the Publisher', *Time*, 10 February 1967, https://time.com/archive/6634900/a-letter-from-the-publisher-feb-10-1967.
9 Ibid.

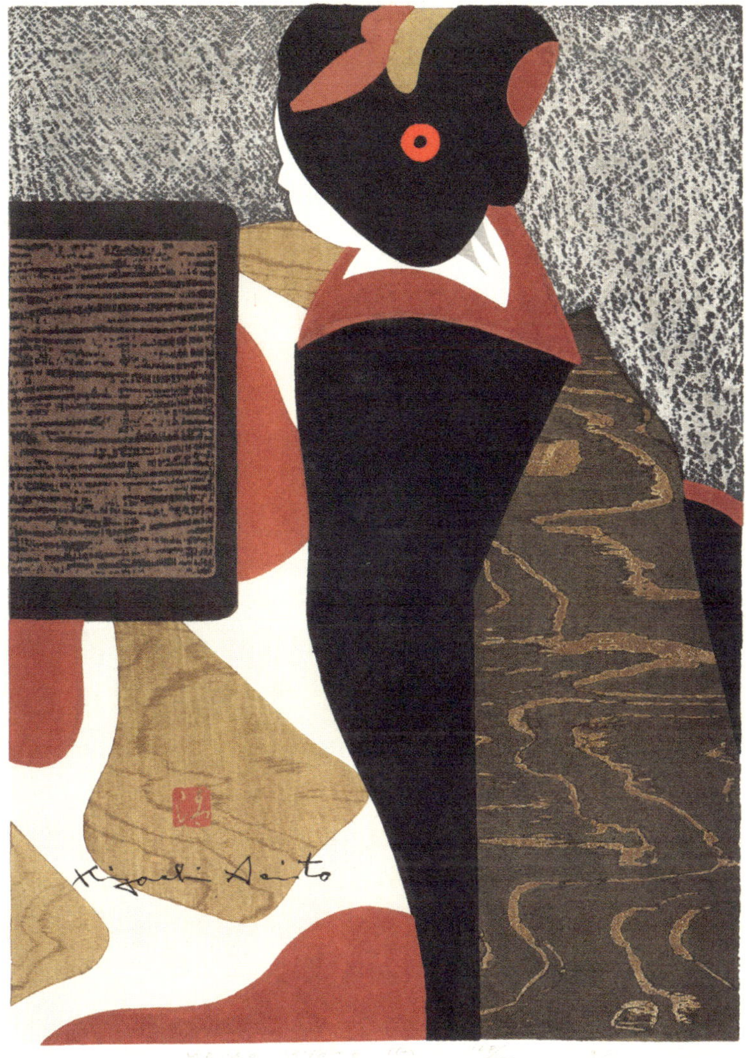

Maiko, Kyoto (G), 1961. Woodblock print

Overleaf
Bisyamonten, Kyoto, 1965. Woodblock print

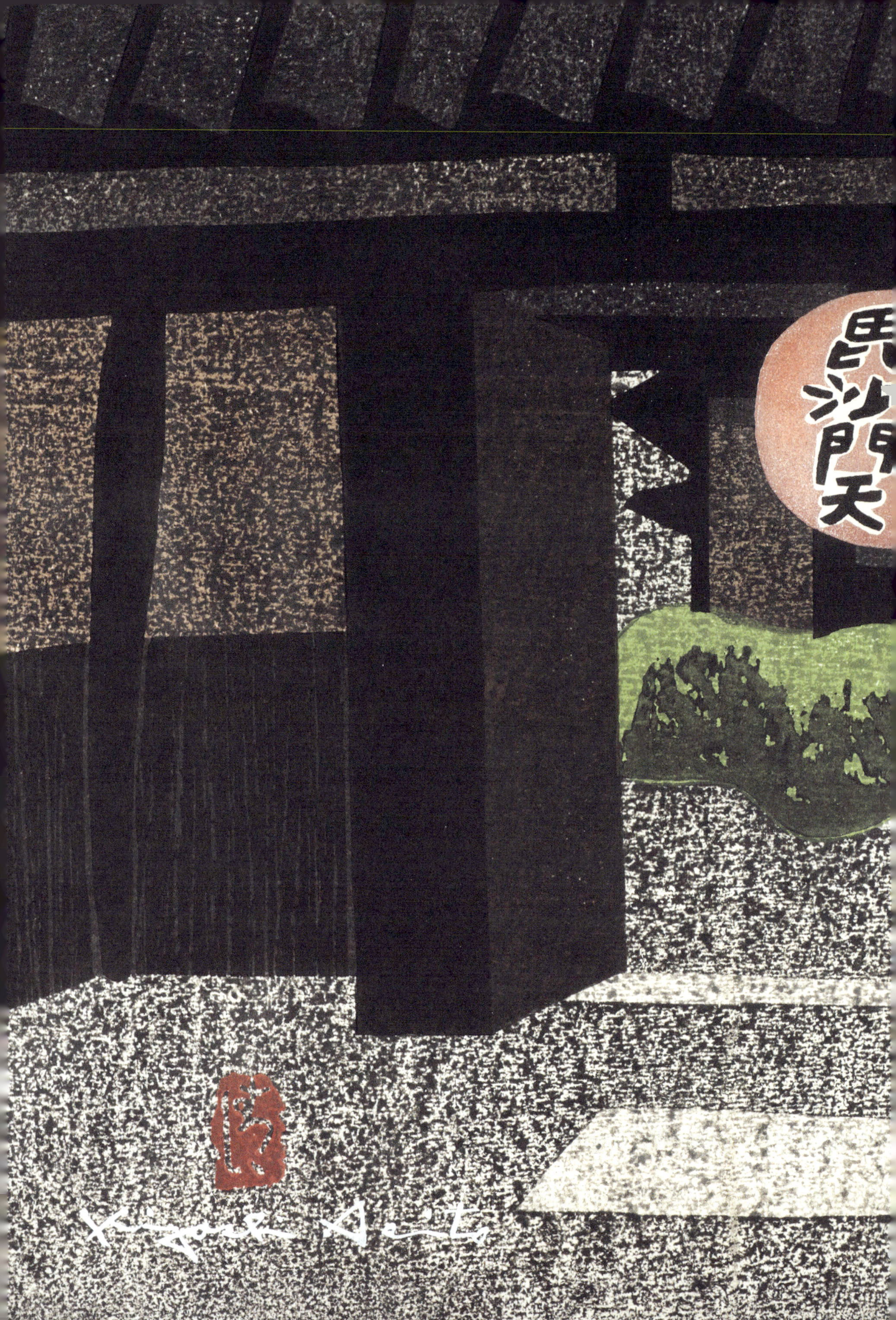
毘沙門天

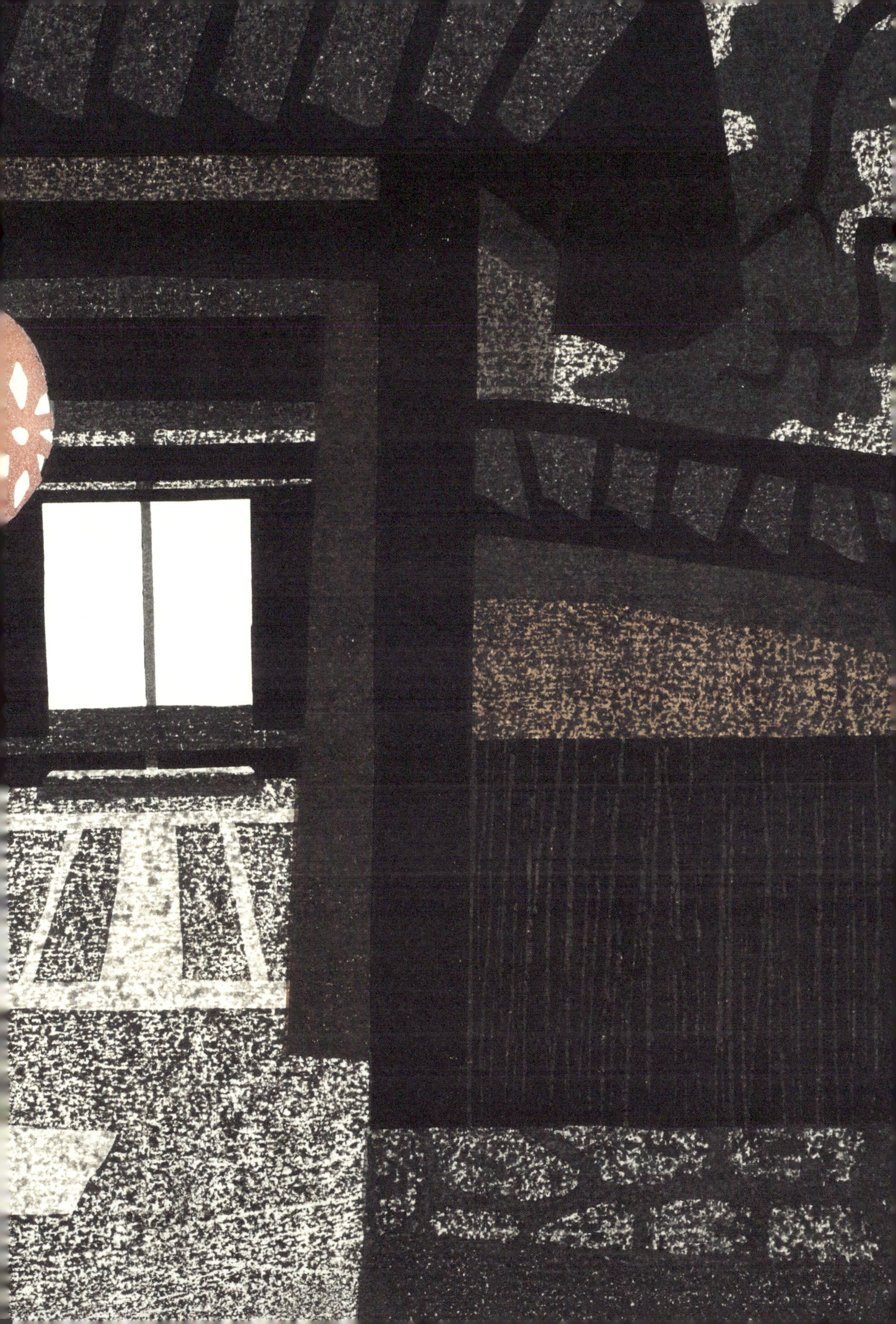

subjects, *maiko* (trainee geisha), puppets and *haniwa* (funerary ceramics), and scenes from Aizu throughout the seasons. He also created series from other countries he visited, such as France, India and Mexico.

Dog (1954), a print from a rather comical series featuring sausage dogs, was included in the Museum of Modern Art exhibition *Prints from Europe and Japan* as early as 1955 along with two other prints by the artist. In the following decades, Saitō was represented in numerous national and international exhibitions: *Color Print Artists of Modern Japan* at the Museum of Fine Arts, Boston (1953); the São Paulo Biennial (1953, 1957); the CWAJ Print Show (1956–68, 1970); *Japan's Modern Prints: Sōsaku Hanga* at the Art Institute of Chicago (1960); *Contemporary Japanese Prints* at the Los Angeles County Museum of Art (1972); and *Saitō Kiyoshi Exhibition* at the Kanagawa Prefectural Museum of Modern Art (1983).

The Kiyoshi Saito Museum of Art in Yanaizu, Fukushima prefecture, opened in 1997. It houses more than 850 of his works.

Collections: Art Institute of Chicago; British Museum, London; Kiyoshi Saito Museum of Art, Yanaizu; Museum of Fine Arts, Boston; Museum of Modern Art, New York; Victoria and Albert Museum, London.

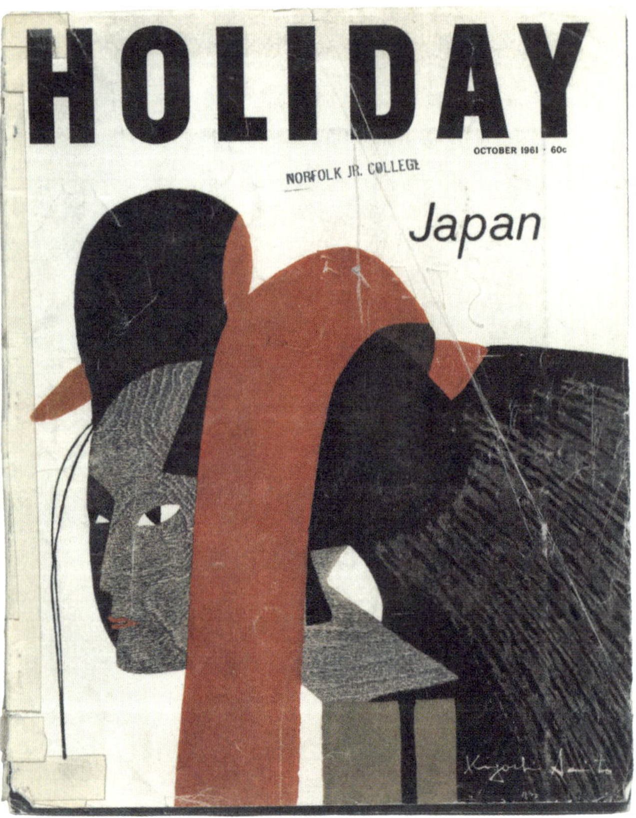

Holiday magazine, October 1961, featuring *Bunraku (B)*, 1959

Installation view of the exhibition *Prints from Europe and Japan; Etchings by Matisse* at the Museum of Modern Art, New York, 4–31 May 1955, showing Saitō's woodblock print *Dachshund*

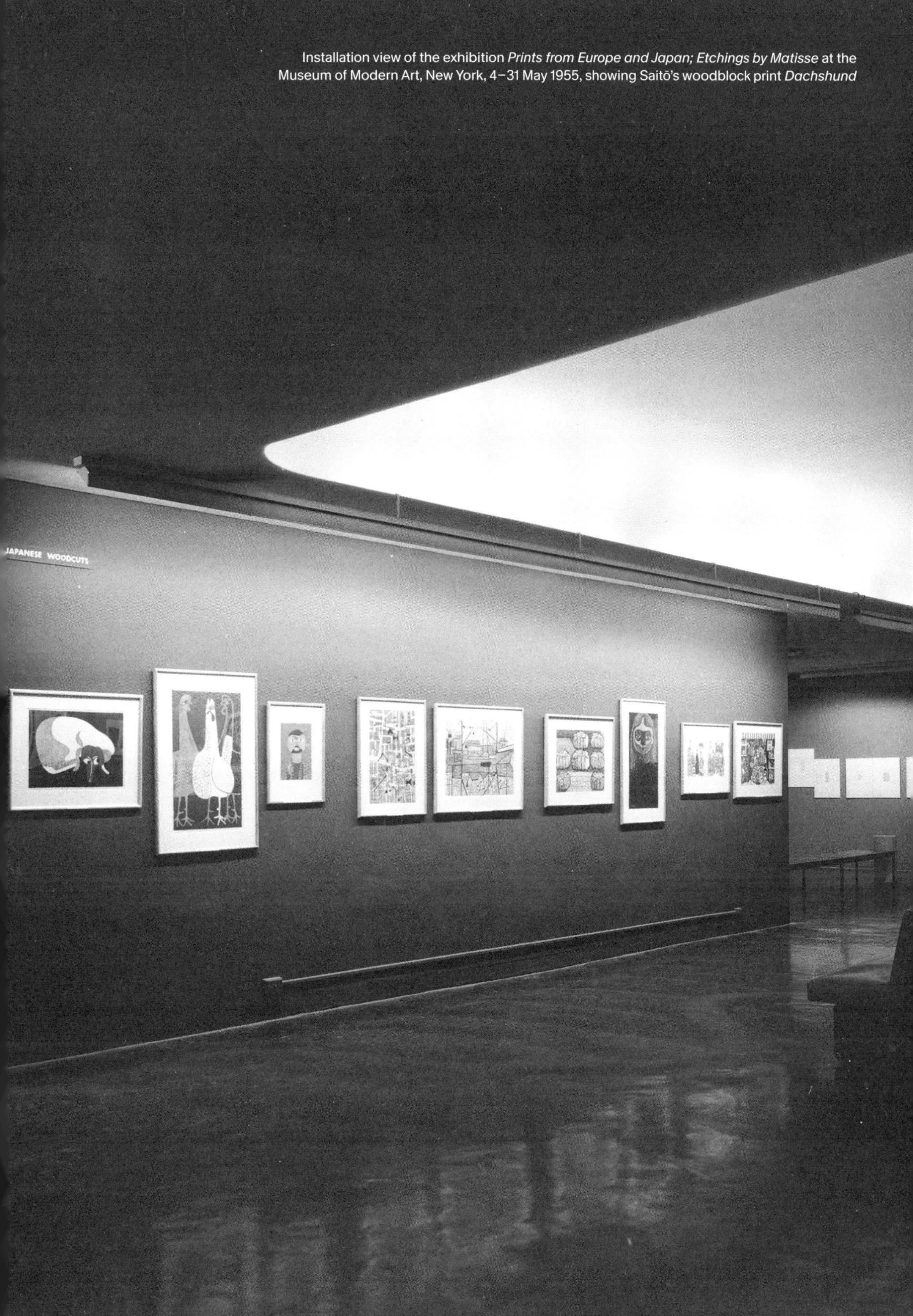

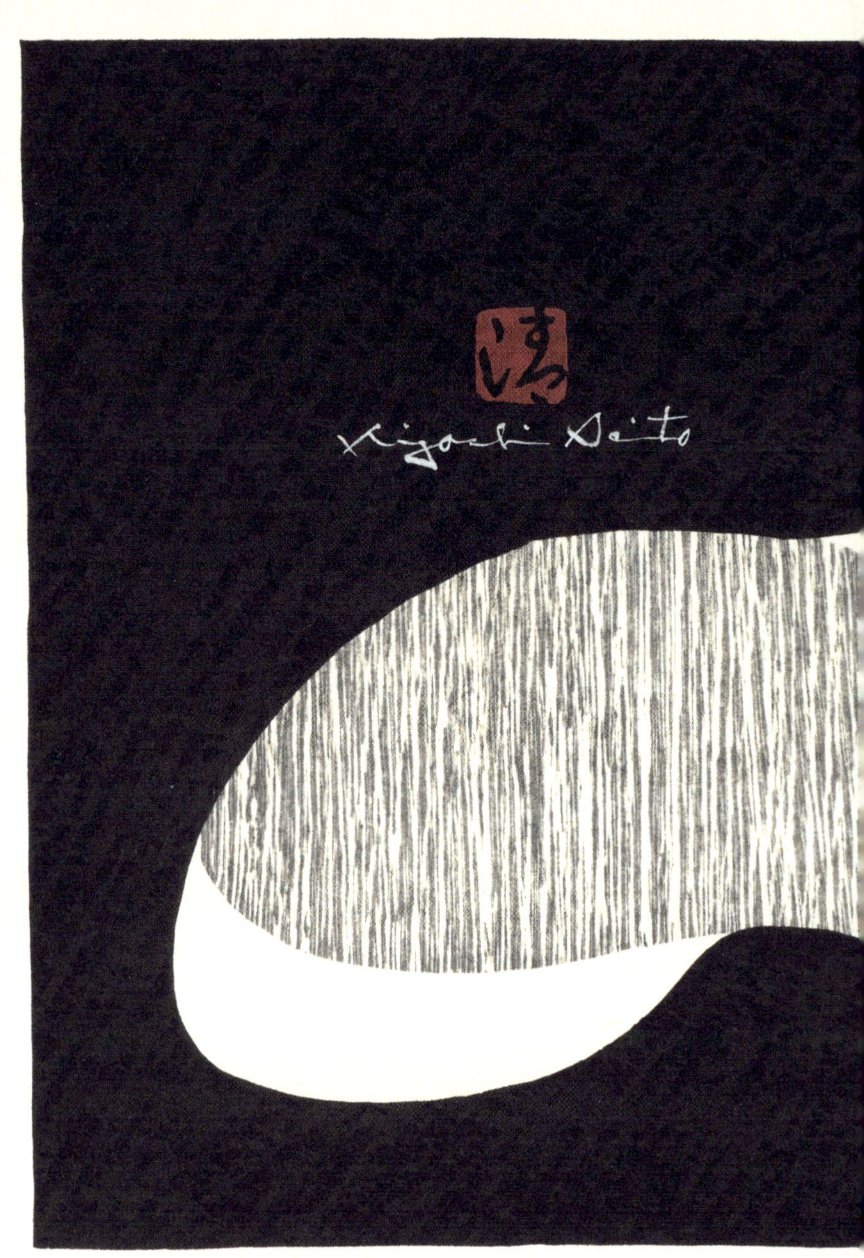
Kiyoshi Saito

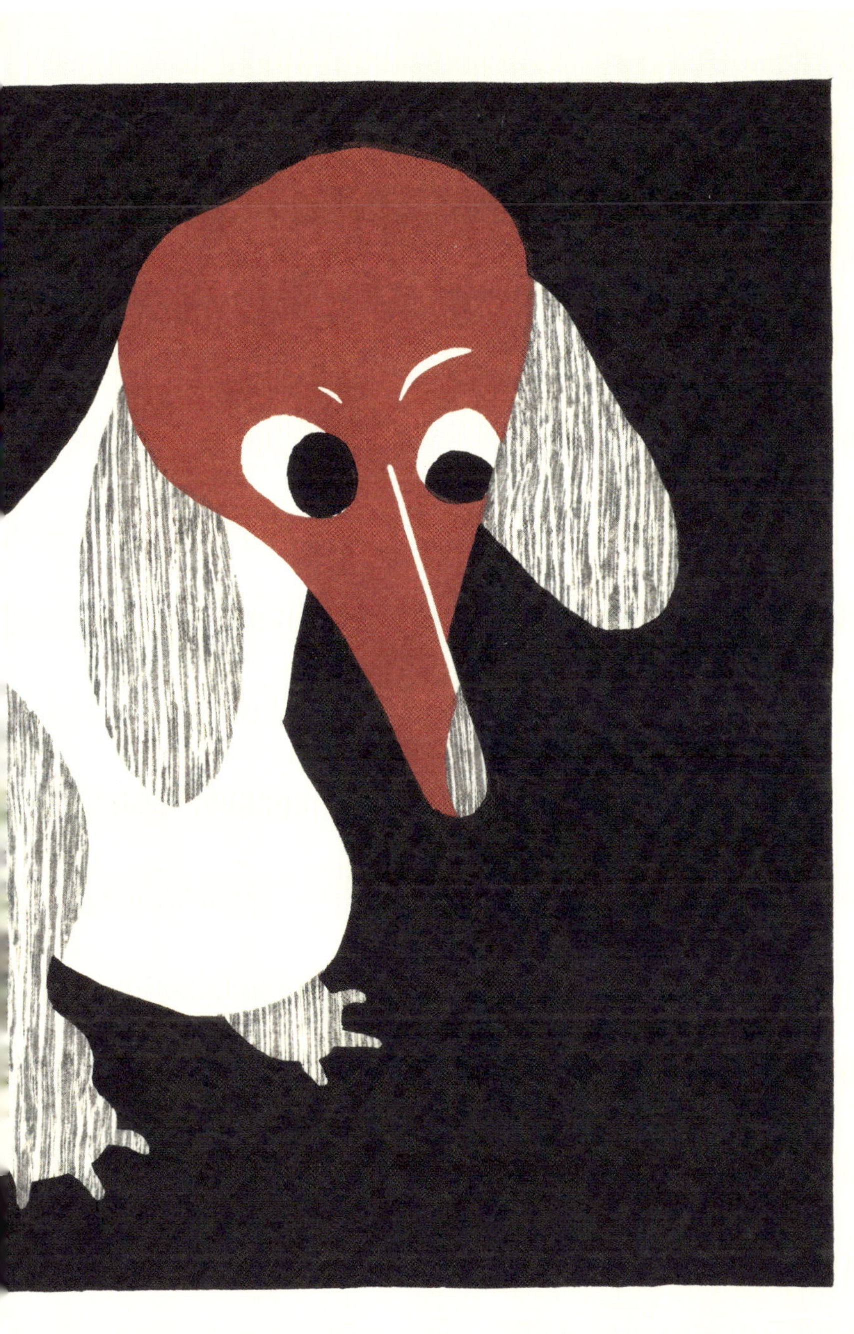

Dachshund, undated. Woodblock print

SATŌ Ado (1936–1995)

Medium:
Silkscreen

We must keep the purity of a child, remain enthusiastic at every moment of life.[1]

Satō Ado, 1975

Born in Yokohama to artist parents, Satō Ado was surrounded by creative minds from the beginning. His mother was the famous opera singer Satō Yoshiko (1903–1982) and his father was the painter Satō Key (1906–1978), who in 1960 represented Japan at the Venice Biennale. A close friend of the family was the renowned Francophile artist Foujita (pp. 48–51), whom Key knew from his time in Paris in the 1930s. Towards the end of the Second World War, the Satō family joined Foujita in the small town outside Tokyo where he had taken refuge. Other artist friends were invited as well. Foujita did a portrait of six-year-old Ado and taught him to fish in the river because of food shortages.[2]

It seems only natural that Ado would take up a creative profession. Winning the Young Artists Prize in 1953 from the Museum of Modern Art in Kamakura at eighteen, he went on to study aesthetics at Keiō University in Tokyo, graduating in 1961. Ado took a job as a designer for an advertising company; however, the following year he decided to move to Paris to pursue a career as a painter.[3] His father, with whom he shared a close relationship, had settled in Paris in 1952. Ado wanted to establish his career independently of his father, so began to sign his works with his given name, Ado.

Ado quickly made a name for himself with solo exhibitions in France and abroad: the first at the Hamilton Galleries, London, in 1964 and then at Galerie Mouffe, Paris, the following year. He exhibited at the Biennale de Paris, first in 1965 and then in 1967, 1969 and 1971. He also showed work at Galerie Horn, Luxembourg (1966), Templon, Paris (1968), Galerie Arnaud, Paris (1969, 1971, 1975), Gallery Bloomingdale, New York, and Gallery Muramatsu, Tokyo (both 1970), and in a group show at the National Museum of Modern Art, Kyoto (1970).

From the late 1960s, Ado began moving from volume paintings – playing with three-dimensionality with the use of wood relief or impasto techniques – to flat canvases, and he started exploring the medium of screenprint as well. In what would become Ado's trademark aesthetic, he created precise, stark yet inviting and joyful geometric compositions investigating the infinity of space: circles, lines, squares and other forms pop in intense, pure oranges, reds, blues, purples and greens (Ado did not like to mix colours).

As early as 1968, Ado took part in the 1st British International Print Biennale in Bradford, and the following year he was represented in the 7th International Biennial Exhibition of Prints in Tokyo with two silkscreen prints, *Institut Hotel I* and *Institut Hotel II*. Along with another of his silkscreens – *The Cage* (1969) – *Institut Hotel II* entered the New York Museum of Modern Art's collection in 1971.[4]

This was also the year when the Musée d'Art Moderne in Paris invited Ado to mount a solo exhibition. *Ado: peintures et photographies* was held from 15 June to 19 September as part of the series L'ARC (Animation – Recherche – Confrontation) and included his silkscreen prints.[5] Reflecting a busy and

1 Satō Ado quoted in exhibition catalogue, Galerie Arnaud, Paris, 1975, n.p.

2 I am grateful to Eko Satō for providing information about her father's work and life.

3 Frédéric Bodet, *Ado 70*, exh. cat. (Paris: Galerie Les Modernistes, 2008).

4 According to MoMA, it was purchased through the Mrs Donald B. Straus Fund in 1971, but if it was the actual print exhibited at the Tokyo print biennale is not clear.

5 See Archives d'expositions de l'ARC (1967–1972), Musée d'Art Moderne de la Ville de Paris, MAM-ARCH-EXPO-ARC 1967–1972, www.parismuseescollections.paris.fr.

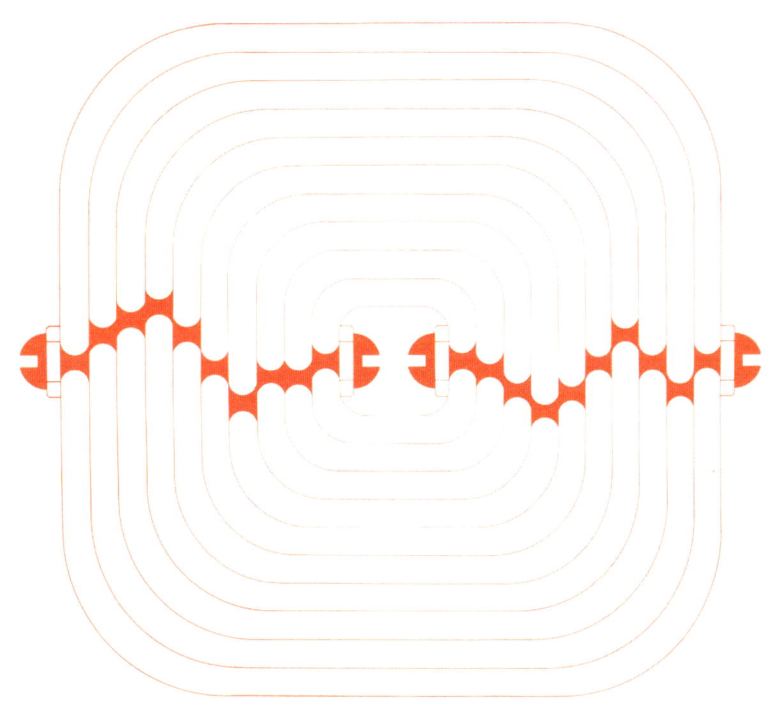

Time Tunnel, 1968. Silkscreen print

bright decade for Ado, the exhibition attracted a lot of positive attention. He was also appreciated by art critics, with Picasso scholar Georges Boudaille writing: 'Behind the perfection of the forms, in a painting of Ado, there is always something happening ... his painting never bores because it is not only decorative, it is also a narrative.'[6]

Ado's paintings and prints were featured in French cult films during the 1960s and '70s, such as Gérard Pirès's *Erotissimo* (1969) with Jean Yanne and Serge Gainsbourg, testifying to the popularity of his optical effects, so fitting for the Op art era. When MoMA put on an exhibition of recent acquisitions of prints and illustrated books in 1973, Ado's *The Cage* was displayed alongside works by Wassily Kandinsky, Alberto Giacometti, Jackson Pollock and Stanley William Hayter, as well as by his contemporaries in the graphic medium Roy Lichtenstein, Jasper Johns, Edward Ruscha (b. 1937), Kurosaki Akira (pp. 90–93) and Noda Tetsuya (pp. 117–23).

In the production of his silkscreen prints, Ado worked with printers in both France and Japan. A significant collaborator of his was master printer Okabe Tokuzō, whom Ado first met in 1975 at the Shinzenbi Gallery in Tokyo. Okabe had established the first screenprinting studio in Japan in 1964 and worked with many well-known artists of Ado's generation, including Ay-O (pp. 31–43), Kusama Yayoi (pp. 94–99) and Yokoo Tadanori (pp. 226–31).

In 1977, Ado invited the photographer Shinoyama Kishin (1940–2024) and writer Ishikawa Jun (1899–1987) to contribute to *Paris*, a print box containing ten silkscreen prints in limited editions of 170, today a collector's item. Ado continued making prints until the end of his career.

Collections: Musée d'Art Moderne, Paris; Museum of Contemporary Art, Tokyo; Museum of Modern Art, New York; Seattle Art Museum; Victoria and Albert Museum, London.

6 Translation kindly provided by Eko Satō.

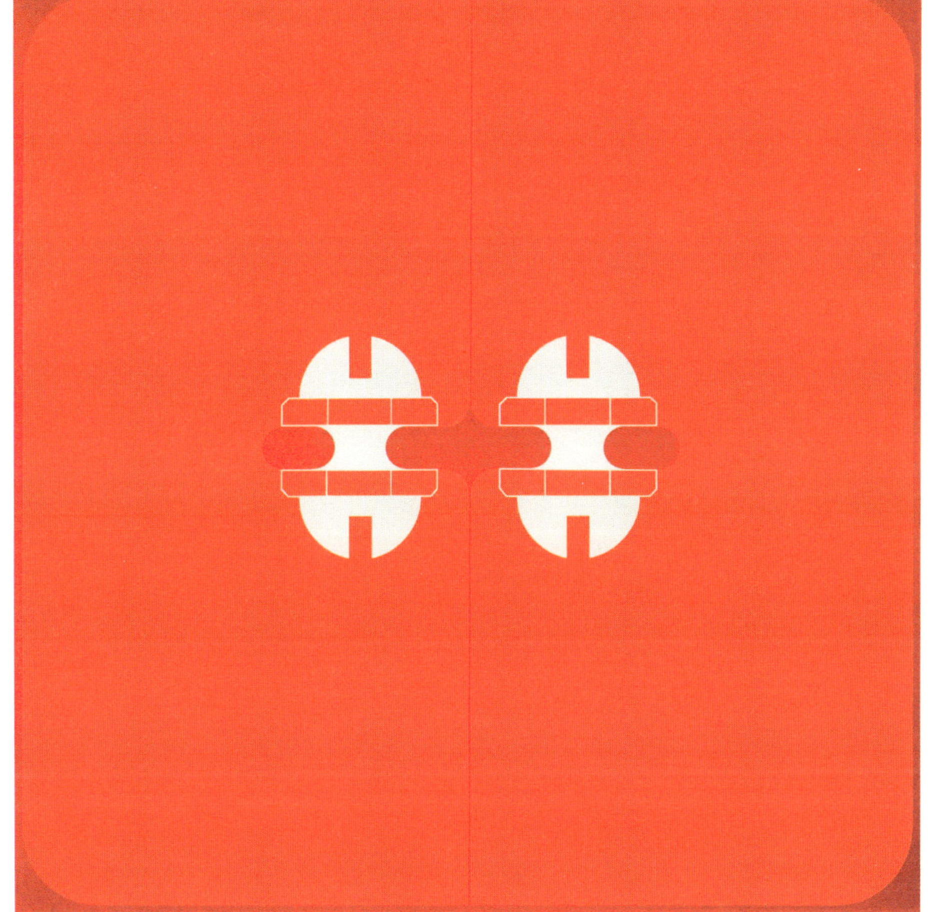

CB70, 1970. Silkscreen print

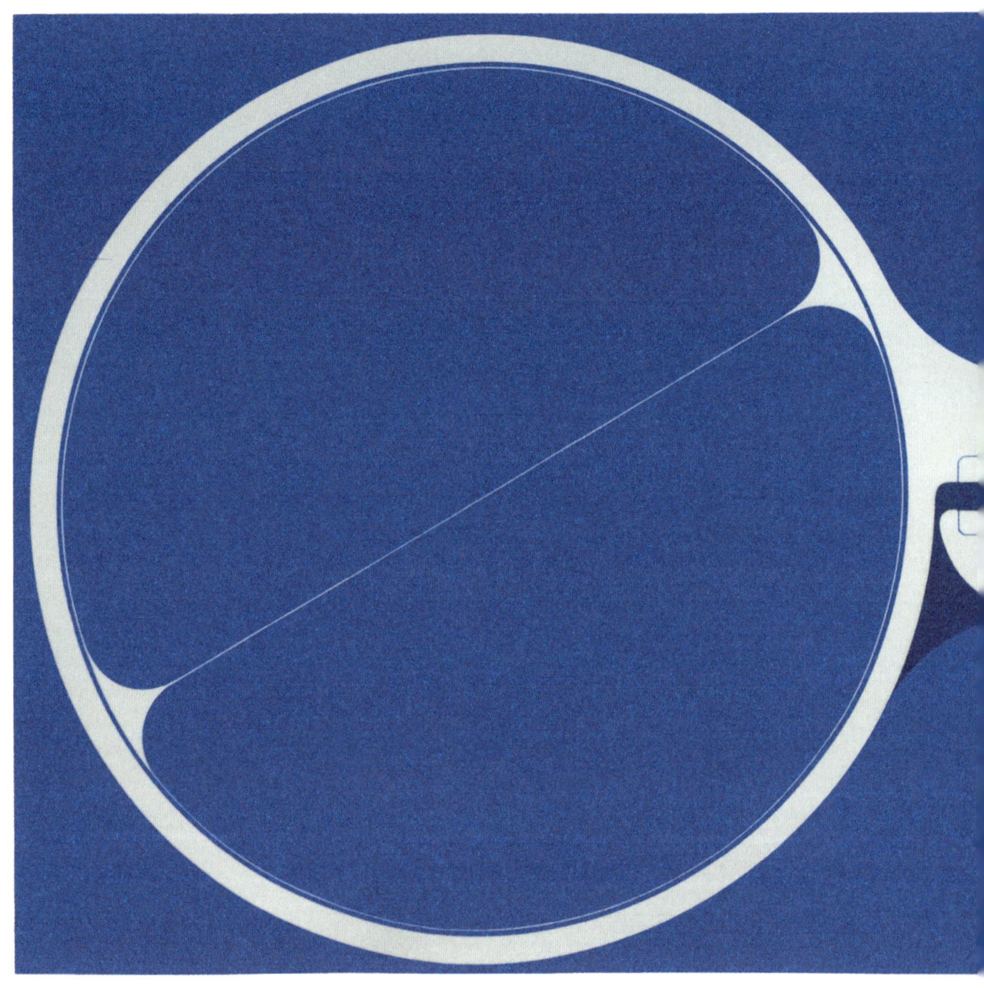

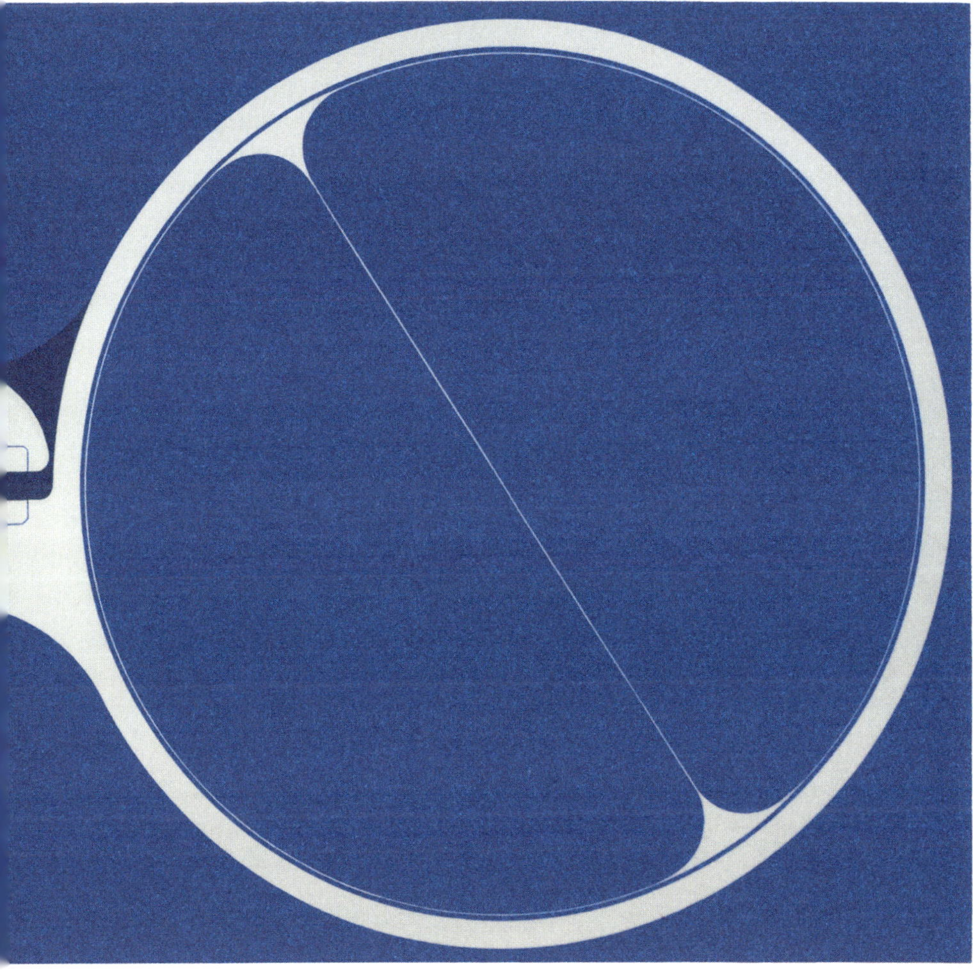

Starter Blue, 1968. Silkscreen print

SHINODA Tōkō (1913–2021)

Medium:
Lithograph

First showing of Abstract Japanese Calligraphy at Museum of Modern Art. Approximately 40 examples of the new abstract calligraphy developed by Japanese artists in the past decade will be on view ... in the first exhibition of its kind presented in this country.[1]

Japanese Calligraphy,
Museum of Modern Art, New York, 1954

One of Japan's leading twentieth-century painters, who gained acclaim for her calligraphic abstractions, Shinoda Tōkō began to exhibit internationally as early as 1954 when a work of hers, *Twilight*, was shown as part of MoMA's exhibition *Japanese Calligraphy*, along with 34 other Japanese calligraphers, the majority male.

Born in Manchuria in 1913, Shinoda moved with her family the following year to Tokyo, where she was raised. She trained in traditional Japanese calligraphy and poetry from the age of six to fifteen. But, Shinoda explained in an article in *Time* magazine in 1983, 'I got tired of it and decided to try my own style. My father always scolded me for being naughty and departing from the traditional way, but I had to do it.'[2]

She had her first solo show in Tokyo in 1940 at the Ginza retail store Kyukyodo. She spent the years 1956–58 in the United States, at a time when Abstract Expressionism was at its height. In 1956 Shinoda was photographed by Hans Namuth (1915–1990), who also captured artists like Jackson Pollock, Mark Rothko (1903–1970) and Robert Rauschenberg. She had her first New York solo show at the Bertha Schaefer Gallery in January 1957.

Artist Pierre Alechinsky's short film *Calligraphie japonaise* (Japanese Calligraphy), made that same year, featured Shinoda with other prominent calligraphers Eguchi Sōgen (1919–2018), Morita Shiryū (1912–1998) and Ōsawa Gakyū (1890–1953), tracing the link between traditional Japanese calligraphy and modern art.

Through Kenzō Okada (1902–1982), who had already moved to New York in 1950, Shinoda met Betty Parsons in 1958 during a trip to Tokyo. The prominent gallerist, who also represented Pollock and Rothko, later took on Shinoda, who had several solo shows at her gallery between 1965 and 1977.[3] Shinoda's distinctive calligraphic abstractions made her one of the few commercially successful Asian artists associated with Abstract Expressionism.[4]

In a lithograph, even though it is my own creation, there exists another sphere realised through the medium of 'plate'. This is the mystery of my inner self, unknown to even me. I glimpse with trepidation.[5]

Shinoda Tōkō

During the 1960s, Shinoda began making lithographs with hand-painted brush strokes, similar in style to her ink paintings, creating more than one thousand works: 'Characteristic brush strokes overlap and angle elegantly in

1 Museum of Modern Art, *Japanese Calligraphy*, press release, 23 June 1954, www.moma.org/calendar/exhibitions/3320.
2 Paul Gray, 'Art: Work of a Woman's Hand', *Time*, 1 August 1983.
3 Alexandra Monroe, *Japanese Art after 1945: Scream against the Sky* (New York: Harry N. Abrams, 1994), p. 311.
4 Kimihiko Nakamura, 'Shinoda Tōkō: Ink, Abstraction, and Radical Individualism', *Woman's Art Journal* 43, no. 1 (Spring–Summer 2022), p. 21.
5 Shinoda Tōkō quoted in *50th CWAJ Print Show* (Tokyo: College Women's Association of Japan, 2005), n.p.
6 Frances Blakemore, *Who's Who in Modern Japanese Prints* (New York and Tokyo: Weatherhill, 1975), p. 185.
7 Shinoda Tōkō, *103-sai ni natte wakatta koto: jinsei wa hitori demo omoshiroi* [Things That I Figured Out about Life by 103: Life Is Fun Even When You Are Alone] (Tokyo: Gentosha, 2015), pp. 96–98, quoted in Nakamura, 'Shinoda Tōkō', p. 21.

every Shinoda presentation.'[6] In the production of prints, she collaborated with master lithographer (and artist) Kimura Kihachi (1934–2014) at the Fuji Bijutsu print workshop. Kimura, who also printed for Kusama Yayoi (pp. 94–99), worked as Shinoda's printer for almost fifty years, until he retired in 2007.

Shinoda was invited to represent Japan at the São Paulo Biennial in 1961 with three large-scale ink murals. In 1983 her work was exhibited as the CWAJ Associate Show, *Shinoda Toko: A Retrospective of Her Prints*. She was also included in the Cincinnati Art Museum exhibition *Innovation and Tradition: Twentieth-Century Japanese Prints from the Howard and Caroline Porter Collection* (1989). This was the same year as her first solo museum show in Japan, at the Seibu Museum of Art in Tokyo. Living to the age of 107, Shinoda, a pioneer in her field, remained active as an artist until the end of her life.

My heart's yearning for freedom has created my own path.
Everything I have done has been because my heart asked for it,
and that is why I am who I am today.[7]

Shinoda Tōkō, 2015

Collections: Art Institute of Chicago; British Museum, London; Cincinnati Art Museum; Gifu Collection of Modern Arts, Seki; Museum of Modern Art, New York; National Museum of Modern Art, Tokyo.

Unfortunately, it has not been possible to obtain permission from the copyright holder to include images of Shinoda Tōkō's prints. However, given her pioneering work as an artist, I still wished to include her in this book. I encourage the reader to look up her work online or in the above-mentioned collections.

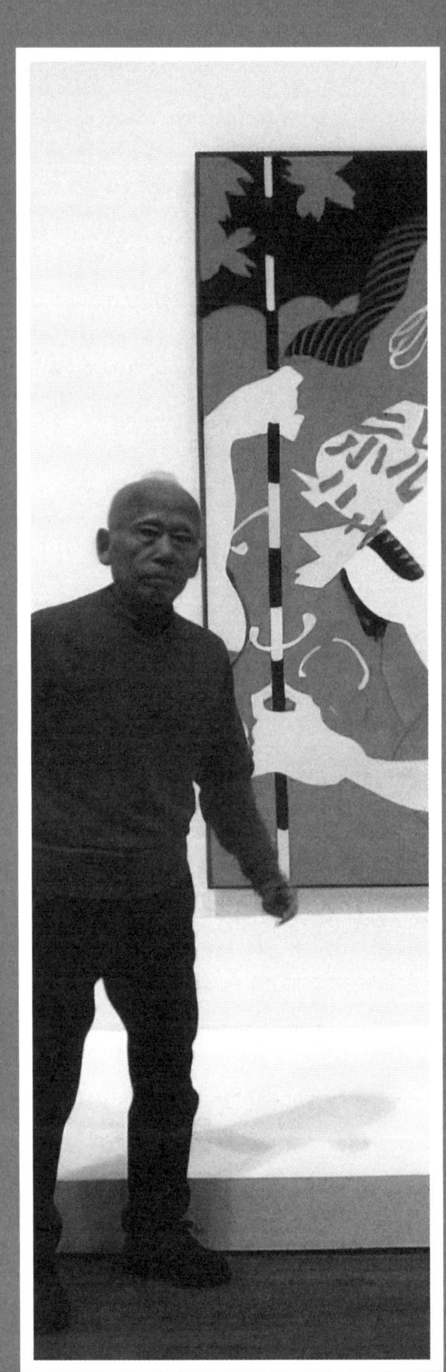

No point in having a serious talk about art in front of a microphone.
Better to attract attention with loud, shocking words.
Or maybe even start dancing naked in front of a camera.[1]

Shinohara Ushio, 1968

SHINOHARA Ushio (b. 1932)

Medium:
Silkscreen

First and foremost a painter, sculptor and performance artist, and best known for his 'boxing' action paintings, Shinohara Ushio was one of the Japanese artists of the post-war generation who became seriously influenced by American culture and was drawn to New York and its avant-garde art scene.

Shinohara had been influenced by Van Gogh since his student days. He attended Tokyo University of the Arts in 1952–57, but because of his 'chaotic' way of drawing, he was told by his teacher, the *yōga* painter Hayashi Takeshi (1896–1975), 'Your works are honest, but you don't need to stay any longer in a school.' And so Shinohara left.[2]

It was following his departure from university that he cut his hair into his trademark mohawk style, which he has kept to this day. In 1960, the Neo-Dada Organizers was established with Shinohara as the leader, and the group held its first exhibition at the Ginza Gallery that year. By that time, Shinohara had already performed his first 'boxing painting', where, 'half-naked with his mohawk haircut, [he] dipped his gloved fists into a bucket of paint and punched his way along an extensive sheet of canvas'.[3]

In 1969, he moved to New York on a grant from the John D. Rockefeller III fund. He didn't return to Japan. In New York he was introduced to fellow Japanese artist Ay-O (pp. 31–43) through a friend and stayed in his loft in Chinatown until Ay-O returned a year later. The building was a base for several Fluxus artists, including Nam June Paik, with whom Shinohara had many conversations during this period.

A couple of years before his move to New York, the Museum of Modern Art had included in the exhibition *The Artist as His Subject* Shinohara's work *Marcel Duchamp* (1965), a blueprint based on a sculpture he had made of the iconic French artist. The exhibition presented the crème de la crème of international modern printmaking: silkscreen prints by Andy Warhol and Roy Lichtenstein, woodblock prints by Munakata Shikō (pp. 104–7), and lithographs by Edvard Munch, Josef Albers and Robert Rauschenberg (the latter Shinohara had met in Tokyo). The exhibition, which ran from 6 June to 17 September 1967, also featured Duchamp's own *Self-Portrait*, a silkscreen print from 1959. The following year, Duchamp, who was an influential figure for Shinohara's generation of Neo-Dada artists, died. MoMA included Shinohara's *Marcel Duchamp* once again for the show *Popular Mechanics in Print Making* in 1970. This was meaningful recognition for the young artist – and Shinohara was proud.

During the 1960s, when almost every major American artist was making graphic work, Shinohara also touched upon the medium, turning to silkscreen printing. This printing technique was how he could best express what he wanted, he later explained.[4] During this period, Shinohara was also inspired by the traditional woodblock prints of his home country, especially those by Yoshitishi Tsukioka, one of the last great masters of *ukiyo-e*. It was

1 Shinohara Ushio, *Zen'ei no michi* [Way of the Avant-Garde] (Tokyo: Bijutsu Shuppan-sha, 1968), quoted in Alexandra Monroe, *Japanese Art after 1945: Scream against the Sky* (New York: Harry N. Abrams, 1994), p. 373.

2 Thanks to Ushio and Norika Shinohara for sharing information and anecdotes. The following stories from New York are based on information shared via email, winter 2024–25.

3 Monroe, *Japanese Art after 1945*, p. 98.

4 Ushio and Norika Shinohara, email, winter 2024–25.

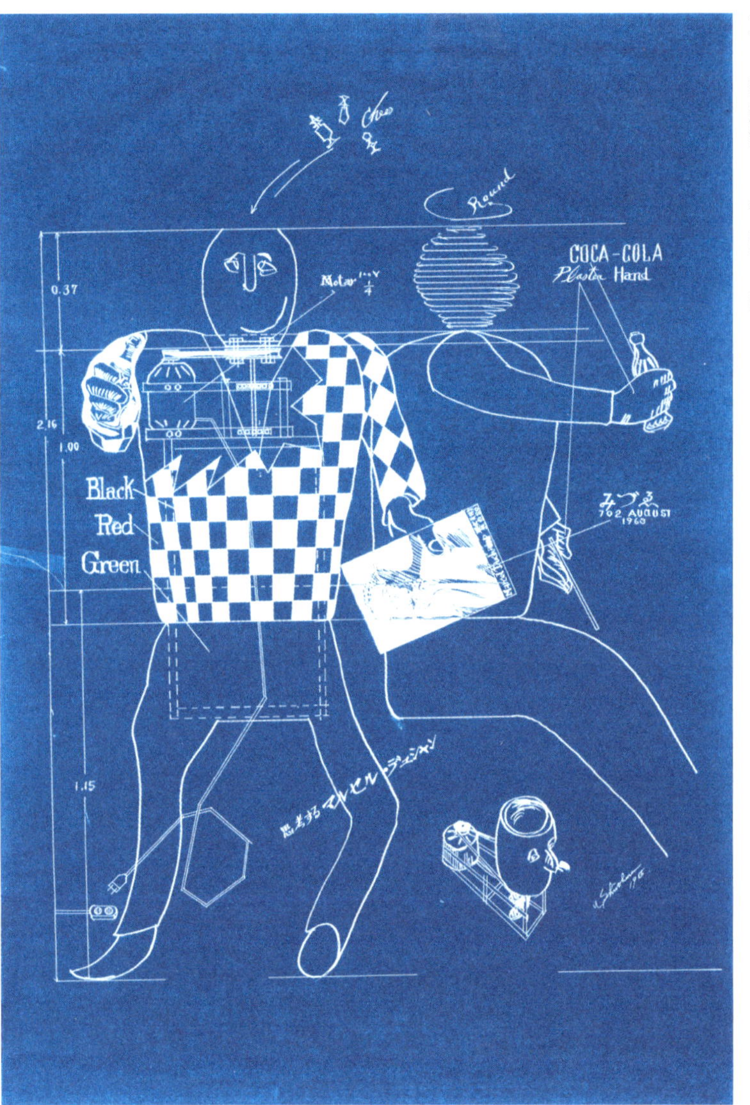

Marcel Duchamp, 1965. Blueprint

Doll Festival, 1966. Triptych of silkscreen prints

Yoshitoshi's series of female portraits from the 1880s that led Shinohara to create his own series, *Oiran*, beginning in 1965. He focused on the classic subject of the *oiran*, the highest-ranking courtesans of the 'red-light districts' of Edo (Tokyo), the most famous being Yoshiwara. Not to be mistaken for geisha (a reserved entertainer) or *maiko* (a trainee geisha), *oiran* were prostitutes, yet revered as the pinnacle of beauty and elegance. They were the 'pop stars' and flamboyant trendsetters of the day, recognisable by their elaborate ornamental hair pins (*kanzashi*).

Shinohara decided to leave the figures of his *ukiyo-e*-inspired works faceless to eliminate the sentimental mood while heightening the imagination of the audience. He used the same *ukiyo-e* themes for both prints and paintings, bringing the traditional Japanese motif into the modern day with his 1960s Pop aesthetics: bold colours and compositions and geometric shapes. For another silkscreen print, titled *Doll Festival* (1966), which he also made as a painting, he borrowed the triptych format common in *ukiyo-e*. Shinohara's interpretation at once reflects the influence of contemporary American Pop art and that of the 'floating world' and *ukiyo-e*, the original Japanese 'pop art' of the Edo period. Shinohara is still active as an artist today. He lives in New York with his wife Noriko (b. 1953), who is a painter and printmaker as well.

Collections: Centre Georges Pompidou, Paris; Metropolitan Museum of Art, New York; Museum of Modern Art, New York; Tate Modern, London.

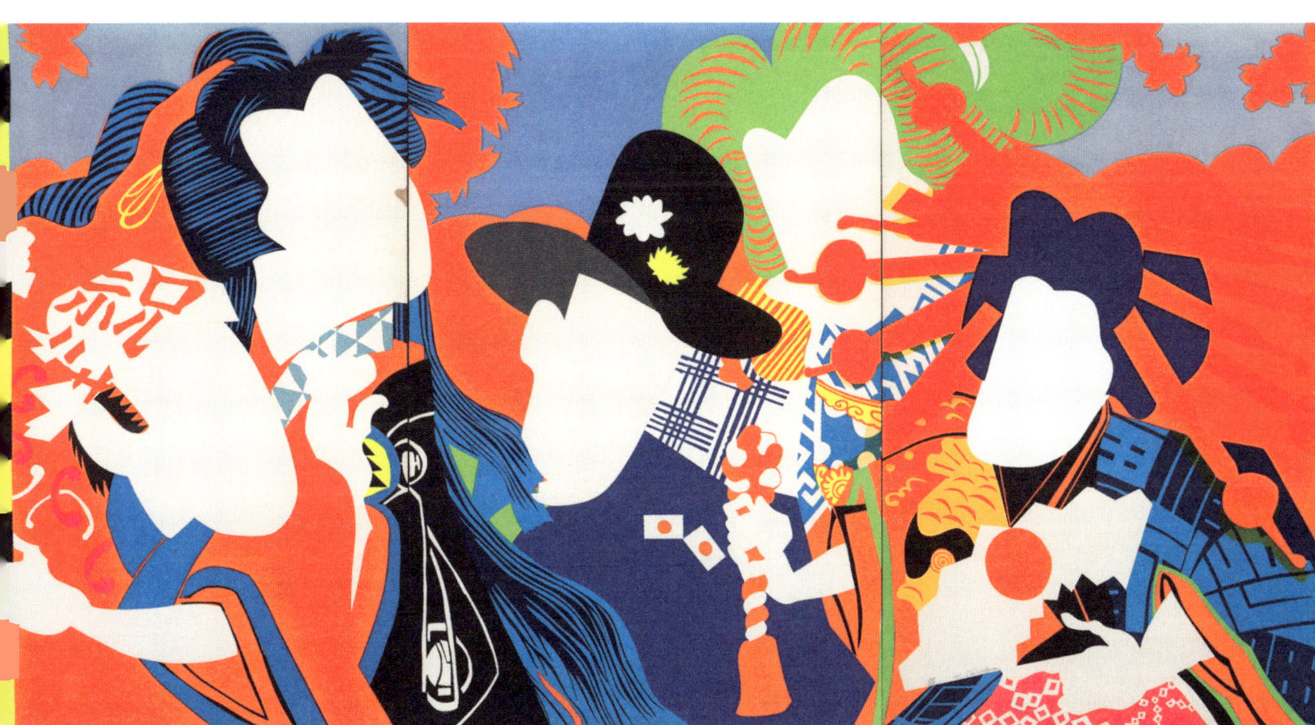

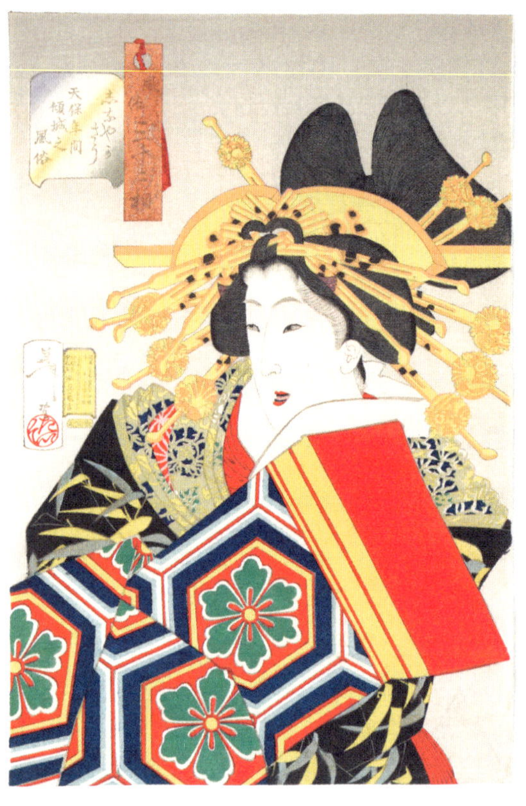

1 TSUKIOKA Yoshitoshi

Appearing Graceful, Behaviour of a High-Ranking Prostitute of the Tenpō Era, 1888. Woodblock print

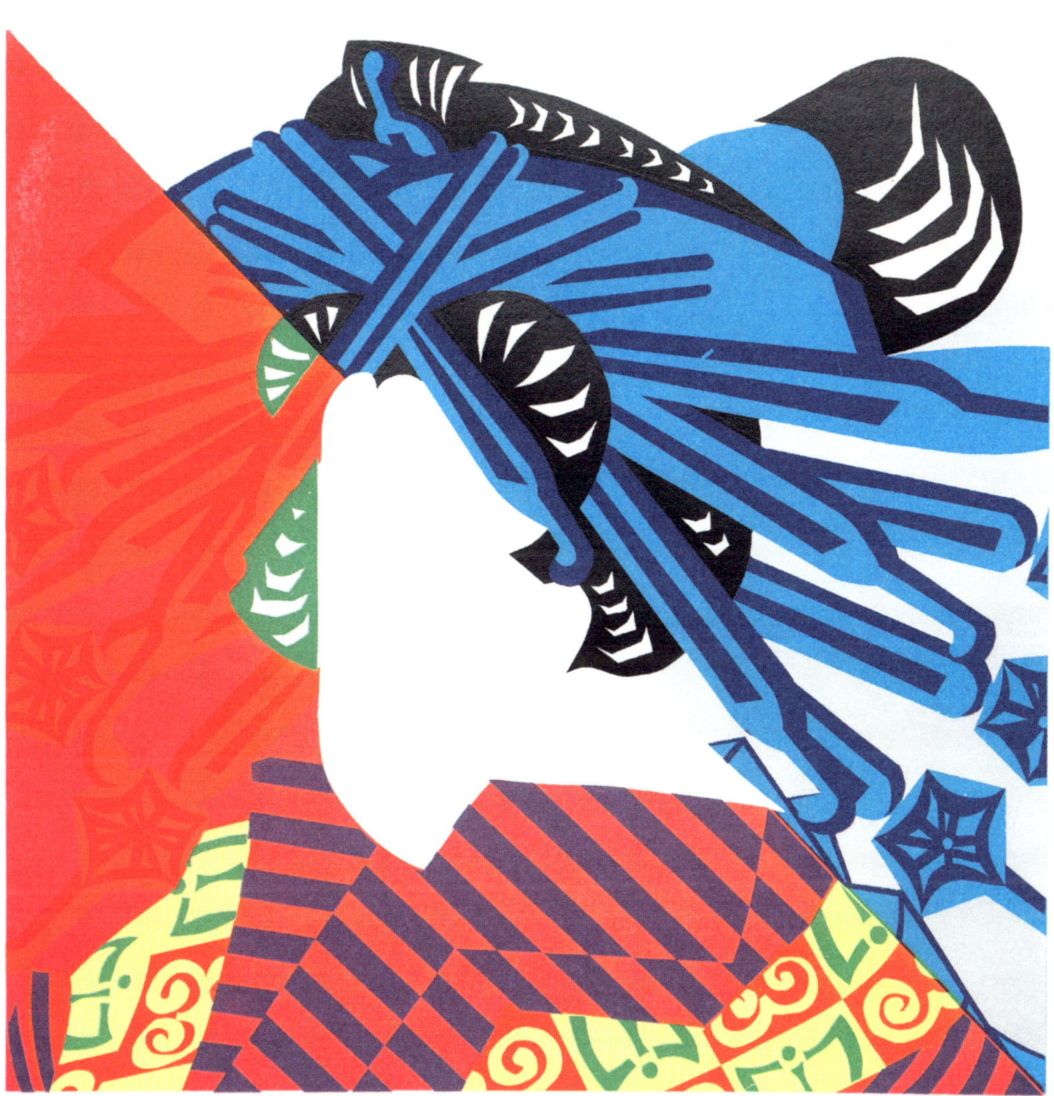

Oiran, undated. Silkscreen print

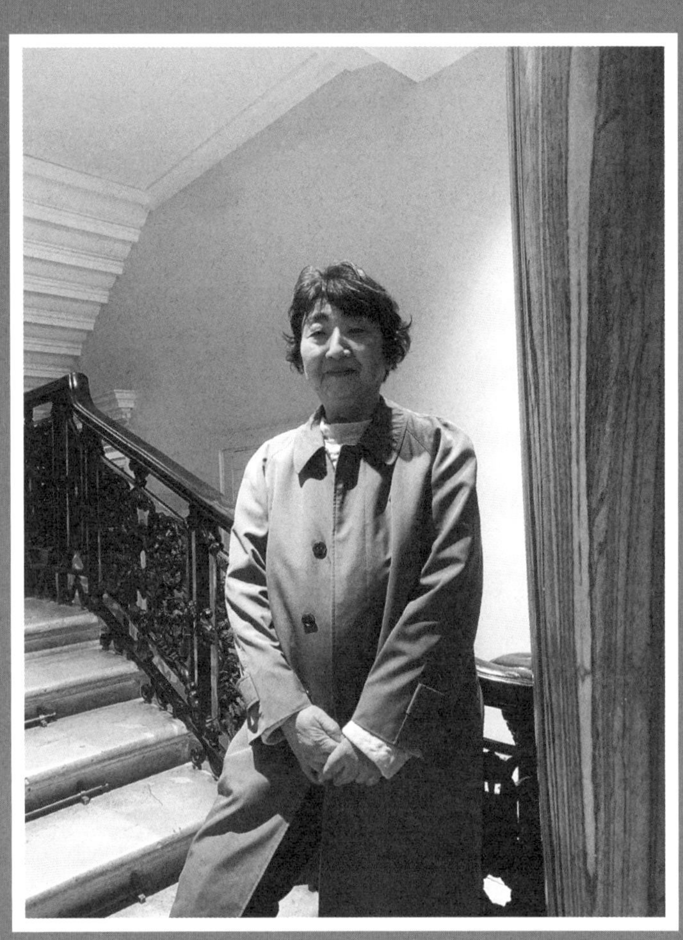

SHIOMI Nana (b. 1956)

Medium: Woodblock

As a printmaker, I have become addicted to thinking about ... dualisms. It is no coincidence that most of my work comprises two opposing sides, right and left.[1]

Shiomi Nana, 2024

Born in Osaka, Shiomi Nana began painting in oils when she was fourteen years old and developed an interest in modern art. After attending a seminar on Marcel Duchamp, an influential figure for many artists of the post-war generation, her interest moved to conceptual art. Shiomi studied oil painting and printmaking at the prestigious Tama Art University from 1975 to 1981, one of her teachers being Fukita Fumiaki (pp. 52–55). As a young student in Tokyo, her main influences were Western artists such as Jasper Johns and Andy Warhol.

Shiomi decided to continue her studies at the Royal College of Art in London. It was while studying there in 1989–91 that she discovered her 'Japaneseness', Shiomi explains. She decided on woodblock printing as her medium, combining the traditional technique with modern materials and tools. The technique being an important part of her process, Shiomi carves and prints her works herself, using large, thin pieces of plywood.

From an early age, Shiomi had a strong interest in Western culture, which was emphasised by her attending Christian schools. While abroad, Shiomi could begin to look at Japanese culture from an outside perspective and learned to appreciate her heritage. This meeting of cultures has naturally impacted her work and evoked a fascination for opposites, mirroring, and the idea of East and West, which are constant themes in her prints.

Shiomi began her most notable woodblock print series, *One Hundred Views of Mitate*, in 1998 and completed it in 2016. *Mitate* refers to a process of thought in Japanese culture, a form of analogy comparing one thing to another. The theme of 'one hundred views' is especially known from the three-volume book *One Hundred Views of Mt Fuji* (c. 1834–49) by Katsushika Hokusai, which included one of his many wave motifs, as well as Utagawa Hiroshige's single-sheet print series *One Hundred Famous Views of Edo* (1856–58).

In Shiomi's series, each 'view' is depicted as a theatre stage where an object or element that refers to an aspect of Japanese culture and daily life – such as the tea ceremony, Shintoism, noh and kabuki theatre, *shōji* sliding doors, Mt Fuji – is presented as the protagonist of a play. Taken out of their original context, these symbols of Japanese culture may take on a new meaning depending on the viewer.

1 Unless noted, the information and quotes in this text are based on an interview with Shiomi Nana in London, winter 2024–25.

Shiomi explains the meaning behind six of the elements in the series *One Hundred Views of Mitate*:

No. 35, *Front of the Back*:
'"Who is standing in front of your back?" is a lyric from a children's song, "Kagome, kagome", or, "who is in front of you when you look behind?" I matched the lyrics to this cat curled up and asleep.'

No. 45, *Peach*:
'Momotaro, the boy who was born from a peach and goes to exterminate demons, is a popular tale from Japanese folklore. Peaches have long been a familiar fruit to the Japanese.'

No. 46, *Tea Bowl*:
'Not only at the tea ceremony, but always people in Japan drink tea. So the tea bowl is one of the most familiar objects for Japanese people. Tea Bowl is a tiny existence in your hand. But when you look at it carefully, you can find the world. Hold your Tea Bowl. Hold your Universe.'

No. 53, *Fuji*:
'Mt Fuji is the highest and the most popular mountain in Japan. It is central to the Japanese belief in mountains and has long been the subject of poetry, paintings and prints.'

No. 84, *Night*:
'Before electric lights lit up the streets and houses, the night was long and dark. The darkness stimulated people's imagination, and many stories have been born from it. Japanese literature and drama cannot be discussed without the dark hours of the night.'

No. 93, *Mirror Cake*:
'*Kagami-mochi* is a traditional Japanese New Year decoration offered to the gods. It usually consists of two round rice cakes on top of each other with a Japanese orange on the top. The name *kagami-mochi* is due to its resemblance to the shape of an old mirror. The mirror was seen as the boundary between this world and the next. As a mirror-image-collector, I am interested in this kind of story.'

1 *Mitate No. 35 – Front of the Back (Ushiro no shōmen)*, 2000. Woodblock print
2 *Mitate No. 45 – Peach (Momo)*, 2001. Woodblock print
3 *Mitate No. 46 – Tea Bowl (Cha-wan)*, 2001. Woodblock print
4 *Mitate No. 53 – Fuji (Fuji)*, 2002. Woodblock print
5 *Mitate No. 84 – Night (Yoru)*, 2007. Woodblock print
6 *Mitate No. 93 – Mirror Cake (Kagami-mochi)*, 2015. Woodblock print

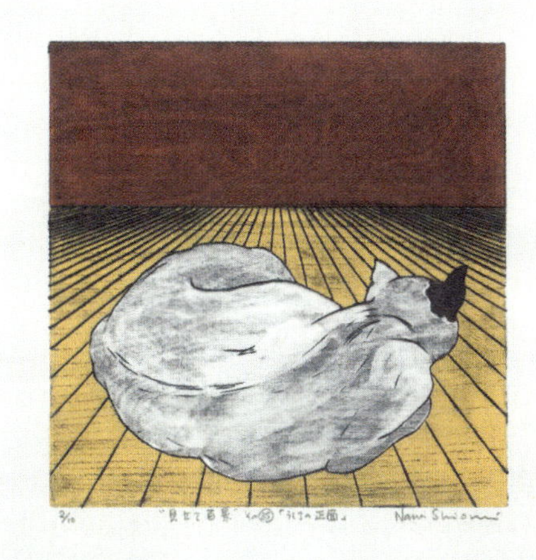

1

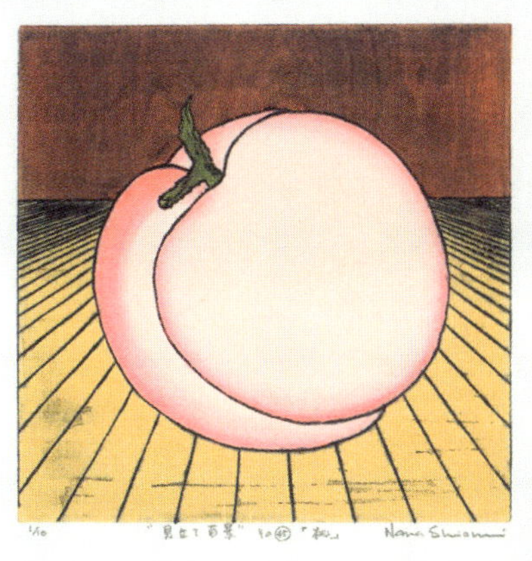

2

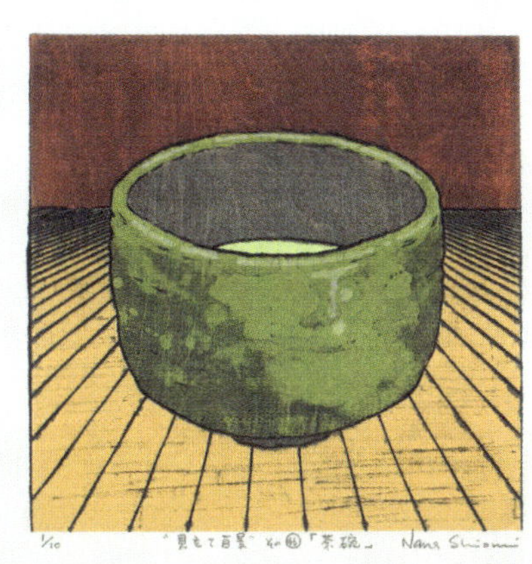

3

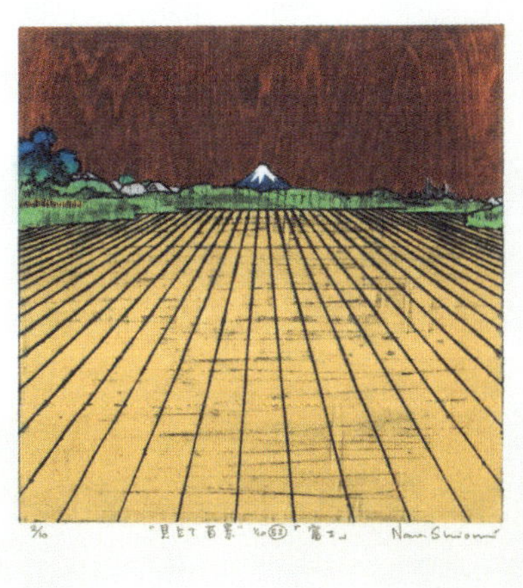

4

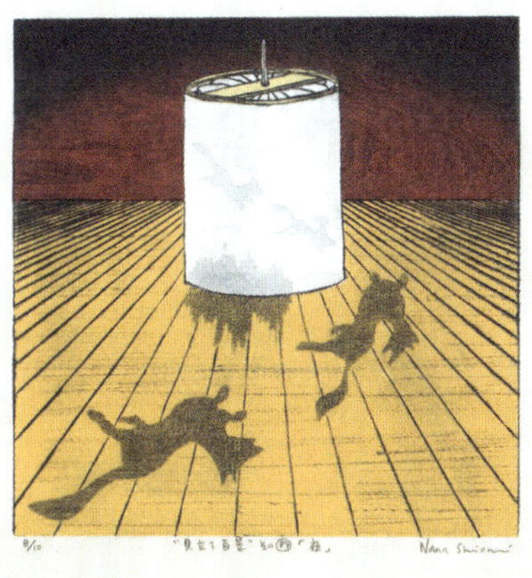

5

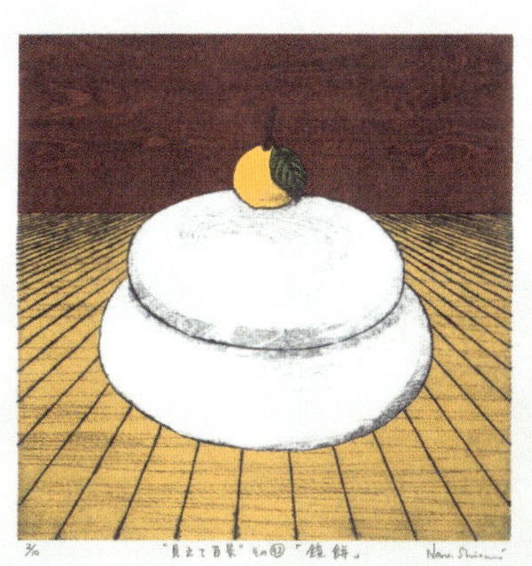

6

For her later prints *Hokusai's Wave (Right) – Happy Carp* and *Hokusai's Wave (Left) – Happy Dog*, from 2001, Shiomi plays with iconic Japanese imagery yet again. Here she pays tribute to Hokusai, whose influence Shiomi often refers to in her work, and to one of the most iconic motifs in art today (and the only one with its own emoji), Hokusai's *Under the Wave off Kanagawa*, published as a commercial endeavour. The series *Thirty-six Views of Mount Fuji*, of which *The Great Wave* was one of the first motifs, paid homage to Japan's holy mountain by depicting it from different perspectives and throughout the seasons. 'I cannot help thinking that the series is a set of self-portraits, as one's vantage point changes so the view of the mountain will also change,' Shiomi says. Today, Hokusai's iconic wave lives on as a global brand, featured on everything from travel brochures, posters, underwear and T-shirts to wine bottles, food packaging and book covers, all in various interpretations beyond its Japanese origins. It has also inspired numerous artists since the nineteenth century, who have taken up the subject in painting, printmaking, ceramics, design, fashion, music and more. In her work, Shiomi has brought the iconic image back to the woodblock medium – back to its roots, one could say. In *Hokusai's Wave*, Shiomi has set the stage once again, but the wave plays the main character. As opposed to the original image, where Hokusai brilliantly designed the cresting wave to emphasise the main figure of the series, Mt Fuji, seen in the distance, in Shiomi's work Fuji is not to be seen. Instead, the mountain has been replaced with rock formations that lead the viewer's eye to the back of the stage.

In *Happy Carp* – a symbol of luck in Japanese culture – Shiomi's wave is depicted from the right, the opposite direction of the wind-driven wave in Hokusai's print, which the boats, carrying fresh fish to the capital of Edo, are desperately trying to cut through. Shiomi returns to the theme of opposites, investigating right and left: 'One prerequisite of printmaking is that the plate and the print always exist in opposing configurations. Everywhere I look, I encounter similar dualistic principles such as left and right, front and back, up and down, East and West, male and female.'

Shiomi has had several group and solo exhibitions, including at Rabley Drawing Centre, Marlborough (2017), Pallant House Gallery, Chichester (2024) and the Embassy of Japan, London (2025). Shiomi has lived and worked in London since 1989. She plans to return to Japan in 2026.

Collections: British Museum, London; Bronx Museum of the Arts, New York; Pallant House Gallery, Chichester; Victoria and Albert Museum, London.

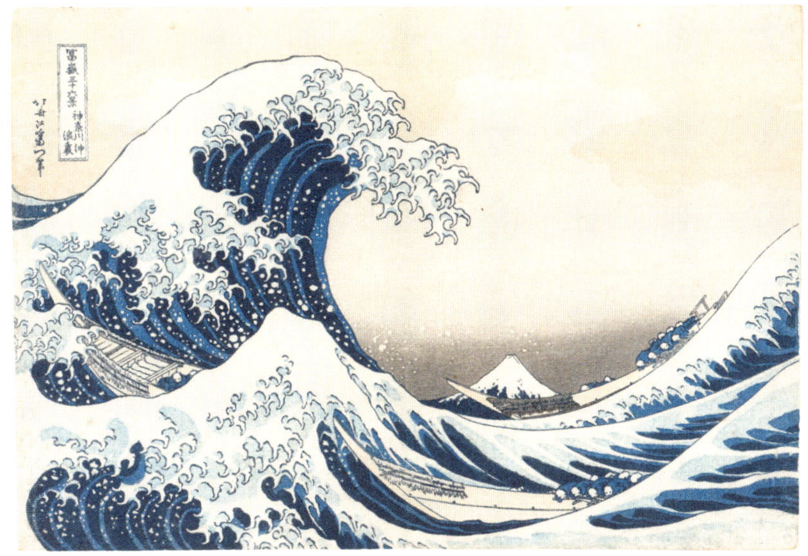

KATSUSHIKA Hokusai *Under the Wave off Kanagawa*, c.1830–32. Woodblock print

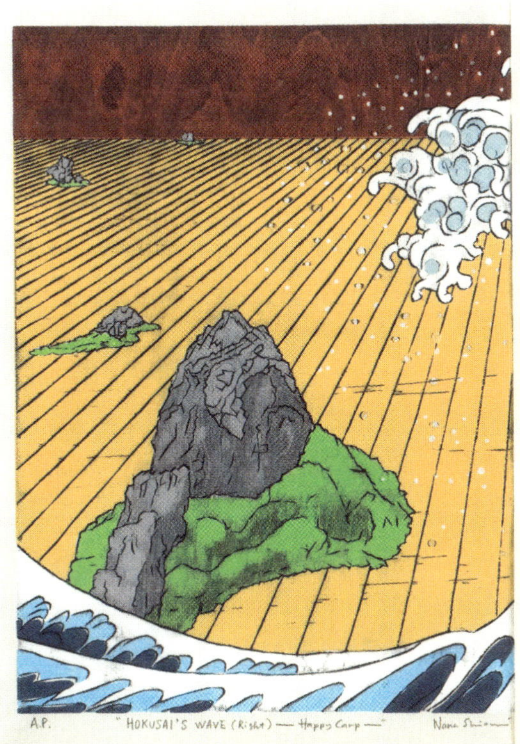

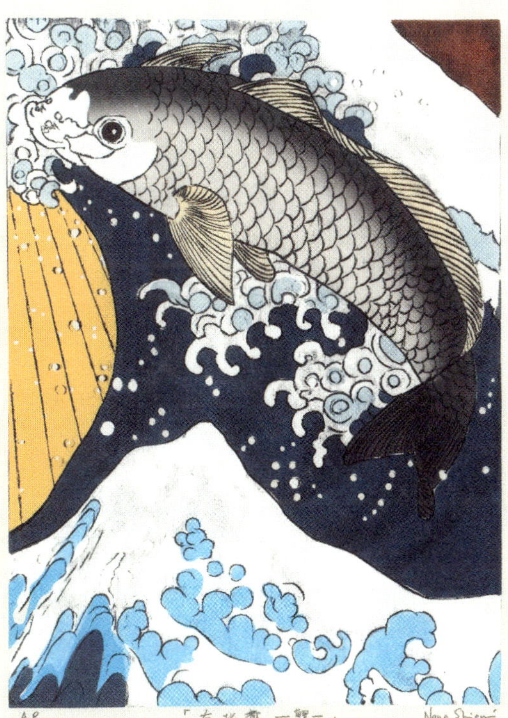

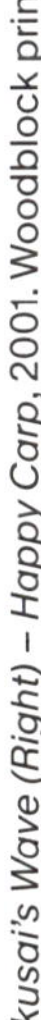
Hokusai's Wave (Right) – Happy Carp, 2001. Woodblock print

SHIOMI Nana

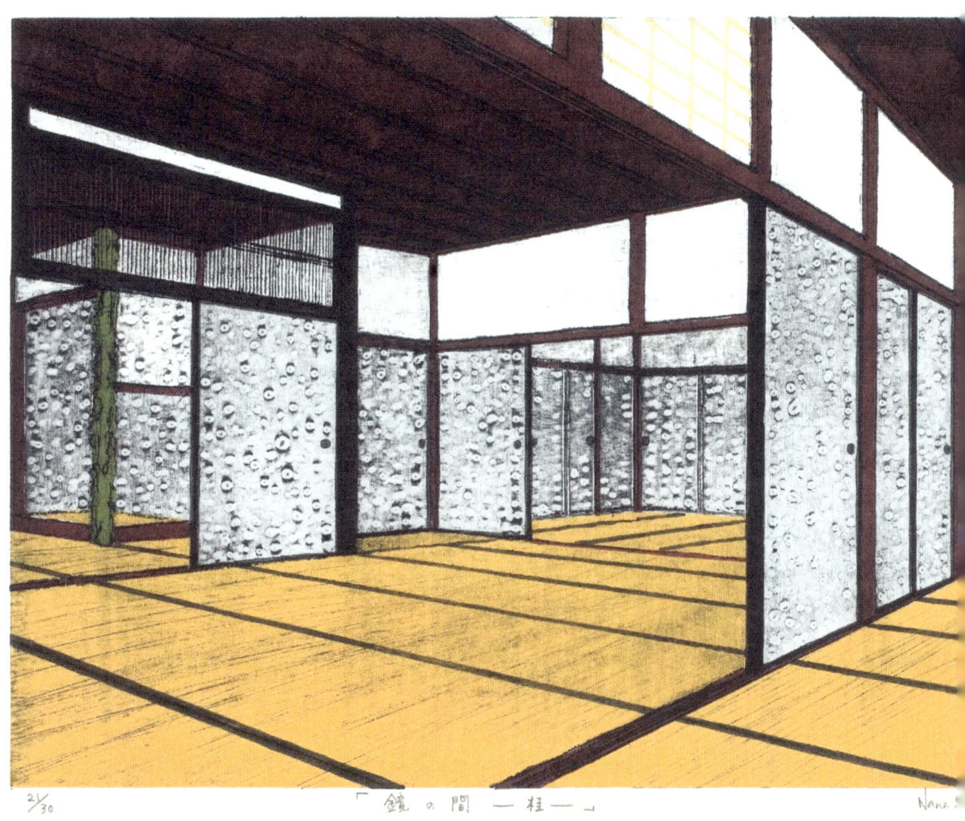
21/30
「鏡の間 ―柱―」

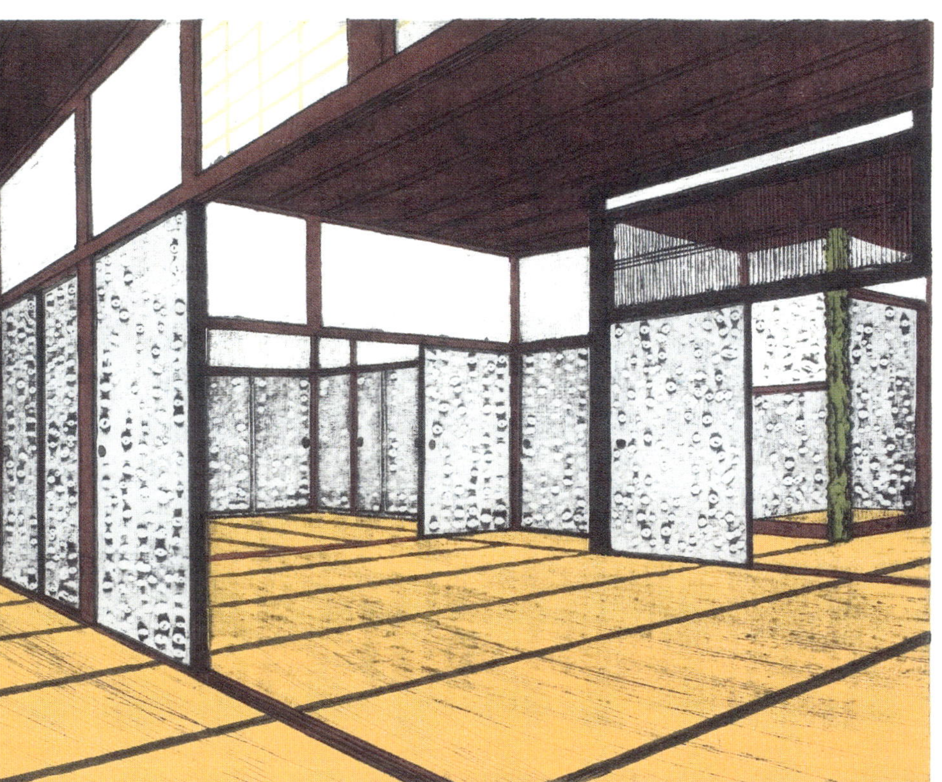

Mirror Room – Katsura, 2006. Woodblock print

SUGAÏ Kumi (1919–1996)

Medium:
Lithograph and silkscreen

He considers himself a painter first and foremost, but his vision seems superbly adapted to the print medium, as well. He likes the idea of selling a great many copies of his prints as very low prices.[1]

Frances Blakemore, 1975

A painter, sculptor and printmaker, Sugaï Kumi was born in Kobe and became a student at the Osaka School of Fine Arts in 1933, when he was fourteen, having first experimented with oil painting at the age of nine. He left art school, however, and, like many other artists at the time, he started working in advertising, working for Hankyu Railway and the *Asahi shimbun* newspaper during the Second World War.

In 1952 Sugaï settled in Paris, driven by an interest in European avant-garde painting. He became part of the École de Paris (School of Paris) and quickly established an international reputation. He enrolled at the Académie de la Grande Chaumière, which had been home to artists like Foujita (pp. 48–51) and Amedeo Modigliani.

From 1955 Sugaï studied lithography with Jean Pons (1913–2005), who had founded a studio in 1938, working with artists such as Wassily Kandinsky and Robert Delaunay (1885–1941). Sugaï also trained at Stanley William Hayter's print studio Atelier 17, where other renowned Japanese artists like Yoshida Masao (b. 1934) and Yayanagi Go (pp. 219–25) also learned printmaking techniques.

The 1950s and 1960s were busy decades for Sugaï both as a painter and printmaker, as he participated in numerous exhibitions in Paris and abroad. He had his first one-man show in Paris at Galerie Craven in 1954 and showed his work at the avant-garde Salon de Mai and Salon des Réalités Nouvelles from 1956. From 1957 he participated in every Tokyo International Biennial Exhibition of Prints and in 1960 won a National Museum of Modern Art award for his lithographs. He showed at Expo 58 in Brussels and at Documenta in Kassel (1959, 1964).

In 1959, he had a show at Kootz Gallery, one of the leading galleries at the time. That same year, two of Sugaï's works entered the MoMA collection: *Woman* (1957), a lithograph, and *Kabuki* (1958), a painting; the latter was included that same year in the exhibition *Recent Acquisitions*, which also counted among its works a large-scale example of Claude Monet's famous *Water Lillies* (1914–26).[2] In 1964, *Kabuki* was exhibited again, this time side by side with similar gestural abstract works by Hans Hartung (1904–1989) and Willi Baumeister (1889–1955), in MoMA's *Art in a Changing World, 1884–1964*. The Tate Gallery in London also included Sugaï with four paintings in the exhibition *Painting and Sculpture of the Decade* in 1964,[3] as did MoMA once again in its groundbreaking exhibition *The New Japanese Painting and Sculpture* two years later, where Onosato Toshinobu (pp. 134–37) was also presented. In 1965 Sügai participated in the São Paulo Biennial with fifteen large paintings,[4] winning the prize for best foreign painting.[5]
Sugaï's work could seemingly be found everywhere during these decades.

The 1960s saw a natural shift in Sugaï's work from mainly abstract calligraphic forms in subdued tones – 'a painterly use of lithography'[6] – to hard-edge

1 Frances Blakemore, *Who's Who in Modern Japanese Prints* (New York and Tokyo: Weatherhill, 1975), p. 190.
2 Museum of Modern Art, New York, *Recent Acquisitions*, 1959–60, master checklist, www.moma.org/calendar/exhibitions/2841.
3 *54–64: Painting and Sculpture of a Decade*, exh. cat., Tate Gallery, London (London: Calouste Gulbenkian Foundation, 1964), cat. nos. 218–21.
4 'JAPÃO', in *VIII Bienal de São Paulo: Catálogo* (Fundação Bienal de São Paulo, 1965), p. 305.
5 Ibid., p. 458.
6 Pat Gilmour, *Modern Prints* (London: Studio Vista, 1970), p. 112.
7 '1968: Tomio Miki, Kimi Sugai, Jiro Takamatsu, Katsuhiro Yamaguchi', Japan Pavilion Official Website, La Biennale di Venezia, https://venezia-biennale-japan.jpf.go.jp/e/art/1968.
8 *Kumi Sugaï: Les plus grands tableaux de ses dernières années*, exh. cat. (Paris: Maison de la Culture du Japon à Paris, 1999), p. 35.

geometry in vivid colours, leaning towards a Pop art style as well as evoking sign painting. When he represented Japan at the Venice Biennale in 1962 his 'abstract paintings composed of luculent tones and forms' won him the David E. Bright Foundation Award. He participated in the Venice Biennale again four years later with 'nine oil paintings composed of curved lines and geometric patterns, and four sculptural works that appeared like paintings emerging in three-dimensional form'.[7]

From the 1970s onwards, Sugaï began working in series, and from 1977 he focused mainly on the production of lithographs.[8] Sugaï created more than four hundred prints and continued to do so until 1995, the year before he died.

A major retrospective travelling exhibition was held at the Seibu Museum of Art, Tokyo (1983), and Ōhara Museum of Art, Kurashiki (1984). *Sugai / Matsutani: Print Works* was held at the Ashiya City Museum of Art and History in Hyōgo prefecture in 2013. The Umi-Mori Art Museum in Hiroshima celebrated the 100th anniversary of his birth with *Kumi Sugai: The Eternal Challenger* in 2019.

Collections: British Museum, London; Museum of Modern Art, New York; National Museum of Modern Art, Tokyo; Solomon R. Guggenheim Museum, New York; Victoria and Albert Museum, London.

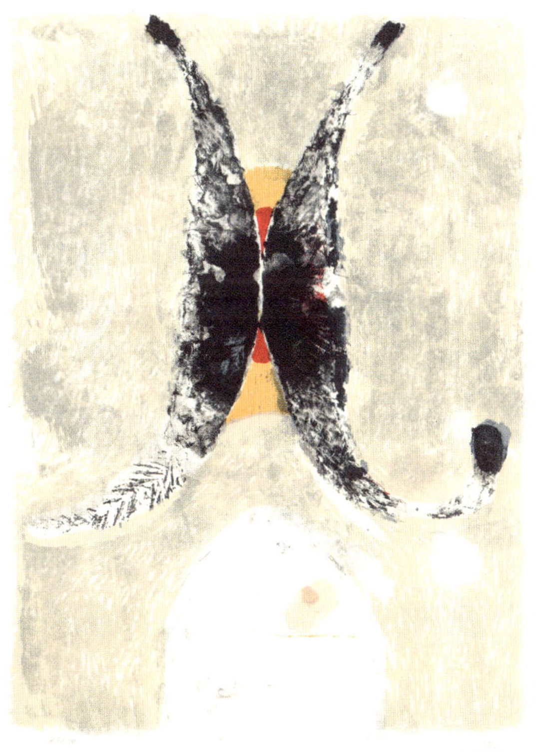

Woman (La Femme), 1957. Lithograph

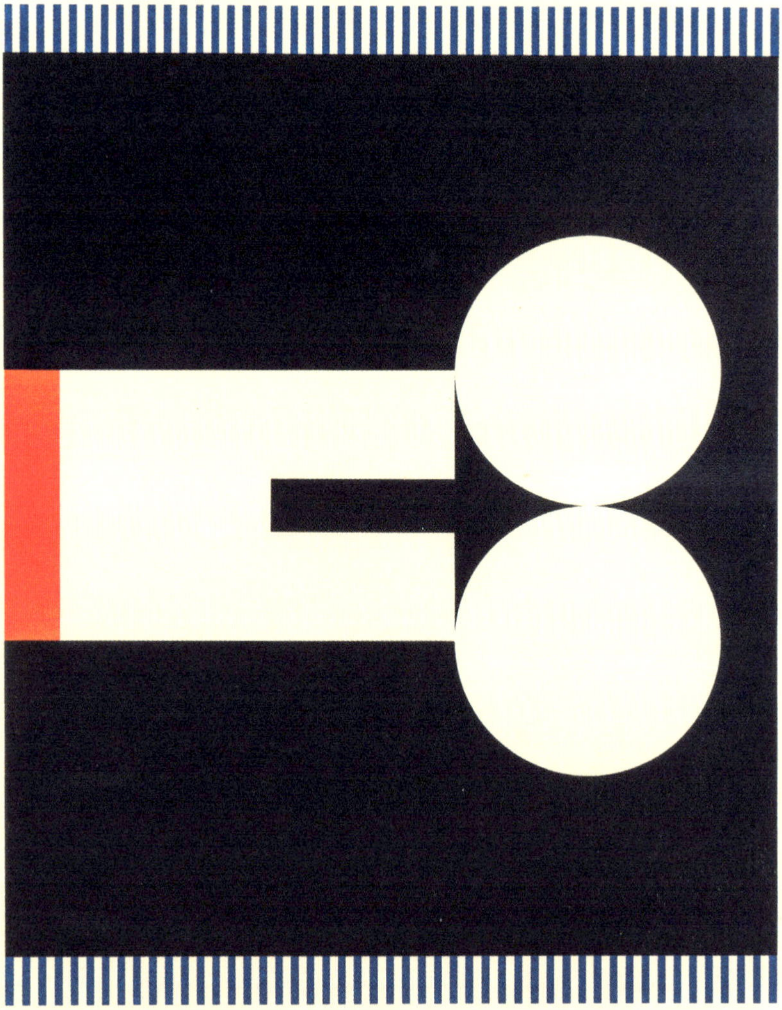

Untitled (Homage to Picasso), 1973. Silkscreen print

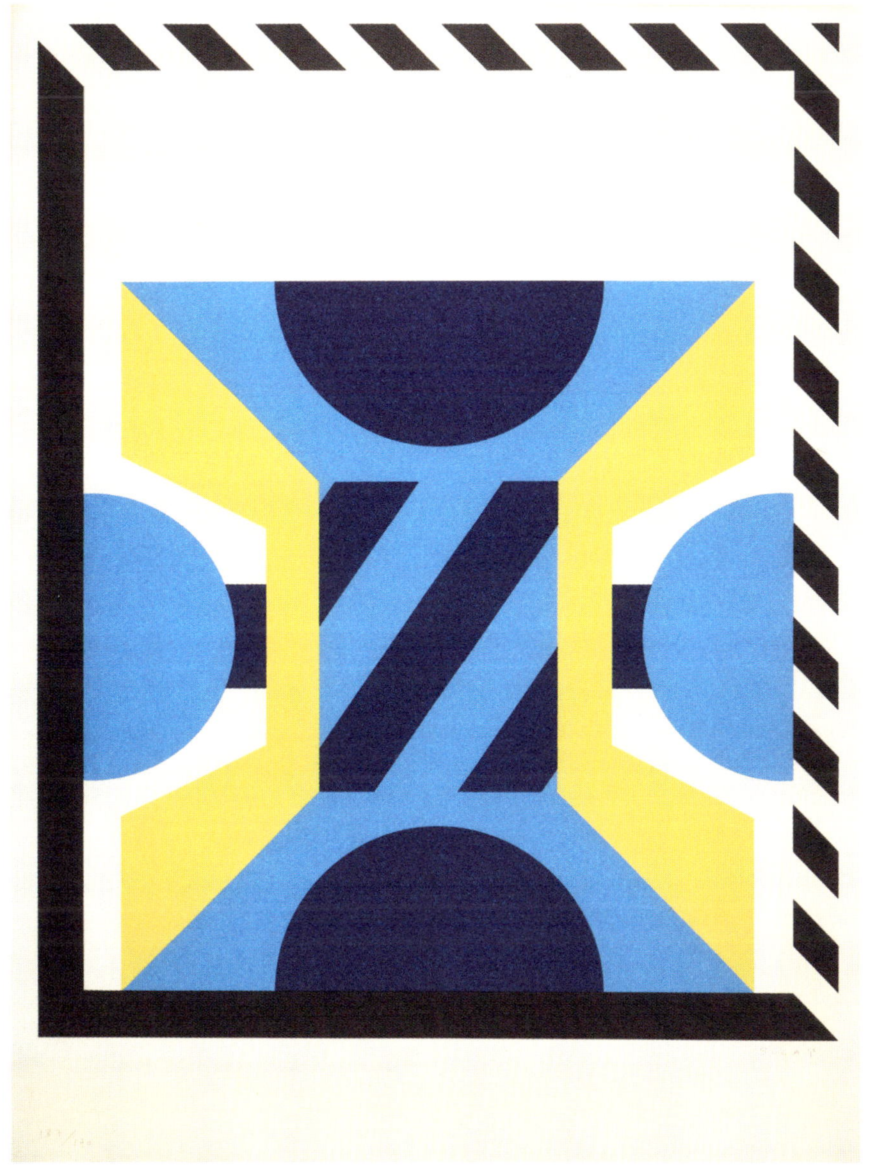

Signal A, 1974. Lithograph

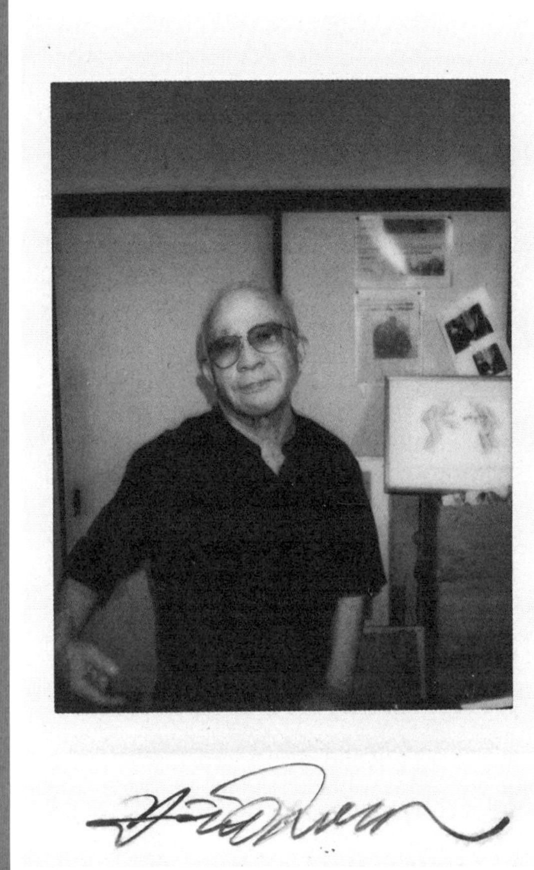

TAKEDA Hideo (b. 1948)

Medium:
Silkscreen

Takeda Hideo was born in Osaka and studied sculpture at Tama Art University in Tokyo, graduating in 1973. A visit to a bookshop, where he discovered the captivating illustrations in an issue of *Playboy*, changed his direction, influencing the repeated use of sexuality in his future work. Delving into the world of graphic art, he had his first collections of cartoons – expressing a Western influence – published in the 1970s under the titles *Madame Chang's Chinese Restaurant* (1973), *Yogi* (1974) and *Opera Glasses* (1977). 'When I was 21 and studying sculpture at university, I started drawing cartoons. I decided not to draw things that only Japanese people can understand.'[1]

In 1993, the British Museum in London held the first solo exhibition of Takeda's work in a museum. True to Takeda's self-perception, it was called *Takeda Hideo and the Japanese Cartoon Tradition*; 'I am a cartoonist and a thinker, not an artist,' he insists. Throughout his artistic career, Takeda has worked in many different media: sculpture, painting, drawing and printmaking – which, one could argue, does make him an artist, even a multifaceted one. But, artist or not, Takeda's works are created by strong lines and a mixture of genius, humour, the grotesque and the bizarre.

In his work, Takeda comments on Japanese history and traditional culture with a modern-day twist. He created his first series of silkscreen prints in 1976 in collaboration with the printer and silkscreen artist Taninaka Kazuo, resulting in eleven designs. The series is titled *Monmon*, which is Japanese slang for 'tattoo'. Takeda has taken the classic Japanese tattoo design synonymous with the yakuza, covering the arms, chest, back and upper legs, and presented it in an absurd, frequently comical fashion by depicting male bodies stripped naked, their full-body tattoos exposed, in a series of unconventional poses – one is even wearing pink women's panties. In another print, one character is busy defecating on the floor; the pile of faeces is also tattooed. A clever but brutal motif from the series is of a tattooed human skin hanging on a line to dry on a red background. The series won Takeda the Bungeishunjū Manga Award, an award supporting satirical and comic manga artists since 1955.

Takeda began his most famous series of silkscreen prints, *Genpei*, in 1985, again collaborating with Taninaka. In 2001, it was featured on the cover of the 46th annual College Women's Association catalogue. It is based on the civil war between the Minamoto (Genji) and Taira (Heike) clans during the Heian period (794–1185). The war, which lasted from 1180 to 1185, was the culmination of a decades-long conflict over military power and thus control over Japan. In 1179, in a coup d'état, the Taira clan removed their rivals from all government posts and established themselves as a sitting power with headquarters in Fukuhara (now Kobe). But the following year, the Minamoto clan, led by Minamoto Yoritomo, rebelled against the Taira, who had become complacent in their position of power. They beat the Taira in one battle after another.

This medieval feud has traditionally been a popular theme in Japanese art, with artists of the traditional Tosa and Kanō schools taking it up in paintings from the fourteenth century onwards, and *ukiyo-e* artists depicting the historical battles in woodblock prints. Takeda has continued the tradition, bringing Japanese history into the modern day with a humorous and somewhat grotesque approach. In his chaotic battle scenes, the warriors wear helmets and weapons from the medieval period, but they are almost naked, only 'armoured' with full-body tattoos like yakuza gangsters and the traditional

1 Unless noted, information in this text is based on interviews with Takeda Hideo in Osaka, 2022–23, and email correspondence, 2022–25.

Japanese *fundoshi* undergarment. Some are riding horses, while others are 'riding' on women in dominating poses. In the midst of the chaos and clashing bodies, it can be difficult to distinguish between the sexes.

Takeda's graphic style, 'combining clear, firm black line with bright, almost garish colour',[2] bears a strong resemblance to the nineteenth-century *ukiyo-e* artists, especially the woodblock prints of kabuki actors and samurai warriors by the Utagawa school. The Japanese print tradition undoubtedly echoes throughout Takeda's work, which also contains references to classic Japanese iconography, such as the setting sun and the wave motif so well known from Hokusai and later artists. However, Takeda continually claims that the world of Japanese things does not interest him, specifically the *Genpei* series – which gained him international acclaim – and seeks to distance himself from these things. Instead, he acknowledges the British cartoonist Ronald Searle (1920–2011) and French caricaturist Tomi Ungerer (1931–2019) as influences in his work. Ungerer especially, known for his explicit motifs, spurred Takeda to continue drawing, 'with the goal of beating him'. Takeda and Ungerer had a two-man show in Paris in 2006.

Another of Takeda's print series is *Altamira: Moving Sculptures*, begun as illustrations in 1979, which features animal skeletons in motion in often humorous settings. He made around forty different designs for this series, which was exhibited in Tokyo in 1994. Takeda's trademark absurdity and satirical approach is even more present in the *Inferno* series, begun in 2000, which depicts 'hell for women'. The sarcastic moral is that if a woman doesn't take good care of her partner, she can end up there. Again, Takeda works with the contrast between the grotesque and violent and the erotic and pleasurable, producing 'a kind of brutal sexuality'.[3] Takeda's absurd visual world is to be taken with a large dose of irony and humorous distance.

The interplay of the absurd, the satirical, the grotesque and the erotic is typical of Takeda, whose work could be characterised at times as modern *shunga*. This erotic art genre, arising in the Edo period, depicted many facets of sex and sexuality in Japan and was enjoyed in *ukiyo-e* prints, books and paintings by both men and women of all social classes, not bound by any strict moral or religious code relating to sex.[4] Indeed, the images were often meant to be humorous. Many *ukiyo-e* artists took up *shunga* during their careers, and its artworks are of the same high artistic and technical quality as other genres. Artists such as Kitagawa Utamaro and Hokusai created some of the most famous *shunga* motifs (p. 194).[5]

Takeda's works play an important role in the story of modern Japanese printmaking. Both with his first series of prints, *Monmon*, and in the later *Genpei*, Takeda continues a tradition of printmaking in Japan dating back centuries. Takeda lives and works in Osaka and continues to develop new styles of painting and drawing for many different themes, though he has not created prints in the last couple of decades. However, it seems only a matter of time before he finds the right printer to collaborate with.

Collections: British Museum, London; Harvard Art Museums, Cambridge, MA; National Museum of Asian Art, Washington, DC; Portland Art Museum.

2 Lawrence Smith and Sasaki Seiichi, eds, 'Preface', in *Takeda Hideo and the Japanese Cartoon Tradition at the British Museum*, exh. cat. (London: Minato Ishikawa Associates and British Museum, 1993), n.p.

3 Ibid.

4 See Rosina Buckland, *Shunga: Erotic Art in Japan* (London: British Museum Press, 2010), p. 12.

5 The meaning of the word *shunga* is explained ibid., pp. 16–17.

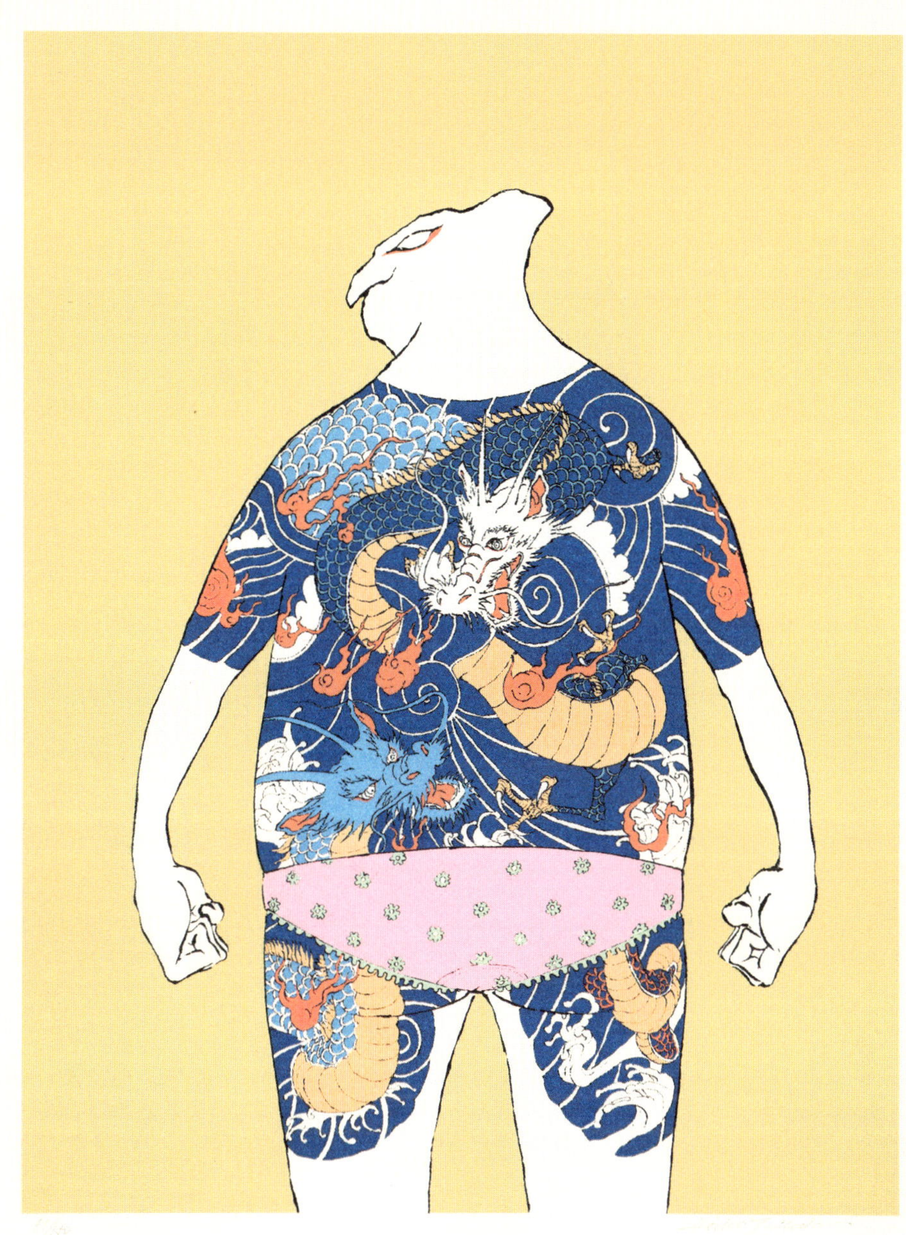

Monmon (panties), 1976. Silkscreen print

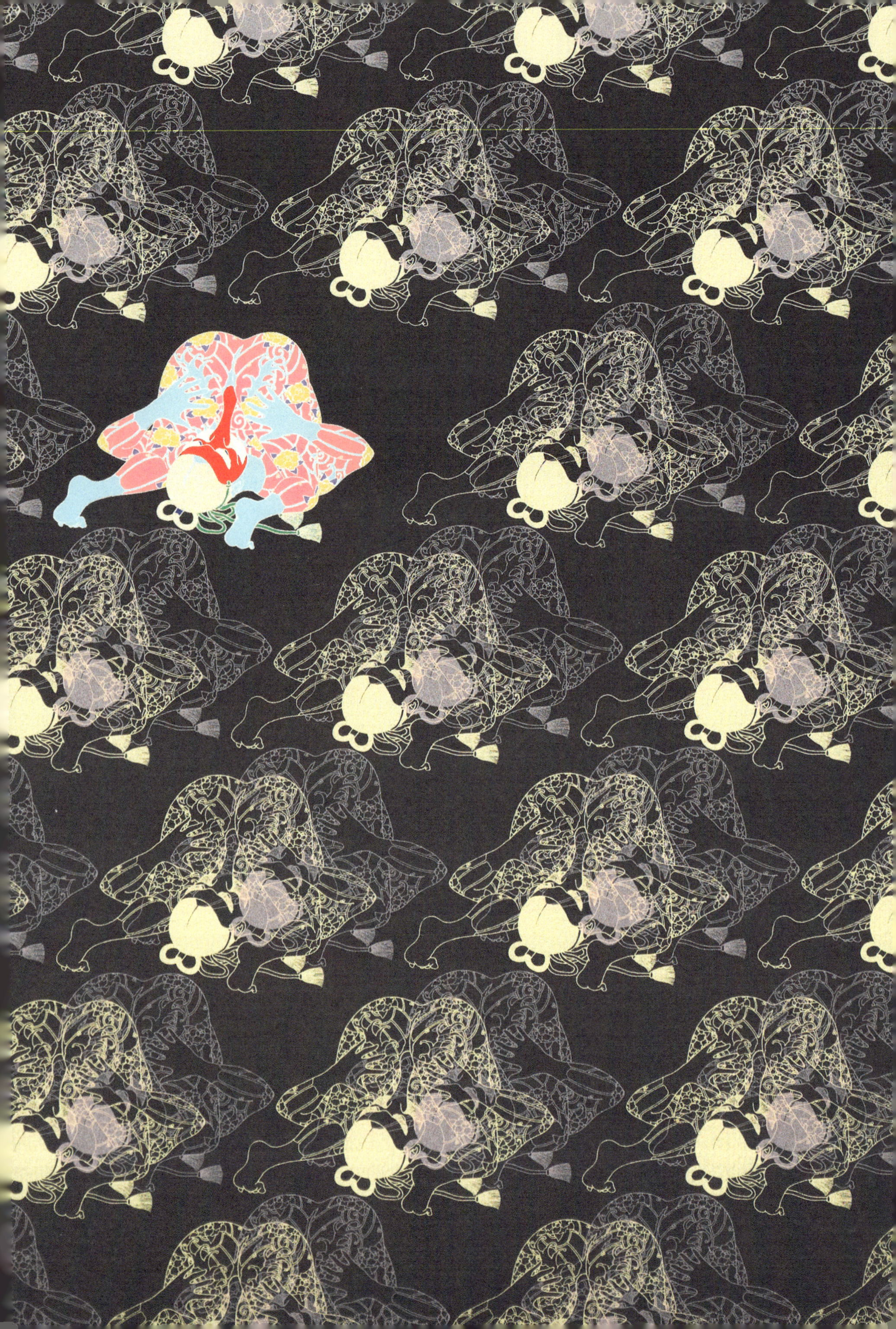

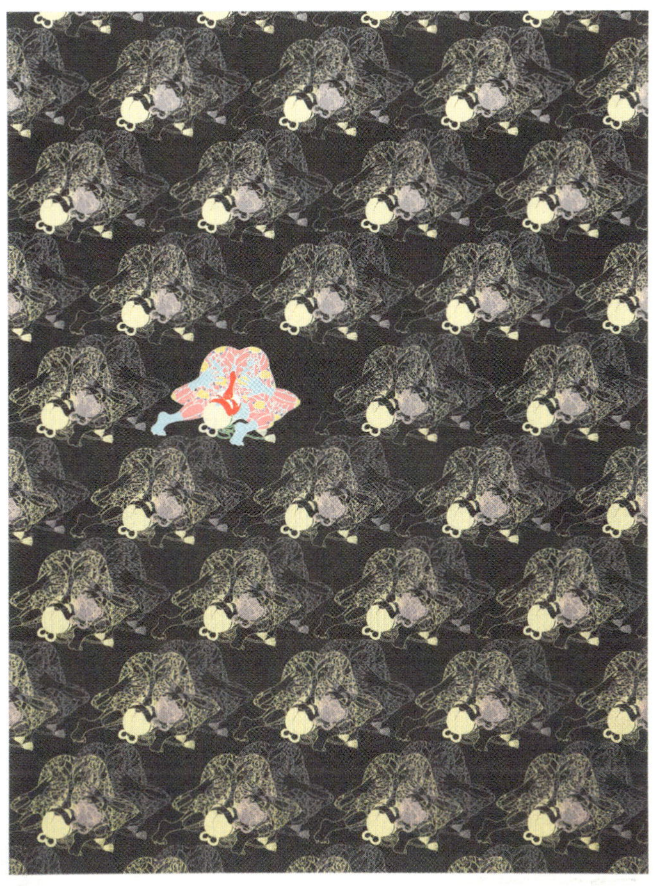

Ushiwaka-maru, 1985–99. Silkscreen print

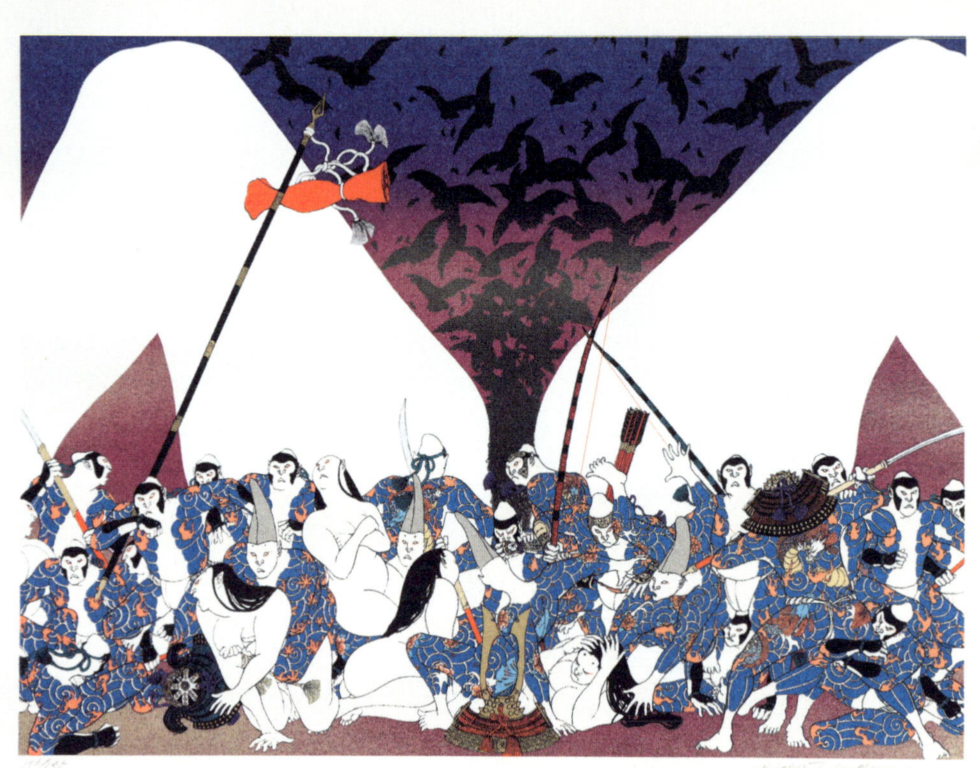

The Battle at Fuji River, 1985–99. Silkscreen print

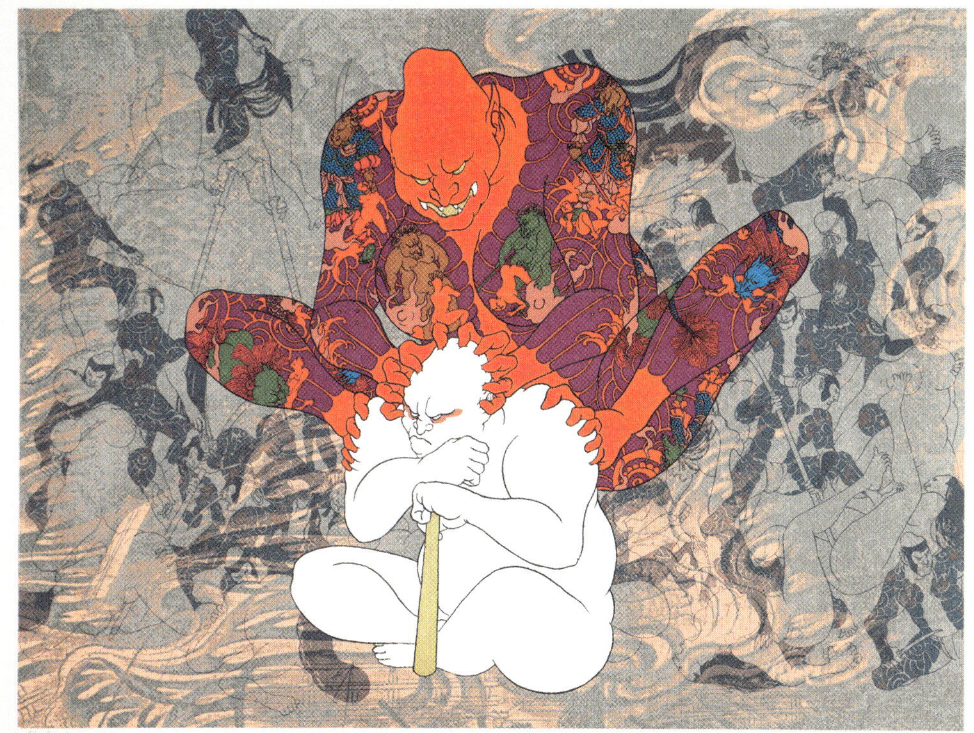

Taira no Kiyomori Dies of Illness, 1985–99. Silkscreen print

The Heike Clan's Capital. In July 1183, as the forces of Minamoto Yoshinaka (cousin and rival of Minamoto Yoritomo) approached Kyoto, the Taira clan fled the capital, taking with them Emperor Antoku, grandson of the military leader Taira no Kiyomori, and the Three Sacred Treasures of imperial Japan.

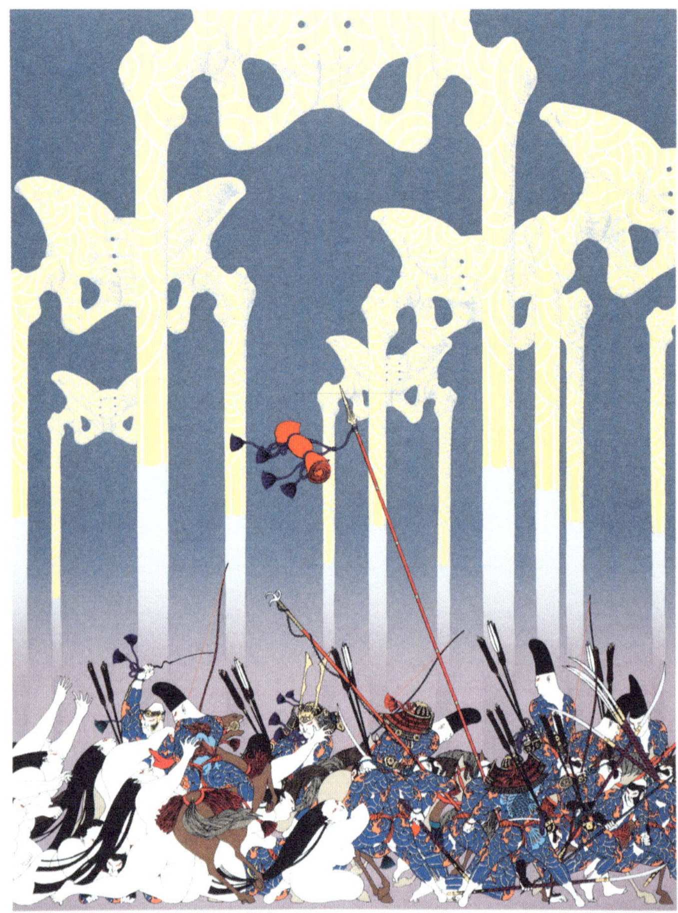

The Heike Clan's Capital, 1985–99. Silkscreen print

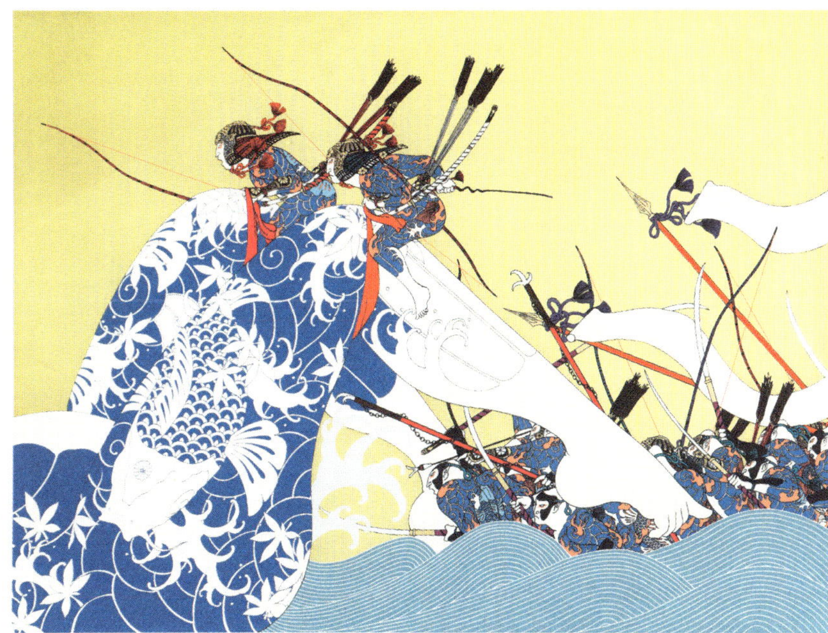

The Battle of the First Guard at Uji River, 1985–99. Silkscreen print

The Battle of the First Vanguard at Uji River. In January 1184, Minamoto no Yoshitsune, half-brother of Yoritomo and one of the most skilled and popular samurai in Japanese history, led his horsemen across the river and defeated his cousin Yoshinaka, who was trying to take command of the Minamoto clan.

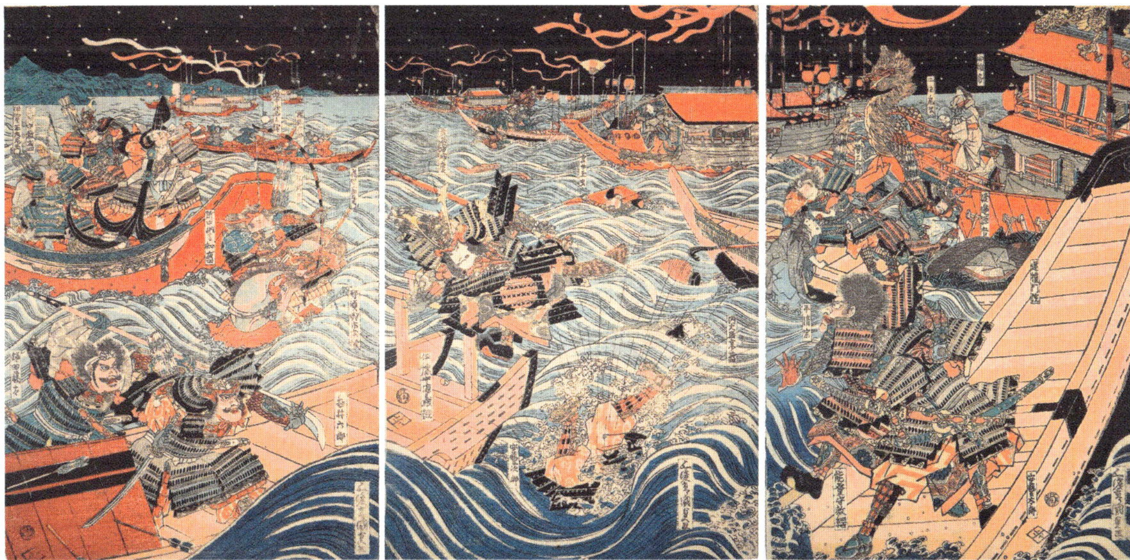

UTAGAWA Kunisada

The Battle of Yashima in the Genpei War, c. 1838. Woodblock print

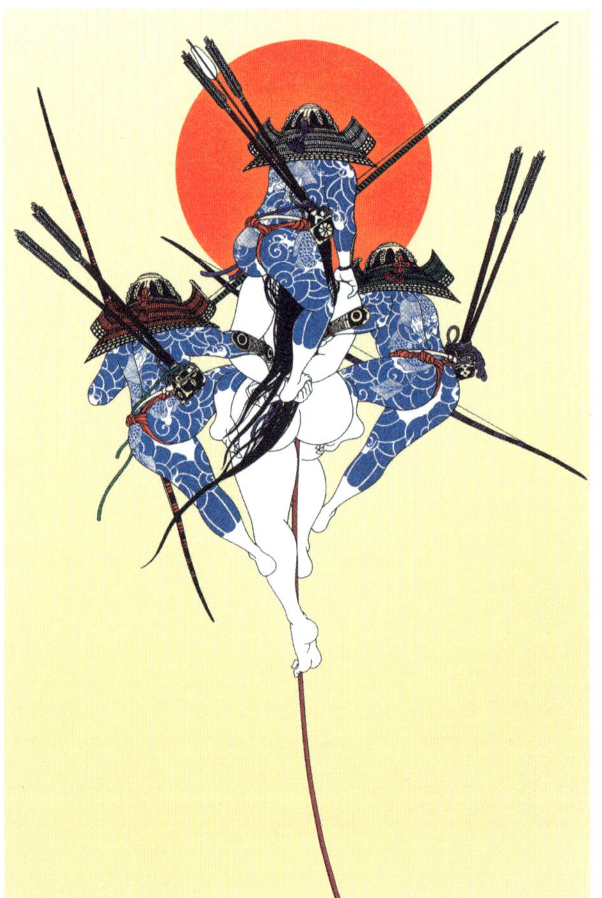

Dan-no-ura Genji, 1985–99. Silkscreen print

After five years of war, in March 1185 the Minamoto family were finally victorious over the Taira clan, and Yoritomo took over the government. This marked the end of the Heian period and the beginning of the Kamakura period (1185–1333), when the capital moved to Kamakura in eastern Japan and Yoritomo became head of Japan's first shogunate (*bakufu*).

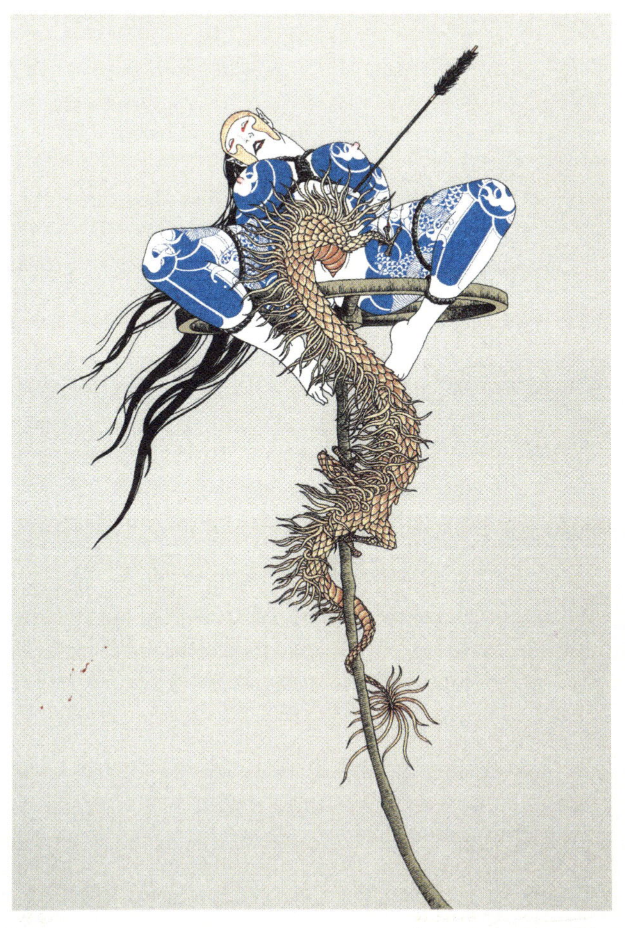

Inferno, 2000. Silkscreen print

TAKEI Takeo (1894–1983)

Medium:
Stencil, woodblock and others

His work is very stylish, along Western-style sophisticated lines. His engraving is very accurate and beautiful, and his printing is skilful, clear and severe.[1]

Onchi Kōshirō, 1965

Takei Takeo was born in Okaya in Nagano prefecture and began drawing as a child. He studied Western-style painting at the Tokyo School of Fine Arts, graduating in 1919. Here he had a brief exposure to etching when he was recruited for a course in the technique that lacked students due to a shortage of interest.[2] He found his early influences in the art and literary magazine *Shirakaba*, through which, like many of his contemporaries, he learned about Paul Cézanne, Paul Gauguin and Vincent van Gogh.[3] Later he gained an interest in Paul Klee (1879–1940), whose influence can be clearly detected in part in Takei's imaginative dreamworlds.

Although Takei worked both as a painter and a print artist throughout his prolific career, he left the biggest mark as an illustrator of children's books and magazines. The father of *dōga*, Takei coined and popularised the term, which can be translated as 'pictures for children'.[4] His aim was for children to come into contact with real art through imagination and creativity.

Following the Meiji period, the Taishō period (1912–26) saw the spread of a Westernised culture of consumption among urban middle-class families and their children. This manifested in a boom in exhibitions, department stores and, not least, literature aimed at children, including the launch of several illustrated magazines that mixed Western and Japanese culture: *Kodomo no tomo* (Children's Friend) in 1914, *Akai tori* (Red Bird) in 1918 and *Kodomo no kuni* (Children's Country) in 1922.[5] This new genre of artistic and educational children's magazines included pictures, stories, songs, dances, plays and articles on handicrafts and played a central role in the culture of children in Japan in the pre-war period. After graduating, Takei began illustrating for *Kodomo no kuni*, among others, contributing numerous illustrations as well as original stories throughout its run, including the cover of the first edition.

In 1925, Takei organised the *Takeo Takei Dōga Exhibition* at the Ginza Shiseido Gallery, which marked the first use of the term *dōga*. Two years later he founded the Japan Association of Illustration for Children (Nihon Dōgaka Kyōkai) with fellow artists and illustrators Okamoto Kiichi (1888–1930) and Shimizu Yoshio (1891–1954).

Takei also knew Onchi Kōshirō (pp. 130–33), who had been a contributor to *Kodomo no kuni*. Onchi was a member of Han no Kai, a group of print artists organised by Takei from 1935, who met and exchanged printed New Year's cards.[6] From 1935 until his death, Takei also self-published a series of miniature print art books, *Kanpon*, for which he used an impressively wide range of printing techniques, from self-carved woodblock to colour stencil, wood engraving, letterpress, tile printing and colour gravure.[7]

Takei exhibited two prints at the first CWAJ show in 1956 (*Snow* and *White and Black*), as well as at the two following shows. He was represented in the

1 Kōshirō Onchi, 'The Modern Japanese Print: An Internal History of the *Sosaku Hanga* Movement', *Ukiyo-e Art* (Japan Ukiyo-e Society), no. 11 (1965), p. 18.
2 Oliver Statler, *Modern Japanese Prints: An Art Reborn* (Rutland, VT: Charles E. Tuttle Co., 1956), p. 95.
3 Ibid., pp. 95–96.
4 Takei merged the words *dōwa* (children's stories) and *dōyō* (children's songs). See Jinnō Yuki, 'Consumer Consumption for Children: Conceptions of Children in the Work of Taishō-Period Designers', in *Child's Play: Multi-Sensory Histories of Children and Childhood in Japan*, ed. Sabine Frühstück and Anne Walthall (Oakland, CA: University of California Press, 2017), p. 99, n. 9.
5 See Jinnō, 'Consumer Consumption for Children', for an in-depth examination of the subject.
6 Lawrence Smith, *Japanese Print during the Allied Occupation, 1945–1952: Onchi Kōshirō, Ernst Hacker and the First Thursday Society*, exh. cat. (London: British Museum Press, 2002), p. 32.
7 The various techniques are listed in detail in Rachel Saunders, 'Gyre and Gimble: The Artist Books of Takei Takeo', *Print Quarterly* 30, no. 1 (2013), pp. 37–39, and Statler, *Modern Japanese Prints*, pp. 94–95.

first International Biennial Exhibition of Prints in Tokyo in 1957. *The Takeo Takei Exhibition Celebrating 130 Years of His Birth: Welcome to the World of Fantasy* was held at Meguro Museum of Art, Tokyo, in 2024.

Collections: Art Institute of Chicago; British Museum, London; ILF Douga Museum of Art, Nagano; Meguro Museum of Art, Tokyo; National Museum of Modern Art, Tokyo.

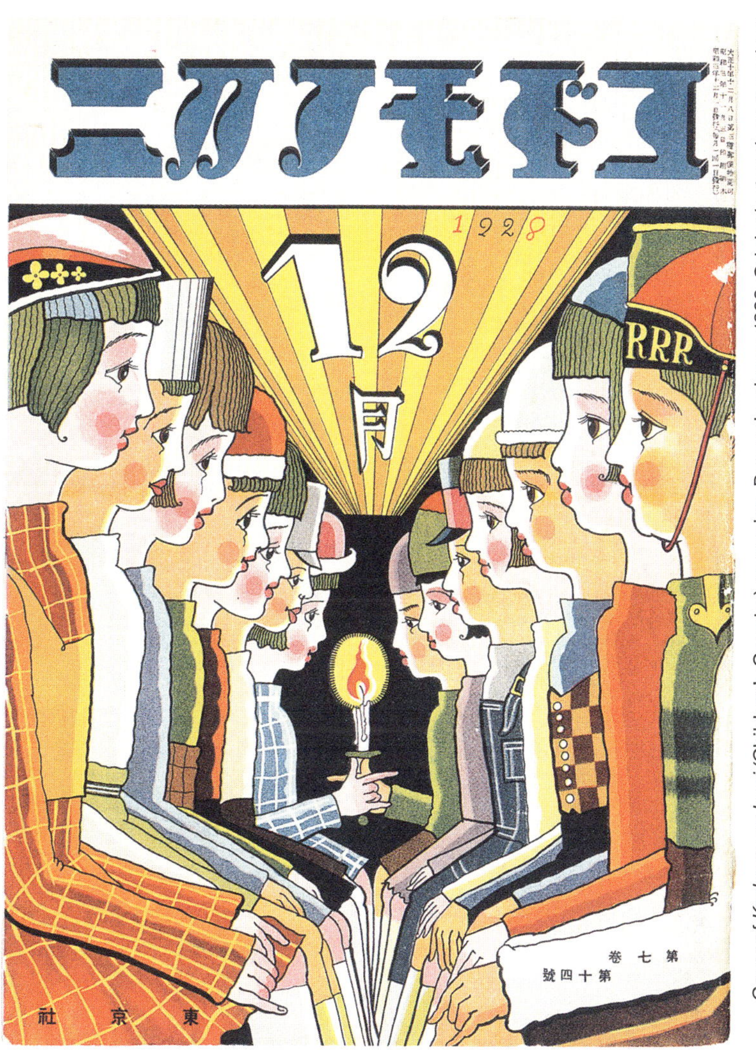

Cover of *Kodomo no kuni* (Children's Country) magazine, December issue, 1928. Original artwork: watercolour

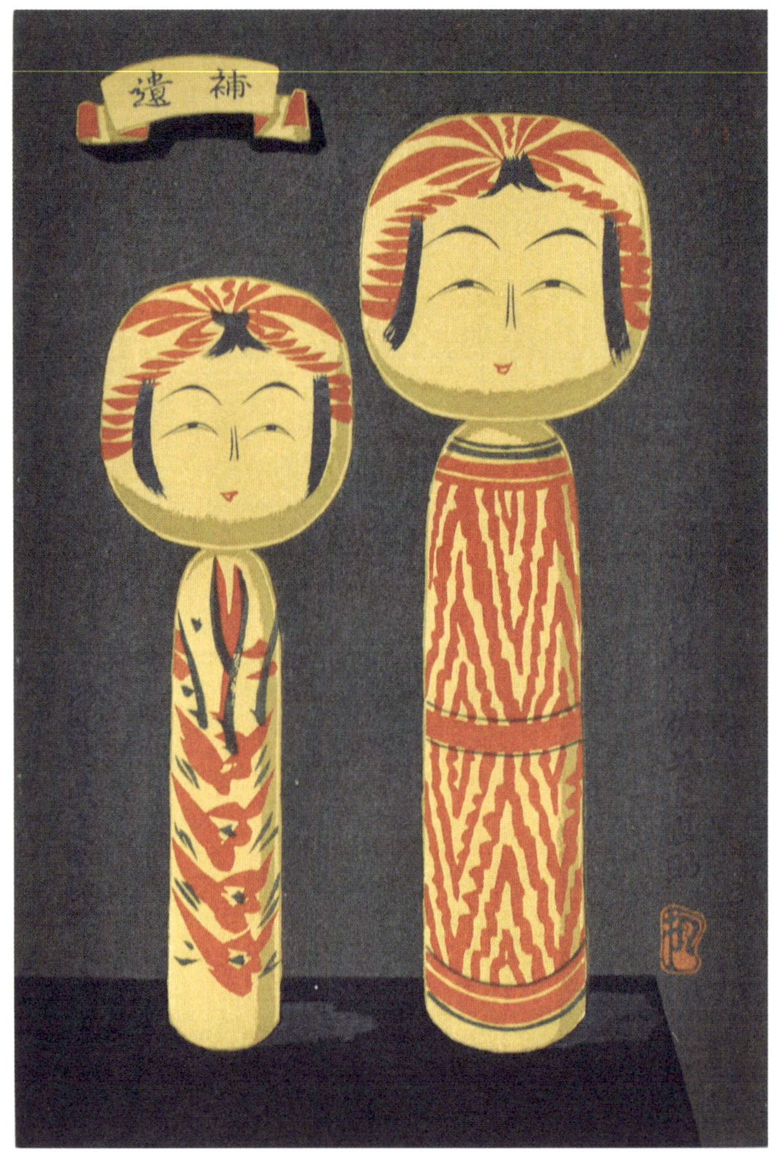

Treasured Kokeshi Dolls, undated. Woodblock print

Rock-Paper-Scissors, 1952. Woodblock print

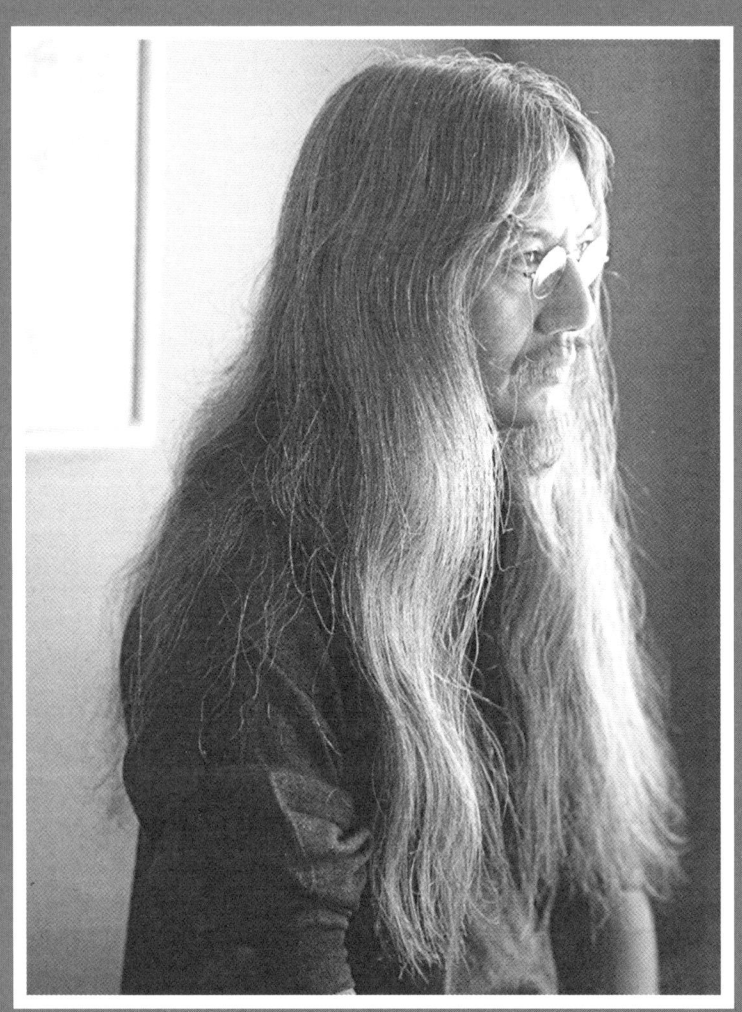

TERAOKA Masami (b.1936)

Medium:
Etching, silkscreen, woodblock and others

Masami Teraoka is more than a genius; he is a hero. His work is an inspiration.[1]

Roger Keyes, 1988

Born in the harbour town of Onomichi in southwest Honshu, Teraoka Masami has spent most of his adult life in the United States, and since 1980 he has lived and worked in Honolulu. The clash between Japanese and American culture has been an ongoing theme in Teraoka's work. Both his paintings as well as his prints investigate modern-day Western themes combined with *ukiyo-e*-style aesthetics and iconography of the Edo period, making Teraoka's work a significant link to the centuries-old print tradition of Japan.

Like others of his Japanese contemporaries such as Ay-O (pp. 31–43), Kusama Yayoi (pp. 94–99) and Shinohara Ushio (pp. 155–59), Teraoka was drawn to American art and culture in his youth. Following his studies of aesthetics at Kwansei Gakuin University in Kobe, in 1961, at the age of 25, Teraoka moved to the United States, where he graduated in fine arts from the Otis Art Institute in Los Angeles in 1968.

Primarily a painter, from 1966 Teraoka also dived into printmaking using a number of different techniques and processes, which he has continued throughout his career. These include *Ukiyo-e Series* (1972), *New Views of Mt Fuji* (1977) and *McDonald's Hamburgers Invading Japan* (begun in the 1970s). However, Teraoka's work is connected not only to the medium but also to the aesthetics of the classic Japanese woodblock print. His bold and graphic style is a modern take on *ukiyo-e* by artists such as Katsushika Hokusai and Utagawa Kunisada.

Teraoka sees his works as like modern-day kabuki plays: 'The people and props that I use are symbols of both the contemporary life I experience and of the venerable Japanese traditions I admire. I also look at my paintings as *Kabuki* plays, the ancient Japanese equivalent to movies.'[2]

In his works Teraoka comments, often with a humorous approach, on modern-day society and its dilemmas – including serious topics, as seen in his *AIDS Series*, begun in the 1980s. He combines traditional Japanese elements and aesthetics borrowed from *ukiyo-e* with contemporary pop culture. His visual world is inhabited by Japanese archetypes like the geisha, samurai, ghosts and foxes, transporting the viewer back to Edo-period Japan. That is, until the numerous anachronisms reveal themselves: a hamburger, a condom wrapper, a scuba-diving mask or a woman in kimono with an ice cream cone.

Subjects referring to the traditional Japanese erotic genre of *shunga* (see p. 174) are also numerous in Teraoka's prints, including in *Woman and Iris* (silkscreen, 1980); *Geisha and Ghost Cat* from the *AIDS Series* (aquatint and sugar-lift etching, 1989) and *Sarah and Octopus/Seventh Heaven* (woodblock print, 2001). In *Sarah and Octopus/Seventh Heaven*, also called *Giant Octopus Flower Opening Series*,[3] Teraoka takes up the subject of a female diver and an octopus, an image also found in his earlier watercolour *Wave Series* (1984). He places himself in the *ukiyo-e* tradition of depicting *ama* ('sea women', free divers who collect abalone and pearls) in eroticised,

1 Quoted in Howard A. Link, *Waves and Plagues: The Art of Masami Teraoka*, exh. cat., The Contemporary Museum, Honolulu (San Francisco: Chronicle Books, 1988), p. 7.

2 Teraoka Masami quoted in 'Masami Teraoka and Japanese Ukiyo-e Prints', https://nga.gov.au/exhibitions/masami-teraoka-and-japanese-ukiyo-e-prints.

3 The 'series' is a pun written in two characters that mean 'butt exposed'. Thank you to Catharine Clark Gallery, San Francisco, for sharing the information related to Teraoka's prints.

fantastical images by artists such as Utagawa Kuniyoshi, Toyohara Chikanobu (1838–1912) and, not least, Hokusai.

In fact, Teraoka's print is a contemporary take on Hokusai's erotic image popularly known as *The Dream of the Fisherman's Wife*. Perhaps the most famous of all *shunga* images – inspiring Pablo Picasso,[4] among others – it was originally published in the book *Pine Seedlings on the First Rat Day* in 1814 as an erotic parody of a medieval tale. The work depicts an *ama* being pleasured by two octopuses. Contrary to the nineteenth-century interpretation by French writer Edmond de Goncourt, who described the woman's body as *sicut cadaver* (like a corpse) in his book on Hokusai,[5] the unlikely *ménage à trois* is one of mutual consent, which the accompanying humoristic dialogue also reveals.[6] Teraoka's interpretation is also an expression of female pleasure and empowerment, indicated not least by the print's title and the featured dialogue:

Takonosukehichi:
She looks delicious, if I eat her as she is. Perhaps starting from here?
Wow! Feels like slippery *nuru-nuru*!!!![7]

Sarah:
Love, you shouldn't rush, but enjoy my clitoris area
slowly with gentle pleasure.

Takonosukehichi:
You mean this area, or much deeper inside here?
How about here or there?!?!

Sarah:
Your suction cups are not at all dependable, but wimps.
Don't hesitate to suck me!

As a double homage to the artist, Teraoka has set *Sarah and Octopus/ Seventh Heaven* in a landscape of Hokusai-inspired waves. Hokusai's wave motif would become an icon for the nineteenth-century avant-garde artists of Paris, with Vincent van Gogh describing it in a letter to his brother Theo in 1888: 'in his case with his *lines*, his *drawing* … these waves are *claws*, the boat is caught in them, you can feel it'.[8]

Catfish Envy from the *Hawaii Snorkel Series* (1992–93) also plays on the sexual dynamic between a woman and 'the other'. Set in an *ukiyo*-esque seascape similar to the watercolours of Teraoka's *Hanauma Bay Series* (1984), a samurai with a snorkel mask stares jealously at a modern-day Western woman, who is holding a catfish close to her naked chest. The catfish (*namazu*), which according to Japanese mythology lives deep under the islands of Japan and causes earthquakes, was a theme that became popular following the Ansei Edo earthquake of 1855, resulting in the production of catfish prints (*namazu-e*).[9] A woodblock print, *The Cause of the Great Catfish at Shin Yoshiwara*, by an unknown *ukiyo-e* artist, depicts women blaming the catfish for the earthquake, but the catfish is delighted to have these women touch him and threatens to squirm again and thereby cause an aftershock. Teraoka's *Catfish Envy* – which combines several print techniques: woodblock,

4 See for example Ricard Bru, 'Tentacles of Love and Death: From Hokusai to Picasso', in *Secret Images: Picasso and the Japanese Erotic Print*, exh. cat., Museu Picasso de Barcelona (London: Thames & Hudson, 2010), pp. 54–81.

5 Edmond de Goncourt, *Hokousaï: l'art japonais au XVIIIe siècle* (Paris: G. Charpentier & E. Fasquelle, 1896), p. 175. Goncourt (1822–1896) was an important figure among the early 'japonistes' in Paris, publishing books on Kitagawa Utamaro as well as Hokusai.

6 See Rosina Buckland, *Shunga: Erotic Art in Japan* (London: British Museum Press, 2010), p. 134.

7 Teraoka explains the name of the octopus: 'Takonosukehichi is the nickname I gave to the giant octopus. It loosely translates as "Octopus Pervert Seven".' Information provided by Catharine Clark Gallery. *Nuru-nuru* is a Japanese onomatopoeic phrase translating to 'slippery' or 'slimy'.

8 Vincent van Gogh to Theo van Gogh, Arles, 8 September 1888, letter 676, Van Gogh Museum, Amsterdam, https://vangoghletters.org/vg/letters.html.

9 Gregory Smits, 'Conduits of Power: What the Origins of Japan's Earthquake Catfish Reveal about Religious Geography', *Japan Review*, no. 24 (2012), p. 41.

10 Ken Tyler (b. 1931) began his career in printmaking in 1963 at the Tamarind Lithography Workshop, which was also attended by Ruth Asawa (pp. 26–29).

etching, aquatint and ink on paper – is one of four prints from the *Hawaii Snorkel Series* that were made in collaboration with Tyler Graphics.[10] The carving and printing was done by Shibata Yasuyuki, who later also collaborated with Nara Yoshitomo (pp. 112–15).

Masami has had more than seventy one-man shows, including at the Whitney Museum of American Art, New York (1979), Yale University Art Gallery, New Haven (1998), New Albion Gallery in Sydney (2012), Honolulu Museum of Art (2015) and the National Gallery of Australia, Canberra (2024–25).

Collections: Honolulu Museum of Art; Fine Arts Museums of San Francisco; National Gallery of Australia, Canberra; Smithsonian Institution, Washington, DC; Tate Modern, London.

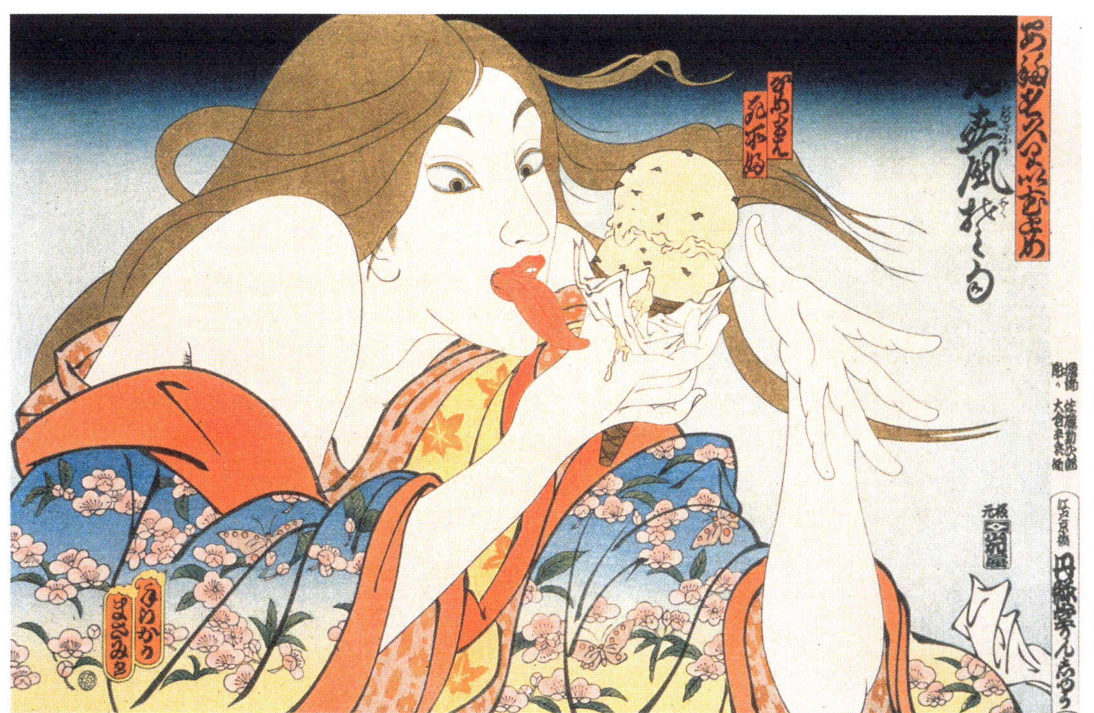

31 Flavors Invading Japan/Today's Special, 1980–82. Woodblock print

Overleaf
Sarah and Octopus/Seventh Heaven, 2001. Woodblock print

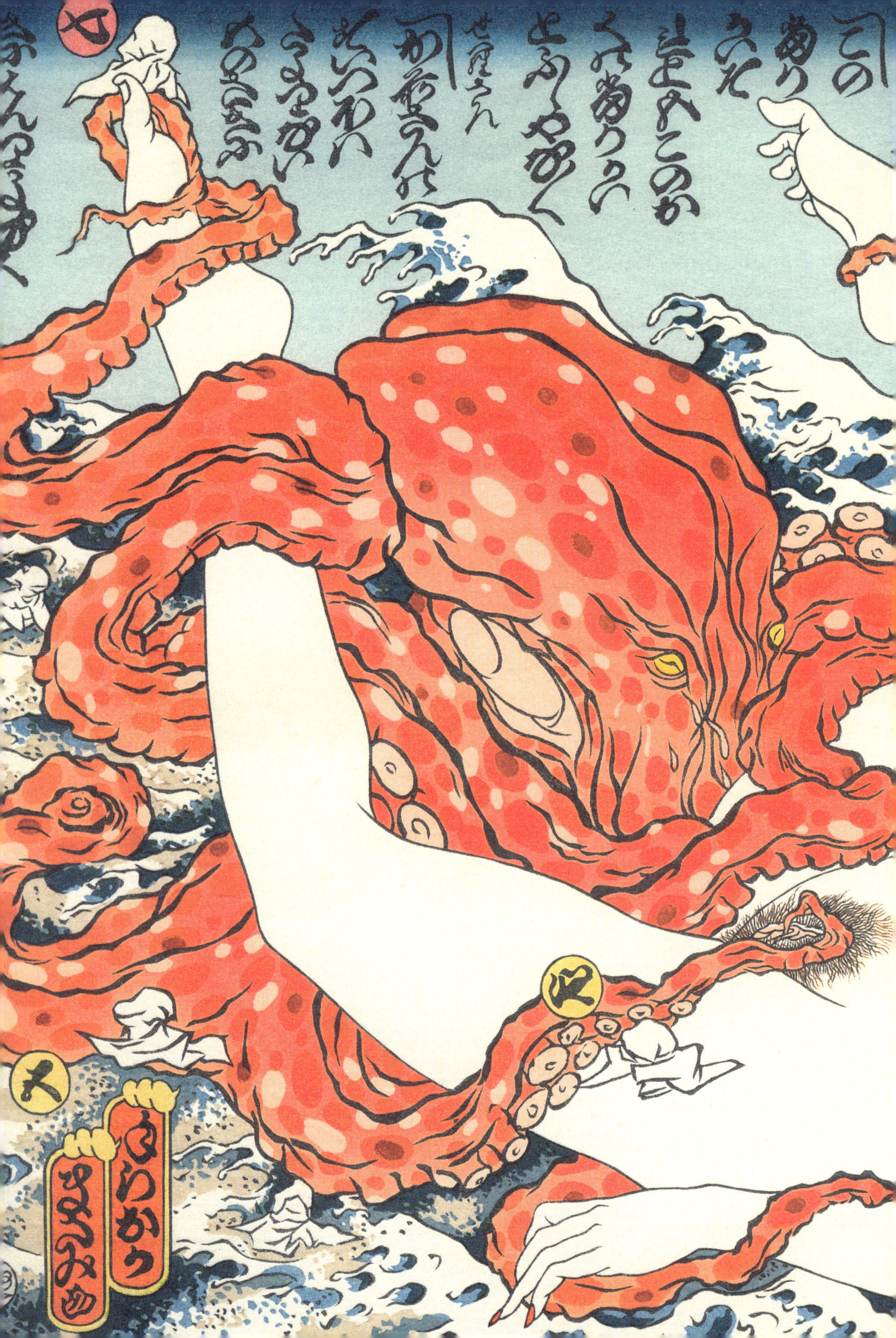

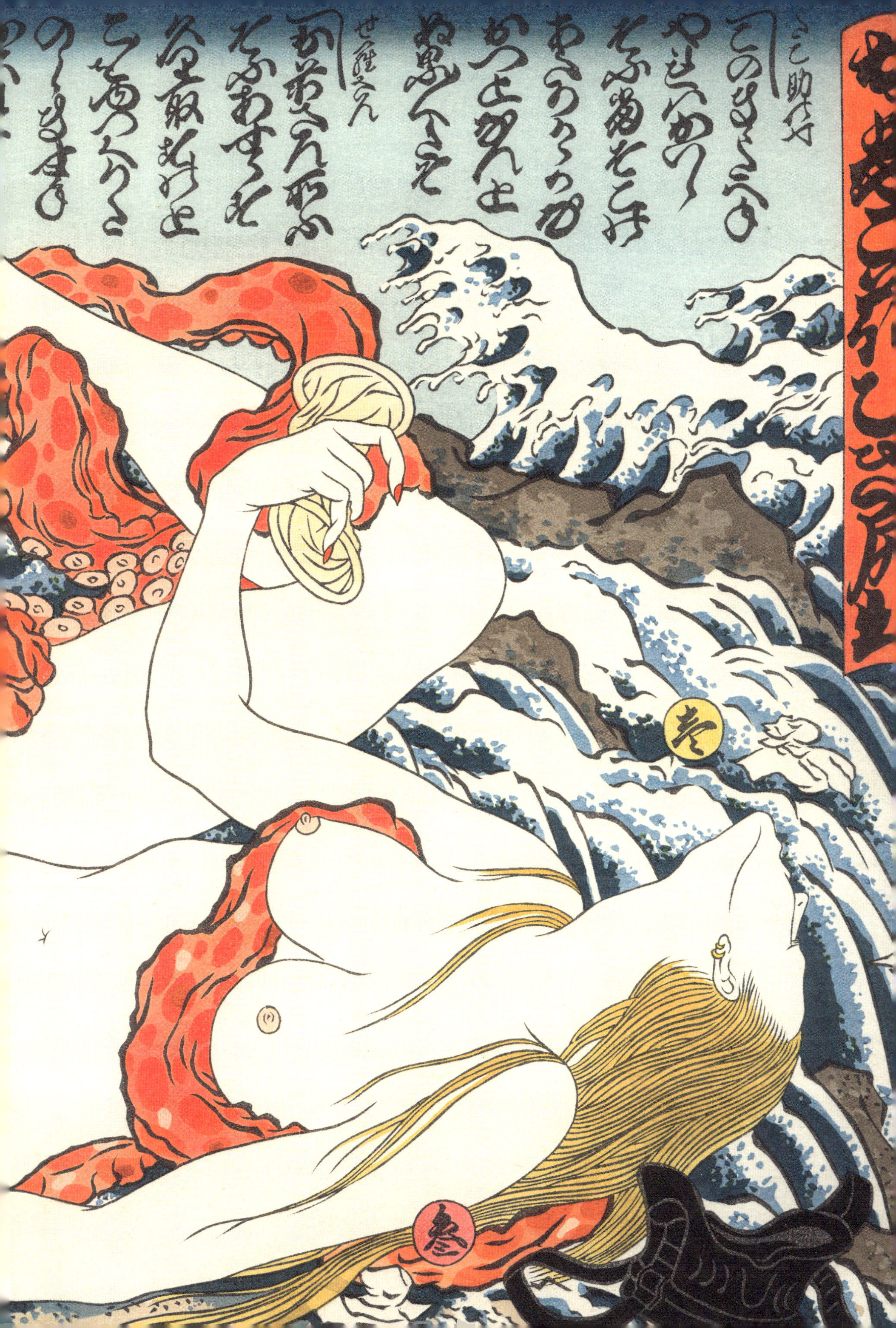

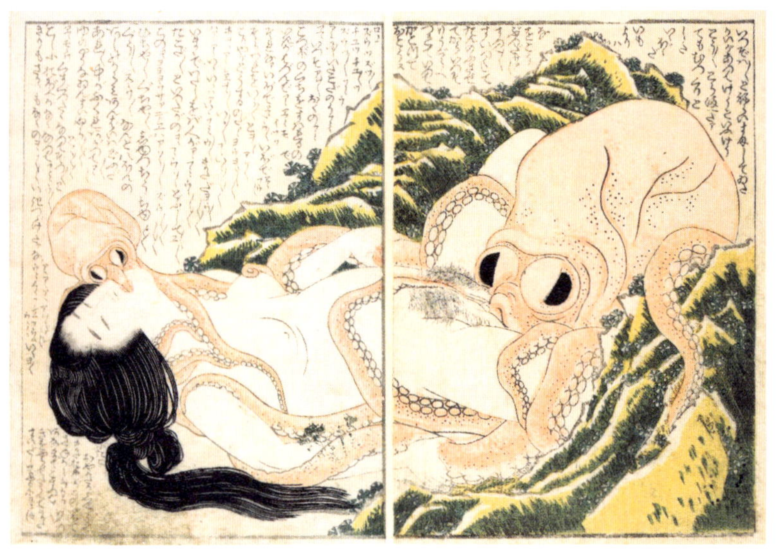

1

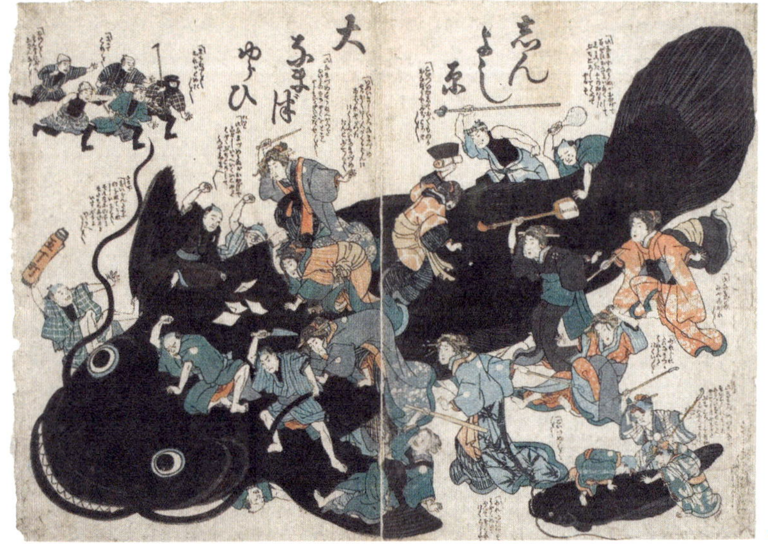

2

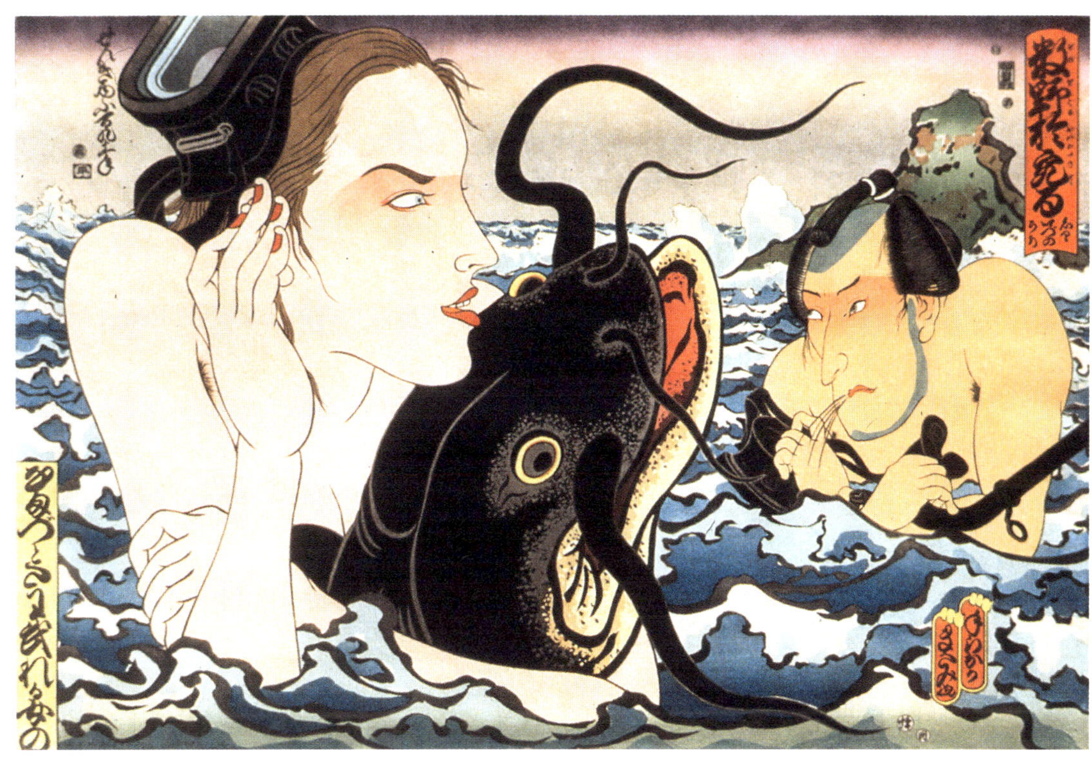

3

1 KATSUSHIKA Hokusai — *Female Diver being Pleasured by a Small and Large Octopus*, 1814, from the book *Pine Seedlings on the First Rat Day*. Woodblock print

2 Unknown artist — *Angry Ansei earthquake victims take revenge on a giant catfish responsible for the destruction*, 19th century. Woodblock print

3 TERAOKA Masami — *Catfish Envy*, 1993. Etching, aquatint and woodblock print

TOKURIKI Tomikichirō (1902–2000)

Medium:
Woodblock

Tokuriki despite his traditionalism, is a modern print master. His palette is Fauvist (i.e., vivid) and the strong, expressive lines are gouged with a knife to produce jagged contours.[1]

George Kuwayama, 1972

In 1972, the then seventy-year-old Tokuriki Tomikichirō was included in the exhibition *Contemporary Japanese Printmakers* at Los Angeles County Museum of Art, side by side with works by the younger generation of contemporary print artists such as Nagai Kazumasa (pp. 108–11), Ay-O (pp. 31–43) and Noda Tetsuya (pp. 117–23). In 1934 he had participated in the first major *sōsaku hanga* exhibition held in Paris, which showed artists of the first generation, including Yamamoto Kanae (pp. 212–17) and Ishii Hakutei. Tokuriki's representation as a contemporary artist in both exhibitions, held almost forty years apart, testifies not only to his long career but, more importantly, to the longevity and modernity of his work.

Tokuriki was born into a long line of Kanō school artists in Kyoto – the most influential school of painting in Japan – and graduated from Kyoto City School of Fine Arts and Crafts in 1924. He first studied painting with his grandfather, who also made woodblock prints and sparked the young Tokuriki's interest in the print medium. In 1929 Tokuriki began making woodblock prints, becoming the first professional print artist in the family: 'Fate made me an artist, but I made myself a hanga artist.'[2] Having learned printmaking both from traditional artisans, including a printer who had reputedly worked for Utagawa Hiroshige III (1842–1894),[3] as well as by taking short courses with Hiratsuka Un'ichi (pp. 68–71), Tokuriki was a unique link between the bygone world of *ukiyo-e* and that of modern-day printmaking.

Tokuriki was the unofficial 'leader' among the *sōsaku hanga* artists in Kyoto and a member of the Japan Print Association from 1932. Tokuriki's portrait from 1947 of his wife combing her hair was described by Oliver Statler as one of 'the best of his creative prints', which 'show a resolute effort to design with the knife'.[4]

While active in the creative print movement, for a living Tokuriki also designed traditional landscapes in the *shin hanga* style, which were more in demand among tourists. He created perhaps the best known of his series, *Thirty-six Views of Mount Fuji* (c. 1939–41), in collaboration with the publisher Uchida Bijutsu Shoten. A little more than one hundred years after Hokusai led the way for serial views of the sacred mountain with his famous series of the same title, Tokuriki took on the classic subject too. Showing Fuji throughout the seasons and from different vantage points, like Hokusai's series, Tokuriki's was commercially very successful, selling a thousand copies of each set within a short amount of time.[5]

After the war, Tokuriki established the publishing company Matsukyū, producing and distributing his own prints. He continued to design scenes from around Kyoto and Nara, but these were self-printed, self-carved and self-published according to the *sōsaku hanga* ideal. In 1948 Tokuriki also set up the sub-company Kōrokusha, which published works by artists such as Takahashi Tasaburō (1904–1977) and Kamei Tōbei (1901–1977).

1 George Kuwayama, *Contemporary Japanese Prints*, exh. cat. (Los Angeles: Los Angeles County Museum of Art, 1972), p. 36.
2 Quoted ibid., p. 118.
3 Tokuriki mentions the printer Ōiwa Tokuzō as one of his teachers, but he does not write if he had actually worked with Hiroshige III. See Tōmikichirō Tokuriki, *Wood-block Printing* (Osaka: Hoikusha Publishing Co., 1968), p. 126.
4 Oliver Statler, *Modern Japanese Prints: An Art Reborn* (Rutland, VT: Charles E. Tuttle Co., 1956). Statler dates the print, *Woman Combing Her Hair*, to 1947, while other sources, including the Honolulu Museum of Art, date it to 1935. But as it was published by Tokuriki's publishing company, Matsukyū, established following the war, 1947 must be correct.
5 Helen Merritt, *Modern Japanese Woodblock Prints: The Early Years* (Honolulu: University of Hawai'i Press, 1990), pp. 88–89.
6 Quoted from the blurb, Tōmikichirō Tokuriki, *Wood-block Print Primer* (Tokyo: Japan Publications, 1970).

The technical aspect of printmaking was always significant to Tokuriki. He taught artisans and artists, including Westerners, and through articles and books published in both Japanese and English he did much to emphasise the technical side of printmaking. In 1962 he was invited to Germany, the UK and USA to perform woodblock print demonstrations. On the occasion of the publication of his book in 1970, he wrote: 'Since I consider the propagation of traditional Japanese woodblock techniques one of my greatest happinesses, not only do I continue to teach, but I have also written this book in the hope that it will serve a useful purpose for all my students and for all those people who want to begin studying the ancient art form.'[6]

Collections: Art Institute of Chicago; British Museum, London; Los Angeles County Museum of Art; National Museum of Modern Art, Tokyo.

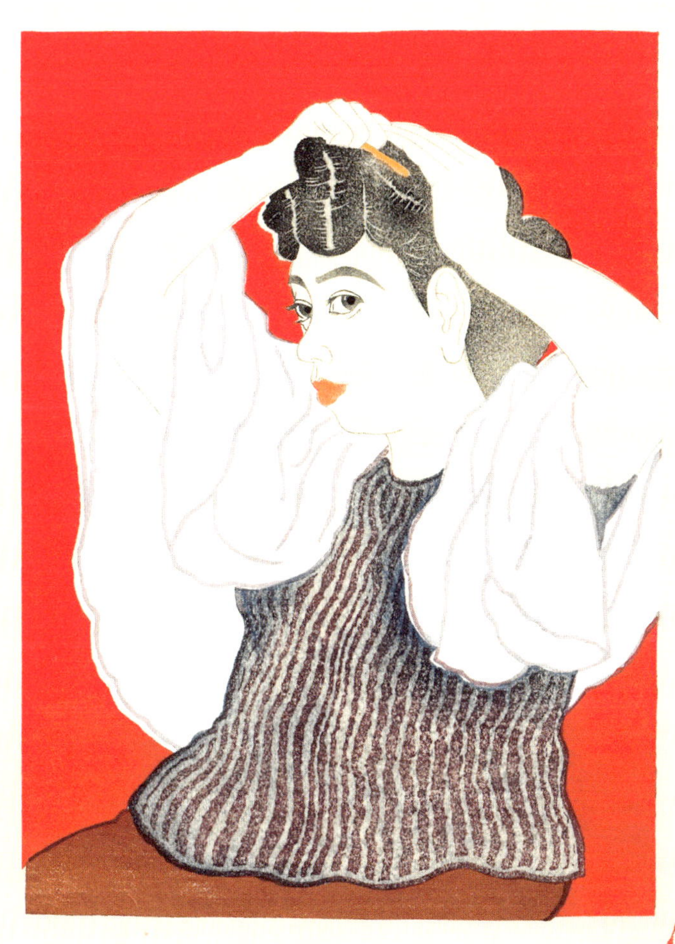

Woman Combing her Hair, 1935. Woodblock print

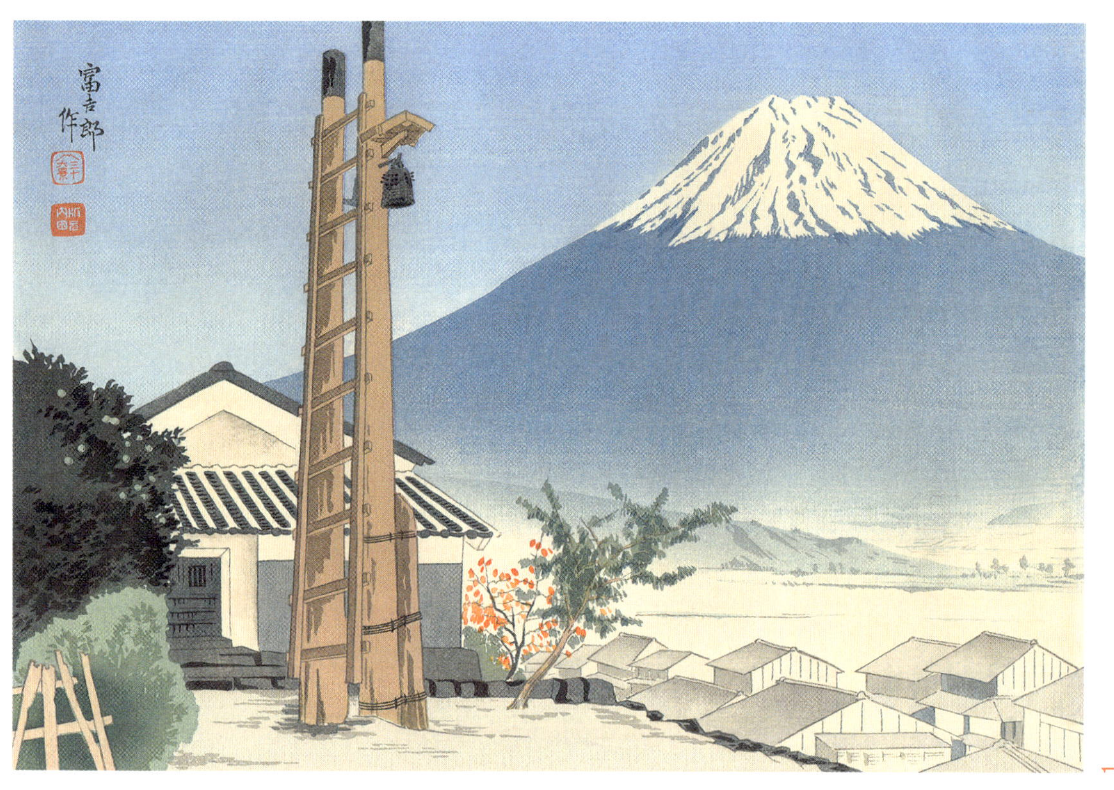

1

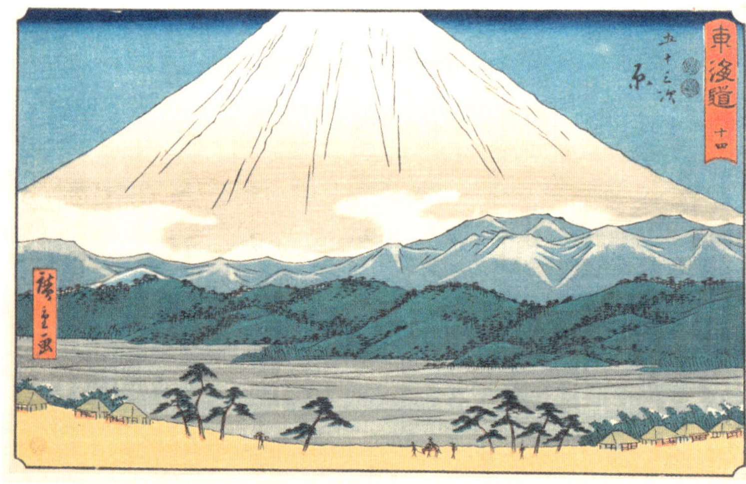

2

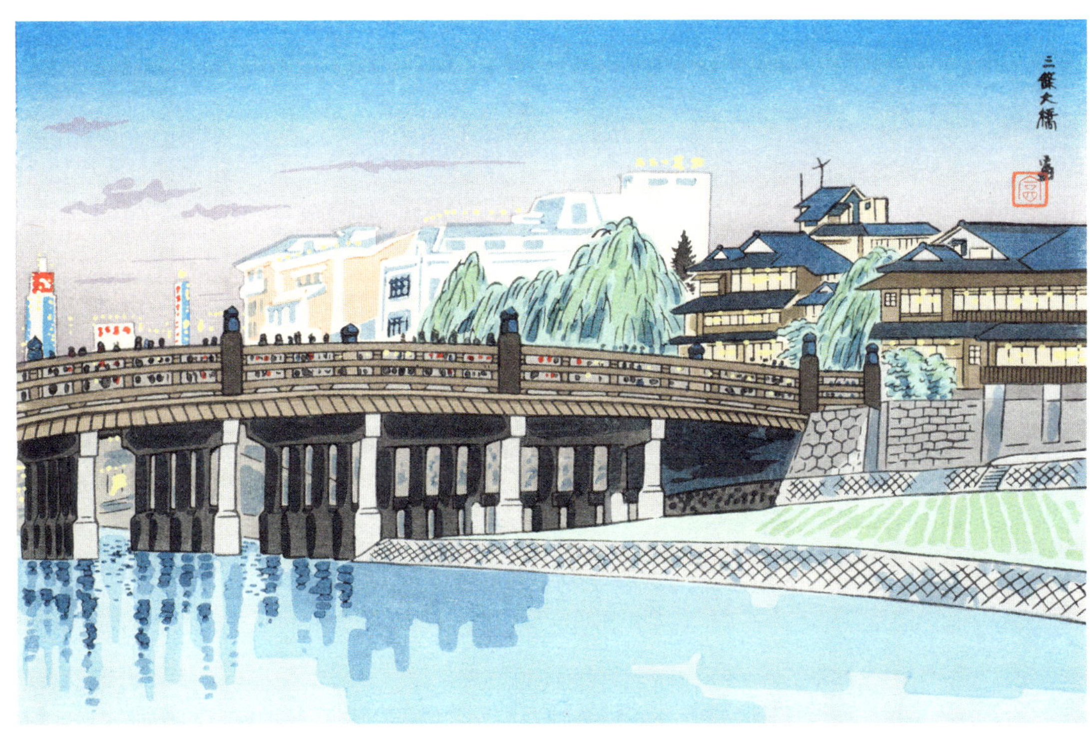

3

1 TOKURIKI Tomikichirō — *Fuji from Iwabuchi*, 1939–41. Woodblock print
2 UTAGAWA Hiroshige — *Hara*, 1847–52. Woodblock print
3 TOKURIKI Tomikichirō — *Sanjo Bridge, Kyoto*, c. 1950s. Woodblock print

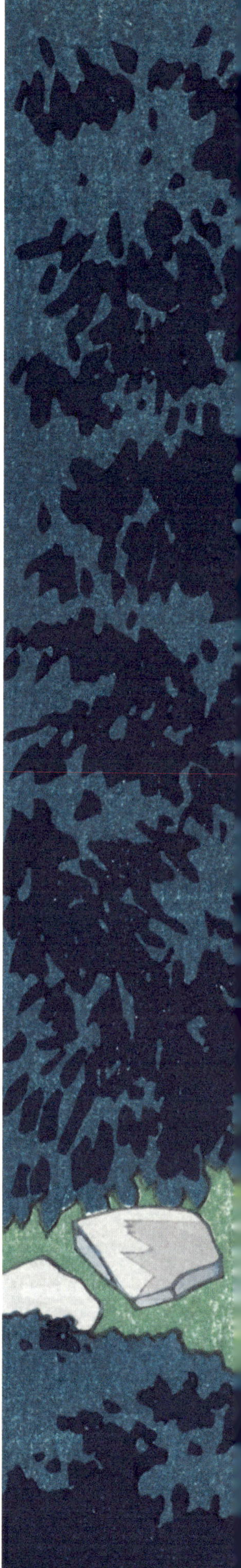

Katsura Imperial Villa, c. 1960s. Woodblock print

TOKURIKI Tomikichirō

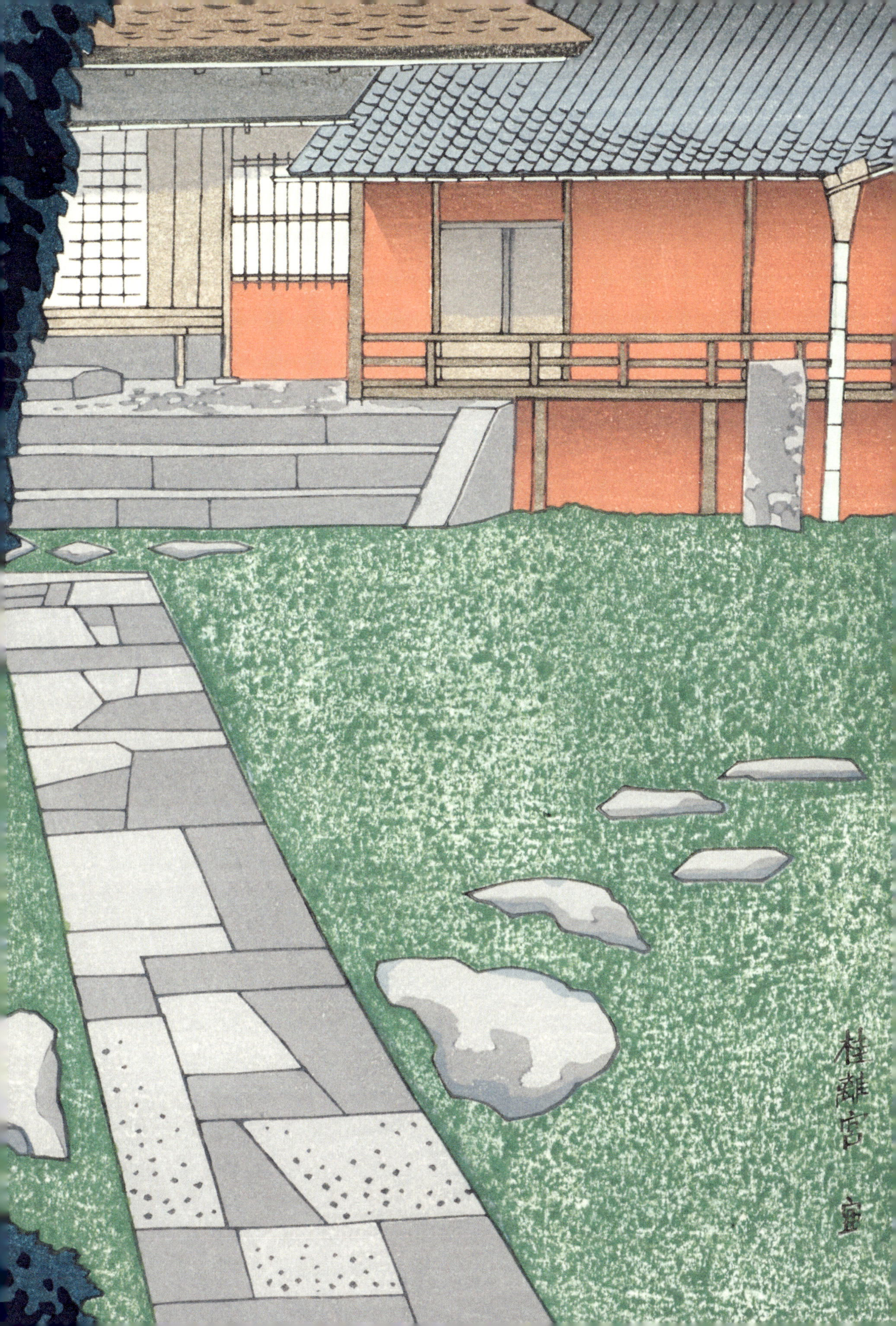
桂離宮

TSURUYA Kōkei (b. 1946)

Medium:
Woodblock

Until seeing Kōkei's work, I had believed that all the vigour of contemporary Japanese prints had passed to those working in international style.[1]

Lawrence Smith, 1988

Also referred to as 'the modern Sharaku', Tsuruya Kōkei is as bold and distinctive in his style as his Edo-period predecessor, the *ukiyo-e* artist Tōshūsai Sharaku (active 1794–95), known for his unique portraits of kabuki actors.

About 150 years after Sharaku, Mitsui Gen (Kōkei's birth name) was born in Chigasaki, Kanagawa prefecture, to an artist family. Both his father and grandfather were oil painters; the latter was Nakazawa Hiromitsu (1874–1964), recognised as a Person of Cultural Merit by the Japanese government in 1957. 'I grew up with the aroma of turpentine until I was fifteen,' Kōkei would later recollect about his childhood.[2] He liked sketching as a child but never received formal art training. It was his brother, nine years his senior, who went to an arts and crafts high school where he made woodblock prints and sculpted in wood, who would influence Kōkei. As a young man, Kōkei would also visit Jimbōchō, the Tokyo neighbourhood famed for its old bookstores and publishing houses, where he could view and buy woodblock prints, especially *ukiyo-e*.

Kōkei first began making his own woodblock prints in 1978 after seeing kabuki – the traditional theatre form that originated in the Edo period – performed for the first time. This gave him the idea to make prints of actors just like the *ukiyo-e* artists. Within a year, Kōkei began his collaboration with Shōchiku, the theatre and film production company that runs Tokyo's iconic Kabuki-za theatre in Ginza. Here Kōkei would sell his prints as souvenirs to begin with, much like the *ukiyo-e* in the Edo period, but later his reputation grew and institutions such as the British Museum began to collect his works.

Kōkei designs, carves and prints his own works, and although that is in line with the *sōsaku hanga* ideal, he is an independent artist and does not associate with any movement. Usually, one limited edition of 72 prints will take forty days to make: ten days to create the design, another ten days to carve a set of woodblocks (carving being his favourite part of the creative process) and twenty days of printing.[3]

In 2016, Kōkei created the series *Five Subjects Dedicated to Arcimboldo*, depicting the dragon, insect, dog, *kumadori* (the make-up worn by kabuki actors) and cat. As the title suggests, the series is inspired by the Italian Renaissance painter Giuseppe Arcimboldo (1526–1593), known for his fantastical portrait heads composed of objects such as books, vegetables, fish and flowers. Similarly, in the 1840s, Utagawa Kuniyoshi created somewhat grotesque faces by combining multiple figures in his caricatures known as *yose-e* ('gather-together pictures').

In 1989, the Pacific Asia Museum in Pasadena held the first exhibition of Kōkei's work outside Japan, which it celebrated thirty years later, in 2019, with *Tsuruya Kōkei: Modern Kabuki Prints Revised and Revisited*, which also travelled to the Asia Society Texas Center in Houston. Kōkei was

1 Lawrence Smith, then Keeper of Oriental Antiquities at the British Museum, London, quoted in *The 100th Anniversary of the Kabuki-za Theatre – Tsuruya Kokei: Kabuki Actor Prints* (Tokyo: Shochiku Co., 1988), p. 10.
2 Ibid., p. 101.
3 See ibid., p. 99.

included in the British Museum's publication *Modern Japanese Prints, 1912–1989: Woodblocks and Stencils* (1994). He is now working on *Five Styles of Banzai-Ukiyoe*, a series of portraits of famous *ukiyo-e* artists.

Collections: British Museum, London; Ohio State University Libraries; USC Pacific Asia Museum, Pasadena.

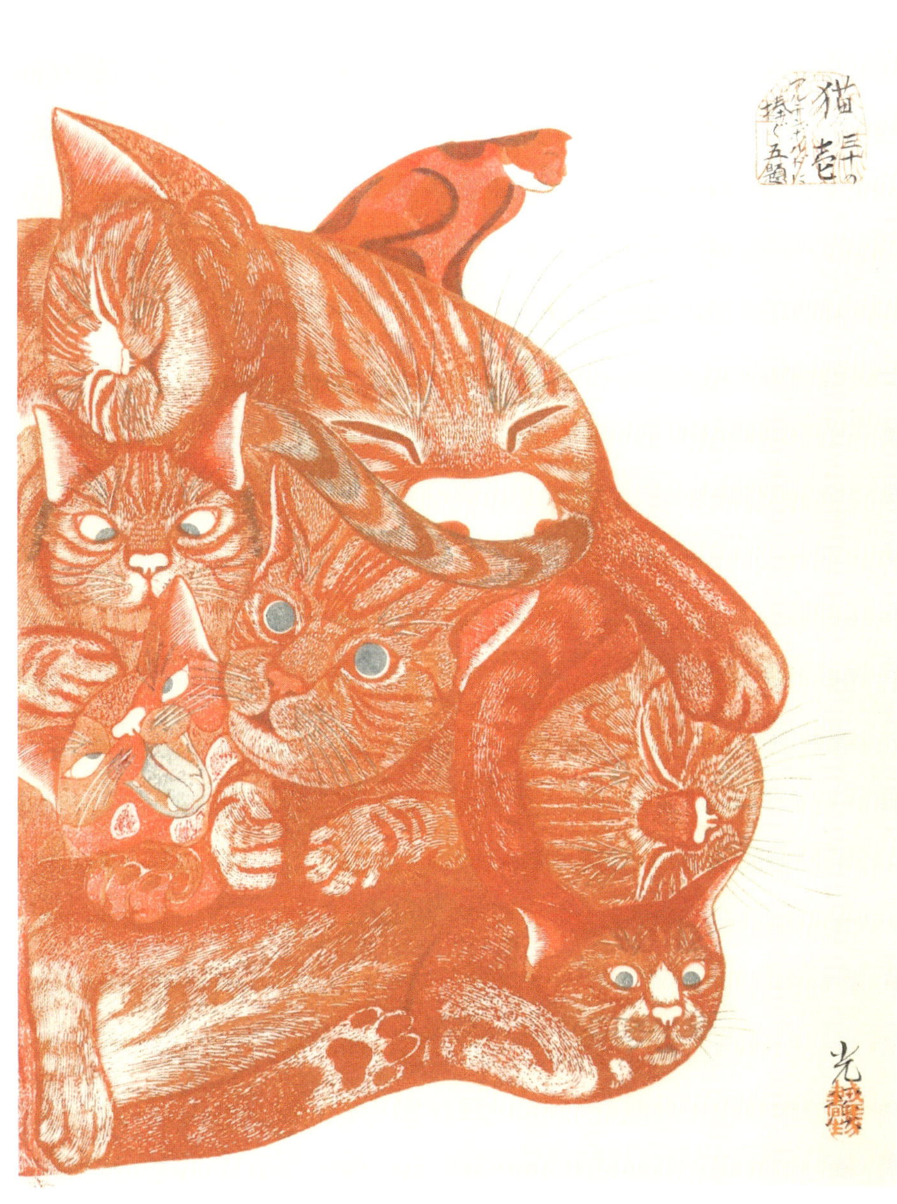

Cat, 2013. Woodblock print

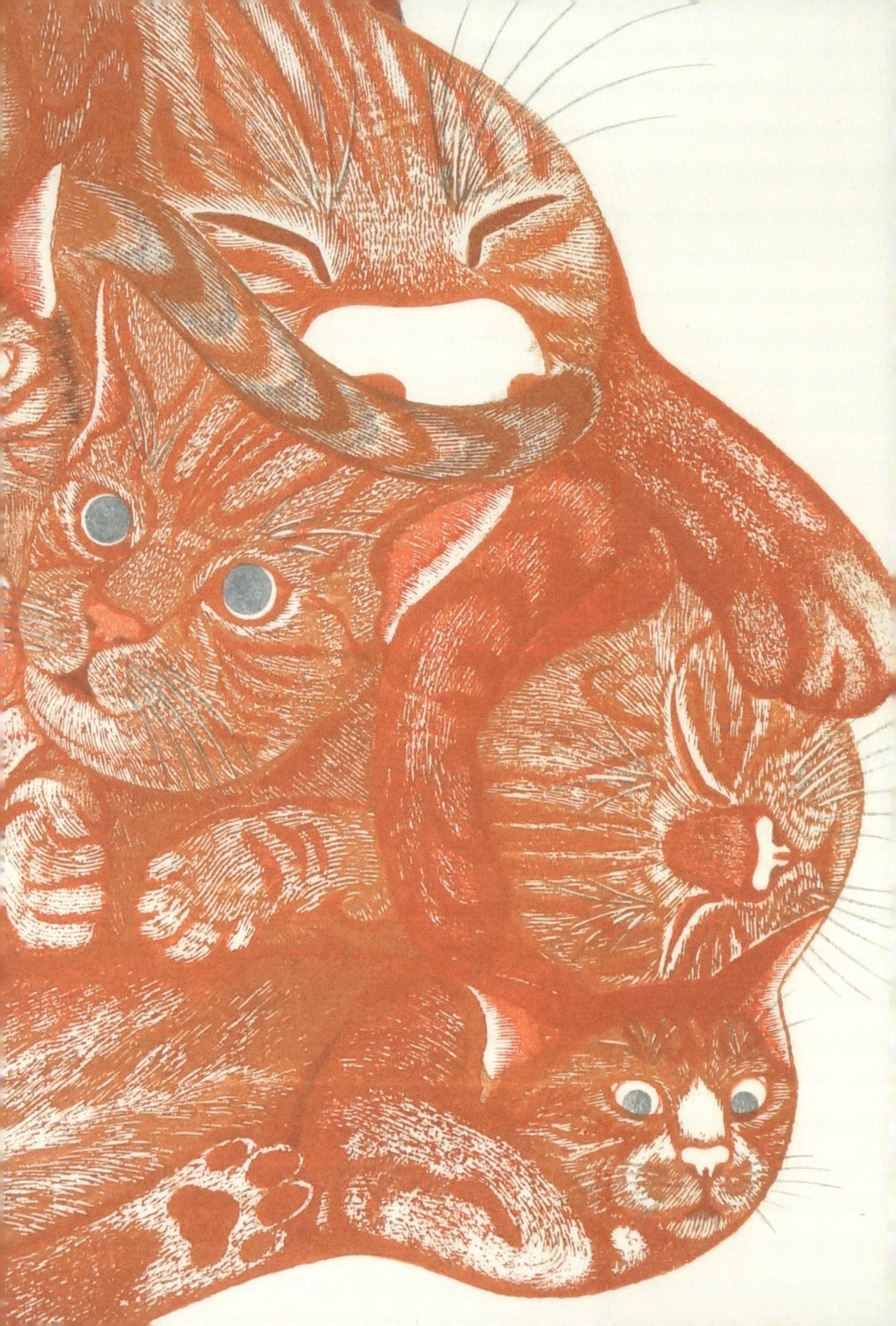

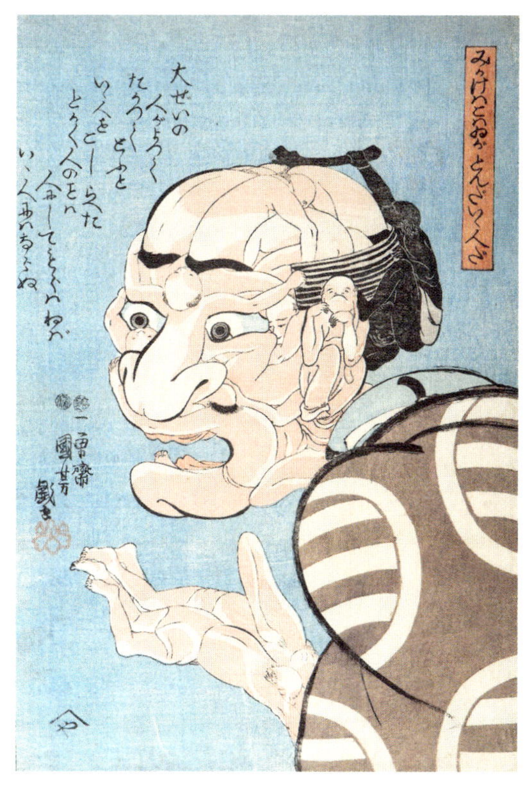

UTAGAWA Kuniyoshi *Looks Fierce but is Really Nice*, c. 1847–52. Woodblock print

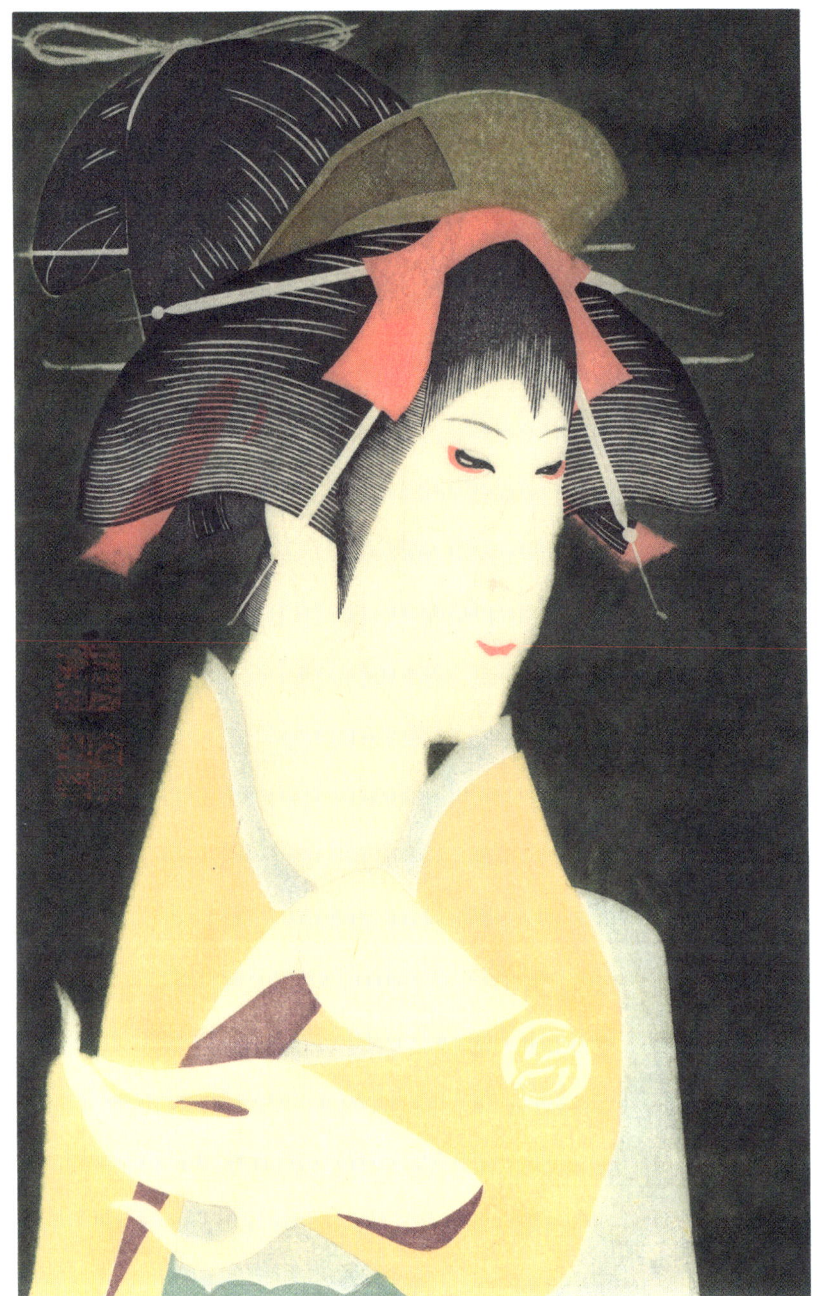

Nakamura Jakuemon IV as Hanako in 'Bungo Dōjōji', 1982. Woodblock print

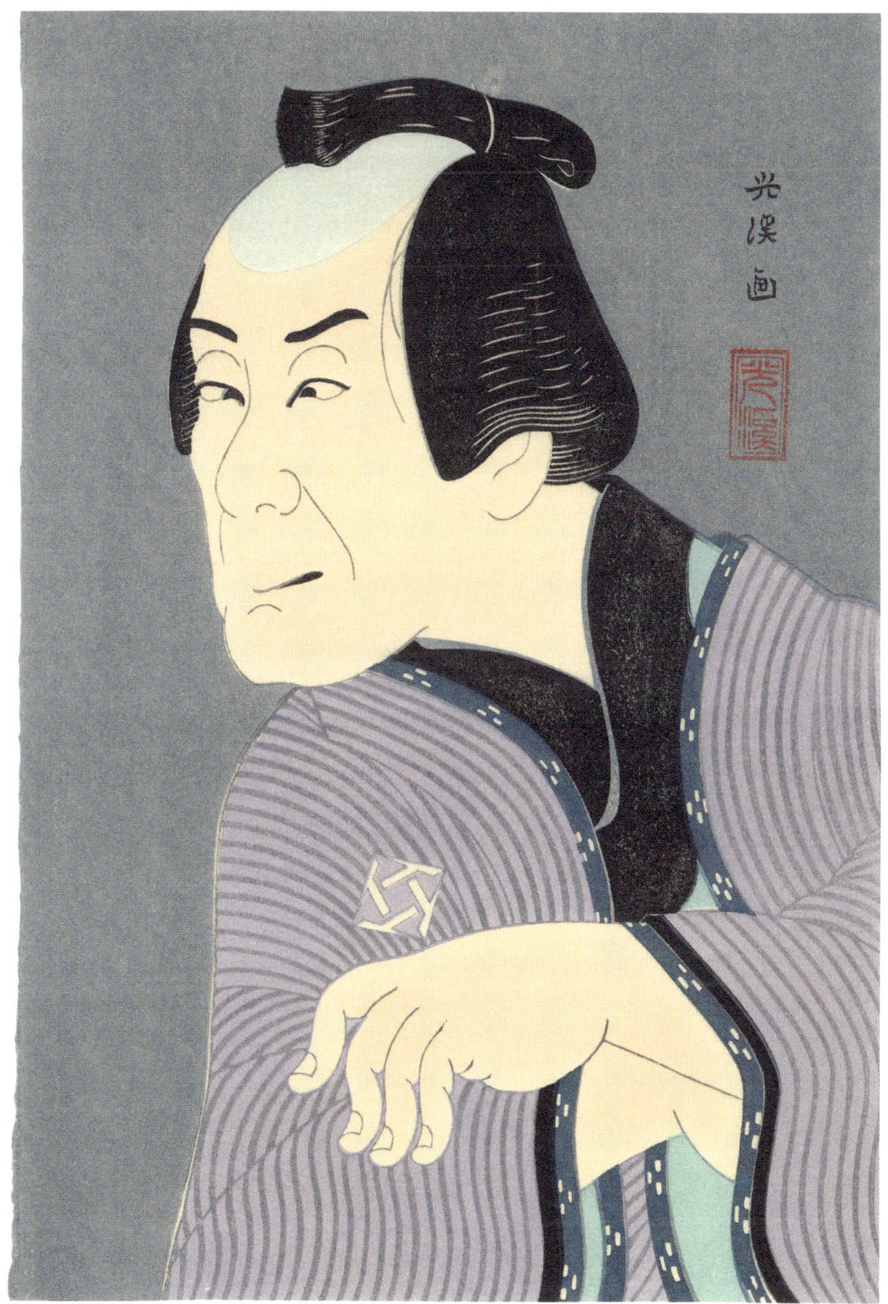

Nakamura Ganjiro II as Kamiya Jihei in 'Kawasho', 1979. Woodblock print

URUSHIBARA Yoshijirō (1889–1953)

Medium:
Woodblock

The story of Urushibara Yoshijirō, also known by his artist name Mokuchū, is slightly unusual when compared to the other print artists in this book. As an artisan turned teacher and artist, Urushibara played a pioneering role in the revival of the colour woodblock print in the early twentieth century – not in Japan, though, but in Europe.

Urushibara lived and worked in London for almost thirty years. He was trained as a printmaker and worked for the Tokyo publisher Shimbi Shoin Ltd, who specialised in old master reproductions, including the volumes *Selected Relics of Japanese Art, One Hundred Masterpieces of Japanese Pictorial Art* as well as *Masterpieces Selected from the Ukiyo-e School.* This led Urushibara to London in 1910 to demonstrate the technique of woodblock printing at the major Japan-British Exhibition held at White City.[1] Urushibara ended up staying in London and was offered work at the British Museum, where he made reproductions of classic *ukiyo-e,* including works by Hokusai, as well as helping to restore Asian prints and paintings. The critic Malcolm Charles Salaman wrote in 1924: 'When Mr Yoshijiro Urushibara came some years ago from his native Tokyo to London he brought with him not only an extraordinarily practical knowledge of the Japanese craftsman's technique on the wood-block, but a very adaptable artistic spirit.'[2]

At the exhibition in 1910, Urushibara had encountered the French artist Prosper-Alphonse Isaac (1858–1924), who asked the young Urushibara to teach him the technique of traditional Japanese woodblock printing. This led Urushibara to Paris in 1911, where he lived for several months.[3] Through Isaac, Urushibara was introduced to the Société des Amis de l'Art Japonais, initially established by Siegfried Bing.[4] Urushibara designed and collaborated with Isaac on a number of invitation cards for their monthly dinners – all Japanese-style woodblock prints, of course (see p. 15, fig. 10). During his thirty years in Europe, Urushibara was significant in encouraging the production and appreciation of the Japanese woodblock print by taking on students like Isaac,[5] Jules Chadel (1870–1941) and painter Walter J. Phillips (1884–1963).[6]

Urushibara collaborated on a considerable number of prints as carver and printer with other artists, such as fellow Japanese expatriate Makino Yoshio (known as Yoshio Markino, 1869–1956) and the Welsh artist Frank Brangwyn (1867–1956), the latter collaboration being Urushibara's longest and most successful. A former apprentice to William Morris (1834–1896), the leader of the British Arts and Crafts movement, Brangwyn witnessed the first wave of Japonisme in the late nineteenth century. In 1895, Brangwyn was commissioned by none other than Bing to decorate the exterior of his new Paris gallery, Maison de l'Art Nouveau, which would give its name to the art movement of the same name.

About twenty years later, in 1917, Brangwyn began collaborating with Urushibara, who would make woodblock prints after Brangwyn's drawings, such as *The Devil's Bridge* and the *Bruges* series. This way of collaborating was similar to the classic *hanmoto* system, although Urushibara did both the carving and printing parts of the process.

During the 1920s and 1930s, Urushibara focused on making his own designs, creating numerous still-lifes, arrangements of flowers (often using the same vases for different setups) and European cityscapes and landscapes; later his subject became horses in simple black and white. Though technically

1 Hilary Chapman and Libby Horner, *Yoshijiro Urushibara: A Japanese Printmaker in London, a Catalogue Raisonné* (Leiden: Hotei Publishing, 2017), p. 10.

2 Malcolm C. Salaman, 'Mr Urushibara's Wood-Block Colour-Prints', *Studio: International Art* 86, no. 368 (November 1923), p. 258.

3 Émilie Vabre, 'Prosper-Alphonse Isaac (1858–1924)', *Nouvelles de l'estampe,* no. 237 (2011), pp. 4–21.

4 Following Bing's death in 1905, the society was continued by jeweller Henri Vever (1854–1942) and the other members into the 1930s.

5 In 1913, Isaac wrote an article based on Urushibara's instructions: 'La gravure sur bois à la manière japonaise', *Art et décoration* (May 1913), pp. 155–62.

6 Walter J. Phillips, 'Making a Wood-Cut', in 'Another Wood-Cut', unpublished and undated typescript, https://wjphillips.ca.

in line with the *sōsaku hanga* ideal of the artist as the sole creator of the print, Urushibara was aesthetically closer to the *shin hanga* movement.

Collections: British Museum, London; Glenbow, Calgary; Museum of Fine Arts, Boston; National Museum of Asian Art, Washington, DC; Victoria and Albert Museum, London.

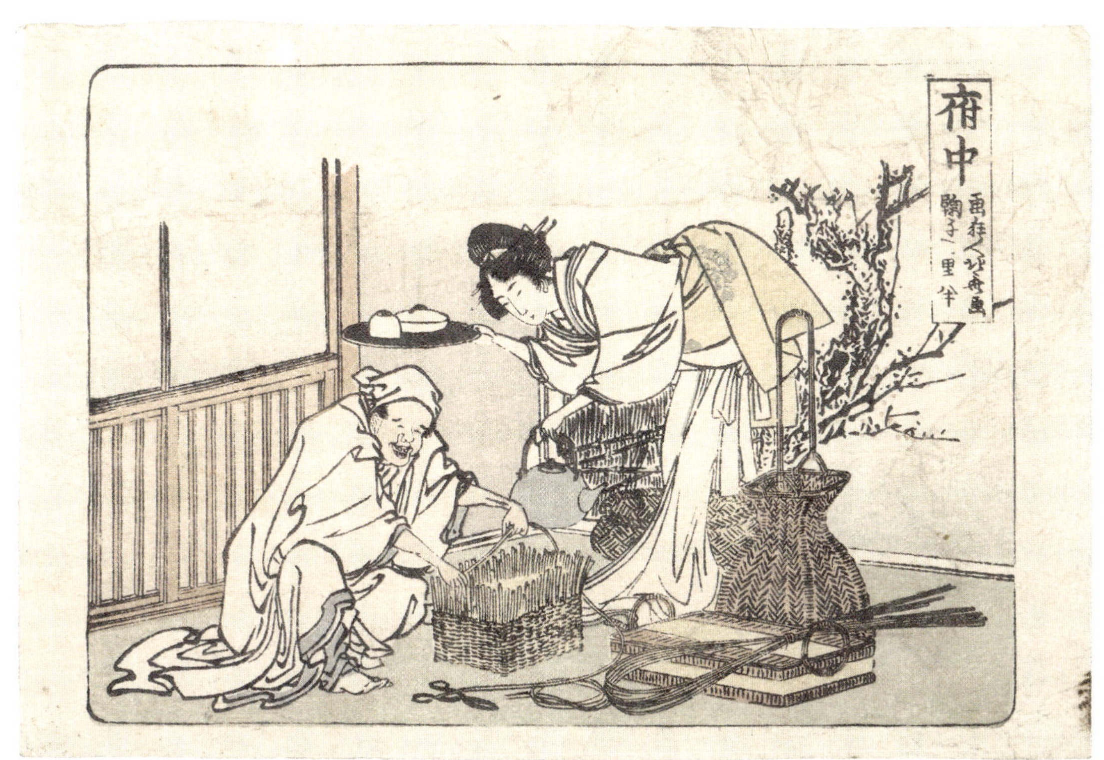

Fuchu, after Katsushika Hokusai, c. 1912. Woodblock print

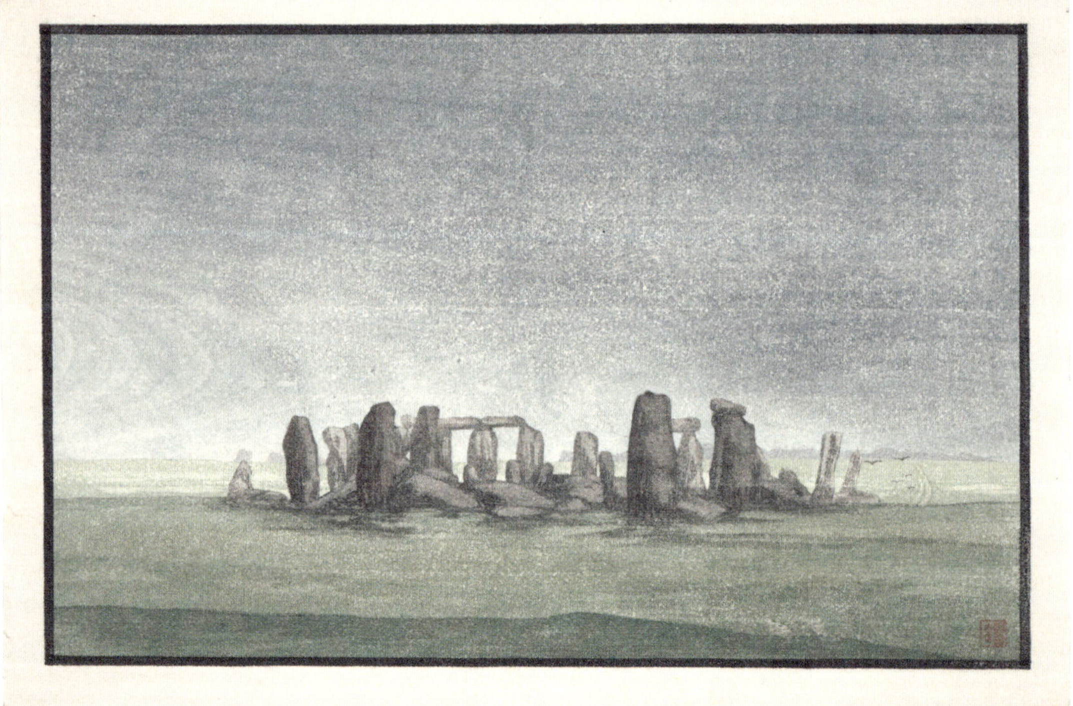

Stonehenge, c. 1915. Woodblock print

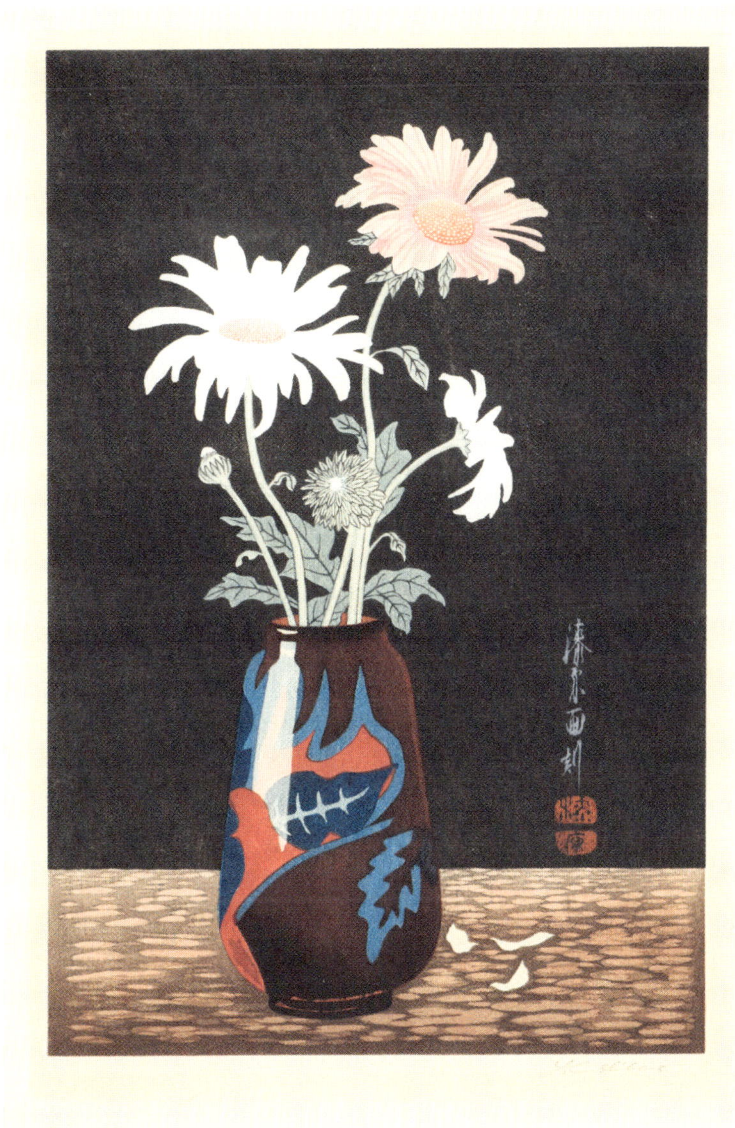

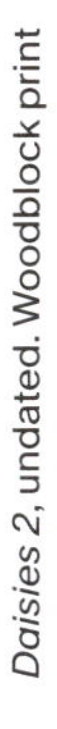

Daisies 2, undated. Woodblock print

YAMAMOTO Kanae (1889–1953)

Medium:
Woodblock

When an idea excited him he would bury himself in it. Sacrifice meant nothing. It was the same with the creative hanga, his school, and his free-art movement. He was a selfless man, a passionate man, a man of great sensitivity. I guess if I had to describe himin one word it would be – artist.[1]

Ishii Tsuruzō, 1956

A pioneer of *sōsaku hanga*, Yamamoto Kanae paved the way for a new approach to printmaking when he created the first 'creative' print, emphasising the artist's self-expression by designing, carving and printing his own work, thereby distancing himself from the old collaborative *hanmoto* system.

It all began in 1904, while Yamamoto was still a student of Western-style painting (*yōga*) at Tokyo School of Fine Arts. Returning from a trip in Chiba prefecture, Yamamoto carved a design from two cherry woodblocks based on a sketch he had made of a fisherman.[2] By producing a print from start to finish, he laid the foundation for the ideal of the print artist as sole creator of a work, similar to the European *peintre-graveur* (painter-engraver). Furthermore, the print was carved similarly to a Western-style wood engraving, by cutting out white lines against the black background, rather than the traditional Japanese mode of *moku hanga*. He had learned this technique during an apprenticeship from age eleven to nineteen at the workshop of the wood engraver Sakurai Torakichi.

Fisherman (*Gyofu*), as the print was titled, was published in the art and literary magazine *Myōjō* in July 1904. Its editor Ishii Hakutei (1882–1958), a friend of Yamamoto's, coined the word *tōga* ('knife picture') to describe the work, giving emphasis to the new and groundbreaking cutting technique. The year after, they used the word *hanga*, which became the general term for 'print', to describe their works.[3]

In 1907 Ishii and Yamamoto, along with others, established the magazine *Hōsun*, modelled on the German art periodical *Jugend*. Yamamoto designed illustrations using both woodblock print and lithograph, filling its pages with creative prints. The magazine would become a cornerstone of the *sōsaku hanga* movement, seeking to break the stigma against printmaking as a second-class medium.

Driven by his interest in European art (and to heal a broken heart[4]), in 1912 Yamamoto left for Paris, following in the footsteps of Ishii, who had lived in the French capital the previous year. Spending four years abroad, Yamamoto studied Western printing techniques, including etching for a few months at the École des Beaux-Arts. This turned out to be a prolific period, and Yamamoto created most of his prints during this time. *On the Deck* (1912), a scene from aboard the ship *Tango Maru* heading to Marseilles, was one of the first. But unlike *Fisherman*, carved eight years earlier and similar to a wood engraving, *On the Deck* broke with both traditional Japanese technique and that of wood engraving, as Yamamoto carved out the white to create not lines, but planes of colour and shadow.[5]

In Paris, Yamamoto witnessed first-hand the impact *ukiyo-e* had left on European avant-garde art during the first wave of Japonisme. He was especially

1 Oliver Statler, *Modern Japanese Prints: An Art Reborn* (Rutland, VT: Charles E. Tuttle Co., 1956), p. 17.
2 Ibid., p. 12.
3 Helen Merritt, *Modern Japanese Woodblock Prints: The Early Years* (Honolulu: University of Hawai'i Press, 1990), p. 17 and note 2. This is also discussed in Roger S. Keyes, *Break with the Past: The Japanese Creative Print Movement, 1910–1960*, exh. cat. (San Francisco: Fine Arts Museums of San Francisco, 1988), p. 8.
4 See Merritt, *Modern Japanese Woodblock Prints*, p. 156.
5 See Statler, *Modern Japanese Prints*, p. 13.
6 Janine Bailly-Herzberg, *Dictionnaire de l'estampe en France, 1830–1950* (Paris: Flammarion, 1985), pp. 323–24.
7 See Onchi Kōshirō, 'The Modern Japanese Print: An Internal History of the Sosaku Hanga Movement', *Ukiyo-e Art*, no. 11 (1965), p. 8.

inspired by the Nabis artist Félix Vallotton, who was a collector of *ukiyo-e*. As a key figure in the development of the modern woodblock print in Europe,[6] Vallotton left a mark on an entire generation of artists, including Edvard Munch and Wassily Kandinsky, who in turn inspired the early generations of *sōsaku hanga* artists.

Upon his return to Japan, Yamamoto helped establish the first real organisation of print artists in 1918. The Japan Creative Print Association held its first exhibition at the Mitsukoshi department store in Tokyo in 1919, where Yamamoto exhibited twenty of the prints he had made during his time abroad. According to Onchi Kōshirō (pp. 130–33), 25 artists and 189 prints of various techniques (woodblock, etching, lithograph) were represented and about 20,000 people attended the show. It was an unexpected success.[7]

The Municipal Museum Kanae Yamamoto was founded in 1962, but it has since closed and the collection is now part of Ueda City Museum of Art in Nagano prefecture.

Collections: British Museum, London; Cleveland Museum of Art; National Museum of Modern Art, Tokyo; Ueda City Museum of Art.

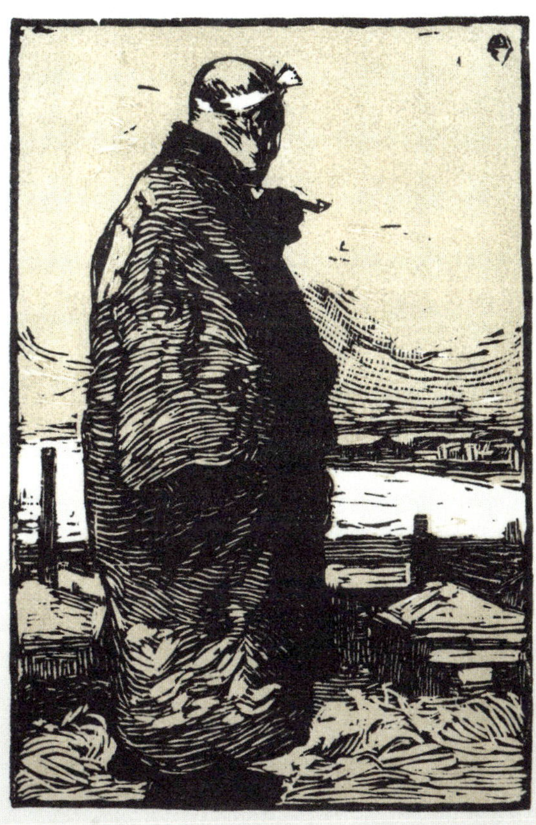

Fisherman, 1904. Recarved 1960. Woodblock print

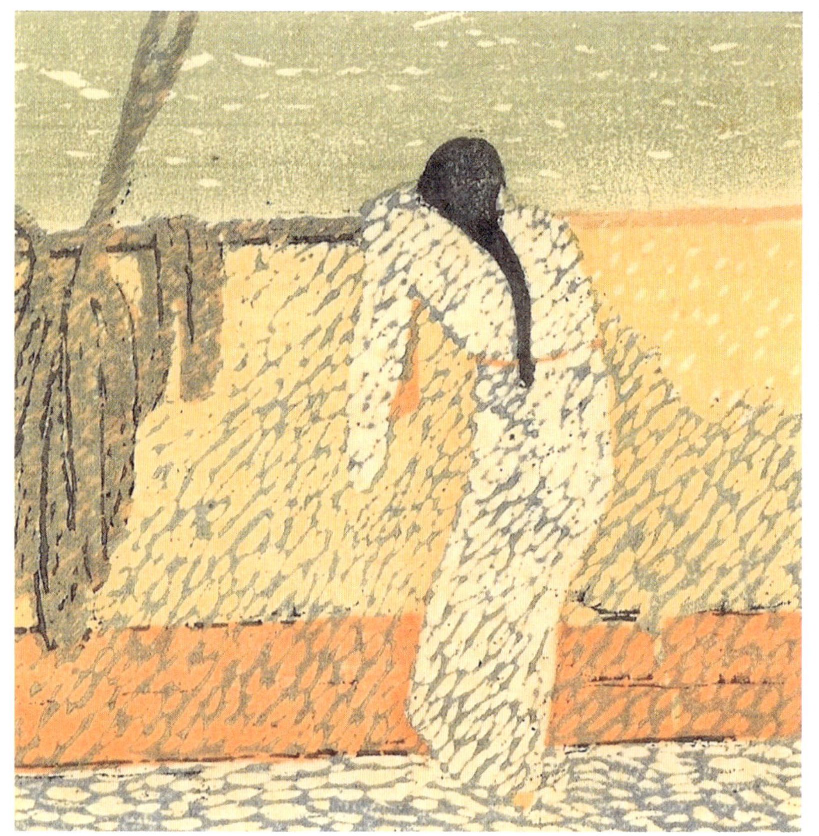

On the Deck, 1912. Woodblock print

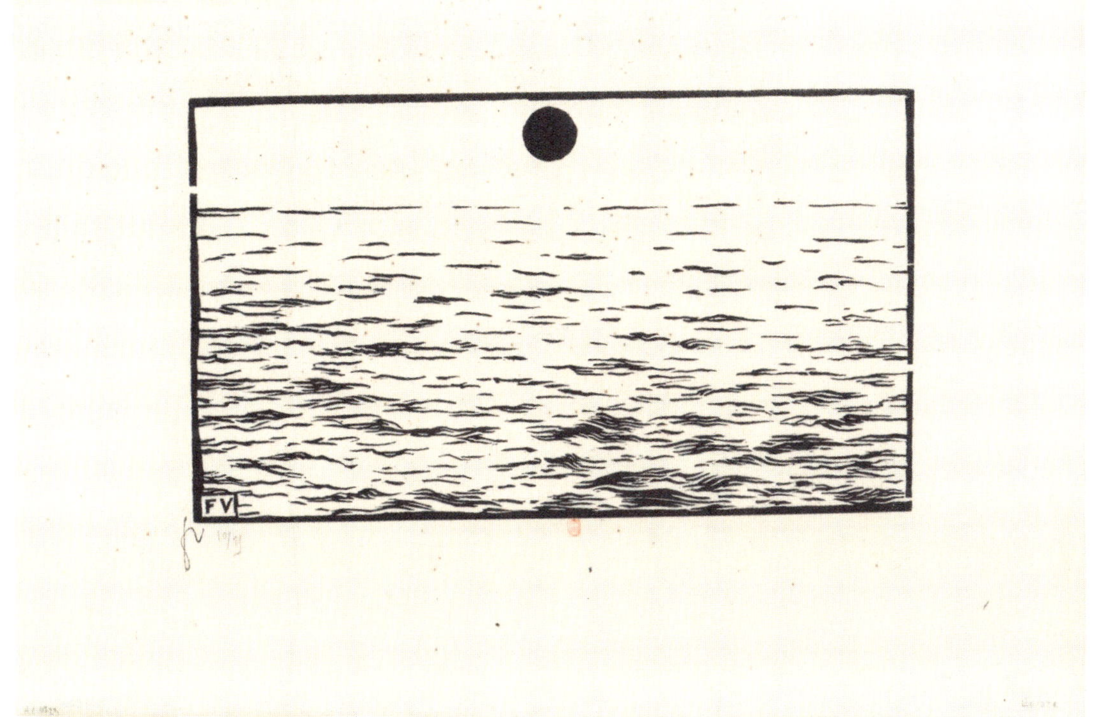

The Sea (La Mer), 1893. Engraving

Félix Vallotton

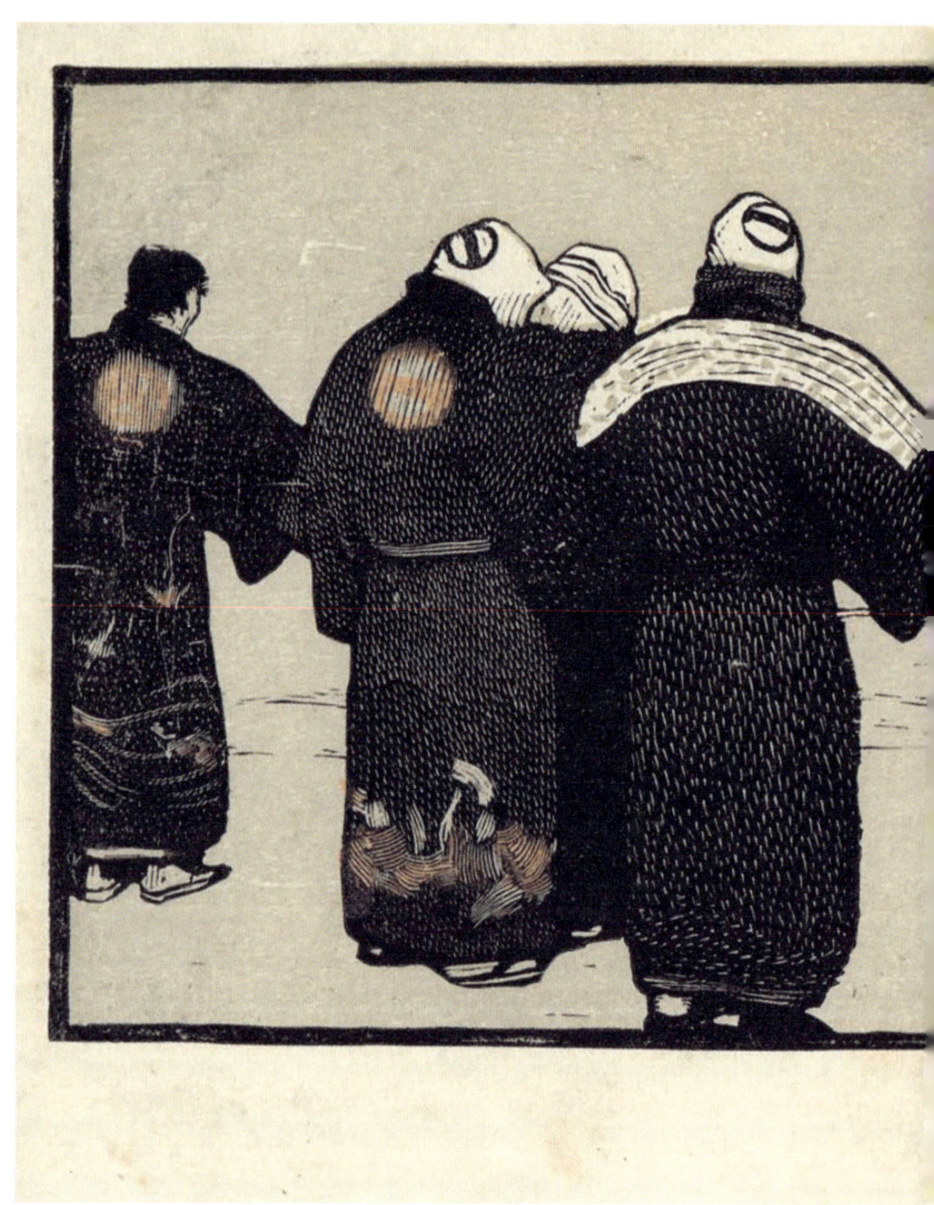

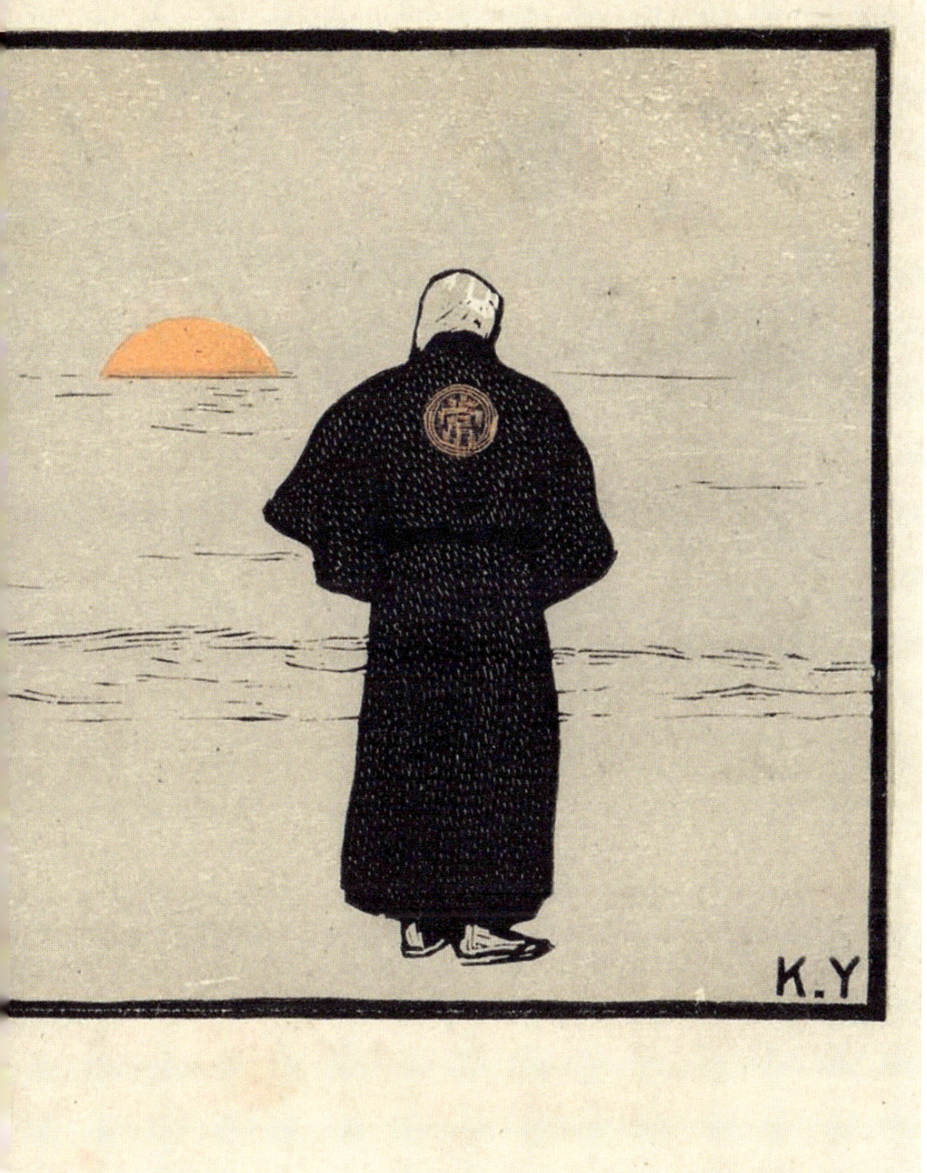

Fishermen, c.1900s. Woodblock print

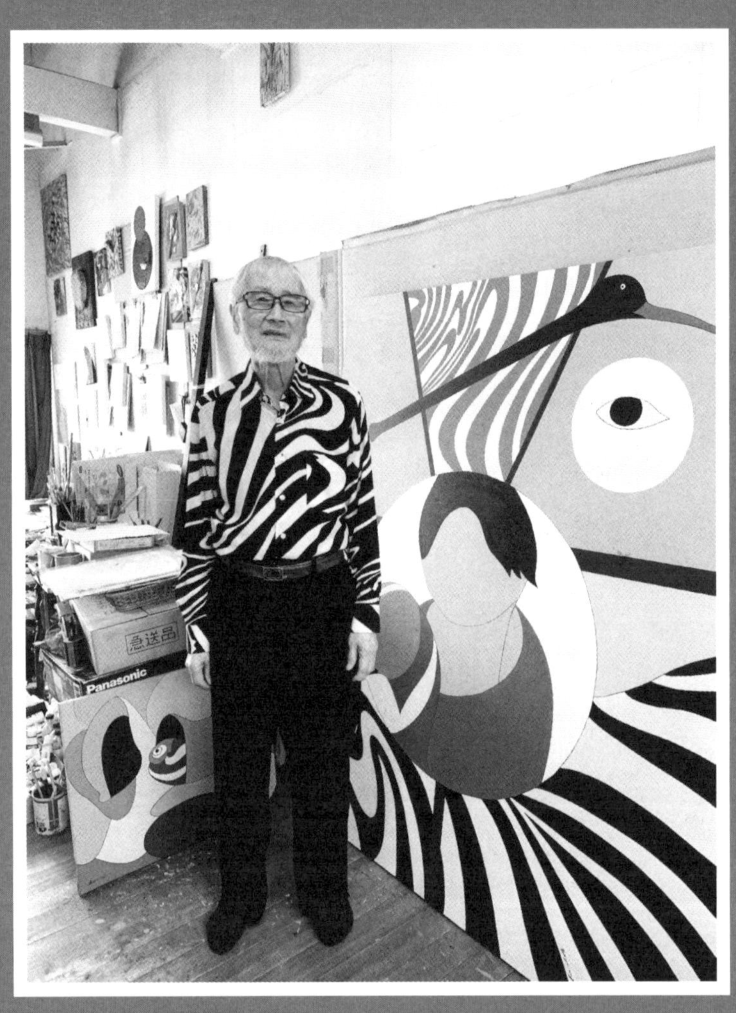
急送品
Panasonic

YAYANAGI Go (Tsuyoshi) (b.1933)

Medium:
Etching, silkscreen

He always works with splendid vitality and intensity and his skilful treatment of the value of colors, his high refinement in the control of forms, and his moderate expression of eroticism remind one of the traditional ukiyo-e, *which seem to be renewed in his unique modern version.*[1]

Ogura Tadao,
Japanese curator at the São Paulo Biennial, 1971

Both in his paintings and prints, Yayanagi Go's eye-catching signature style is defined by bright, intense colours, bold shapes and a linear sharpness, combining modern Pop art aesthetics with those of the Edo-period *ukiyo-e* – a style Yayanagi named 'pop-uki'.[2]

Yayanagi Go (Tsuyoshi) was born in Atsunai, in the Tokachi region of Hokkaido, where he graduated from an agricultural high school in 1951. He went on to study physics at Hoshi University in Tokyo, but when he came upon the work of Vincent van Gogh at an exhibition, a real interest in art was sparked, and with a desire to pursue a career as an artist, he dropped out of university. Imagining himself being like Van Gogh, he taught himself to paint in oils while working as a dishwasher and a milkman to make a living.

In 1957, Yayanagi left Japan for two years. At a time when the majority of artists of his generation were drawn to either New York or Paris, Yayanagi decided on a very different destination: São Paulo, Brazil. After 49 days aboard the immigrant ship *Brazil Maru* from Yokohama, passing through the Panama Canal, he arrived in São Paulo. Yayanagi became mesmerised by the bright colours of the Amazon and the exotic animals and birds that met him there: 'Nature is beautiful, especially its colours. The plants are beautifully green, and the soil is not only brown but also red,' he recalls. This 'exoticism' would leave clear traces in Yayanagi's later work.

The year of his arrival was also that of the 4th São Paulo Biennial, which had pushed forward modern Japanese printmaking since its beginning in 1951. Yayanagi visited the exhibition and was especially taken by the work of Jackson Pollock. The famous Abstract Expressionist, known for his drip paintings, had died the year before and had a special exhibition dedicated to him.[3] Also represented at the biennial that year were Japanese print artists of the older generation: Azechi Umetarō (pp. 44–47), Saitō Kiyoshi (pp. 138–45) and Hamaguchi Yōzō (pp. 64–67), who won a prize.[4]

Following his time in Brazil, Yayanagi visited Africa, Singapore and the Philippines. Travelling through Africa he found further inspiration, particularly in the black and white stripes of the zebra, which left a strong impression on him: 'The colours of zebras ... Black and white represent everything. Black is death and white is life.' Yayanagi adopted the monochromatic stripes as his trademark, and they feature in the majority of his paintings and prints, as well as in textiles that he has designed as part of fashion collaborations throughout his career. Yayanagi himself has often been photographed wearing silk shirts bearing his characteristic stripes. 'Etching is rendered in black and white. The colours black and white are amazingly beautiful. I first tried to grasp black and white in etching. There are whole colours in this. Japanese woodblock prints also started with black and white, from which colours were born,' Yayanagi recalls of his route into printmaking, which started with etching.

1 Ogura Tadao in 'Japão', in *XI Bienal de São Paulo: Catálogo* (Fundação Bienal de São Paulo, 1971), p. 134.

2 Unless noted, the information and quotations in this text are based on an interview with Yayanagi Go in Tokyo, May 2024. I thank Mr Yayanagi Go and his son Yayanagi Seiichi, as well as Matsuhashi Eiichi for translating the interview.

3 *IV Bienal do Museu de Arte Moderna, São Paulo, Brasil, 1957*, exh. cat. (Prefeitura de São Paulo, 1957), pp. 198–202.

4 Ibid., pp. 314–15.

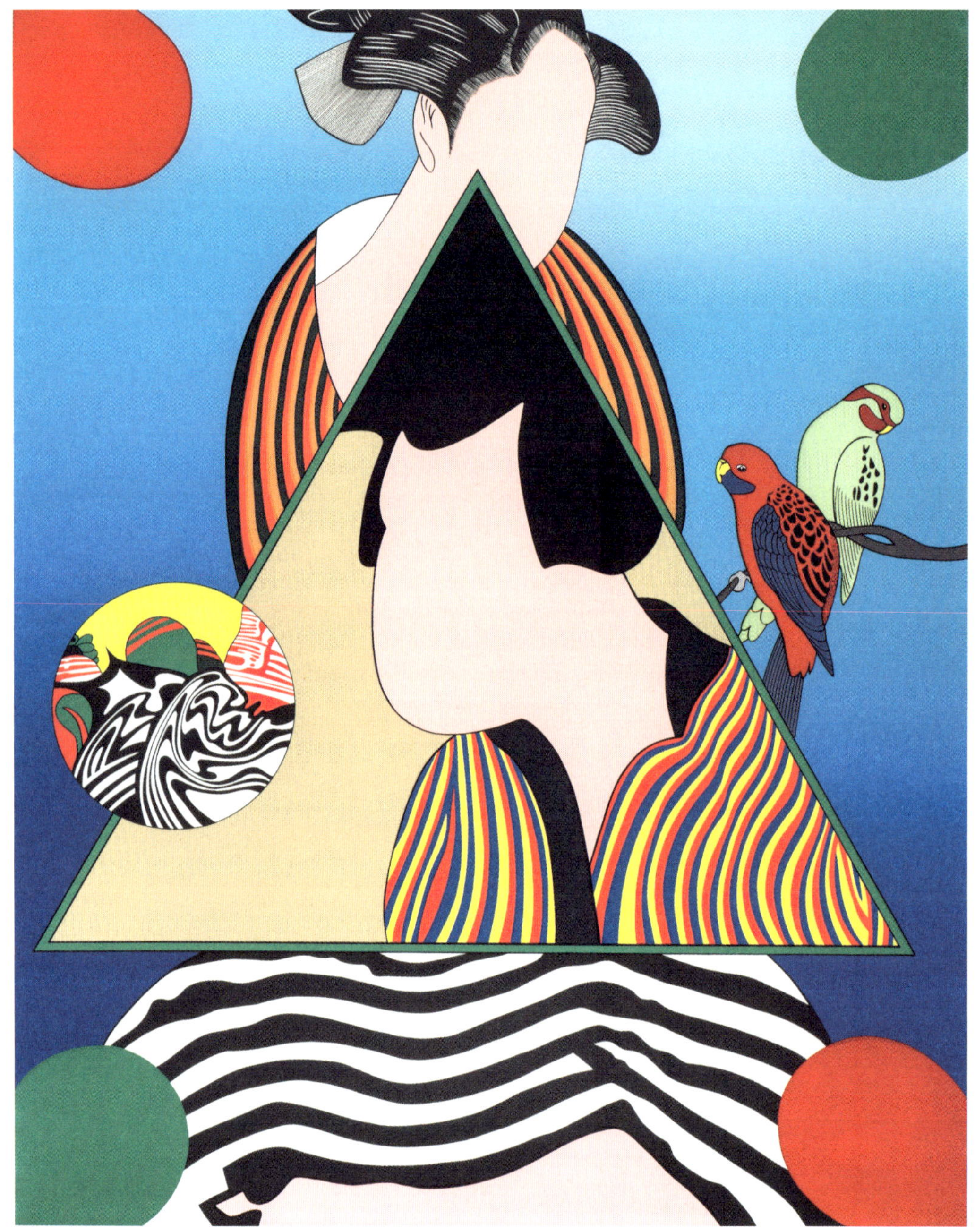

Edo Games, 1979. Silkscreen print

In 1965 Yayanagi moved to Paris, where he lived and studied for three years. His formal training in printmaking began in 1966 with an apprenticeship at the famous print studio Atelier 17, run by the master printer Stanley William Hayter, where he learned etching. Yayanagi joined a long line of artists studying printmaking under Hayter, including fellow Japanese artists Sugaï Kumi (pp. 168–71) and Yoshida Masao (b. 1934). Following his training there, he took up silkscreen printing in 1968, the year he returned to Japan. As the forms of his works changed and became more expansive, he began looking for colour, and silkscreen was the perfect medium: 'My sense of colour expanded as colours from all over the world came into my eyes, and there were things that could not be expressed in etching, so in 1968, I decided that silkscreen printing was the way to go.'

From the late 1960s, Yayanagi's 'pop-uki' style started to emerge, adopting from *ukiyo-e* the arrangement of the subject on a flat surface without the use of shadows: geometric forms, black-and-white stripes, exotic animals, shapes that clearly evoke the human body, soft flesh and women's breasts in abstract form. 'When Mr Hayter saw my silkscreen works, he said they were very nice,' he remembers.

One of Yayanagi's early silkscreen prints in his new style, *Reflecting Image* (1968), entered the collection of the Museum of Modern Art, New York, as early as 1970. Also in 1970, Yayanagi participated in the 7th International Biennial Exhibition of Prints in Tokyo with two large silkscreens in his already established signature 'pop-uki' style, *Female Body A* and *Female Body B*, which received a full-page colour illustration in the exhibition catalogue, designed by Nagai Kazumasa (pp. 108–11).[5] Visitors to the major print exhibition that year could also enjoy other bright, colour-pop prints by Japanese artists Ay-O (pp. 31–43), Onosato Toshinobu (pp. 134–37) and Satō Ado (pp. 146–51), as well as Gordon Rayner (1935–2010) and Roy Lichtenstein, to mention just a few.

The following year, Yayanagi was one of the artists representing Japan at the 11th São Paulo Biennial. He was reuniting with the country that had such a strong influence on his artistic development when he was just twenty years old. In 1971, alongside four other Japanese print artists – Ay-O, Noda Tetsuya (pp. 117–23), Kimura Kosuke (b. 1936) and Nagai Kazumasa – Yayanagi showed twenty large silkscreen prints. *Female Body A* and *Female Body B*, shown at the Tokyo print biennale the previous year, were included. Yayanagi's unique aesthetics captured the audience's interest, and his prints sold very well.[6]

Believing that he must understand his native country's art and traditions to become truly innovative, in 1974 Yayanagi turned to the classic Japanese theme of the *Tale of Genji*, a novel written by the lady-in-waiting Murasaki Shikibu around 1021. The story, which has been interpreted in various media throughout Japanese art history, was taken up by the *ukiyo-e* artists Utagawa Kuniyoshi and Toyohara Kunichika (1835–1900), who both created whole series based on the theme. Yayanagi created his own 'pop-uki' version, consisting of ten silkscreen prints. He reinterpreted the classic tale, turning it into colourful, psychedelic scenes that reference both *ukiyo-e* as well as the erotic genre of *shunga*, from which Yayanagi also borrowed a humorous approach. 'I broke [the story] down and then expressed it in modern prints,' he explains. The series received much recognition abroad and won Yayanagi awards.

5 Catalogue published by the National Museum of Modern Art, Tokyo, 1970, n.p.

6 Yayanagi Go et al., *Ai no dōbutsushi: hanga zensakuhinshū, 1965–1981* [Animals of Love: Complete Collection of Prints, 1965–1981] (Tokyo: Sōbunsha, 1981), p. 7.

Yayanagi has been represented at several international exhibitions, such as the 2nd International Exhibition of Graphic Art in Frechen, Germany (1972); the Los Angeles County Museum of Art's *Contemporary Japanese Prints* (1972); *Contemporary Japanese Prints: Symbols of a Society in Transition* at the British Museum, London (1985); and the Cincinnati Museum of Art's *Innovation and Tradition: Twentieth-Century Japanese Prints from the Howard and Caroline Porter Collection* (1989).

Feeling more closely aligned to Hokusai than to Picasso, Yayanagi aims to express a strong connection to his cultural heritage in his work, while also embracing Western art and culture. The meeting of the two, the artist says, 'can create something wonderful'. Today Yayanagi Go lives in Tokyo and is still active as a painter.

Collections: British Museum, London; Cincinnati Museum of Art; Hokkaido Museum of Modern Art; Museum of Modern Art, New York; National Museum of Modern Art, Tokyo.

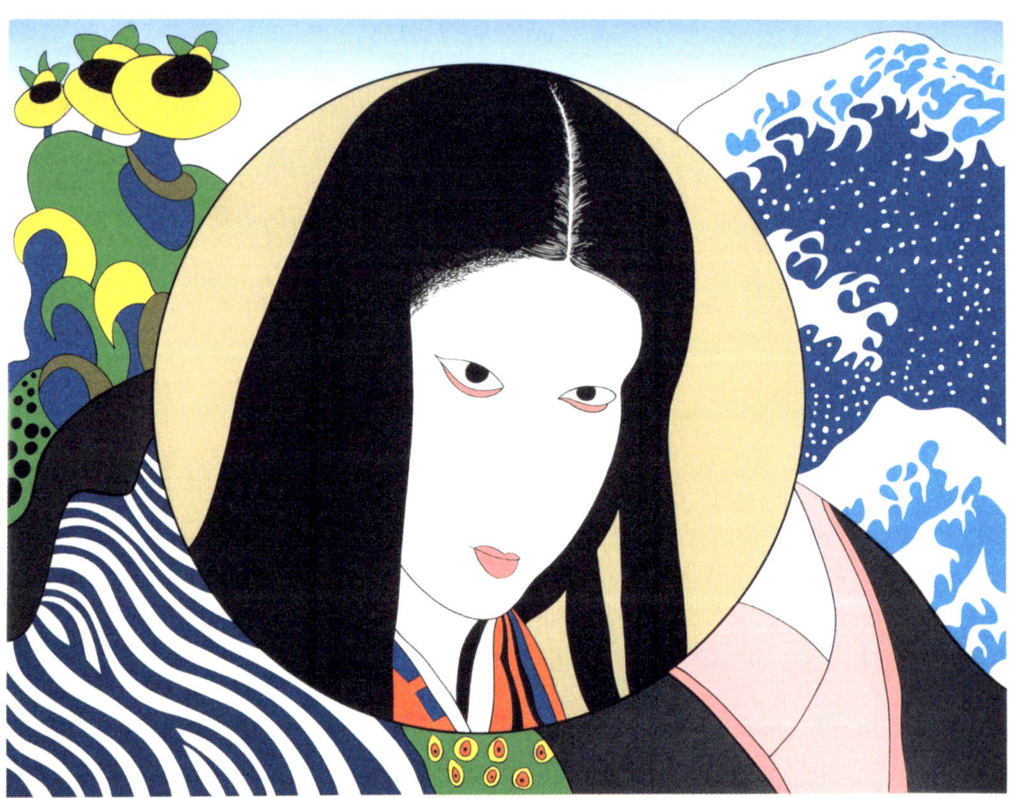

Sentier Fleuri, 1978. Silkscreen print

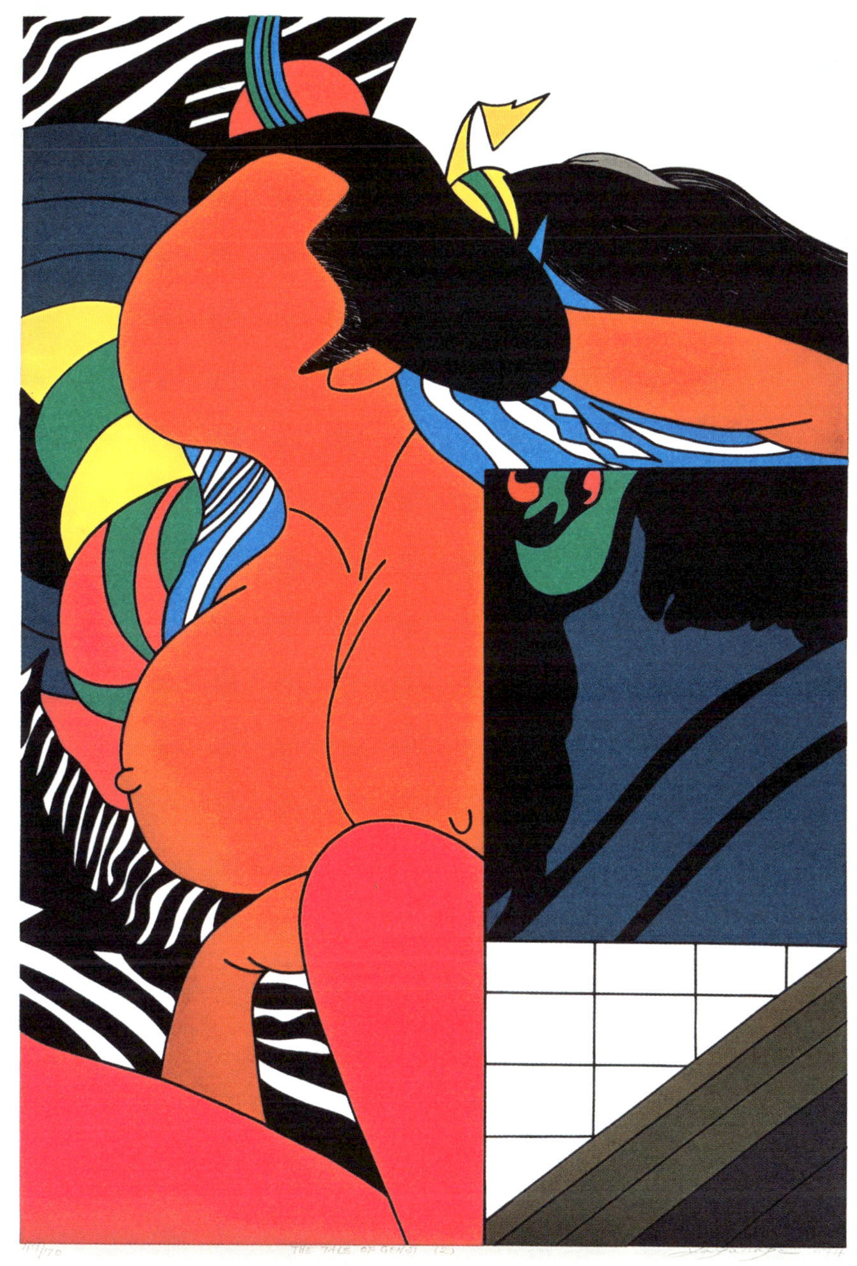

The Tale of Genji (2), 1974. Silkscreen print

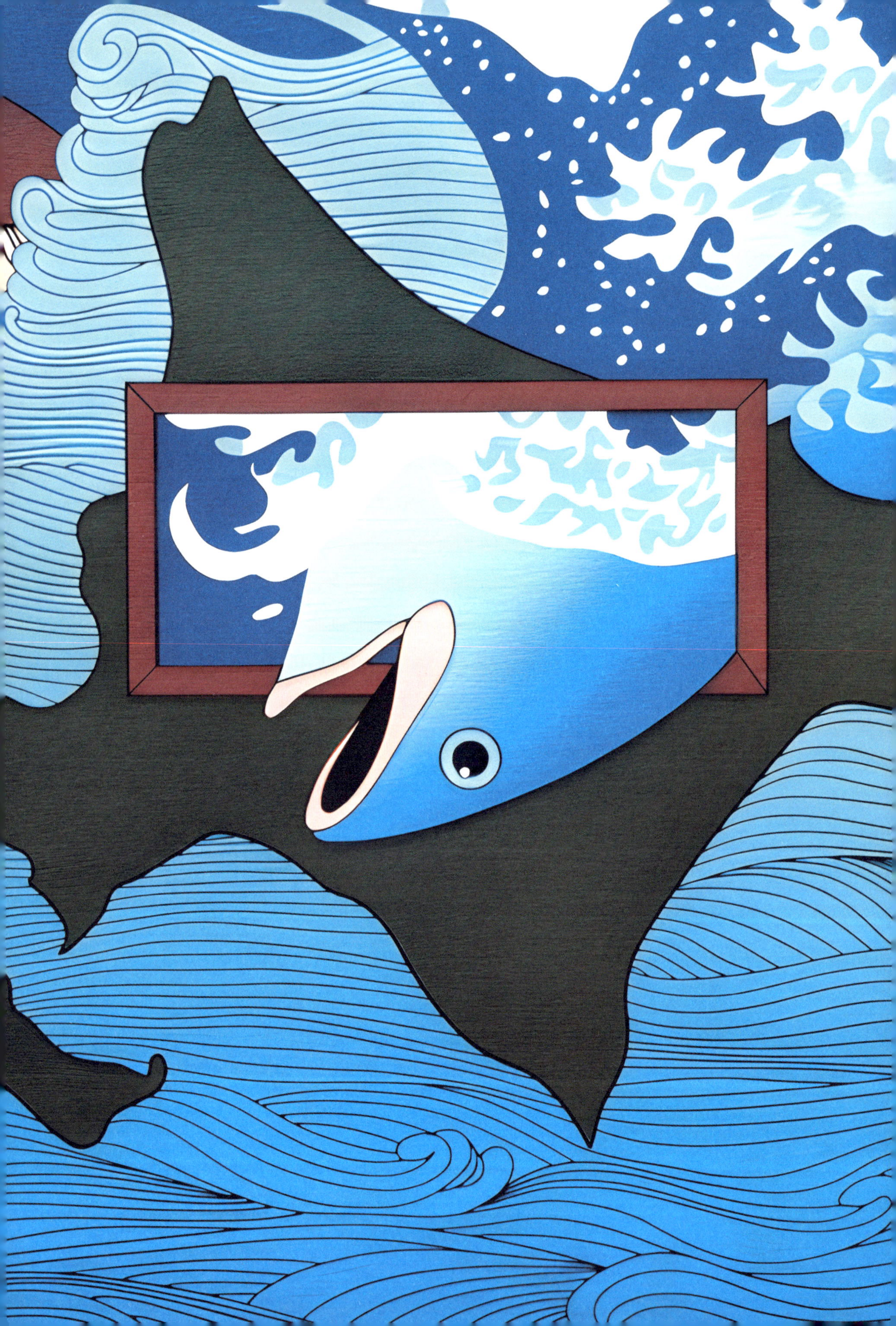

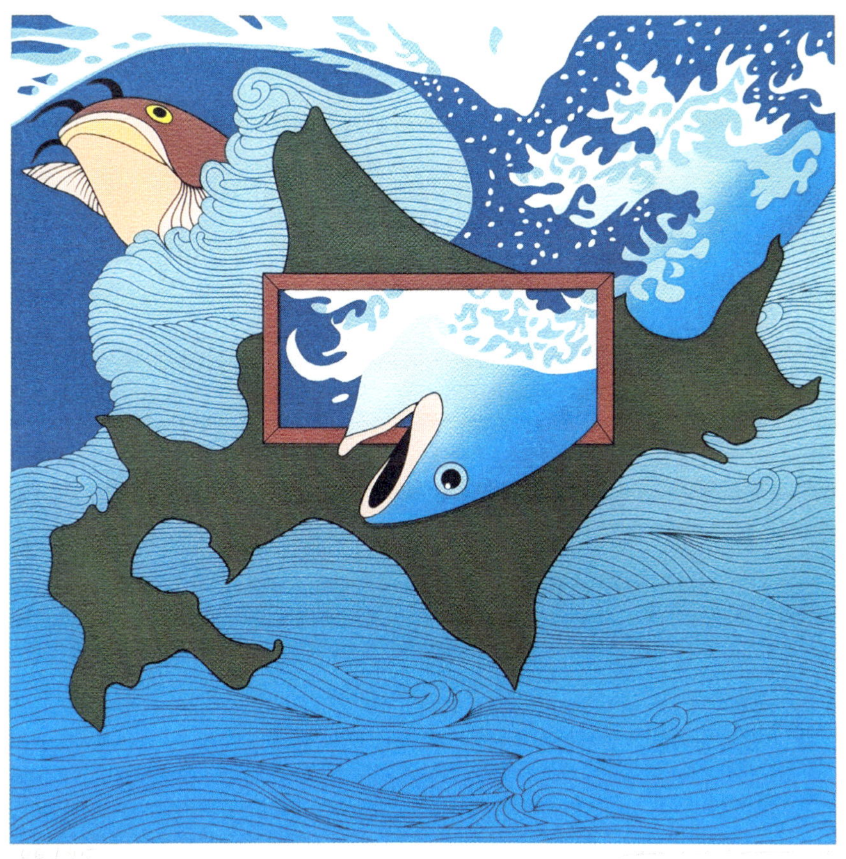

Flower Like the Blue Sky, 1982. Silkscreen print

YOKOO Tadanori (b.1936)

Medium:
Silkscreen, woodblock

Yokoo is completely uninhibited – for him nothing is unspeakable … He is as likely to shock and repel as to amuse and delight.[1]

Graphics by Tadanori Yokoo,
Museum of Modern Art, New York, 1972

Yokoo Tadanori, painter, printmaker, illustrator and graphic designer, has produced some of Japan's most iconic works of graphic design. Taking his cues from both traditional *ukiyo-e* and contemporary pop culture, Yokoo inhabits a nostalgic, humorous, psychedelic and often absurd visual world – one that takes *ukiyo-e* back to its roots as a form of commercial art.

Beginning his career as a stage and graphic designer for theatre, in 1960 Yokoo moved to Tokyo and started working for the Nippon Design Center, co-founded by Nagai Kazumasa (pp. 108–11), and during the 1960s and '70s was perhaps Japan's most famous graphic designer. In 1966 he created advertisements for Asahi beer, the Exhibition of Japan Advertising Artists Club, the Takarazuka Grand Revue, the Jōkyō Gekijo (Situation Theatre) troupe, as well as for art critic Kurita Isamu's book *The City and Design, The Wonders of Life on Earth* and for the essay 'The Aesthetics of End' by Mishima Yukio (1925–1970). Indeed, Yokoo collaborated with the controversial author and playwright several times. For Mishima's kabuki production *Strange Tales of the Bow Moon* (1969), Yokoo created a poster in his distinctive graphic style, combining Edo iconography with vivid psychedelic colours and a fragmented layout, each scene labelled numerically. The four-act play, performed at the National Theatre of Japan in Tokyo in 1969 (a year before Mishima's suicide), was based on the popular story of the medieval hero Minamoto no Tametomo (1139–1170), written by Edo novelist Takizawa Bakin (1767–1848) and illustrated by none other than Katsushika Hokusai in 1807–11.[2] Yokoo borrowed his warrior figures and wave motifs directly from Hokusai's monochrome illustrations in volume 1, taking them out of their original context of popular printed literature (*yomihon*) of the Edo period and into a modern-day silkscreen poster.[3]

Yokoo's psychedelic-pop silkscreens were exhibited in the United States for the first time in 1967, in a New York gallery: 'At the time, as the advertisement style and the Japanese on the works were not understood, some people called them posters and others called them Japanese-style pop art,' he has said.[4] The following year they entered the collection of the Museum of Modern Art, New York.

When the exhibition *Word and Image: Posters and Typography from the Graphic Design Collection of the Museum of Modern Art, 1879–1967* was organised in 1968, seven works by Yokoo were included. Alongside masters of the Belle Époque poster Jules Chéret[5] and Alphonse Mucha (1860–1939) as well as A. M. Cassandre's (1901–1968) iconic interwar design, Yokoo and his contemporaries such as Yamashiro Ryūichi, Bruno Munari (1907–1998), Frank Stella (1936–2024) and Andy Warhol were moving in the cross-section between art and graphic design.

In New York, Yokoo had met some of the Pop art stars who were key figures in pushing the graphic medium onto the art scene: 'I went to New York in 1967 in order to meet these pop artists. Andy Warhol's friend John Wilcock was

1 Museum of Modern Art, New York, *Graphics by Tadanori Yokoo*, press release, 1972, p. 2, www.moma.org/documents/moma_press-release_326787.pdf.

2 See Christine Guth, *Hokusai's Great Wave: Biography of a Global Icon* (Honolulu: University of Hawai'i Press, 2015), pp. 117–18.

3 *Chinsetsu yumiharizuki* (Strange Tales of the Bow Moon), woodblock printed book, vol. 1 (of 30 volumes in five parts), published 1807–11, can be found in the collection of the British Museum, London.

4 Yokoo Tadanori quoted in 'Artist Interview: Tadanori Yokoo', Tate, September 2015, www.tate.org.uk/whats-on/tate-modern/world-goes-pop/artist-interview/tadanori-yokoo.

5 Interestingly, Jules Chéret was the designer behind the poster for the first major Japanese print exhibition in Paris, *Exposition de la gravure japonaise*, held in 1890. See p. 14, fig. 8.

Exhibition of Japan Advertising Artists Club, 1966. Offset print a collector of my screen prints. Andy Warhol was interested in my work so I went to Warhol's factory. Jasper Johns, Rauschenberg and Tom Wesselmann were also interested in my silk screen works so whenever I went to New York I met them as well.'[6]

In 1969 Yokoo presented *Torture*, a set of three silkscreen prints, at the 6th Paris Youth Biennale; the work was awarded the grand prize in the prints category. He also participated in the exhibition *A Prospect of Modern Design in Japan* at the National Museum of Modern Art, Kyoto. In 1972, Yokoo received the UNESCO Award at the 4th International Poster Biennale in Warsaw.

With his return to MoMA in the 1972 solo exhibition *Graphics by Tadanori Yokoo*, Yokoo's international recognition was fully cemented. The 1970s offered collaborations on album covers for Miles Davis (1975) and Santana (1974) as well as posters for The Beatles and Cat Stevens (both 1972), among other major names. The exhibition *Graphic Image '73* was held at the Tokyo Central Museum of Arts, in which Yokoo participated along with Nagai Kazumasa and Sugaï Kumi (pp. 168–71), among others. In 1974 he had a solo exhibition at the Stedelijk Museum in Amsterdam, and he also participated in the Tokyo International Biennial Exhibition of Prints.

Throughout Yokoo's career, woodblock printing has been an important part of his oeuvre. Perhaps Yokoo can be seen as today's 'keeper' of not only the *ukiyo-e* graphic style but also that of the traditional woodblock medium. His portrait series of kabuki actors (*yakusha-e*), from 2021, is based on the work of Edo-period printmaker Tōshūsai Sharaku, who has also influenced the contemporary printmaker Tsuruya Kōkei (see pp. 202–7). In his twenty-first-century interpretation of the eighteenth-century prints, Yokoo combines traditional Japanese technique and imagery with vivid 'Pop' colours and simple lines in semi-abstract compositions, somewhat reminiscent of Picasso's linocut *Portrait of a Woman with a Hat* (1962). By emphasising a deliberate misalignment of lines and colours, Yokoo also plays with the accuracy in traditional printing of multiple colour blocks.[7]

Yokoo has participated in the annual College Women's Association of Japan shows since the 1970s, continuing to this day. A major exhibition titled *Hanga Jungle* was held at Machida City Museum of Graphic Arts in 2017, showing about 250 of Yokoo's works.

Collections: Machida City Museum of Graphic Arts; Museum of Contemporary Art, Tokyo; Museum of Modern Art, New York; Yokoo Tadanori Museum of Contemporary Art, Kobe.

6 Yokoo quoted in 'Artist Interview: Tadanori Yokoo'.

7 When making prints of multiple colours, *ukiyo-e* artisans – and many modern-day artists using the traditional printing technique – would use a *kentō*, a registration mark, in order to know where to place the paper when printing each colour.

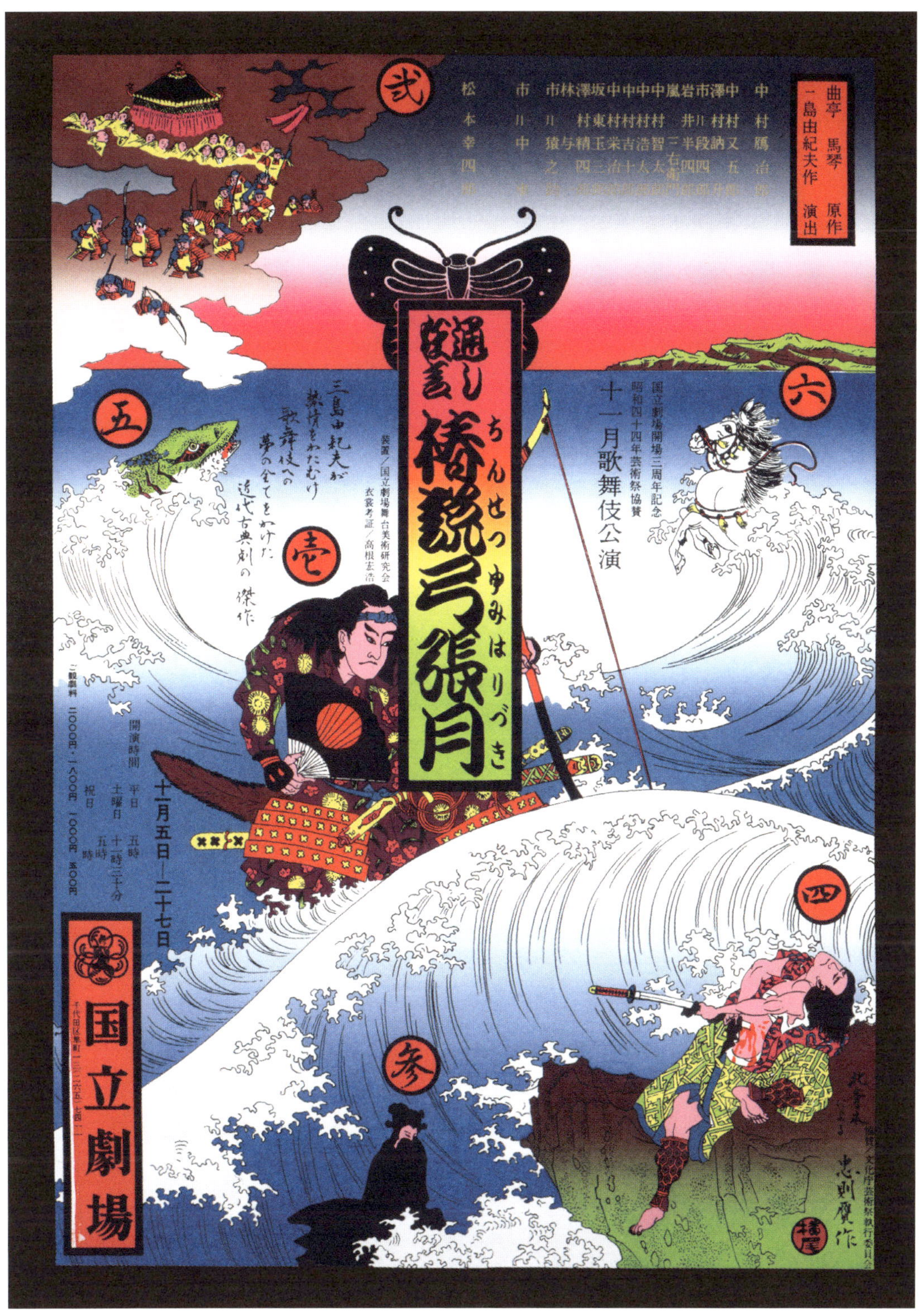

The Kyogen Play 'Chisetsu Yumiharizuki', 1969. Silkscreen print

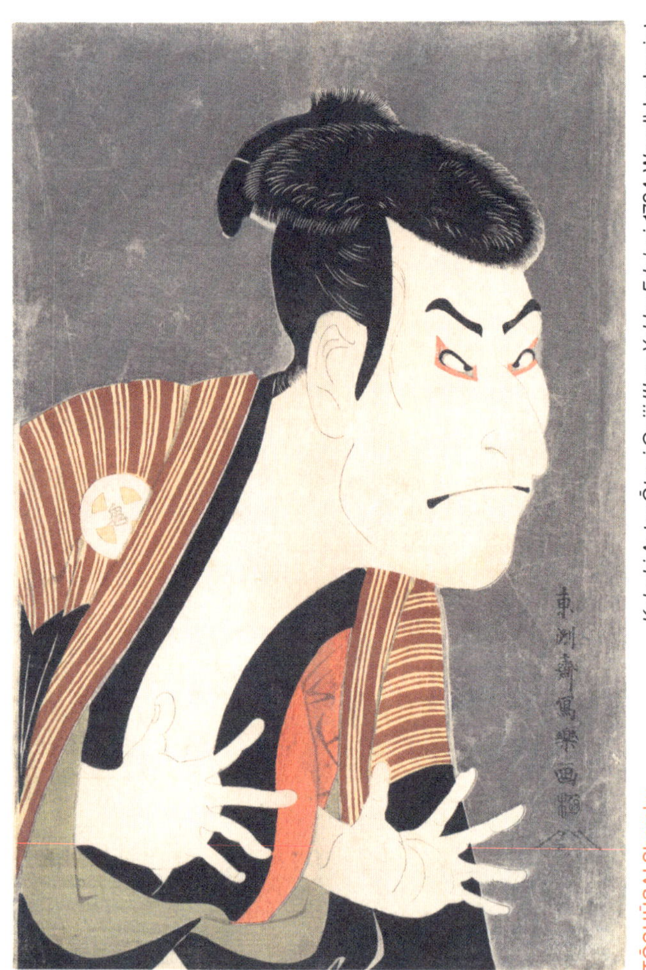

TŌSHŪSAI Sharaku

Kabuki Actor Ōtani Oniji III as Yakko Edobei, 1794. Woodblock print

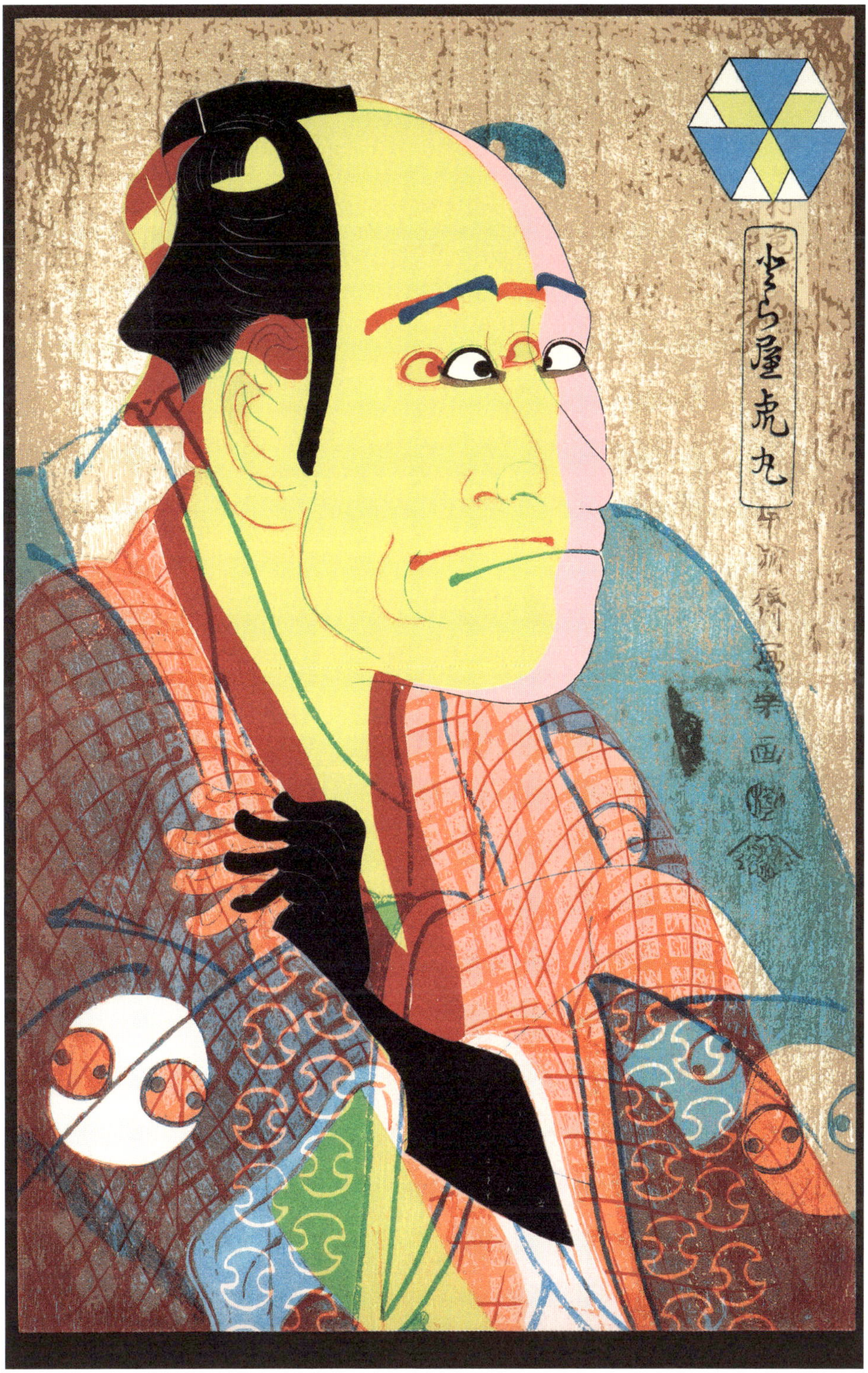

Sharaku – The Five Constellations, 2021. Woodblock print

Yoshida Family: YOSHIDA Hiroshi (1876–1950)

Medium:
Woodblock

When Yoshida Hiroshi visited the Exposition Universelle in 1900, where he was participating with a watercolour for which he won a prize,[1] it had been only ten years since the first major exhibition of Japanese *ukiyo-e* prints in Paris that fuelled the craze for the Japanese graphic medium in Europe (p. 18).

Already a successful artist trained in Western-style painting, at that time Hiroshi was not involved or interested in printmaking. When his contemporary Urushibara Yoshijirō (pp. 208–11), at the time working as a woodblock print craftsman, was demonstrating the traditional technique at the Japan-British Exhibition, London, in 1910, Hiroshi was participating in the 'Western Paintings' section of the same exhibition.[2] But, in 1920, he presented his first woodblock prints at the studio of Watanabe Shōzaburō, the driving force behind Hiroshi's, as well as many other artists', interest in printmaking. It was also through him that Hiroshi had his first *shin hanga* prints published and sold.

As a talented painter of landscapes, it is not surprising that Hiroshi transferred this skill to printmaking. It was his prints that gained him commercial success abroad, and today he is considered one of the masters of modern Japanese landscape printmaking. In 1923–24, Hiroshi and his wife Fujio travelled to the USA on their third visit. Among other things, their objective was to collect money for artists struggling following the Great Kantō earthquake of 1923, in which the original blocks of many print artists were destroyed when Watanabe's shop went up in flames.[3] It was during this trip that Hiroshi realised there was a bigger market for his *shin hanga* prints than for his paintings. Fujio recalled: 'We had shows in several major cities, but we sold discouragingly few pictures. There was a good deal more interest in a few prints ... his first prints, commissioned and published by the house of Watanabe.'[4]

In 1925, Hiroshi set up his own studio of carvers and printers, similar to the practice of *ukiyo-e*, but taking full control of the process: 'He became his own publisher, and the best carvers and printers he could find worked in his studio under his personal supervision.'[5] *Ancient Ruins of Athens (Acropolis – Night)* from 1925 and *Morning on Mount Tsurugi* from 1926 – two very different subjects from Eastern and Western culture – are examples of Hiroshi's self-published prints from this early period, also reflecting the many places around the world he visited and turned into subject matter.

Hiroshi continued travelling and organising exhibitions abroad, promoting works by other *shin hanga* artists as well, including in the two important exhibitions at the Toledo Museum of Art in 1930 and 1936. As curator Dorothy Blair wrote: 'It is due to the splendid co-operation of our friend, Hiroshi Yoshida, wood-block print designer of Tokyo, that our exhibition is so complete.'[6]

In 1952, two years after Hiroshi's death, the Yoshida family was invited to exhibit at the Japan Society in New York. *Wood-block Prints by the Yoshida Family* featured the work of six members of the family, each very different in style: Hiroshi and Fujio, their sons Tōshi and Hodaka, Kobun (son of Tōshi) and Chizuko (wife of Hodaka).[7] Much had changed between the world's fair in Paris in 1900 and this exhibition of a family legacy in mid-twentieth-century New York. The Yoshida family had entered a new era.

Collections: Boston Museum of Fine Arts; British Museum, London; Toledo Museum of Art.

1 Commission impériale à l'Exposition universelle de Paris, *Catalogue spécial officiel du Japon: Exposition universelle internationale de 1900*, exh. cat. (Paris, 1900), cat. no. 51, p. 136.

2 He showed three works: *After the Rain*, *Perpetual Snows* and a third, untitled landscape. See Imperial Japanese Government Commission to the Japan-British Exhibition, *An Illustrated Catalogue of Japanese Modern Fine Arts Displayed at the Japan-British Exhibition, London, 1910*, exh. cat. (Tokyo: Shimbi Shoin, 1910), cat. nos. 52, 56 and 58.

3 See 'Foreword' (1930), in Dorothy Blair, *Modern Japanese Prints: Printed from a Photographic Reproduction of Two Exhibition Catalogues of Modern Japanese Prints Published by the Toledo Museum of Art in 1930 and 1936* (Toledo, OH: Toledo Museum of Art, 1997), and Helen Merritt, *Modern Japanese Woodblock Prints: The Early Years* (Honolulu: University of Hawai'i Press, 1990), p. 60.

4 Yoshida Fujio quoted in Oliver Statler, *Modern Japanese Prints: An Art Reborn* (Rutland, VT: Charles E. Tuttle Co., 1956), p. 171.

5 Statler, *Modern Japanese Prints*, p. 168.

6 'Foreword' (1930), in Blair, *Modern Japanese Prints*.

7 See *A Catalog of Wood-Block Prints by the Yoshida Family*, exh. cat. (New York: Japan Society, 1952).

The Acropolis Ruins at Night, 1925. Woodblock print

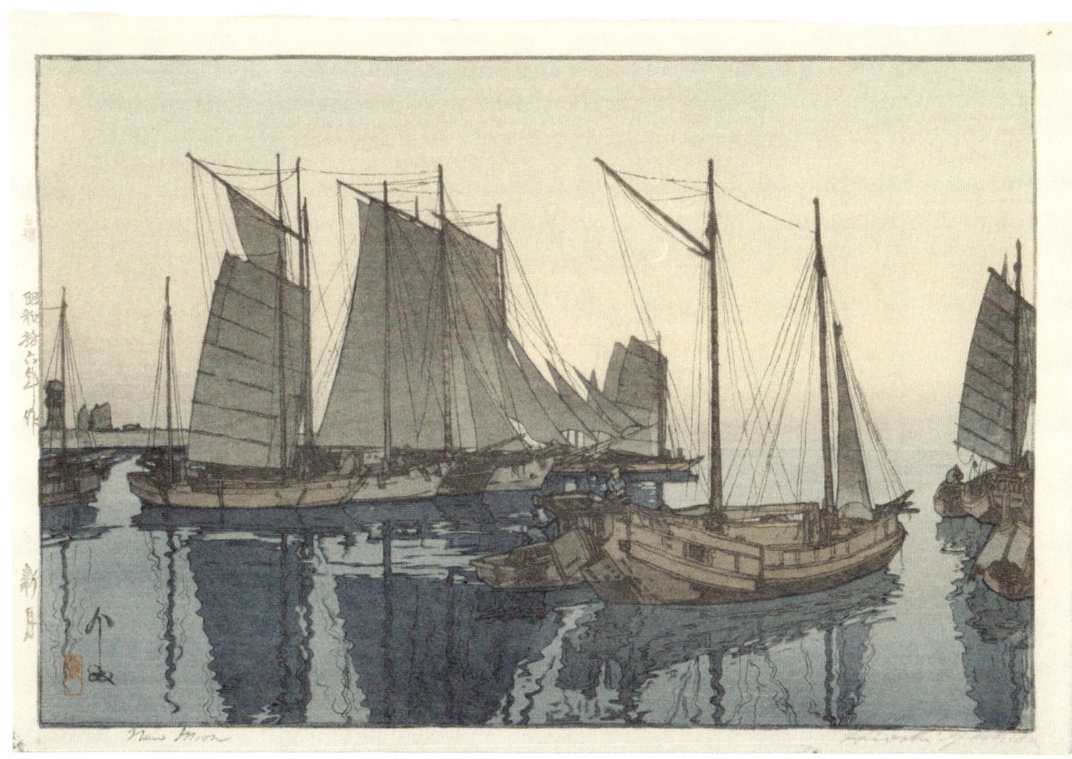

Crescent Moon, 1941. Woodblock print

Yoshida Family: YOSHIDA Fujio (1887–1987)

Medium:
Woodblock

It was following the death of her husband Hiroshi in 1950 that Yoshida Fujio moved into her abstract period. An accomplished painter and the first female artist in her family – her father was the painter Yoshida Kasaburō (1861–1894) – she was also one of the first women to study Western-style painting in Japan, at a time when women were excluded from attending the Tokyo School of Fine Arts (until 1946). She entered the private art school Fudōsha at the age of twelve, where her future husband Hiroshi was also a student.[8] They had two sons, Yoshida Tōshi, born in 1911, and Yoshida Hodaka, born in 1926.

In 1920, Fujio was an establishing member of Shuyōkai (Vermilion Leaf Society), a group for female painters. Later in the decade, Fujio, whose usual medium was watercolour, began making a few woodblock prints. These were traditional still-lifes, such as *Roses* (1927), based on an earlier watercolour.

It was not until the 1950s that she appeared with her 'queer pictures', as she herself described them.[9] These enlarged, semi-abstract flowers and plants first appeared in paintings from 1949 and then in prints from 1953. As pointed out in *A Japanese Legacy: Four Generations of Yoshida Family Artists*, 'they are among the few works by Fujio to be widely known', however at the time the prints sold only in modest numbers.[10] Fujio's later boldness and abstractionism were inspired by her son Hodaka, and in line with the *sōsaku hanga* movement, she also began carving and printing herself in 1954.

Fujio participated in the very first College Women's Association of Japan show in 1956 with two prints in her new signature style, *Myōga* (Ginger) and *Narcissus*, alongside works by both of her sons and her daughter-in-law Chizuko, wife of Hodaka. She was part of the exhibition *Prints by the Yoshida Family* at the Dallas Museum of Art in 1957, and joined the young couple on an extended trip around the world in 1957–58.

Living to the age of 100, Fujio experienced and overcame the restrictions on female artists particularly during the first half of the twentieth century, and was later able to experience both her daughter-in-law's and her granddaughter's successes as modern female artists in a world still largely dominated by men.

Collections: Art Institute of Chicago; Cincinnati Art Museum; Minneapolis Institute of Art; Portland Museum of Art; Rijksmuseum, Amsterdam.

8 Hiroshi had been adopted by Yoshida Kasaburō so that he could take over the painting business from Kasaburō, whose only children were daughters. One of them was Fujio, whom Hiroshi married in 1907. See Laura W. Allen et al., *A Japanese Legacy: Four Generations of Yoshida Family Artists*, exh. cat. (Minneapolis, MN: Minneapolis Institute of Arts, 2002), p. 24.

9 Statler, *Modern Japanese Prints*, p. 172.

10 Allen et al., *A Japanese Legacy*, p. 30.

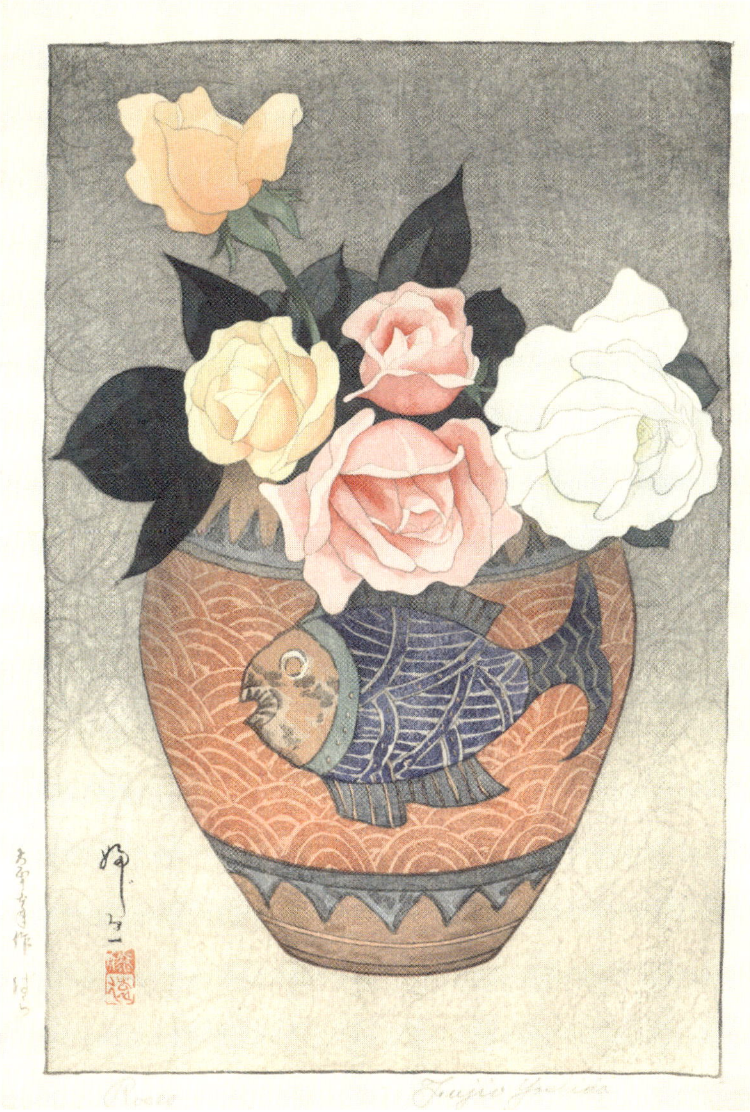

Roses, 1927. Woodblock print

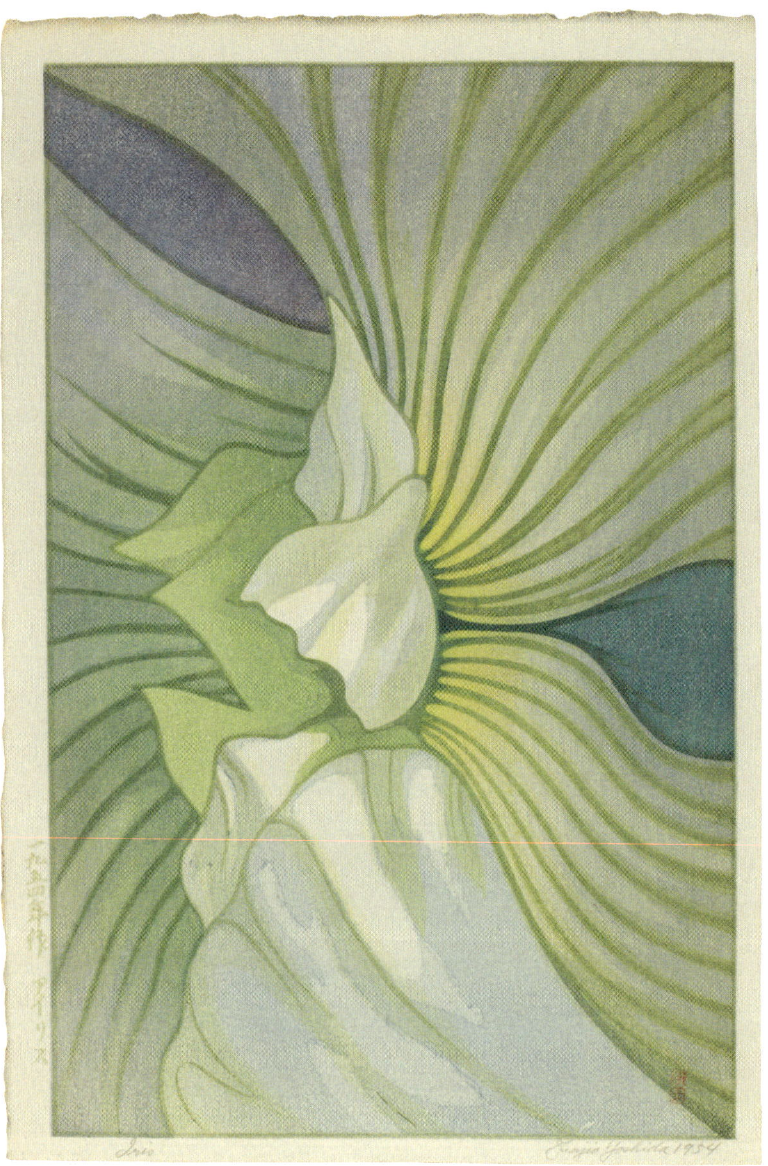

Iris, 1954. Woodblock print

Photograph of YOSHIDA Fujio (left), Hodaka (middle) and Chizuko (right) at Dallas Museum of Fine Arts, 1957

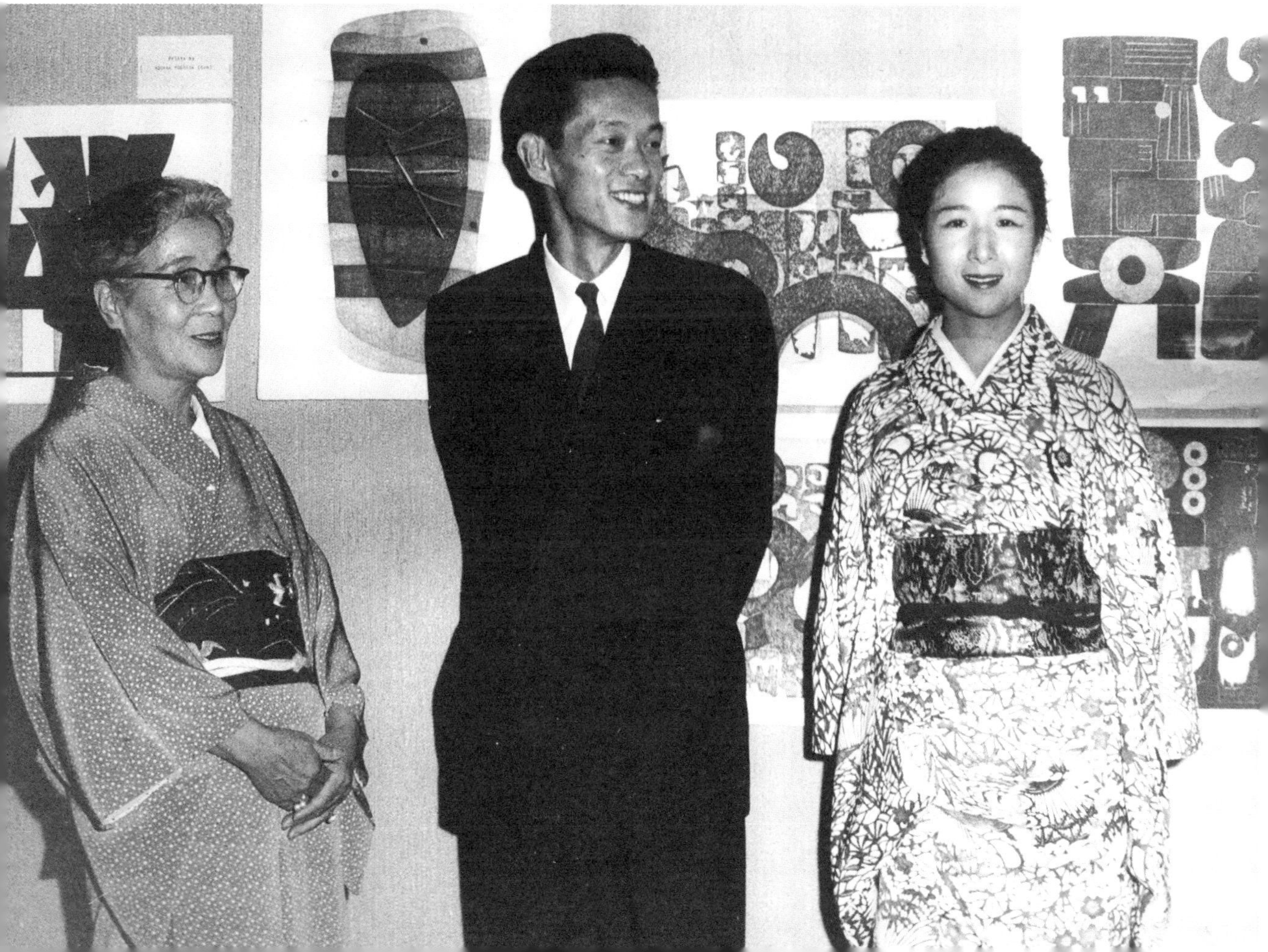

Yoshida Family: YOSHIDA Hodaka (1926–1995)

Medium:
Lithograph, photo etching, silkscreen and woodblock

Yoshida Hodaka was the youngest son of Hiroshi and Fujio, and named after one of his father's favourite mountains, Hodaka-yama. He showed an early interest in art, and painted when he was a child, but his father's decision that he should pursue a career in science led him away from the creative path for a while. However, during his university years he took up art again, experimenting with abstract oil painting in secret. 'My father's opposition made me an abstract artist,' he explained to Oliver Statler in 1956.[11]

Growing up in the studio surrounded by printmaking, it is no surprise that Hodaka began experimenting with woodblock printing, which happened around 1949. But, as opposed to Hiroshi, he would carve and print his own work. Rather than following in his father's footsteps as a *shin hanga* artist, he became active in the *sōsaku hanga* movement, manifesting a strong creative force and belief in self-expression. He exhibited for the first time with the Japan Print Association in 1952.

Over the course of his long career, Hodaka's styles ranged from expressionism to Pop art and photorealism, while working in different techniques besides woodblock printing, including lithography, photo etching and screenprinting.[12] A trip to Mexico in 1955, where he encountered pre-Columbian artefacts, left a strong impression on Hodaka and significantly influenced his subject matter, such as can be seen in *Ancient People* and *Mask* (1956), both exhibited in the first CWAJ print show in 1956.

In 1957, *Mask* was exhibited again as part of the Dallas Museum of Art's exhibition *Prints by the Yoshida Family*, which included works by Hodaka, Chizuko and Fujio. 'Famed Japanese printmaker, Hodaka Yoshida, his wife Chizuko, and mother, Fujio, will give a lecture demonstration of woodblock printmaking Sunday at the Dallas Museum of Fine Arts', the *Dallas Morning News* wrote. The exhibition showcased thirty prints by the three artists, which were also available for sale. In a photograph of the three taken during the exhibition, Hodaka's works appear in the background, including his two large prints *Stones and a Man A* and *B*.

In the 1950s and '60s, Hodaka was also active as a photographer. Between 1960 and 1965, he succeeded in developing a technique combining woodblock with zinc letterpress prints of his own photographs; starting in 1970, and for the rest of his life, he actively combined his own photographs with woodblock prints.

Other early national and international shows that Hodaka participated in include the Tokyo International Biennial Exhibition of Prints (1957–66), *Contemporary Japanese Prints: Sōsaku Hanga* at the Art Institute of Chicago (1960) and the São Paulo Biennial (1967).

Collections: Art Institute of Chicago; British Museum, London; Dallas Museum of Art; National Museum of Asian Art, Washington, DC.

11 Yoshida Hodaka quoted in Statler, *Modern Japanese Prints*, p. 170.
12 See for example Gaston Petit and Amadio Arboleda, *Evolving Techniques in Japanese Woodblock Prints* (Tokyo, New York, San Fransico: Kodansha International, 1977), pp. 132–38.

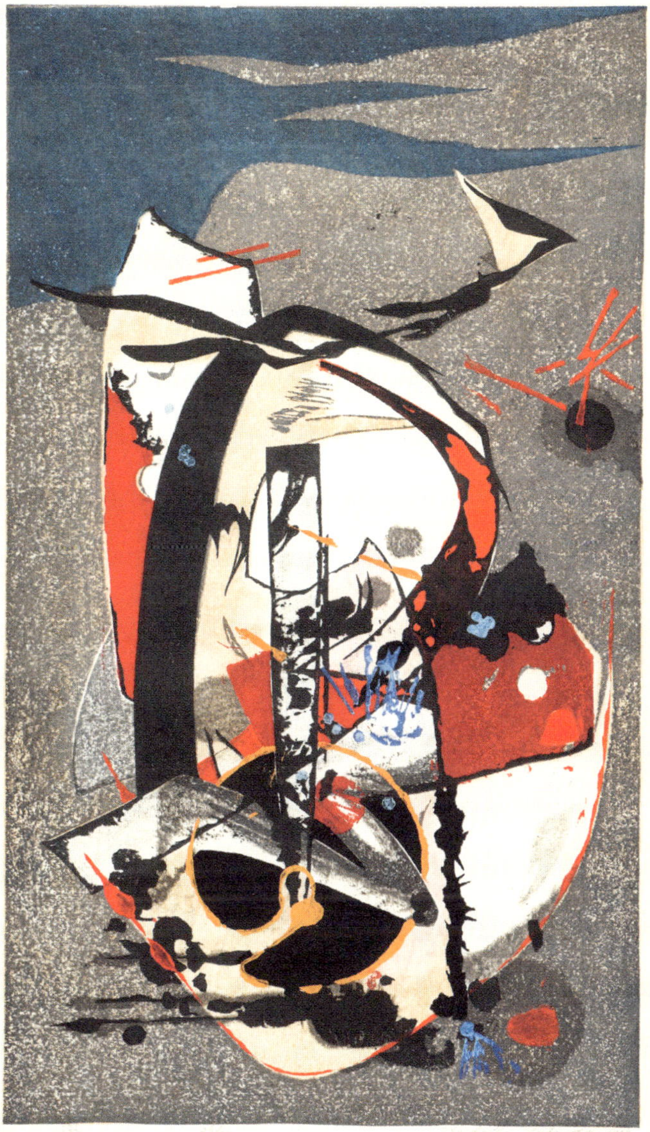

Floating, 1959. Woodblock print

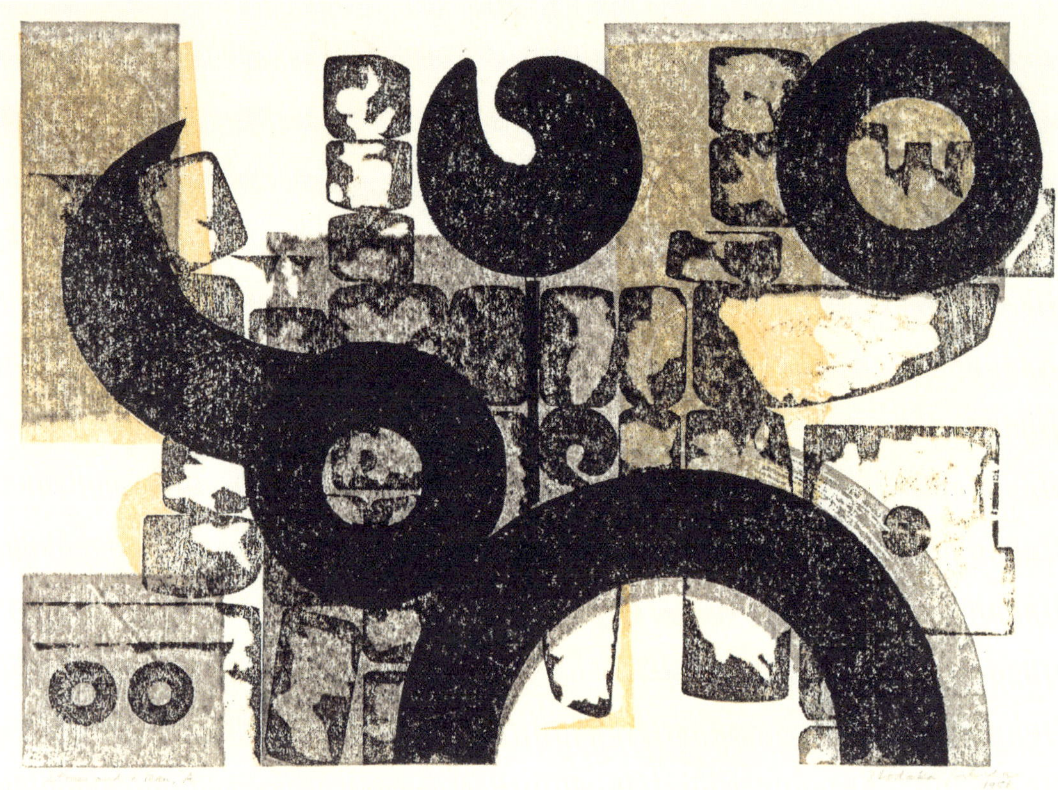

Stones and a Man (A), 1956. Woodblock print

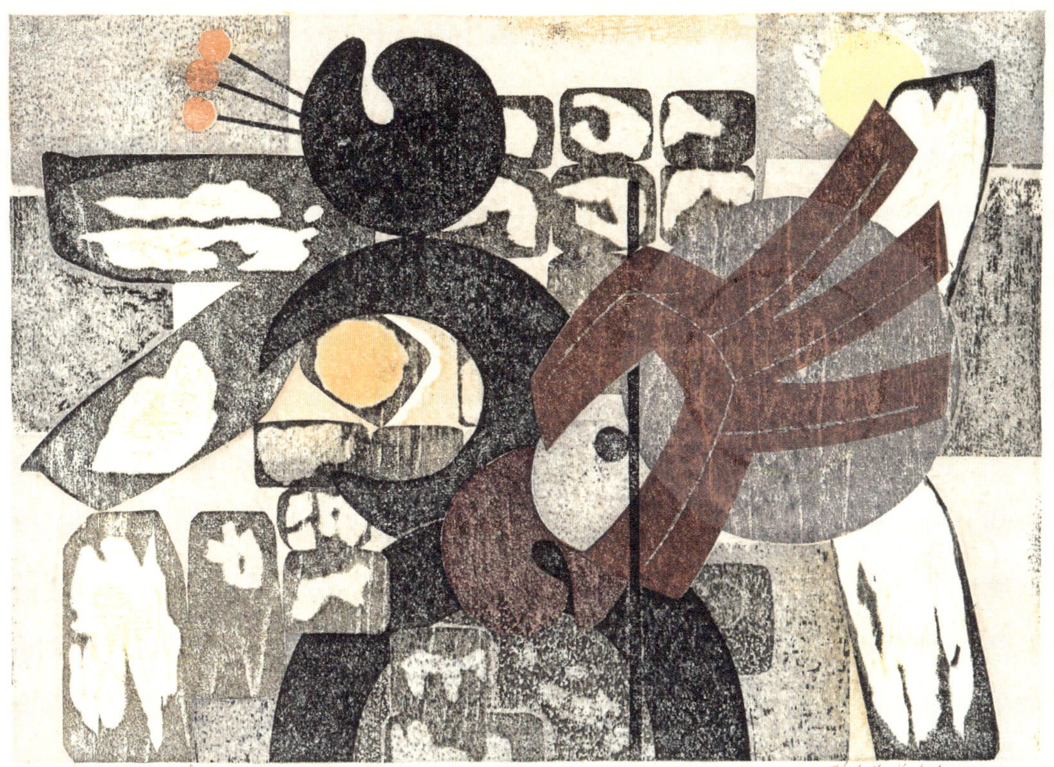

Stones and a Man (B), 1956. Woodblock print

Yoshida Family: YOSHIDA Chizuko (1924–2017)

Medium:
Photo etching and woodblock

Born Inoue Chizuko in Yokohama, Chizuko's formal training in oil painting began at the Sato Girl's High School in Tokyo, a private school specialising in fine arts. Following her graduation in 1941 she studied oil painting privately with Kitaoka Fumio (1918–2007), a renowned *sōsaku hanga* artist, via whom Chizuko was also exposed to printmaking. Later, Chizuko attended meetings of the group Yoru no Kai (Night Society), established in 1948 by the writer Hanada Kiyoteru (1909–1974) and artist and theorist Okamoto Tarō (1911–1996), whose concepts around avant-garde art and abstract painting influenced her.

It was at the Yomiuri Indépendant Exhibition in Tokyo in 1949 that she met Yoshida Hodaka, and in 1951 she exhibited oil paintings in their first two-person exhibition. In June 1953 Hodaka and Chizuko married, and shortly after her focus moved to printmaking.

Another influential figure in her printmaking endeavours was leading *sōsaku hanga* artist Onchi Kōshirō (see pp. 130–33), who held courses that both Chizuko and Hodaka attended. Onchi's experimental printing techniques were to influence Chizuko, but, as she later explained to Oliver Statler when interviewed for his book, 'I want to make it very clear … that it was Hodaka who was my teacher in prints.'[13]

Chizuko participated in the first CWAJ show with her prints *Mambo No. 1* and *Frozen*. Having developed her own personal style, Chizuko's motifs from the 1950s were abstract, using vibrant colours and dynamic compositions. During the 1960s Chizuko began embossing her prints, which can be seen in the Pop-like *Star Star Star A* (1969), which won her a prize at the International Triennial of Original Colour Graphics in Grenchen, Switzerland, in 1969. In her later prints, combining woodblock with zinc letterpress, a more tranquil world is exposed, one of butterflies, irises and chrysanthemums making up poetic dreamscapes.

Chizuko was a founding member of the Women's Print Association (Joryū Hanga Kyōkai, 1956–65). The first association of female printmakers, providing support for women in the graphic arts, the group consisted of nine professional print artists, including Iwami Reika (1927–2020) and Minami Keiko (1911–2004); the latter was the wife of print artist Hamaguchi Yōzō (pp. 64–67).

Two retrospective exhibitions dedicated to Chizuko opened in 2025: *Yoshida Chizuko: Dance, Sing, Paint – A Passionate Artist of Postwar Rebirth* at Mitaka City Gallery of Art, Tokyo, and *Yoshida Chizuko* at Portland Art Museum, Oregon.

Collections: Art Institute of Chicago; British Museum, London;
Cincinnati Art Museum; Dallas Museum of Art;
Minneapolis Institute of Art; Rijksmuseum, Amsterdam.

13 Ibid., p. 170.

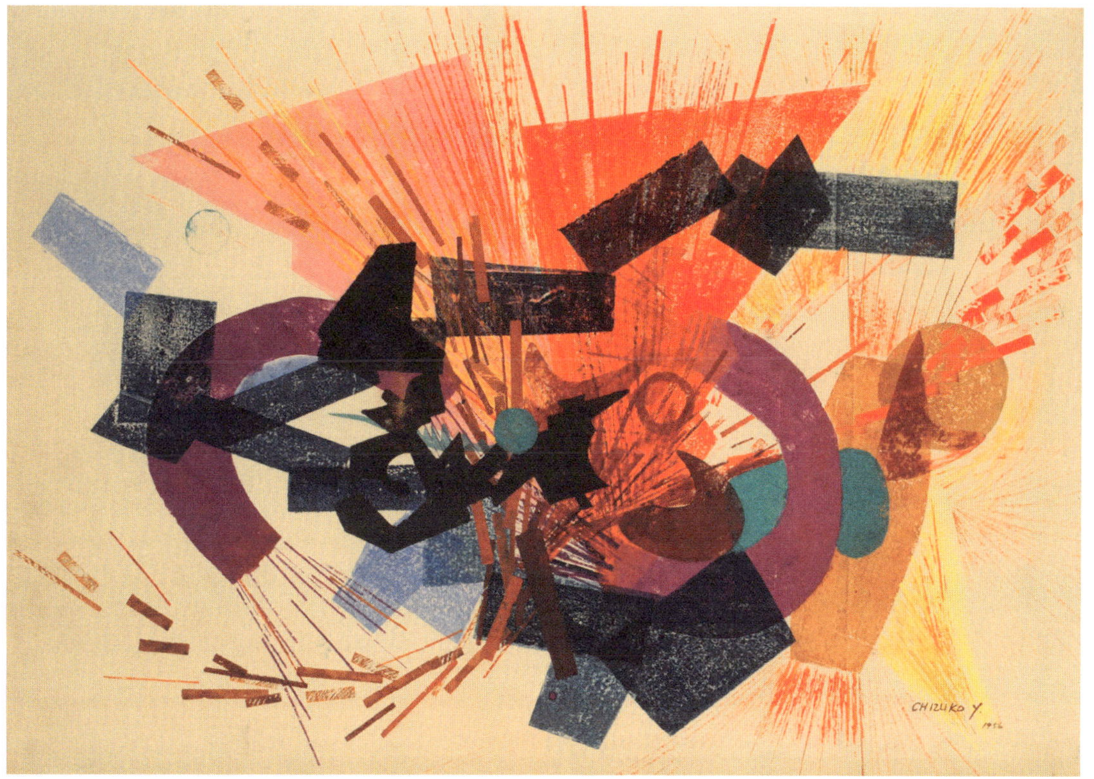

Mambo, 1956. Monoprint

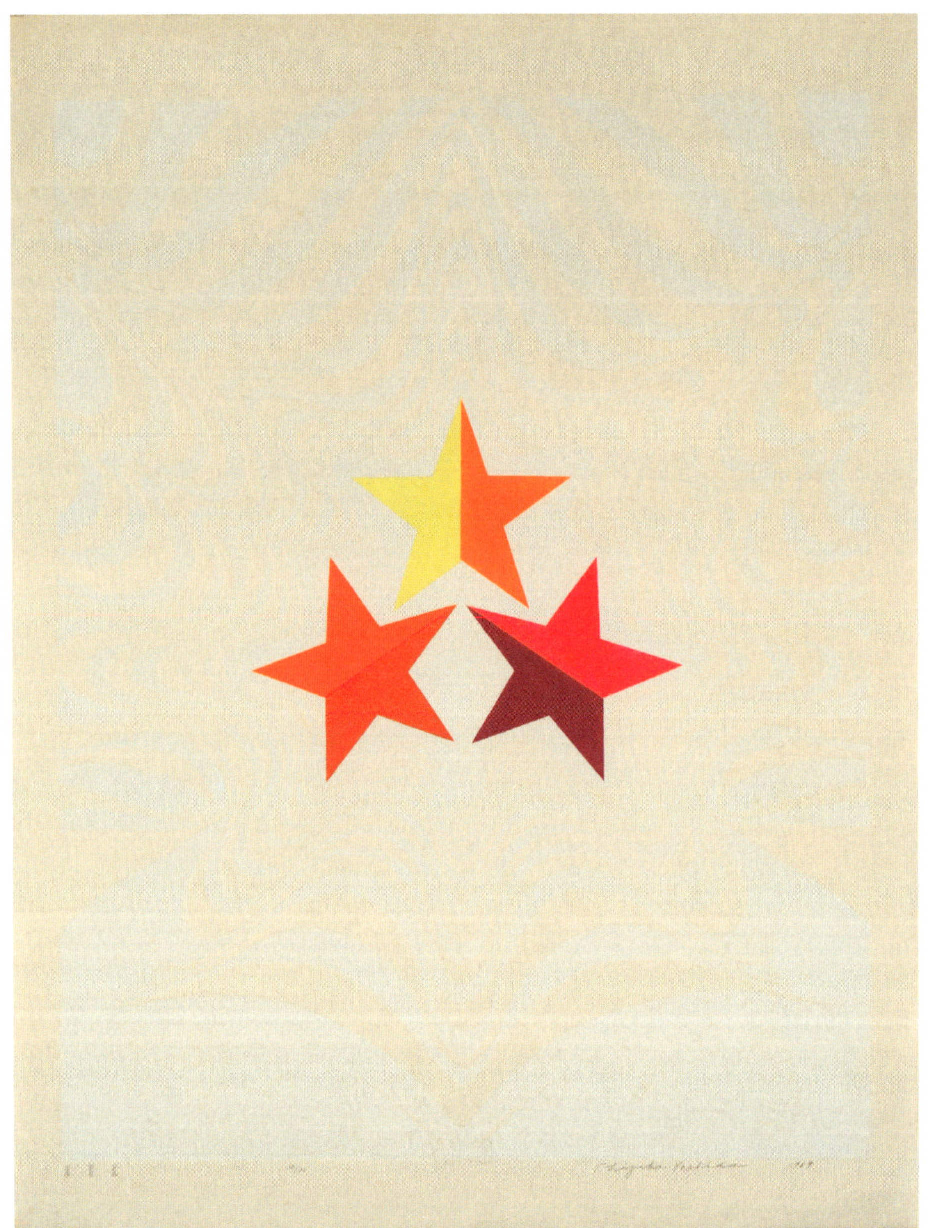

Star Star Star A, 1969. Woodblock print

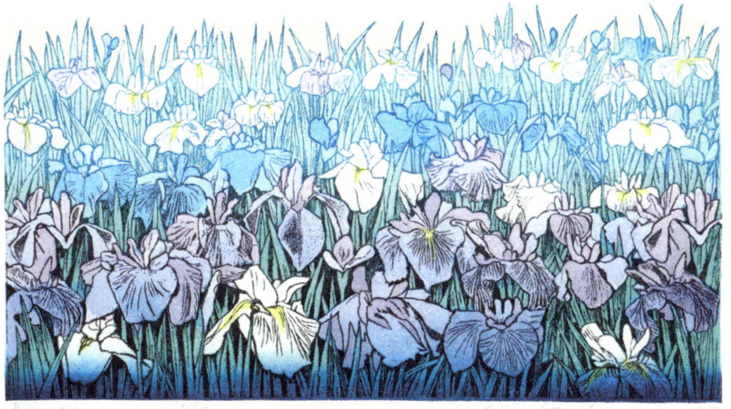

Summer Swallow, 1987. Photo etching and woodblock print

Yoshida Family: YOSHIDA Ayomi (b. 1958)

Medium:
Woodblock

Yoshida Ayomi is the first child of Hodaka and Chizuko. She studied architecture at Wakō University in Tokyo, where she also took art history classes. Growing up, printmaking was of no real interest to Ayomi, and she did not pay much attention to her family's legacy, even though she was surrounded by generations of established printmakers. Neither of her parents encouraged or pushed her into printmaking, although the indirect exposure must have left an impression: in secret, Ayomi began experimenting with woodblock printing on her own. This was much like her own father, who had hidden his canvases from his father. But while her father hid his art out of fear of disapproval, Ayomi hid hers out of shyness. At night, Ayomi, then 23 years old, would sneak into the studio to make prints.[14]

Ayomi's formal training in printmaking did not begin until 1979, when she studied screenprinting at the Mendocino Art Center in California. The layering process involved in silkscreen printing inspired her to try the same effect with woodblock printing, which remained her main medium until 1997.[15]

The theme of water is recurrent in her work, much like in Hokusai's about 150 prior. In her *Surface* series from the late 1980s, Ayomi chose the subject of the Kanda River, which runs from western Tokyo to Tokyo Bay in the east. The river has special significance for the artist because it flows through her birthplace and near the home she moved to when she was ten years old. Ayomi would decide on 36 photographs, on which the motifs are based, to represent each section of the river, selecting the images based on colours. The initials in the titles refer to different parts of the river: 'K.I.' refers to the Kanda River in Inokashira Park (upper course); 'K.O.' the same river in Ochiai (middle course), and 'K.Y.' the Kanda at Yanagibashi (lower course).[16]

Having primarily moved to large-scale, intricate installations in the latter part of her career, Ayomi incorporates traditional Japanese printmaking techniques utilising organic materials, continuing the family legacy in her very own style. In 2024, the Dulwich Picture Gallery in London held a major exhibition of the Yoshida family, for which Ayomi created a site-specific installation. For the Rijksmuseum, Amsterdam, in the same year, she created another paper installation, *Taki*, as part of an exhibition showcasing works by the three generations of Yoshida female artists: Ayomi, her mother Chizuko and her grandmother Fujio. Ayomi also showed another of her latest works, *Sudden Rain* (2024), a woodblock print on handmade indigo-dyed washi paper, which she made herself.

Ayomi's early exhibitions include the Ljubljana Biennale of Graphic Arts (1981, 1983, 1985 and 1987), the 67th Exhibition of the Japan Print Association, Tokyo Metropolitan Art Museum (1999), and the 2nd Seibu Triennial Exhibition of Prints, Seibu Art Museum, Tokyo (1984).

Collections: Art Institute of Chicago; British Museum, London; Portland Art Museum; Rijksmuseum, Amsterdam.

14 Much of the information in this text is based on an interview with Yoshida Ayomi in Copenhagen, winter 2024.
15 Allen et al., *A Japanese Legacy*, p. 196.
16 Ibid., pp. 204–5.

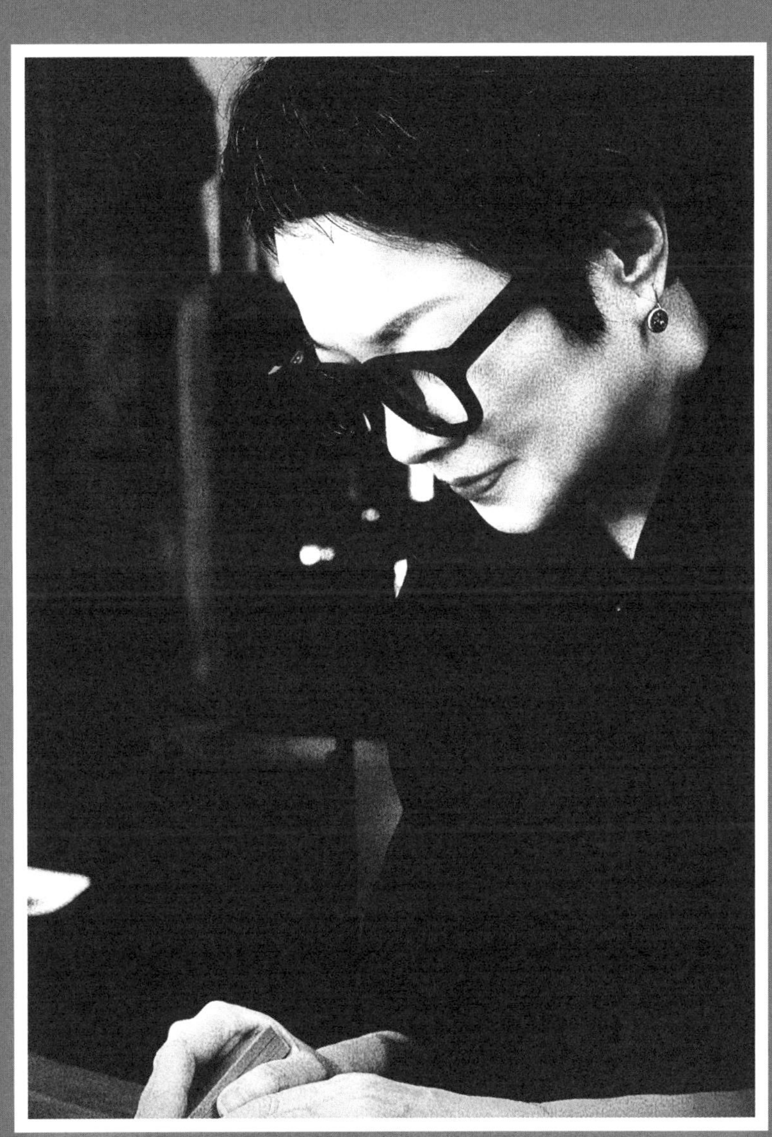

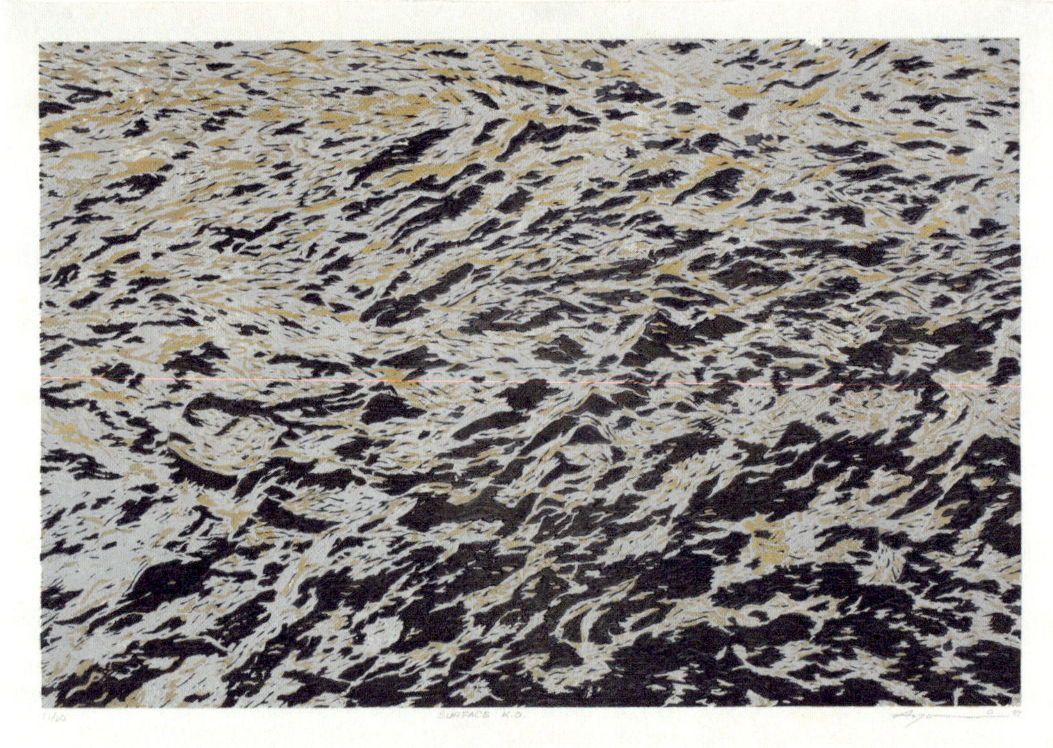

Surface K.O., 1987. Woodblock print

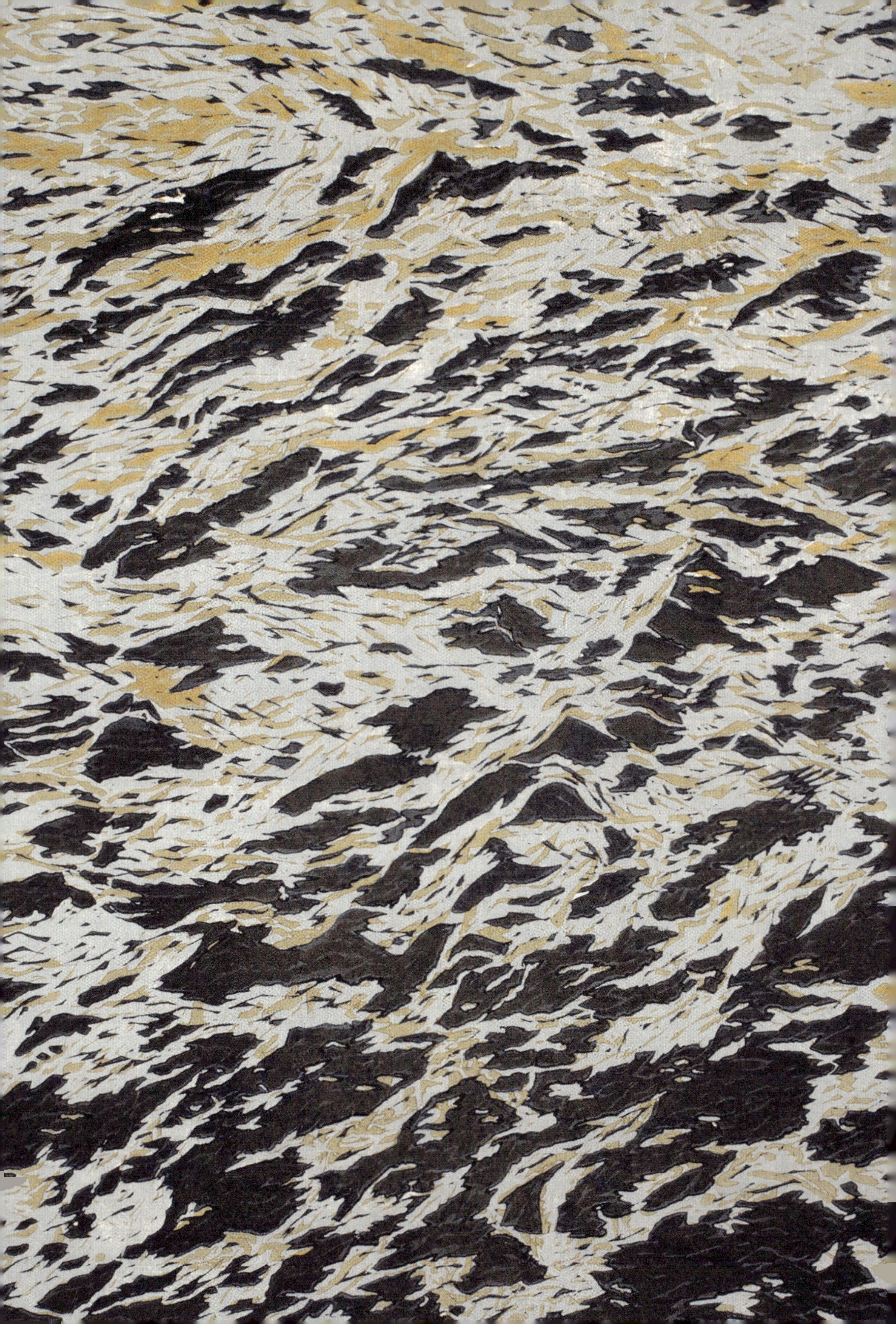

Misty Rain, 2021. Woodblock print

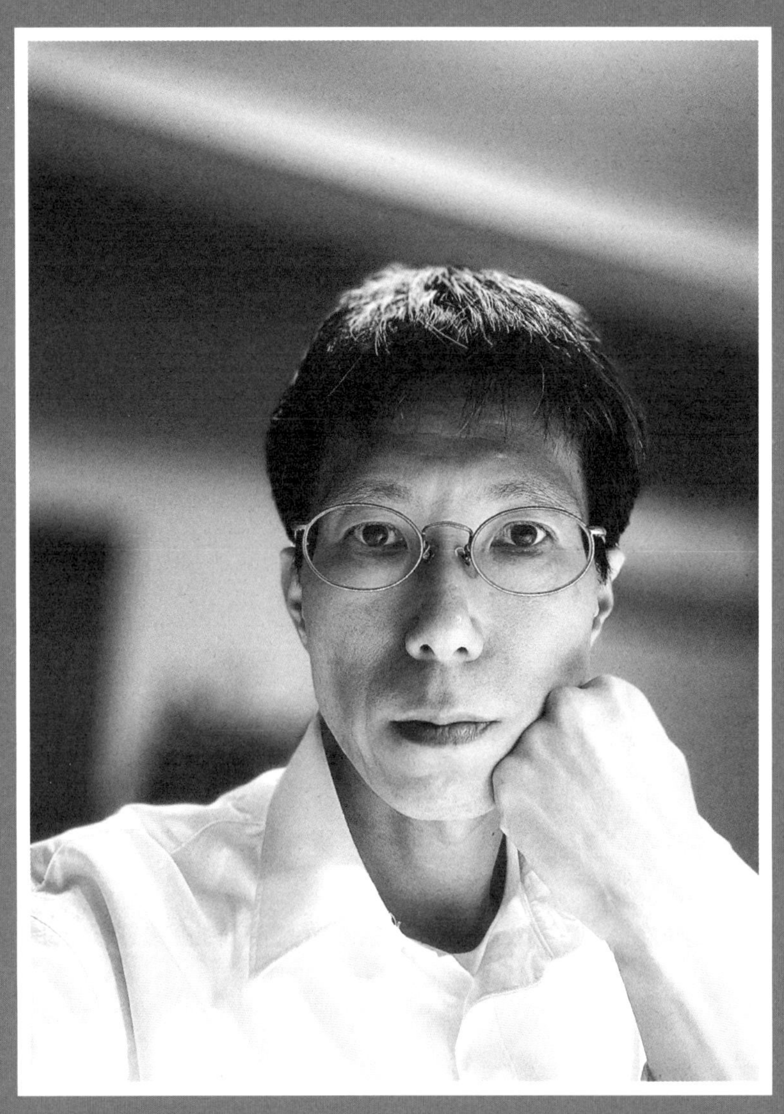

I think I'm unconsciously attracted to duality, like 'black and white' or 'day and night'. After all, most of my works are monochromatic.[1]

Yoshida Hideshi, 2024

YOSHIDA Hideshi (b.1968)

Medium:
Woodblock

Yoshida Hideshi was born in Hokkaido and graduated in 1991 from the English department at Tokyo's Teikyō University. He represents the youngest generation of artists included in this book, and his work is yet to be studied further.

Yoshida's themes range from dark fantasy to sci-fi to *kawaii* animals, and at times all three merge, revealing a surreal world of cute and uncanny darkness and delight. This melding of effects can be seen as a contradiction or, as Yoshida explains, an equilibrium: 'I think creating both "surreal and dark" and "cute" keeps me mentally balanced. It's the same logic as when you want to eat salty things if you eat only sweet things.' In his work we learn that there is more than meets the eye.

We see this in *The whole universe conquest plan by cuteness* (2022) and in *Why is this coffee cup so small?* (2024). Here we are at the Café du Lapin, a small, quaint place run by a rabbit. As Yoshida explains, the coffee brewed by the café owner is known to be very delicious. He chooses carefully from the beautiful coffee cups arranged in the cupboard behind the counter, tailoring the selection to each customer. Usually the café is visited by small animals, but one day a bear, who has been recommended the place, comes in. He is surprised when the coffee is served and asks: 'Why is this coffee cup so small?'

Yoshida is influenced by authors such as Lewis Carroll as well as H. G. Wells, Jules Verne and Arthur Conan Doyle. Classic science fiction in particular plays a role as a reference for the designs of the vehicles and gadgets that appear in his work.

Highly technically accomplished, Yoshida works with both woodblock printing and wood engraving. Whereas the first follows Japanese tradition with the use of the vertical length of the woodblock, Western wood engraving involves carving the end grain of the wood. In 1904, Yamamoto Kanae created the acclaimed print *Fisherman* (p. 213), which would become regarded as the first *sōsaku hanga* print, partly by using the wood engraving technique. But wood engraving is not done on a large scale in Japan, and Yoshida thus follows in a small line of Japanese artists working with this technique, which he studied at the art school Bigakkō, Tokyo, in 1987. As he explains: 'I only knew that it was a type of printmaking in which extremely fine lines are carved into wood cut along the end of the grain, but when I studied it at art school, I was so impressed by the level of detail.' He could not understand why other artists working with the technique at that time were only making 'dark' works. It therefore became his mission to create bright and cute works using wood engraving, but it took him about ten years to achieve a result he was satisfied with: 'One day, I decided to make a cute white cat. The sketch turned out very well, but the finished print was surprisingly gloomy and depressing, not cute at all. What I learned from this is that it is easy to make gloomy and depressing works with wood engraving, but it is extremely difficult to make bright and cute works.' Yoshida uses boxwood and lemonwood for his engravings. He went on to teach wood engraving as a guest instructor at Musashino Art University in 2010–11.

1 The information in this text is based on an interview with Yoshida Hideshi in Tokyo, October 2024, as well as email correspondence, winter 2024–25.

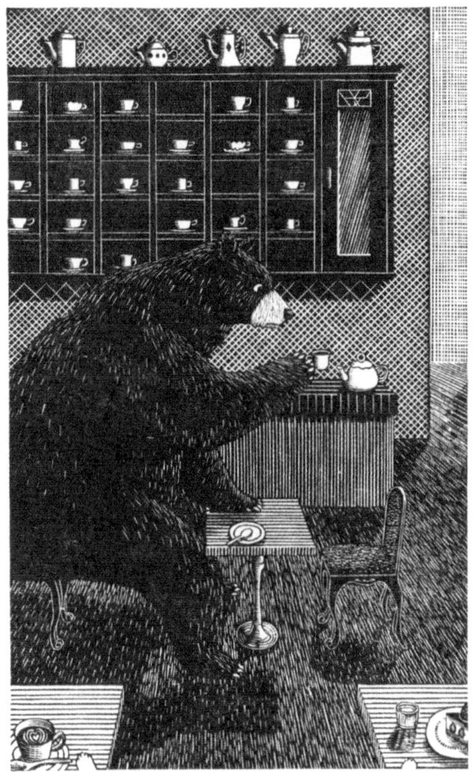

Why is this coffee cup so small!?, 2024. Woodblock print

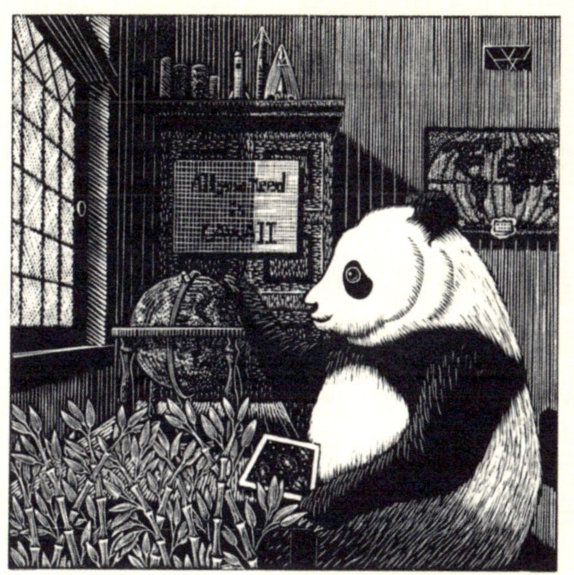

A.P. YOSHIDA Hideshi 2022

The whole universe conquest plan by cuteness, 2022. Wood engraving

Yoshida is self-taught in woodblock printing. Paradoxically, as a child he did not like woodblock printing, which children in Japan are taught in elementary and junior high school for them to experience traditional crafts. 'However, I was lazy,' he explains: 'When I was in elementary school, it was very difficult to write New Year's cards by hand, so I thought, "If I carve a woodblock, it will be easy after that, right?" Before I knew it, I was hooked on the charm and craftsmanship of woodblock printing.' For his woodblock prints, Yoshida uses shina (linden) plywood.

Yoshida believes there are many things to learn from the old *ukiyo-e* masters, and he acknowledges useful technical aspects of the traditional ways: 'Even I use registration marks [*kentō*] and, very rarely, I also use *kyōgō* [impressions from the key block]. I do think there is a succession in terms of technique.' However, perhaps to no surprise when one looks at his prints, it is the work of Dutch graphic artist M. C. Escher (1898–1972) that has had the strongest influence on Yoshida. He first discovered Escher's work in a book when he was ten years old, and this was his first real introduction to wood engraving. Escher, who made lithographs and woodblock prints as well as wood engravings, left a tremendous impact on Yoshida's work. A clear homage to Escher's work can be seen in his woodblock print *Symmetry Variation – Birds* (1998).

Like with Escher, mathematics plays a significant role in Yoshida's work, especially topology, and the play on perspective and impossible spaces is often present in his prints. 'There are very few artists who create sci-fi woodblock prints,' he says. 'Also, my approach to themes is more theoretical, like a mathematician or scientist rather than an artist (or so people think). Except for a few works, I don't create my works by "imagining". I visualise the landscape of the other world, which I call "Agnahuecom-Land".' Every Yoshida print represents a landscape or event in an area of Agnahuecom-Land, such as the region with magical and strange inhabitants, the region where humans live, and the area with animals (most of whom talk like humans). According to Yoshida: 'Currently, in the human area, a company called FROSKEY is considered one of the most successful companies in the human world of Agnahuecom-Land. It is rapidly growing, and I am creating several works based on that theme. However, these images are very vague and difficult to understand, so I spend a long time looking through them, analysing their meaning, and then creating works based on the results. Some works take up to twenty years to complete.'

Yoshida has participated in group exhibitions since the early 1990s, including the 40th Exhibition of Nippon Hangain, Tokyo (1990); *Museum of Extra Sensory Perception*, commemorating the 100th anniversary of M. C. Escher's birth, held in Tokyo and nine other cities in Japan (1999); the 3rd Yamamoto Kanae Print Grand Prix Competition, Nagano (2005); International Print Exchange Project, Japan–Portugal–Holland (2008–9); the 9th Kochi International Triennial Exhibition of Prints (2014); College Women's Association of Japan Exhibition, Tokyo (2012 and 2021); and the 44th Mini Print International of Cadaqués, Spain, UK and France (2024).

Collections: Manggha Museum of Japanese Art and Technology, Krakow.

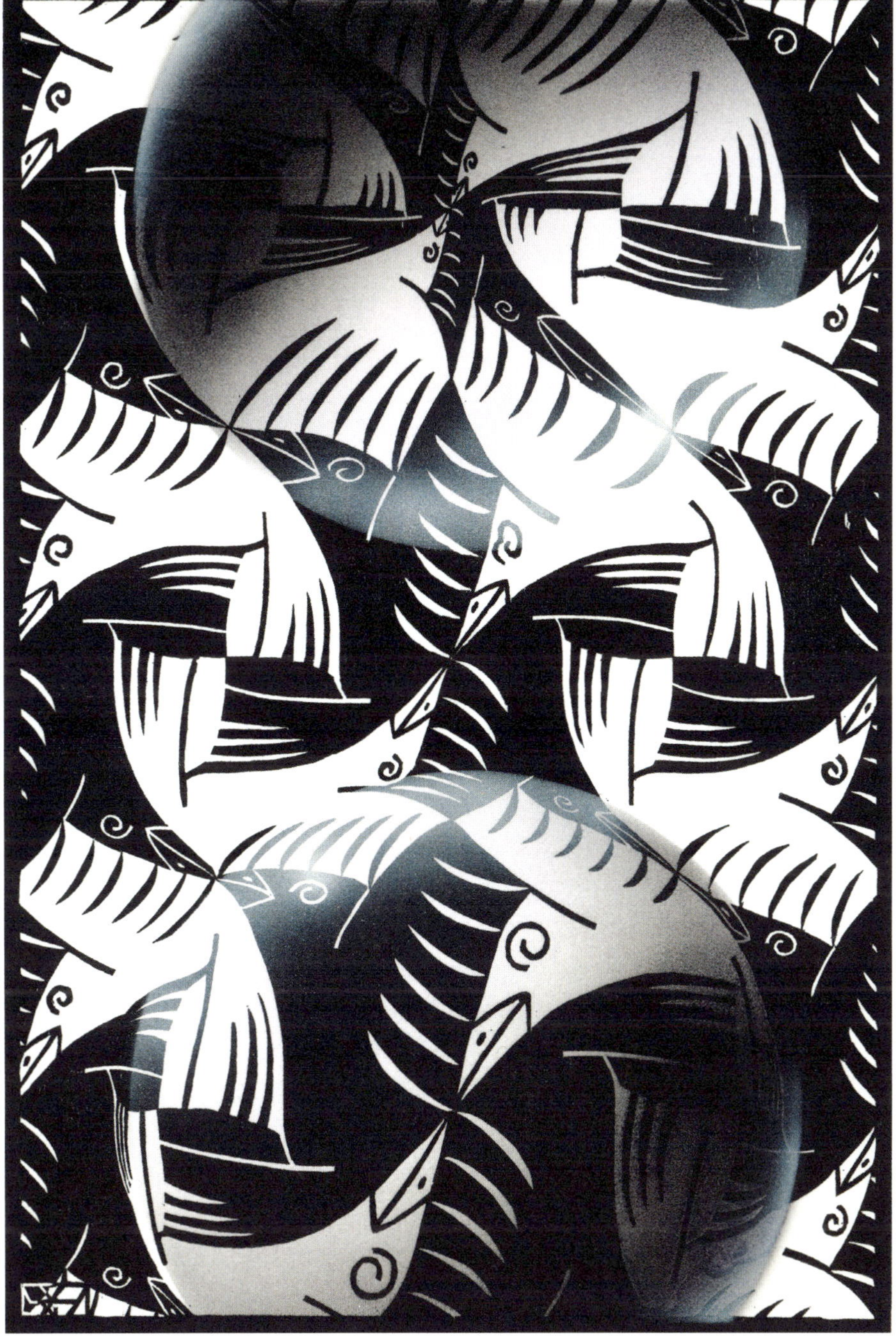

Symmetry Variation – Birds, 1998. Woodblock print with airbrush

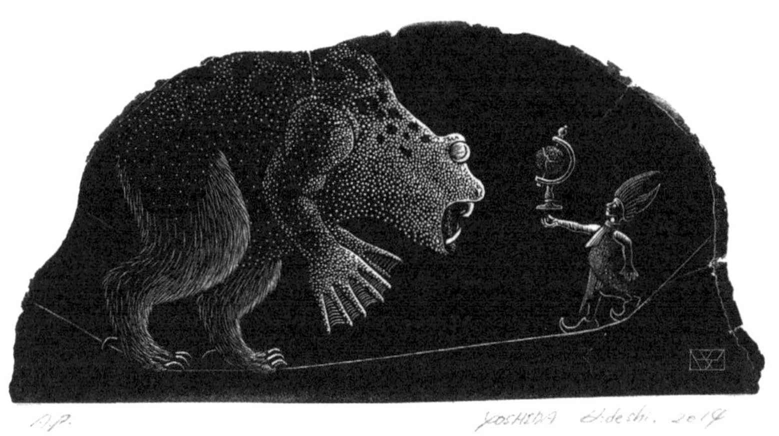

At the Depths, 2014. Wood engraving

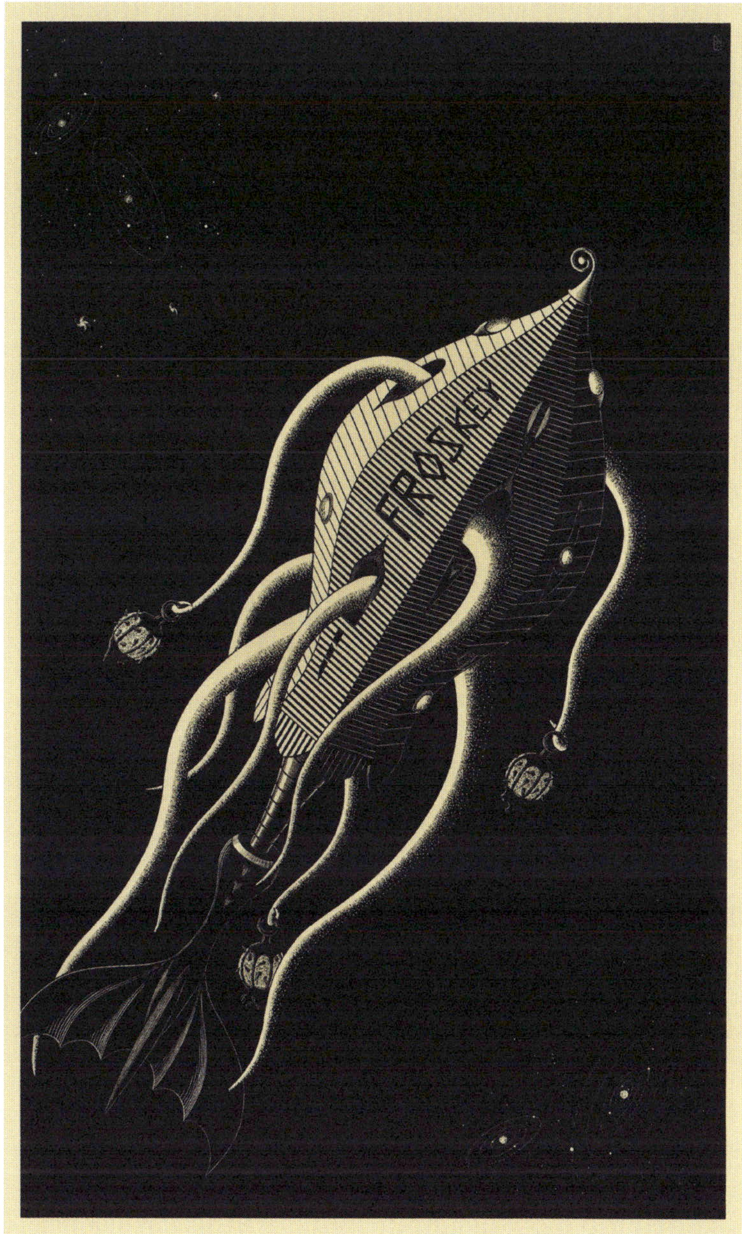

Special cargo ship: Last Resort. Final destination: Undecided, 2012. Woodblock print

Glossary

Aquatint an intaglio printing technique similar to etching, but the design is dusted onto the plate using resin, to imitate the effect of watercolour wash. See 'etching' and 'intaglio'.
Baren a traditional tool wrapped in bamboo skin and used for woodblock printing. It is used to apply pressure to the paper during the printing process. See 'woodblock print'.
College Women's Association of Japan (CWAJ) a non-profit organisation founded in Tokyo in 1949.
Drypoint a non-acid intaglio printing process using a sharp needle to scratch the metal plate. The resulting tiny, raised burrs hold ink during the printing. See 'intaglio'.
Engraving an intaglio printing technique where fine lines are incised directly into the plate and the burrs are removed to produce clean, sharp lines on the print. See 'intaglio'.
Etching an intaglio printing process using a needle to draw or scratch freely on a zinc, brass or copper plate coated with acid-resistant ground. See 'intaglio'.
Hanga the Japanese term for fine art prints (literally 'plate picture').
Intaglio a printmaking process where the incised or cut grooves of a metal plate hold the ink and print the image.
Japan Creative Print Association (Nihon sōsaku hanga kyōkai) founded in 1918 by Yamamoto Kanae, Oda Kazuma, Terasaki Takeo and Tobari Kogan. The society became known as the Japan Print Association in 1931.
Japan Print Association (Nihon hanga kyōkai) formerly the Japan Creative Print Association, it is the largest print association in Japan. See 'Japan Creative Print Association'.
Kappazuri a printing process similar to woodblock printing but with stencils used instead of wooden blocks. See 'woodblock print'.
Kentō registration mark used for woodblock printing to ensure the precise positioning of the paper for the inking of each print.
Letterpress printing a form of relief printing where the raised surface of letters or images is inked and then pressed into paper. See 'relief print'.
Linocut a similar technique to woodblock printing but using a linoleum block instead of wood. See 'woodblock print'.
Lithography a planographic technique where the printing plate of stone or zinc is flat. The preparation of the plate relies on the repellency of grease and water.
Mezzotint an intaglio printing process that distinguishes itself from other printing techniques by working from dark to light, rather than vice versa. The plate is roughened by repeated pressure from a serrated tool that can hold ink. See 'intaglio'.
Moku hanga literally meaning wood (*moku*) print (*hanga*). The Japanese term for traditional woodblock printing. See 'woodblock print'.
Monoprint a print with an edition of one.
Nihonga Japanese-style painting. The term first came into use during the Meiji period (1868–1912) to differentiate this style of painting from Western-style painting. See 'yōga'.
Nishiki-e Japanese full-colour woodblock print (literally 'brocade picture'). See 'woodblock print'.
Photogravure a photomechanical process that creates photographic tones on a plate, which is then etched with acid.
Relief print printing from the top of an incision. Examples include woodblock, wood engraving, linocut and paper block.
Shin hanga a Japanese term literally meaning 'new prints'.
Silkscreen print also known as serigraph or screen print. A method using a frame with fine mesh (silk or nylon fabric) stretched over it, through which the ink is forced using a squeegee onto paper to form an image. The process is repeated for each colour.
Sōsaku hanga a Japanese term literally meaning 'creative prints'.
Stencil printing a process using a system of two surfaces: one acting as a block for the ink and the other porous to allow the flow of ink.
Woodblock print known in Japanese as *moku hanga*. A form of relief printing where the areas of the block that are not needed to make the print are cut away. The traditional Japanese technique of woodblock printing uses water-based inks, Japanese paper (*washi*) and *baren*. See '*baren*' and 'relief print'.
Woodcut another name for woodblock print. See 'woodblock print'.
Wood engraving similar to woodblock printing but the block is cut across the grain. The close grain of the end-block allows for the cutting of fine lines and linear patterns characteristic of wood engravings. See 'woodblock print'.
Yōfū Hangakai Western-Style Print Society formed in 1930 by etchers and lithographers.
Yōga term used in Japan to refer to Western-style painting to differentiate this style of painting from *Nihonga*. See '*Nihonga*'.
***Yūzen* dyeing** a Japanese resist dyeing technique traditionally used for kimono designs.

Bibliography

The 7th International Biennial Exhibition of Prints in Tokyo, exh. cat. (Tokyo: National Museum of Modern Art, 1970)

Abe Setsuko et al., *Mori Yoshitoshi: Kappa-ban*, exh. cat., Ginza Matsuzakaya, Tokyo, and National Museum of Ethnology, Leiden (Tokyo: Mori Yoshitoshi-ten Jikkō Iinkai, 1985)

Aitken, Geneviève, and Marianne Delafond, *Claude Monet's Collection of Japanese Prints* (Giverny: Éditions Claude Monet Giverny / Montreuil: Gourcuff Gradenigo, 2023)

Allen, Laura W., ed., *A Japanese Legacy: Four Generations of Yoshida Family Artists*, exh. cat. (Minneapolis, MN: Minneapolis Institute of Art, 2002)

Ay-O, *Ay-O: Rainbow 88*, exh. cat. (Karuizawa-machi: Karuizawa New Art Museum, 2019)

—, *Over the Rainbow: Retrospective, 1960–2006*, exh. cat., Fukui Fine Arts Museum and Miyazaki Prefectural Art Museum (Tokyo: Bijutsu Shuppan-sha, 2006)

Azechi, Umetaro, *Japanese Woodblock Prints: Their Techniques and Appreciation* (Tokyo: Toto Shuppan, 1963)

Bailly-Herzberg, Janine, *Dictionnaire de l'estampe en France, 1830–1950* (Paris: Flammarion, 1985)

Bell, Kate, ed., *Van Gogh and Japan*, exh. cat. (Amsterdam: Van Gogh Museum, 2017)

Birnbaum, Phyllis, *Glory in a Line: A Life of Foujita, the Artist Caught between East and West* (London: Faber & Faber, 2017)

Blair, Dorothy, *Modern Japanese Prints: Printed from a Photographic Reproduction of Two Exhibition Catalogues of Modern Japanese Prints Published by the Toledo Museum of Art in 1930 and 1936* (Toledo, OH: Toledo Museum of Art, 1997)

Blakemore, Frances, *Who's Who in Modern Japanese Prints* (New York and Tokyo: Weatherhill, 1975)

Buckland, Rosina, *Shunga: Erotic Art in Japan* (London: British Museum Press, 2010)

Castleman, Riva, *From Prints to Blocks: Gauguin to Now*, exh. cat. (New York: Museum of Modern Art, 1983)

Chapman, Hilary, and Libby Horner, *Yoshijiro Urushibara: A Japanese Printmaker in London, a Catalogue Raisonné* (Leiden: Hotei Publishing, 2017)

Clark, Catharine, et al., *Ascending Chaos: The Art of Masami Teraoka, 1966–2006* (San Francisco: Chronicle Books, 2006)

Clark, Timothy, ed., *The Dawn of the Floating World, 1650–1765: Early Ukiyo-e Treasures from the Museum of Fine Arts Boston*, exh. cat. (London: Royal Academy of Arts, 2002)

College Women's Association of Japan, *50th CWAJ Print Show: Japanese Contemporary Prints* (Tokyo: College Women's Association of Japan, 2005)

—, *CWAJ Print Show: A 60-Year Journey, 1956–2015* (Tokyo: College Women's Association of Japan, 2015)

—, *Expanding Horizons: Fifty Years of the College Women's Association of Japan, 1949–1999* (Tokyo: College Women's Association of Japan, 1999)

DeVonyar, Jill, and Richard Kendall, *Degas and the Art of Japan*, exh. cat. (Reading, PA: Reading Public Museum, 2007)

Exposition de la gravure japonaise à l'École nationale des beaux-arts à Paris du 25 avril au 22 mai 1890: catalogue (Paris: École Nationale des Beaux-Arts, 1890)

Falck, Ute Kuhlemann, 'Plates, Stones and Blocks: Munch's Painting Matrices', in *Edvard Munch: Love and Angst*, ed. Giulia Bartrum, exh. cat. (London: British Museum and Thames & Hudson, 2019)

Foujita, *Foujita* (Paris: Éditions FAGE, 2018)

Frick, Thomas, ed., *Love Forever: Yayoi Kusama, 1958–1968*, exh. cat. (Los Angeles: Los Angeles County Museum of Art, 1998)

Fujikake, Shizuya, *Japanese Wood-Block Prints*, 2nd revd edn (Tokyo: Japan Travel Bureau, 1949)

Funasaka Yoshisuke Print Exhibition, 1960–2010: My Space and My Dimension, exh. cat. (Minokamo: Minokamo City Museum, 2011)

Gentles, Margaret O., 'Modern Japanese Prints', *Art Institute of Chicago Quarterly* 53, no. 1 (February 1959), pp. 13–17

Gilmour, Pat, *Modern Prints* (London: Studio Vista, 1970)

Goncourt, Edmond de, *Hokousaï: L'art japonais au XVIIIe siècle* (Paris: G. Charpentier & E. Fasquelle, 1896)

Gonse, Louis, *L'art japonais* (Paris: A. Quantin, 1886)

Graphic Image '73, exh. cat. (Tokyo: Tokyo Central Museum of Arts, 1973)

Guth, Christine, *Hokusai's Great Wave: Biography of a Global Icon* (Honolulu: University of Hawai'i Press, 2015)

Hamaguchi Yōzō, *Hamaguchi Yōzō*, exh. cat. (Tokyo: Musée Hamaguchi Yozo Yamasa Collection, 2022)

—, *Yozo Hamaguchi, Master of Mezzotint*, exh. cat., Tokyo Metropolitan Teien Art Museum (Tokyo: Mainichi Newspapers, 1990)

Hanai Hisaho et al., *The Making of Munakata Shiko: Celebrating the 120th Anniversary of the Artist's Birth*, exh. cat., National Museum of Modern Art, Tokyo (Tokyo: NHK Promotions, 2023)

Hasegawa, Kiyoshi, *L'estampe japonaise modern et ses origines: exposition organisée par la Société des peintres-graveurs japonais de Tokyo* (Paris: Musée des Arts Décoratifs, 1934)

Hiller, Jack, *The Japanese Print: A New Approach* (London: G. Bell & Sons, 1960)

Hinkel, Monika, *Yoshida: Three Generations of Japanese Printmaking*, exh. cat., Dulwich Picture Gallery, London (London: Paul Holberton Publishing, 2024)

Hiraki Ukiyo-e Foundation, *Tsuruya Kōkei: The Complete Woodblock Prints, 1978–2000* (Tokyo: Hiraki Ukiyo-e Museum, 2000)

Ives, Colta Feller, *The Great Wave: The Influence of Japanese Woodcuts on French Prints*, exh. cat. (New York: Metropolitan Museum of Art, 1979)

Japan's Modern Prints: Sōsaku Hanga, exh. cat. (Chicago: Art Institute of Chicago, 1960)

Japanese Twentieth Century Prints from the Collection of C. Adrian Rübel, exh. cat. (Cambridge, MA: Fogg Art Museum, Harvard University, 1966)

Jenkins, Donald, *Images of a Changing World: Japanese Prints of the Twentieth Century*, exh. cat. (Portland, OR: Portland Art Museum, 1983)

Johnson, Margaret K., and Dale K. Hilton, *Japanese Prints Today: Tradition with Innovation* (Tokyo: Shufunotomo Co., 1980)

Kabuki-za, Tokyo, ed., *The 100th Anniversary of the Kabuki-za Theatre – Tsuruya Kokei: Kabuki Actor Prints* (Tokyo: Shochiku Co., 1988)

Kawakita, Michiaki, *Contemporary Japanese Prints*, trans. John Bester (Tokyo and Palo Alto, CA: Kodansha International, 1967)

Keyes, Roger, *Break with the Past: The Japanese Creative Print Movement, 1910–1960*, exh. cat. (San Francisco: Fine Arts Museums of San Franciso, 1988)

Kusama, Yayoi, *Infinity Net: The Autobiography of Yayoi Kusama* (London: Tate Publishing, 2011)

—, *Yayoi Kusama Prints, 1979–2013: A Catalogue Raisonné* (Tokyo: Abe Publishing, 2013)

Kuwayama, George, *Contemporary Japanese Prints*, exh. cat. (Los Angeles: Los Angeles County Museum of Art, 1972)

Lane, Richard, *Images for the Floating World: The Japanese Print* (Oxford, London and Melbourne: Oxford University Press, 1978)

Link, Howard A., *Waves and Plagues: The Art of Masami Teraoka*, exh. cat., The Contemporary Museum, Honolulu (San Francisco: Chronicle Books, 1988)

Matsumoto Tohru et al., *Onchi Kōshirō*, exh. cat. (Tokyo: National Museum of Modern Art / Wakayama: Museum of Modern Art, 2016)

Merritt, Helen, *Modern Japanese Woodblock Prints: The Early Years* (Honolulu: University of Hawai'i Press, 1990)

—, and Nanako Yamada, *Guide to Modern Japanese Woodblock Prints, 1900–1975* (Honolulu: University of Hawai'i Press, 1992)

Michener, James A., *Japanese Prints: From the Early Masters to the Modern* (Rutland, VT, and Tokyo: Charles E. Tuttle Co., 1959)

—, *The Modern Japanese Print: An Appreciation* (Rutland, VT, and Tokyo: Charles E. Tuttle Co., 1968)

Miyamura, Noriko, and Shinko Suzuki, eds, *Yoshitomo Nara: The Complete Works*, vol. 1: *Paintings, Sculptures, Editions, Photographs, 1984–2010* (Tokyo: Bijutsu Shuppan-sha, 2011)

Monroe, Alexandra, *Japanese Art after 1945: Scream against the Sky* (New York: H. N. Abrams, 1994)

Nakamura, Kimihiko, 'Shiyoshida Tōkō: Ink, Abstraction and Radical Individualism', *Woman's Art Journal* (Spring–Summer 2022), pp. 21–31

The New Japanese Painting and Sculpture, exh. cat. (New York: Museum of Modern Art, 1966)

Newland, Amy Reigle, ed., *Waves of Renewal: Modern Japanese Prints, 1900 to 1960* (Leiden: Hotei Publishing, 2016)

Noda, Tetsuya, *Tetsuya Noda: The Works, 1964–1978* (Tokyo: Fuji Television Gallery, 1978)

Okuyama Gihachirō, *Matsudo-shi Kyōiku Inkai shozō* [A Catalogue of Works in the Matsudo City Board of Education Collection] (Tokyo: Matsudo City Board of Education Collection, 2014)

—, *Sōzō to dentō no mokuhnagaka, Okuhama Gihachirō ten* [Okuyama Gihachirō: Woodblock Prints of Creativity and Tradition] (Tokyo: Matsudo City Board of Education Collection, 1999)

Onchi, Kōshirō, *Kōshirō Onchi, 1891–1955: Woodcuts* (San Francisco: Achenbach Foundation for Graphic Arts, 1964)

—, 'The Modern Japanese Print: An Internal History of the *Sosaku Hanga* Movement', *Ukiyo-e Art* (Japan Ukiyo-e Society), no. 11 (1965), pp. 3–24

Ozaki, Masaaki, ed., *Léonard Foujita* (Tokyo: NHK Promotions Co. and Nihon Keizai Shimbun, 2006)

Paget, Rhiannon, *Saitō Kiyoshi: Graphic Awakening*, exh. cat., John and Mable Ringling Museum of Art, Sarasota, FL (New York: Scala Arts Publishers, 2021)

Petit, Gaston, *44 Modern Japanese Print Artists*, 2 vols (Tokyo, New York, San Francisco: Kodansha International, 1973)

—, and Amadio Arboleda, *Evolving Techniques in Japanese Woodblock Prints* (Tokyo, New York, San Francisco: Kodansha International, 1977)

Rimer, Thomas J., *Since Meiji: Perspectives on the Japanese Visual Arts, 1868–2000* (Honolulu: University of Hawai'i Press, 2012)

Rosenthal, Stephanie, ed., *Yayoi Kusama: A Retrospective*, exh. cat., Gropius Bau, Berlin (London: Prestel, 2021)

Shiomi, Nana, *This Side and the Other Side: Woodcuts, 1996–2016* (Marlborough: Rabley Drawing Centre, 2017)

Smith, Lawrence, *Contemporary Japanese Prints: Symbols of a Society in Transition*, exh. cat. (London: British Museum, 1985)

—, *Japanese Prints during the Allied Occupation, 1945–1952: Onchi Kōshirō, Ernst Hacker and the First Thursday Society* (London: British Museum, 2002)

—, and Sasaki Seiichi, eds, *Takeda Hideo and the Japanese Cartoon Tradition at the British Museum*, exh. cat. (London: Minato Ishikawa Associates and British Museum, 1993)

Statler, Oliver, *Japanese Prints: An Art Reborn* (Rutland, VT, and Tokyo: Charles E. Tuttle Co., 1956)

Sugaï, Kumi, *Kumi Sugaï: Les plus grands tableaux de ses dernières années*, exh. cat. (Paris: Maison de la Culture du Japon à Paris, 1999)

Takashina, Shūji, and J. Thomas Rimer, with Gerald D. Bolas, eds, *Paris in Japan: The Japanese Encounter with European Painting* (Tokyo: Japan Foundation / St Louis, MO: Washington University in St Louis, 1987)

Todate Kazuko, *Ay-O, 1950s–2010* (Ibaraki: Tsubaka Museum of Art, 2010)

Tokuriki, Tomikichirō, *Woodblock Print Primer* (Tokyo: Japan Publications, 1970)

—, *Wood-block Printing* (Osaka: Hoikusha Publishing Co., 1968)

Tolman, Mary S., and Norman H. Tolman, *Toko Shinoda: A New Appreciation* (Rutland, VT: Charles E. Tuttle Co., 1993)

Uhlenbeck, Chris, Louis van Tilborgh and Shigeru Oikawa, *Japanese Prints: The Collection of Vincent van Gogh* (London: Thames & Hudson, 2018)

Vabre, Émilie, 'Prosper-Alphonse Isaac (1858–1924)', *Nouvelles de l'estampe*, no. 237 (2011), pp. 4–21

Volk, Alicia, *Made in Japan: The Postwar Creative Print Movement*, exh. cat. (Milwaukee, WI: Milwaukee Art Museum, 2005)

Yanagi, Sōetsu, *Selected Essays on Japanese Folk Crafts*, trans. Michael Brase (Tokyo: Japan Publishing Industry Foundation for Culture, 2020)

Yanagi, Sōri, ed., *The Woodblock and the Artist: The Life and Work of Shiko Munakata*, exh. cat., Hayward Gallery, London (Tokyo: Kodansha International and Japan Folk Crafts Museum / London: South Bank Centre, 1991)

Yayanagi Gō et al., *Ai no dōbutsushi: hanga zensakuhinshū, 1965–1981* [Animals of Love: Complete Collection of Prints, 1965–1981] (Tokyo: Sōbunsha, 1981)

Yokohama Katsuhiko, ed., *Onosato Toshinobu*, exh. cat. (Tokyo: Nerima Art Museum, 1989)

Yuki, Jinnō, 'Consumer Consumption for Children: Conceptions of Childhood in the Work of Taishō-Period Designers', in *Child's Play: Multi-Sensory Histories of Children and Childhood in Japan*, ed. Sabine Frühstuck and Anne Walthall (Oakland, CA: University of California Press, 2017), pp. 83–101

Image Credits

The Japanese Print: Perception and Appreciation

Fig. 1
KATSUSHIKA Hokusai
Under the Wave off Kanagawa, from the series *Thirty-six Views of Mount Fuji*, c. 1830–32. Woodblock print, 25.7 × 37.9 cm ($10\frac{1}{8} \times 14\frac{15}{16}$ in.). Collection of the Metropolitan Museum of Art, New York. Howard Mansfield Collection. Purchase, Rogers Fund, 1936. Image courtesy of the Metropolitan Museum of Art, New York.

Fig. 2
ONCHI Kōshirō
Portrait of Dr Shizuya Fujikake, 1949. Woodblock print, 62.6 × 45.2 cm ($24\frac{5}{8} \times 17\frac{13}{16}$ in.). Collection of the Museum of Fine Arts Boston. Asiatic Curator's Fund. Image courtesy Wikimedia.

Fig. 3
KITAGAWA Utamaro
Courtesans after the Bath, c. 1801. Woodblock print, 39.2 × 25.5 cm ($15\frac{7}{16} \times 10\frac{1}{16}$ in.). Collection of Michael Fornitz. Image courtesy of Michael Fornitz.

Fig. 4
MUNAKATA Shikō
Flower Arrow, 1961. Woodblock print, 252 × 711 cm ($99\frac{1}{4} \times 280$ in.). Collection of Aomori Museum of Art. Courtesy Ryo Munakata.

Fig. 5
Henry Somm
'Fantaisies Japonaises', S. Bing, rue Chauchat 19, c. 1879. Etching and drypoint, 18.2 × 25.6 cm ($7\frac{1}{4} \times 10$ in.). Collection of the Bibliothèque Nationale de France, Paris. Image courtesy of the Bibliothèque Nationale de France, Paris.

Fig. 6
Henri de Toulouse-Lautrec
Divan Japonais, 1893. Lithograph poster, 80.8 × 60.8 cm ($31\frac{13}{16} \times 23\frac{15}{16}$ in.). Collection of the Metropolitan Museum of Art, New York. Bequest of Clifford A. Furst, 1958. Image courtesy of the Metropolitan Museum of Art, New York.

Fig. 7
Cover of *Le Japon artistique*, volume 2, 1888–91, showing Katsushika Hokusai, *Fine Wind, Clear Morning*, from the series *Thirty-six Views of Mount Fuji*, c. 1830–32. Collection of the University of Wisconsin-Madison. Image courtesy of the University of Wisconsin-Madison.

Fig. 8
Jules Chéret
Poster for the *Exposition de la gravure japonaise*, held from 25 April to 22 May 1890. Lithograph, 85 × 125 cm ($33\frac{1}{2} \times 49\frac{1}{4}$ in.). Collection of the Bibliothèque Nationale de France, Paris. Image courtesy of the Bibliothèque Nationale de France, Paris.

Fig. 9
Henri Rivière
The Wave (*La Vague*), from the series *L'Estampe originale*, 1893. Lithograph, 41.1 × 56.9 cm ($16\frac{1}{4} \times 22\frac{1}{4}$ in.). Collection of the Van Gogh Museum, Amsterdam (Vincent van Gogh Foundation). Image courtesy of the Van Gogh Museum, Amsterdam.

Fig. 10
URUSHIBARA Yoshijirō
Invitation card for the Société des Amis de l'Art Japonais, 14 December 1912. Woodblock print, 19.4 × 13.3 cm ($7\frac{1}{2} \times 5\frac{1}{4}$ in.). Collection of the Bibliothèque Nationale de France, Paris. Image courtesy of the Bibliothèque Nationale de France, Paris.

Fig. 11
KOBAYASHI Kiyochika
The Army of the North Melts Away before the Rising Sun, from the series *Long Live Japan: One Hundred Victories, One Hundred Laughs*, 1904–05. Woodblock print, 39.2 × 25.5 cm ($15\frac{1}{2} \times 10$ in.) Collection of the Library of Congress, Washington, DC. Image courtesy of the Library of Congress, Washington, DC.

Fig. 12
YAMAMOTO Kanae
Fisherman, 1904. Woodblock print, 16 × 10 cm ($6\frac{1}{4} \times 4$ in.). Collection of the Cleveland Museum of Art. Anonymous gift in memory of Paul O. Cartun 1960.122. Image courtesy of the Cleveland Museum of Art.

Fig. 13
Pablo Picasso
The Frugal Meal, 1904. Etching, 48 × 38 cm ($18\frac{15}{16} \times 15$ in.). Collection of the Art Institute of Chicago. Clarence Buckingham Collection © Succession Picasso / VG Bild-Kunst, Bonn 2025. Image: Bridgeman Images.

Fig. 14
Edvard Munch
The Kiss, 1898. Woodblock print, 47 × 45.1 cm ($18\frac{1}{2} \times 17\frac{3}{4}$ in.). Collection of the National Gallery of Art, Washington, DC, 1990.26.1. The Epstein Family Collection. Image courtesy of the National Gallery of Art, Washington, DC.

Fig. 15
HASHIGUCHI Goyō
Woman at the Bath, 1915. Woodblock print, 41.5 × 27.5 cm ($16\frac{5}{16} \times 10\frac{13}{16}$ in.). Collection of the Library of Congress, Washington, DC. Image courtesy of the Library of Congress, Washington, DC.

Fig. 16
YOSHIDA Hiroshi
Morning at Mt Tsurugi, from the series *Twelve Prints of the Japan Alps*, 1926. Woodblock print, 37.1 × 25 cm ($14\frac{5}{8} \times 9\frac{13}{16}$ in.). Private collection. © Ayomi Yoshida.

Fig. 17
HASEGAWA Kiyoshi
From the catalogue for *L'estampe japonaise moderne et ses origines*, 1934. Collection of the Bibliothèque Nationale de France, Paris. Image courtesy of the Bibliothèque Nationale de France, Paris.

Fig. 18
TERAOKA Masami
31 Flavours Invading Japan (Macadamia), 1978/2023. Lithograph and etching, 33 × 24 cm ($13 \times 9\frac{1}{2}$ in.). Collection of Catharine Clark Gallery, San Francisco. Courtesy of the artist and Catharine Clark Gallery, San Francisco.

Fig. 19
FUNASAKA Yoshisuke
Untitled, 1998. Woodblock print, 33 × 33.5 cm ($13 \times 13\frac{1}{4}$ in.). Artist's collection. © Yoshisuke Funasaka.

Fig. 20
SHIOMI Nana
Even Monkeys Tea Bowl, 2024. Woodblock print, 45 × 45 cm ($17\frac{3}{4} \times 17\frac{3}{4}$ in.). Collection of the artist. © Nana Shiomi.

ASAWA Ruth

Desert Plant (TAM.1460), 1965. Lithograph, 45.5 × 45.2 cm ($17\frac{15}{16} \times 17\frac{13}{16}$ in.). Printed by John Rock. Collection of the National Gallery of Art, Washington, DC. Gift of Dorothy J. and Benjamin B. Smith. National Gallery of Art, Washington, DC, 1983.18.177. © 2025 Ruth Asawa Lanier, Inc., Courtesy David Zwirner. Image courtesy of the National Gallery of Art, Washington, DC.

Untitled (TAM.1487-II, Blue and Purple Wash), 1965. Lithograph, 50.8 × 67.3 cm (20 × 26½ in.). Printed by John Rock. Collection of the Norton Simon Museum, Pasadena. © 2025 Ruth Asawa Lanier, Inc., Courtesy David Zwirner. Image courtesy of the Norton Simon Museum, Pasadena.

Untitled (TAM.1558-II, Addie's Chair (Reverse)), 1965. Lithograph, 105.2 × 75.7 cm ($41\frac{7}{16} \times 29\frac{13}{16}$ in.). Printed by John Rock. Collection of the National Gallery of Art, Washington, DC. Gift of Dorothy J. and Benjamin B. Smith. National Gallery of Art, Washington, DC, 1983.18.177. © 2025 Ruth Asawa Lanier, Inc., Courtesy David Zwirner. Image courtesy of the National Gallery of Art, Washington, DC.

AY-O

Portrait of the artist by the author, 2022.

Well! Well! Well!, 1974. Silkscreen print, 72.5 × 51 cm (28½ × 20 in.). Private collection. © Ay-O.

Rainbow Volcano, 1974. Silkscreen print, 72.5 × 51 cm (28½ × 20 in.). Private collection. © Ay-O.

Installation view of *Rainbow Environment*, 1966, at the 33rd Venice Biennale. © Ay-O. Provided by The Japan Foundation.

EISEN Keisai, *Buddha*, from the series *Pictures of Ten Openings*, c. early 19th century. Woodblock print, dimensions not known. Collection of the Art Research Center, Ritsumeikan University, Kyoto, hayE7-0011. Image courtesy of the Art Research Center, Ritsumeikan University, Kyoto.

Rainbow Hokusai, Position A, 1970. Silkscreen print, 90 × 135 cm (35½ × 53 in.). Collection of the Art Gallery of New South Wales, purchased 1971. © Ay-O. Image © Art Gallery of New South Wales 127.1971.

HO (ほ), 2024. Silkscreen print, 27.9 × 20.9 cm (11 × 8¼ in.). Artist's collection. © Ay-O.

RI (り), 2024. Silkscreen print, 27.9 × 20.9 cm (11 × 8¼ in.). Artist's collection © Ay-O.

NU (ぬ), 2024. Silkscreen print, 27.9 × 20.9 cm (11 × 8¼ in.). Artist's collection © Ay-O.

RU (る), 2024. Silkscreen print, 27.9 × 20.9 cm (11 × 8¼ in.). Artist's collection © Ay-O.

AZECHI Umetarō

Fuji, 1951. Woodblock print, 26 × 35 cm (10¼ × 13¾ in.) Collection of the British Museum, London. Courtesy of Atelier-U.

Bird and Pickle, c. 1970s. Woodblock print, dimensions not known. Collection of the Honolulu Museum of Art. Gift of Philip H. Roach, Jr, 2007 (31212). Courtesy of Atelier-U.

Mountaineer in Snow, undated. Woodblock print, 29 × 42 cm (11½ × 16½ in.). Collection of the British Museum, London. Courtesy of Atelier-U.

FOUJITA Léonard Tsuguharu

Self-Portrait with Cat, c. 1920s. Woodblock print, 38.8 × 28.5 cm (15⅛ × $11\frac{3}{16}$ in.). Collection of the Art Institute of Chicago. Gift of Cornelius Crane. © Fondation Foujita / VG Bild-Kunst, Bonn 2025. Image: The Art Institute of Chicago / Art Resource, NY / Scala, Florence.

Untitled (Reclining Nudes), undated. Etching and roulette, 49.8 × 69.8 cm (19⅝ × 27½ in.). Collection of the Art Institute of Chicago. Gift of Elizabeth Stein. © Fondation Foujita / VG Bild-Kunst, Bonn 2025. Image: The Art Institute of Chicago / Art Resource, NY / Scala, Florence.

White Persian Cat, c. 1929. Woodblock print, 33 × 45 cm (13 × 17¾ in.) Collection of the Art Institute of Chicago. Gift of Cornelius Crane. © Fondation Foujita / VG Bild-Kunst, Bonn 2025. Image: The Art Institute of Chicago / Art Resource, NY / Scala, Florence.

FUKITA Fumiaki

Pearl, 1970. Woodblock print, 31.5 × 24.5 cm (12½ × 9½ in.). Private collection. © Fumiaki Fukita 2025 / JAA 2500024.

Thunder in Spring, 1966. Woodblock print, 60 × 45 cm (23½ × 17¾ in.). Private collection. © Fumiaki Fukita 2025 / JAA 2500024.

Constellation, 1974. Woodblock print, 21.2 × 20 cm (8¼ × 8 in.). Private collection. © Fumiaki Fukita 2025 / JAA 2500024.

FUNASAKA Yoshisuke

Portrait of the artist by the author, 2024.

Lemon, Black and White, No. MM171, 2015. Woodblock print, 21 × 20 cm (8¼ × 8 in.). Artist's collection. © Yoshisuke Funasaka.

Lemon, Black and White, No. M731, 2006. Woodblock print, 21 × 20 cm (8¼ × 8 in.). Artist's collection. © Yoshisuke Funasaka.

Lemon, Black and White, No. M741, 2007. Woodblock print, 21 × 20 cm (8¼ × 8 in.). Artist's collection. © Yoshisuke Funasaka.

Lemon, Black and White, No. MM170, 2015. Woodblock print, 21 × 20 cm (8¼ × 8 in.). Artist's collection. © Yoshisuke Funasaka.

Lemon, Black and White, No. MM328, 2018. Woodblock print, 21 × 20 cm (8¼ × 8 in.). Artist's collection. © Yoshisuke Funasaka.

White Space No. 374, 1974. Woodblock and silkscreen print, 27 × 27 cm (10½ × 10½ in.). Artist's collection. © Yoshisuke Funasaka.

Untitled, 1971. Woodblock print, 33 × 33.5 cm (13 × 13¼ in.). Artist's collection. © Yoshisuke Funasaka.

HAMAGUCHI Yōzō

Pitcher, Grapes and Lemon, 1957. Mezzotint, 29.5 × 34.5 cm (11⅝ × $13\frac{9}{16}$ in.). Collection of the National Museum of Asian Art, Smithsonian Institution, Washington, DC. Purchase and partial gift of the Kenneth and Kiyo Hitch Collection form Kiyo Hitch with funds from the Mary Griggs Buke Endowment. Courtesy of the Musée Hamaguchi Yozo: Yamasa Collection.

Roofs of Paris, 1956. Mezzotint, 18.3 × 18.4 cm (7¼ × 7¼ in.). Collection of the National Museum of Asian Art, Smithsonian Institution, Washington, DC. Arthur M. Sackler Collection. Courtesy of the Musée Hamaguchi Yozo: Yamasa Collection.

Fourteen Cherries, 1966. Mezzotint, 51.5 × 24.4 cm (20¼ × 9½ in.). Private collection. Courtesy of the Musée Hamaguchi Yozo: Yamasa Collection.

HIRATSUKA Un'ichi

Nude on a Red Chair, 1939. Woodblock print, 25 × 33.5 cm (10 × 13¼ in.). Private collection. © Un'ichi Hiratsuka. Image courtesy Wikimedia.

Fukagawa Timberyards, from the series *Views of Tokyo after the Earthquake*, 1924. Woodblock print, 26.3 × 34.9 cm (10½ × 13¾ in.). Collection of Mead Art Museum, Amherst College, Massachusetts. © Un'ichi Hiratsuka. Image: Mead Art Museum, Amherst College, MA, USA. © Mead Art Museum / Purchase with William K. Allison (Class of 1920) Memorial Fund / Bridgeman Images.

Portrait of James Michener, 1957. Woodblock print, 82.6 × 63.4 cm (32⁹⁄₁₆ × 25 in.). Collection of the Art Institute of Chicago. Gift of Theodore and Louann Van Zelst, Hiratsuka Un'ichi – Van Zelst Family Collection. © Un'ichi Hiratsuka. Image: The Art Institute of Chi-cago / Art Resource, NY / Scala, Florence.

INAGAKI Tomoo

Pumpkins (Record of My Crop), 1955. Woodblock print, 34.5 × 45.1 cm (13⁹⁄₁₆ × 17¾ in.). Collection of the Hood Museum of Art, Dartmouth College, Hanover. Image courtesy of the Hood Museum of Art, Dartmouth College, Hanover.

Poster for *100 Estampes japonaises contemporaines*, 1963. Lithograph, 58 × 45.5 cm (22¾ × 18 in.). Private collection.

Cat Mandala, 1960s. Woodblock print, 62 × 44.5 cm (24½ × 17½ in.). Private collection.

KASAMATSU Shirō

Group photograph in the garden at Itō Shunsui's home in Ikegami, 2 April 1940. Left to right, back row: Moriyama Tetsutarō (Watanabe's assistant), Kawase Hasui, Robert O. and Inge Muller, Itō Yoshiko and Shinsui; front row: Kasamatsu Shirō and Watanabe Shōzaburō. Image courtesy Wikimedia.

Tokyo Tower, 1959. Woodblock print, 36.7 × 24.3 cm (14½ × 9½ in.). Collection of Unsōdō, Japan. © UNSODO CO., LTD.

Sunset Glow, 1955. Woodblock print, 36.5 × 24.5 cm (16¾ × 11 in.). Private collection. © Kasamatsu Family.

Onion Flowers, 1958. Woodblock print, 37 × 24.8 cm (16¾ × 11 in.). Private collection. © Kasamatsu Family.

KAWANO Kaoru

Small Birds, undated. Woodblock print, 37.7 × 25.6 cm (14¾ × 10 in.). Private collection. © Etsu Kobayashi.

Buddha and Bird, undated. Woodblock print, 55.5 × 37.5 cm (22 × 14¾ in.). Private collection. © Etsu Kobayashi.

Flora (red), undated. Woodblock print, 37.7 × 24.7 cm (14¾ × 9¾ in.). Private collection. © Etsu Kobayashi.

KINOSHITA Tomio

Alone, 1958. Woodblock print, 66.4 × 50.5 cm (26⅛ × 19⅞ in.). Collection of the Minneapolis Institute of Art. Gift of Sue Y.S. Kimm and Seymour Grufferman. © Kinoshita Family. Image © Minneapolis Institute of Art / Bridgeman Images.

Face, 1970. Woodblock print, 69.1 × 55.3 cm (27³⁄₁₆ × 21¾ in.). Collection of the Minneapolis Institute of Art. Gift of Sue Y.S. Kimm and Seymour Grufferman. © Kinoshita Family. Image © Minneapolis Institute of Art / Bridgeman Images.

Clowns, 1965. Woodblock print, 56.7 × 42.2 cm (22⁵⁄₁₆ × 16⅝ in.). Collection of the Cleveland Museum of Art. Gift of Mr and Mrs William E. Ward 1982.359. © Kinoshita Family. Image courtesy of the Cleveland Museum of Art.

KUROSAKI Akira

Mysterious Night, 1972. Woodblock print, 33 × 32 cm (13 × 12½ in.). Private collection. Courtesy of the Estate of Akira Kurosaki.

Twilight II, 1971. Woodblock print, 28.4 × 41.9 cm (11³⁄₁₆ × 16½ in.). Collection of the Cincinnati Art Museum. Courtesy of the Estate of Akira Kurosaki. Image © Cincinnati Art Museum / Bridgeman Images.

The End of Dream A, W-209, 1976. Woodblock print, 54.6 × 38.7 cm (21½ × 15¼ in.). Collection of the Portland Art Museum, Portland, Oregon. Purchase: Funds provided by James Tobin, © 1976 Kurosaki Akira, 80.75.2. Courtesy of the Estate of Akira Kurosaki. Image courtesy of the Portland Art Museum, Portland, Oregon.

KUSAMA Yayoi

Pumpkin (BSQ), 1998. Silkscreen print, 29.9 × 29.8 cm (11¾ × 11¾ in.). Private collection. © YAYOI KUSAMA. Image courtesy YAYOI KUSMA Inc.

Infinity Nets (A · B), 1994. Etching, 17.8 × 11.6 cm (7 × 4⁹⁄₁₆ in.). Collection of the Cleveland Museum of Art. Gift of Lewis J. Greenwald 2022.127. © YAYOI KUSAMA. Image courtesy of the Cleveland Museum of Art.

Mt Fuji in Seven Colours, 2014. Woodblock print, 30.3 × 90 cm (12 × 35½ in.). Private collection. © YAYOI KUSAMA. Image courtesy YAYOI KUSMA Inc.

MORI Yoshitoshi

Cityscape, 1958. Stencil print, 54 × 38 cm (21¼ × 15 in.). Private collection. © Yoshitoshi Mori.

Kabuki C: Shibaraku (Just a Moment), 1967. Stencil print, 69.6 × 85.2 cm (27½ × 33½ in.). Collection of the Cleveland Museum of Art. Gift of the Artist 1984.83. © Yoshitoshi Mori. Image courtesy of the Cleveland Museum of Art.

Geisha, 1970. Woodblock print, 47.7 × 30.4 cm (18¾ × 12 in.). Collection of the British Museum, London. © Yoshitoshi Mori.

MUNAKATA Shikō

Bodhisattva Manjusri, from the series *Ten Great Disciples of the Buddha Sakyamuni*, undated. Woodblock print, 98.9 × 50.2 cm (38¹⁵⁄₁₆ × 19¾ in.). Collection of Harvard Art Museums / Arthur M. Sackler Museum, Gift of Mr and Mrs C. Adrian Rübel. Courtesy

Ryo Munakata. Image © President and fellows of Harvard College.

Self-Portrait, 1959. Woodblock print, 40 × 30 cm (15¾ × 11¹³⁄₁₆ in.). Collection of Harvard Art Museums / Arthur M. Sackler Museum, Gift of Mr and Mrs C. Adrian Rübel. Courtesy Ryo Munakata. Image courtesy Harvard Art Museums.

Hara: A Straight Line at the Foot of Mt Fuji (Suso ichimonji), no. 14, from the series *Munakata's Tōkaidō*, 1963. Woodblock print, 48.5 × 61 cm (19¹⁄₁₆ × 24 in.). Collection of the Art Institute of Chicago. Courtesy Ryo Munakata. Image: The Art Institute of Chicago / Art Resource, NY / Scala, Florence.

NAGAI Kazumasa

Poster for *The Cell*, 1966. Silkscreen print, 102 × 71.2 cm (40⅛ × 29³⁄₁₆ in.). Collection of the Merrill C. Berman Collection, New York. © Kazumasa Nagai.

Untitled, 1968. Zinc relief print, 43.7 × 39.8 cm (17³⁄₁₆ × 15¹¹⁄₁₆ in.). Collection of the Los Angeles County Museum of Art. © Kazumasa Nagai.

Untitled, 1982. Woodblock print, 49.8 × 33.9 cm (19½ × 13¼ in.). Private collection. © Kazumasa Nagai.

NARA Yoshitomo

Mirror, from the series *In the Floating World*, 1999. Fuji Xerox copy, 41.5 × 29.5 cm (16¼ × 11½ in.). Collection of the Bernard Buffet Museum, Nagaizumi. © Yoshitomo Nara. Image courtesy Yoshitomo Nara Foundation.

KITAGAWA Utamaro, *Naniwa Okita Admiring Herself in a Mirror*, c. 1790–95. Woodblock print, 36.8 × 25.1 cm (14½ × 9⅞ in.). Collection of the Metropolitan Museum of Art, New York. Image courtesy of the Metropolitan Museum of Art, New York.

I Am Alone..., 2003. Lithograph, 49.8 × 40 cm (19½ × 15¾ in.). Private collection. © Yoshitomo Nara. Image courtesy Yoshitomo Nara Foundation.

Life is Only One, 2010. Woodblock print, 42 × 29.5 cm (16½ × 11½ in.). Collection of the Machida City Museum of Graphic Arts, Tokyo. © Yoshitomo Nara. Image courtesy Yoshitomo Nara Foundation.

NODA Tetsuya

Portrait of the artist by the author, 2023.

Diary: May 8th '70 in New York (a), 1970. Woodblock and silkscreen print, 51.9 × 67.7 cm (20½ × 26¾ in.). Collection of the National Museum of Modern Art, Tokyo. © Tetsuya Noda. Photo: MOMAT/DNPartcom.

Diary: Oct. 25th '73, 1973. Woodblock and silkscreen print, 49.5 × 71.7 cm (19½ × 28 in.). Collection of the artist. © Tetsuya Noda.

Diary: Mar. 5th '79 (a), 1979. Woodblock and silkscreen print, 49.5 × 71.7 cm (19½ × 28 in.). Collection of the artist. © Tetsuya Noda.

Diary: Mar. 13th '20, 2020. Woodblock and silkscreen print, 51.8 × 79.7 cm (20⅜ × 31⅜ in.). Collection of the artist. © Tetsuya Noda.

OKUYAMA Gihachirō

Nikke, c. 1930. Lithograph, 76.2 × 52.1 cm (30 × 20½ in.). Collection of the Merril C. Berman Collection. © Mrs Okuyama Yuki. Image courtesy of the Merrill C. Berman Collection.

Snow Scene in Yamagata, c. 1950s–'60s. Woodblock print, 24 × 48 cm (9½ × 19 in.). Private collection. © Mrs Okuyama Yuki.

UTAGAWA Hiroshige, *Seki*, no. 48, from the series *Fifty-three Stations of the Tokaido*, c. 1848–49. Woodblock print, 22.2 × 34.9 cm (8¾ × 13¾ in.). Collection of the Metropolitan Museum of Art, New York. The Francis Lathrop Collection. Purchase, Frederick C. Hewitt Fund, 1911. Image courtesy of the Metropolitan Museum of Art, New York.

Landscape with Moon, 1954. Woodblock print, 25.5 × 55.5 cm (10 × 22 in.). Private collection. © Mrs Okuyama Yuki.

OKUYAMA Gijin, *Rock Garden*, 1976. Woodblock print, 50.5 × 25.5 cm (20 × 10 in.). Private collection. © Mrs Okuyama Yuki.

Le Père Tanguy (Old Man Tanguy – Van Gogh), c. 1950s. Woodblock print, 27 × 34.3 cm (10⅛ × 13½ in.). Private collection. © Mrs Okuyama Yuki.

ONCHI Kōshirō

Mother and Child, c. 1915–55. Woodblock print, 30.1 × 23.2 cm (12 × 9 in.). Collection of the Cleveland Museum of Art. Image courtesy of the Cleveland Museum of Art.

Tokyo Station, from the series *Recollections of Tokyo*, 1945. Woodblock print, 25.9 × 19.7 cm (10³⁄₁₆ × 7¾ in.). Collection of the Museum of Fine Arts Boston. Gift of Robert Treat Paine, Jr. through Mrs. Robert Treat Paine, Jr.

Lyric No. 23, 1955. Woodblock print, 18.7 × 13.2 cm (7⅜ × 5³⁄₁₆ in.). Collection of the Honolulu Museum of Art. Gift of James A. Michener, 1955 (13566). Image courtesy of the Honolulu Museum of Art, Hawai'i.

ONOSATO Toshinobu

Installation view of the exhibition *The New Japanese Painting and Sculpture*, 19 October 1966 – 2 January 1967, Museum of Modern Art, New York, showing works by Onosato Toshinobu. © Rokumaru Onosato. Image: The Museum of Modern Art, New York / Scala, Florence.

Lithograph B, 1973. Lithograph, 21 × 29 cm (8¼ × 11½ in.). Private collection. © Rokumaru Onosato.

71-K, 1971. Silkscreen print, 49.8 × 50.5 cm (19⅝ × 19⅞ in.). Collection of Cincinnati Art Museum, Ohio. The Howard and Caroline Porter Collection. © Rokumaru Onosato. Image © Cincinnati Art Museum / Bridgeman Images.

SAITŌ Kiyoshi

Maiko, Kyoto (G), 1961. Woodblock print, 53 × 38 cm (21 × 15 in.). Private collection. © Hisako Watanabe.

Bisyamonten, Kyoto, 1965. Woodblock print, 38 × 53 cm (15 × 21 in.). Private collection. © Hisako Watanabe.

Holiday magazine, no. 375, Japan issue, October 1961, featuring Saitō's *Bunraku (B)*, 1959. © Hisako Watanabe. Photograph by Alfredo Piola, image courtesy *Holiday* magazine.

Installation view of the exhibition *Prints from Europe and Japan: Etchings by Matisse* at the Museum of Modern Art, New York, 4–31 May 1955, showing Saitō's woodblock print *Dachshund*. Collection of the Museum of Modern Art Archives, New York. Image: The Museum of Modern Art, New York / Scala, Florence.

Dachshund, undated. Woodblock print, 29.5 × 44 cm (11½ × 17¼ in.). Private collection. © Hisako Watanabe.

SATŌ Ado

Time Tunnel, 1968. Silkscreen print, 65 × 76 cm (25½ × 30 in.). Private collection. © Ado Sato. Courtesy of the Ado Sato family.

CB70, 1970. Silkscreen print, 58 × 50 cm (22¾ × 19¾ in.). Private collection. © Ado Sato. Courtesy of the Ado Sato family.

Starter Blue, 1968. Silkscreen print, 49 × 95 cm (19¼ × 37½ in.). Private collection. © Ado Sato. Courtesy of the Ado Sato family.

SHINOHARA Ushio

Portrait of the artist, 2015. Photo © Ushio Shinohara.

Marcel Duchamp, 1965. Blueprint, 80.5 × 55.5 cm ($31\frac{11}{16}$ × 21⅞ in.). Collection of the Museum of Modern Art, New York. Gift of the artist. © Ushio Shinohara. Image: The Museum of Modern Art, New York / Scala Florence.

Doll Festival, 1966. Triptych of silkscreen prints, each 71.1 × 48.3 cm (28 × 19 in.). Collection of the Metropolitan Museum of Art, New York. Felix and Helen Juda Foundation Fund. © Ushio Shinohara. Image courtesy of the artist and Tokyo Gallery + BTAP.

TSUKIOKA Yoshitoshi, *Appearing Graceful, Behaviour of a High-Ranking Prostitute of the Tenpō Era*, 1888. Woodblock print, 36.7 × 24.6 cm ($14\frac{7}{16}$ × $9\frac{11}{16}$ in.). Collection of the Minneapolis Institute of Art. The Mary Griggs Burke Endowment Fund established by the Mary Livingston Griggs and Mary Griggs Burke Foundation, gifts of various donors, by exchange, and gift of Edmond Freis in memory of his parents, Rose and Leon Freis. Image courtesy of the Minneapolis Institute of Art.

Oiran, undated. Silkscreen print, 47 × 47 cm (18½ × 18½ in.). Private collection. © Ushio Shinohara.

SHIOMI Nana

Portrait of the artist by the author, 2024.

Mitate No. 35 – Front of the Back (Ushiro no shōmen), from the series *100 Views of Mitate*, 2000. Woodblock print, 46 × 46 cm (18 × 18 in.). Artist's collection. © Nana Shiomi.

Mitate No. 45 – Peach (Momo), from the series *100 Views of Mitate*, 2001. Woodblock print, 46 × 46 cm (18 × 18 in.). Artist's collection. © Nana Shiomi.

Mitate No. 46 – Tea Bowl (Chawan), from the series *100 Views of Mitate*, 2001. Woodblock print, 46 × 46 cm (18 × 18 in.). Artist's collection. © Nana Shiomi.

Mitate No. 53 – Fuji (Fuji), from the series *100 Views of Mitate*, 2002. Woodblock print, 46 × 46 cm (18 × 18 in.). Artist's collection. © Nana Shiomi.

Mitate No. 84 – Night (Yoru), from the series *100 Views of Mitate*, 2007. Woodblock print, 46 × 46 cm (18 × 18 in.). Artist's collection. © Nana Shiomi.

Mitate No. 93 – Mirror Cake (Kagami-mochi), from the series *100 Views of Mitate*, 2015. Woodblock print, 46 × 46 cm (18 × 18 in.). Artist's collection. © Nana Shiomi.

KATSUSHIKA Hokusai, *Under the Wave off Kanagawa*, from the series *Thirty-six Views of Mount Fuji*, c. 1830–32. Woodblock print, 25.7 × 37.9 cm (10⅛ × $14\frac{15}{16}$ in.). Collection of the Metropolitan Museum of Art, New York. Howard Mansfield Collection. Purchase, Rogers Fund, 1936. Image courtesy of the Metropolitan Museum of Modern Art, New York.

Hokusai's Wave (Right) – Happy Carp, 2001. Woodblock print, 65 × 98 cm (25½ × 38½ in.). Artist's collection. © Nana Shiomi.

Mirror Room – Katsura, 2006. Woodblock print on paper, 59.5 × 134 cm (23½ × 52¾ in.). Artist's collection. © Nana Shiomi.

SUGAÏ Kumi

Woman (La Femme), 1957. Lithograph, 54.5 × 40.2 cm ($21\frac{7}{16}$ × $15\frac{13}{16}$ in.). Collection of the Museum of Modern Art, New York. © VG Bild-Kunst, Bonn 2025. Image: The Museum of Modern Art, New York / Scala, Florence.

Untitled, from the series *Homage to Picasso (Hommage à Picasso)*, 1973. Silkscreen print, 62.5 × 49.5 cm (24½ × 19½ in.). Private collection. © VG Bild-Kunst, Bonn 2025. Image: © QUITTENBAUM Kunstauktionen GmbH.

Signal A, 1974. Lithograph, 67 × 52 cm (26½ × 20½ in.). Private collection. © VG Bild-Kunst, Bonn 2025.

TAKEDA Hideo

Portrait of the artist by the author, 2023.

Monmon (panties), 1976. Silkscreen print, 46 × 34.5 cm (18 × 13½ in.). Artist's collection. © Hideo Takeda.

Ushiwaka-maru, from the series *Genpei*, 1985–99. Silkscreen print, 52.5 × 39 cm (20¾ × 15½ in.). Artist's collection. © Hideo Takeda.

The Battle at Fuji River, from the series *Genpei*, 1985–99. Silkscreen print, 39 × 52.5 cm (15½ × 20¾ in.). Artist's collection. © Hideo Takeda.

Taira no Kiyomori Dies of Illness, from the series *Genpei*, 1985–99. Silkscreen print, 39 × 52.5 cm (15½ × 20¾ in.). Artist's collection. © Hideo Takeda.

The Heike Clan's Capital, from the series *Genpei*, 1985–99. Silkscreen print, 52.5 × 39 cm (20¾ × 15½ in.). Artist's collection. © Hideo Takeda.

The Battle of the First Vanguard at Uji River, from the series *Genpei*, 1985–99. Silkscreen print, 39 × 52.5 cm (15½ × 20¾ in.). Artist's collection. © Hideo Takeda.

UTAGAWA Kunisada, *The Battle of Yashima in the Genpei War*, c. 1838. Woodblock print, 36.8 × 73.7 cm (14½ × 29 in.). Image courtesy Wikimedia.

Dan-no-ura Genji, from the series *Genpei*, 1985–99. Silkscreen print, 52 × 35 cm (20½ × 13¾ in.). Artist's collection. © Hideo Takeda.

Inferno, 2000. Silkscreen print, 52.5 × 39 cm (20¾ × 15½ in.). Artist's collection. © Hideo Takeda.

TAKEI Takeo

Cover of *Kodomo no kuni* (Children's Country) magazine, December issue, 1928. Original artwork: watercolour, 26 × 18 cm (10¼ × 7 in.). Collection of ILF Douga Museum of Art, Okaya. © Okaya City / ILF Douga Museum of Art.

Treasured Kokeshi Dolls, undated. Woodblock print, 26.5 × 18 cm (10½ × 7 in.). Collection of ILF Douga Museum of Art, Okaya. © Okaya City / ILF Douga Museum of Art.

Rock-Paper-Scissors, 1952. Woodblock print, 28.8 × 27 cm (11½ × 10½ in.). Collection of ILF Douga Museum of Art, Okaya. © Okaya City / ILF Douga Museum of Art.

TERAOKA Masami

Portrait of the artist, c. 2019. Courtesy the artist and Catharine Clark Gallery, San Francisco.

31 Flavors Invading Japan/Today's Special, 1980–82. Woodblock print, 28.1 × 42.1 cm (11¹⁄₁₆ × 16⁹⁄₁₆ in.). Collection of the National Museum of Asian Art, Smithsonian Institution, Washington, DC. The Pearl and Seymour Moskowitz Collection. Courtesy the artist and Catharine Clark Gallery, San Francisco.

Sarah and Octopus/Seventh Heaven, 2001. Woodblock print, 26.4 × 39.7 cm (10⅜ × 15⅝ in.). Collection of Queensland Art Gallery / Gallery of Modern Art, Queensland. Purchased 2005. The Queensland Government's Gallery of Modern Art Acquisitions Fund. Courtesy the artist and Catharine Clark Gallery, San Francisco.

KATSUSHIKA Hokusai, *Female Diver being Pleasured by a Large and Small Octopus*, from the book *Pine Seedlings on the First Rat Day*, 1814. Woodblock print, 19 × 27 cm (7½ × 10½ in.). Collection of Michael Fornitz. Image courtesy Wikimedia.

Unknown artist, *Angry Ansei Earthquake Victims Take Revenge on a Giant Catfish Responsible for the Destruction*, 19th century. Woodblock print, 25 × 38 cm (10 × 15 in.). Image courtesy Wikimedia.

Catfish Envy, from the series *Hawaii Snorkel*, 1993. Etching, aquatint and woodblock print, 68 × 98 cm (26¾ × 38½ in.). Collection of Tate, London. Presented by Tyler Graphics Ltd in honour of Pat Gilmour, Tate Print Department 1974–7, 2004. Courtesy the artist and Catharine Clark Gallery, San Francisco.

TOKURIKI Tomikichirō

Woman Combing her Hair, 1935. Woodblock print, 40.4 × 27 cm (15⅞ × 10⅝ in.). Collection of the Honolulu Museum of Art. Gift of Philip H. Roach, Jr, 1997 (26377). Courtesy Ishijima Katsuya.

Fuji from Iwabuchi, no. 27 from the series *Thirty-six Views of Mt Fuji*, 1939–41. Woodblock print, 26.5 × 38.5 cm (14½ × 15¼ in.). Private collection. Courtesy Ishijima Katsuya.

UTAGAWA Hiroshige, *Hara*, Number 14, from the series *Fifty-Three Stations of the Tōkaidō*, 1847–52. Woodblock print, 22.2 × 34.9 cm (8¾ × 13¾ in.). Collection of the Metropolitan Museum of Art, New York. The Francis Lathrop Collection, Purchase, Frederick C. Hewitt Fund, 1911. Image courtesy of the Metropolitan Museum of Art, New York.

Sanjo Bridge, Kyoto, c. 1950s. Woodblock print, 27.5 × 40 cm (11 × 15¾ in.). Private collection. Courtesy Ishijima Katsuya.

Katsura Imperial Villa, c. 1960s. Woodblock print, 29.1 × 25.8 cm (11½ × 10¼ in.). Private collection. Courtesy Ishijima Katsuya.

TSURAYA Kōkei

Cats, from the series *Five Subjects Dedicated to Arcimboldo*, 2013. Woodblock print, 41.5 × 32.5 cm (16¼ × 12¾ in.). Private collection. © Tsuraya Kōkei.

UTAGAWA Kuniyoshi, *Looks Fierce but is Really Nice*, c. 1847–52. Woodblock print, 38 × 35.5 cm (15 × 14 in.). Collection of the Tokyo Fuji Art Museum. Image courtesy Wikimedia.

Nakamura Jakuemon IV as Hanako in 'Bungo Dōjōji', from the series *Bust Portraits III*, 1982. Woodblock print, 40 × 25 cm (15¾ × 9¾ in.). Private collection. © Tsuraya Kōkei.

Nakamura Ganjiro II as Kamiya Jihei in 'Kawasho', from the series *Bust Portraits I*, 1979. Woodblock print, 38 × 25.5 cm (15 × 10 in.). Private collection. © Tsuraya Kōkei.

URUSHIBARA Yoshijirō

Fuchu, after Katsushika Hokusai, c. 1912. Woodblock print, 12.7 × 19 cm (5 × 7½ in.). Collection of the British Museum, London. Image courtesy of the British Museum, London.

Stonehenge, c. 1915. Woodblock print, 56 × 40.6 cm (22 × 16 in.). Collection of the British Museum, London. Image courtesy of the British Museum, London.

Daisies 2, undated. Woodblock print, 34.7 × 23.5 cm (13¾ × 9¼ in.). Private collection.

YAMAMOTO Kanae

Fisherman, 1904. Woodblock print, 16 × 10 cm (6¼ × 4 in.). Collection of the Cleveland Museum of Art. Anonymous gift in memory of Paul O. Cartun 1960.122. Image courtesy of the Cleveland Museum of Art.

On the Deck, 1912. Woodblock print, 19.4 × 18.5 cm (7⅝ × 7¼ in.). Collection of the Art Institute of Chicago. Kate S. Buckingham Endowment. Image courtesy Wikimedia.

Félix Vallotton, *The Sea* (*La Mer*), 1893. Wood engraving, 14.2 × 24.5 cm (5½ × 9½ in.). Collection of the Bibliothèque nationale de France, Paris. Image courtesy of the Bibliothèque nationale de France, Paris.

Fishermen, undated. Woodblock print, 8.8 × 13.8 cm (3⁷⁄₁₆ × 5⁷⁄₁₆ in.). Collection of the Museum of Fine Arts Boston. Leonard A. Lauder Collection of Japanese Postcards. Image courtesy Wikimedia.

YAYANAGI Go (Tsuyoshi)

Portrait of the artist by the author, 2024.

Edo Games, 1979. Silkscreen print, 89.4 × 71.3 cm (35³⁄₁₆ × 28¹⁄₁₆ in.). Collection of the Cincinnati Art Museum, Ohio. © Tsuyoshi (Go) Yayanagi. Photo © Cincinnati Art Museum / Bridgeman Images.

Sentier Fleuri, 1978. Silkscreen print, 45.7 × 60.3 cm (18 × 23¾ in.). Collection of the Cincinnati Art Museum, Ohio. © Tsuyoshi (Go) Yayanagi. Photo © Cincinnati Art Museum / Bridgeman Images.

The Tale of Genji (2), 1974. Silkscreen print, 79.5 × 55 cm (31¼ × 21¾ in.). Private collection. © Tsuyoshi (Go) Yayanagi. Image courtesy of Kumo Arts.

Flower Like the Blue Sky, 1982. Silkscreen print, 39 × 39 cm (15½ × 15½ in.). Private collection. © Tsuyoshi (Go) Yayanagi. Image courtesy of Kumo Arts.

YOKOO Tadanori

Exhibition of Japan Advertising Artists Club, 1968. Offset lithograph, 72.8 × 51.5 cm (28¾ × 20¼ in.). Collection of the Museum of Modern Art, New York. Gift of the designer. © Tadanori Yokoo.

The Kyogen Play 'Chinsetsu Yumiharizuki', 1969. Silkscreen print,

103 × 72.8 cm (40½ × 28¾ in.). Collection of the British Museum, London. © Tadanori Yokoo.

TŌSHŪSAI Sharaku, *Kabuki Actor Ōtani Oniji III as Yakko Edobei*, 1794. Woodblock print, 38.1 × 25.1 cm (15 × 9⅞ in.). Collection of the Metropolitan Museum of Art, New York. Henry L. Phillips Collection, Bequest of Henry L. Phillips, 1939. Image courtesy of the Metropolitan Museum of Art, New York.

Sharaku – The Five Constellations, 2021. Woodblock print, 80 × 52 cm (31½ × 20½ in.). Private collection. © Tadanori Yokoo.

Yoshida Family: YOSHIDA Hiroshi

The Acropolis Ruins at Night, 1925. Woodblock print, 25.4 × 37.1 cm (10 × 14⅝ in.). Collection of the Saint Louis Art Museum. The Langenberg Endowment Fund. © Ayomi Yoshida. Image courtesy of the Saint Louis Art Museum.

Crescent Moon, 1941. Woodblock print, 24 × 37 cm (9½ × 14⅝ in.). Private collection. © Ayomi Yoshida.

Yoshida Family: YOSHIDA Fujio

Roses, 1927. Woodblock print, 35.6 × 24.8 cm (14 × 9¾ in.). Collection of the Minneapolis Institute of Art. Gift of the Clark Center for Japanese Art and Culture; formerly given to the Center by H. Ed Robinson, in memory of his beloved wife Ulrike Pietzner Robinson. © Ayomi Yoshida. Image © Minneapolis Institute of Art / Bridgeman Images.

Iris, 1954. Woodblock print, 37.5 × 24.5 cm (14¾ × 9⅝ in.). Collection of the Portland Art Museum, Portland, Oregon, © Ayomi Yoshida, 2015.32.4. Image courtesy of the Portland Art Museum, Portland, Oregon.

Photograph of Yoshida Fujio (left), Hodaka (middle) and Chizuko (right) at Dallas Museum of Fine Arts, 1957. Image courtesy of the Dallas Museum of Art Archives.

Yoshida Family: YOSHIDA Hodaka

Floating, 1959. Woodblock print, 49.5 × 28.7 cm (19½ × 11¼ in.).

Private collection. © Ayomi Yoshida.

Stones and a Man (A), 1956. Woodblock print, 94 × 63.5 cm (37 × 25 in.). Collection of Mitaka City Art Gallery, Tokyo. © Ayomi Yoshida.

Stones and a Man (B), 1956. Woodblock print, 94 × 63.5 cm (37 × 25 in.). Collection of Mitaka City Art Gallery, Tokyo. © Ayomi Yoshida.

Yoshida Family: YOSHIDA Chizuko

Mambo, 1956. Monoprint, 83 × 118 cm (32¾ × 46½ in.). Private collection. © Ayomi Yoshida.

Star Star Star A, 1969. Woodblock print, 77 × 59.5 cm (30¼ × 23½ in.). © Ayomi Yoshida.

Summer Swallow, 1987. Photo etching and woodblock print, 56 × 42 cm (22 × 16½ in.). Private collection. © Ayomi Yoshida.

Yoshida Family: YOSHIDA Ayomi

Portrait of the artist, 2025. Photo © Mareo Suemasa.

Surface K.O., 1987. Woodblock print, 52 × 73 cm (20½ × 28¾ in.). Collection of the Art Institute of Chicago. Gift of Chizuko, Takasuke and Ayomi Yoshida. © Ayomi Yoshida. Image: The Art Institute of Chicago / Art Resource, NY / Scala, Florence.

Misty Rain, 2021. Woodblock print, 65 × 89.7 cm (25 9/16 × 35 5/16 in.). Collection of the Portland Art Museum, Portland, Oregon. Gift of Yoshida Ayomi, © Ayomi Yoshida, 2024.32.14.

YOSHIDA Hideshi

Portrait of the artist, 2024.

Why is this coffee cup so small?, 2024. Woodblock print, 33 × 24 cm (13 × 9½ in.). Private collection. © Hideshi Yoshida.

The whole universe conquest plan by cuteness, 2022. Wood engraving, 15 × 15 cm (6 × 6 in.). Private collection. © Hideshi Yoshida.

Symmetry Variation – Birds, 1998. Woodblock print with airbrush, 38 × 26 cm (15 × 10¼ in.). Artist's collection. © Hideshi Yoshida.

At the Depths, 2014. Wood engraving, 18.9 × 26.8 cm (7½ × 10½ in.). Private collection. © Hideshi Yoshida.

Special Cargo Ship: Last Resort. Final Destination: Undecided, 2012. Woodblock print, 70 × 110 cm (27½ × 43¼ in.) Artist's collection. © Hideshi Yoshida.

Index

This index is in alphabetical, word by word order. It does not cover the Foreword, Preface, Glossary, Bibliography or Image Credits. Location reference is to page number and page/figure number (in italics). Abbreviations: fig. = figure.

A member of Penguin Random House Verlagsgruppe GmbH
Neumarkter Strasse 28 · 81673 Munich
produktsicherheit@penguinrandomhouse.de

(The above information is mandatory information according to GPSR and should be used for all queries relating to the safety of our books)

First printed in 2025

Library of Congress Control Number is available; a CIP catalogue record for this book is available from the British Library.

Editorial direction
Rochelle Roberts

Copyediting
Aimee Selby

Indexing
Elaine Taylor MA

Design
Wolfe Hall

Production management
Corinna Pickart

Separation
Schnieber Graphik GmbH, Putzbrunn

Printing and binding
Livonia Print SIA, Riga

Paper
Munken Print White

Penguin Random House Verlagsgruppe
FSC® N001967

Printed in Latvia
ISBN 978-3-7913-7784-1
www.prestel.com

Cover
Ay-O, *Rainbow Volcano*, 1974.
© Ay-O. See p. 35

Back cover
Teraoka Masami, *31 Flavours Invading Japan (Macadamia)*, 1978–2023.
Courtesy the artist and Catharine Clark Gallery, San Franscisco.
See p. 21

Frontispiece
Tokuriki Tomikichirō, *Sanjo Bridge*, 1945.
Courtesy Ishijima Katsuya

p. 2
Ay-O, *Rabbit*, 1999. © Ay-O

p. 4
Noda Tetsuya, *Diary: Mar. 5th '79 (a)*, 1979. © Tetsuya Noda. See p. 122

Endpapers, front
Satō Ado, *Allo Ako*, 1970.
© Ado Sato. Courtesy of the Ado Sato family

Endpapers, back
Ay-O, *Rainbow Bridge A*, 1979.
© Ay-O

Opposite
Funasaka Yoshisuke, *Lemon, Black and White, No. M424*, 2002.
© Yoshisuke Funasaka

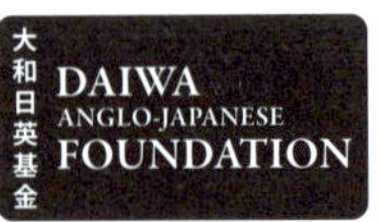

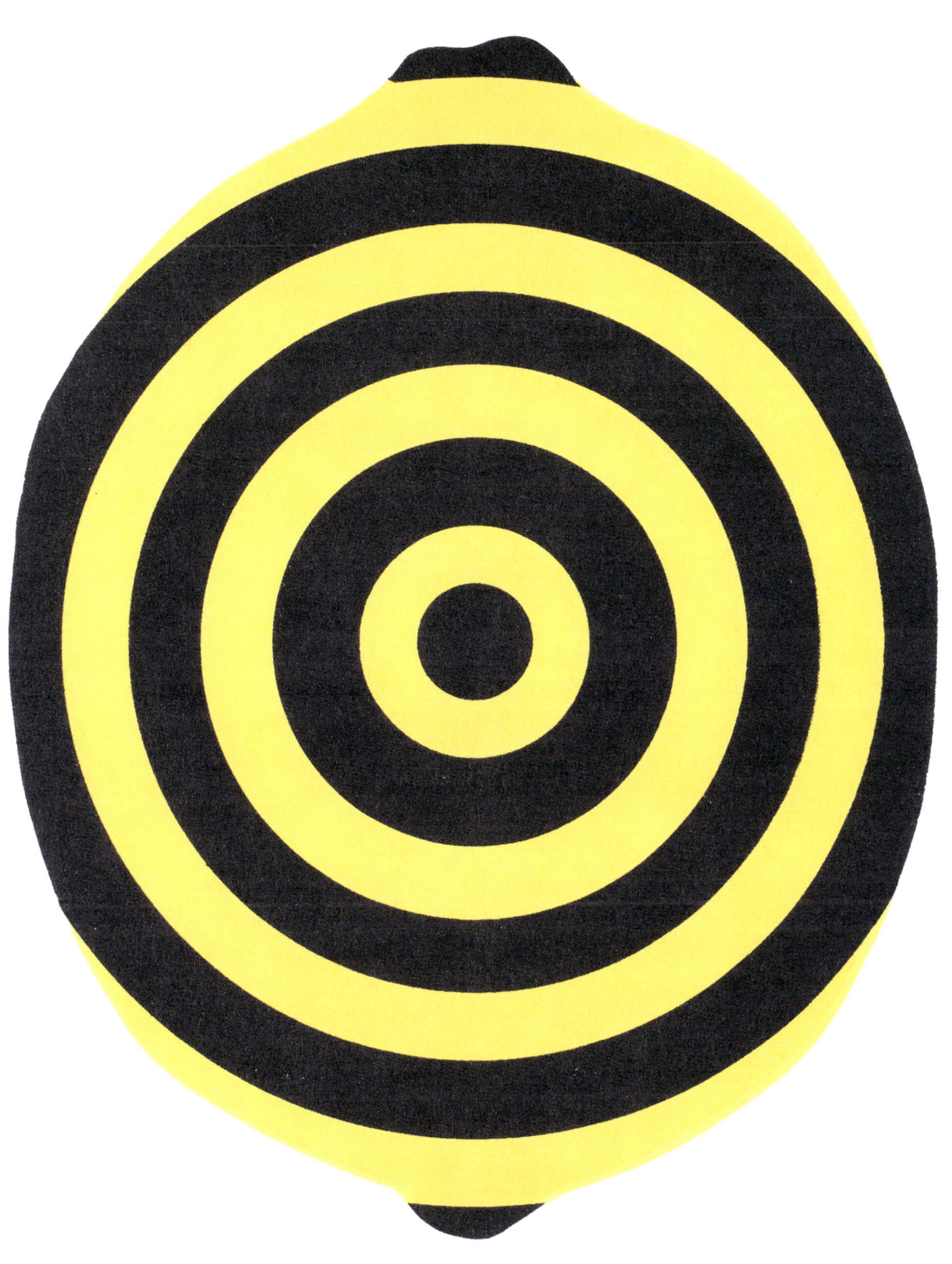

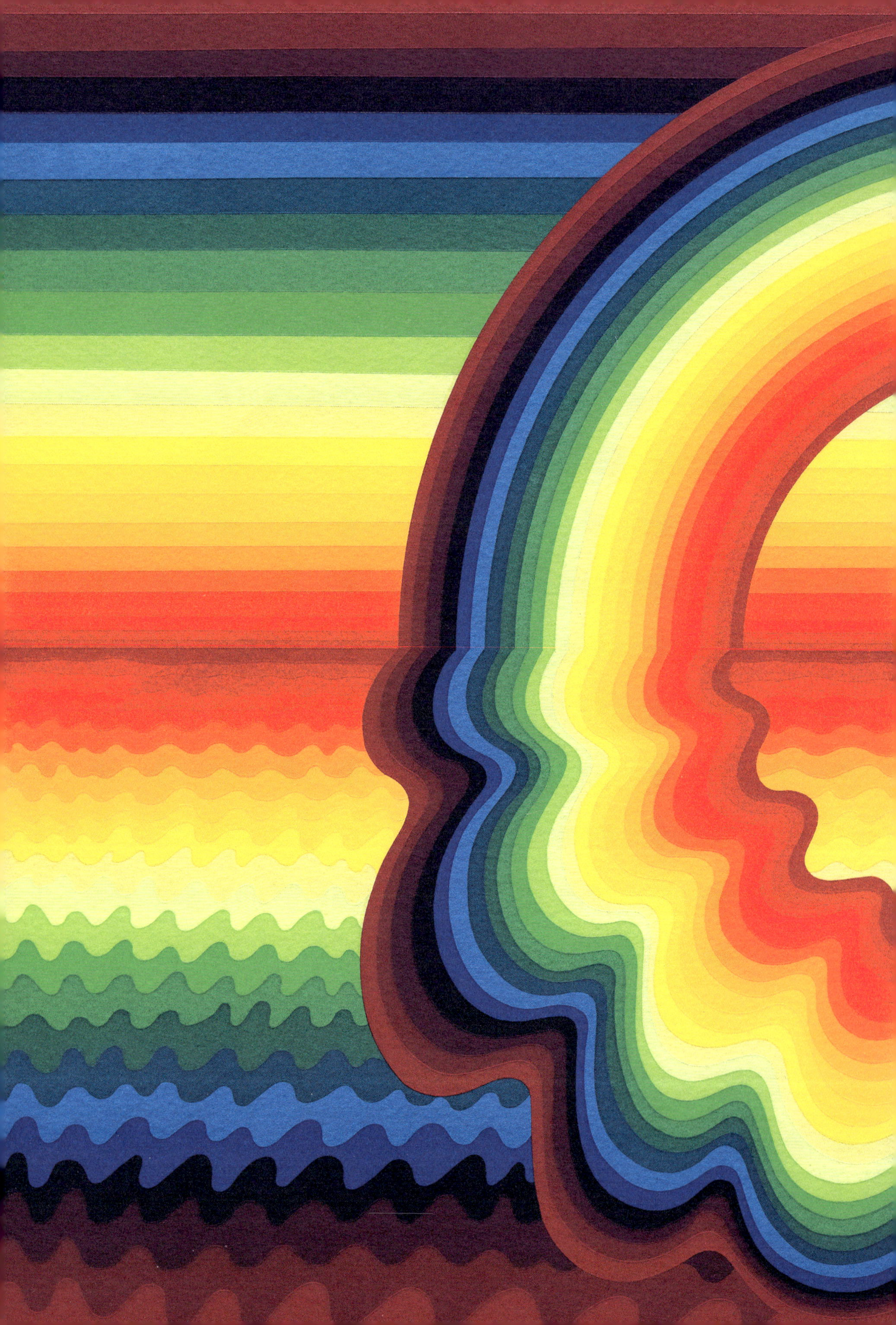